FIRE FORCE

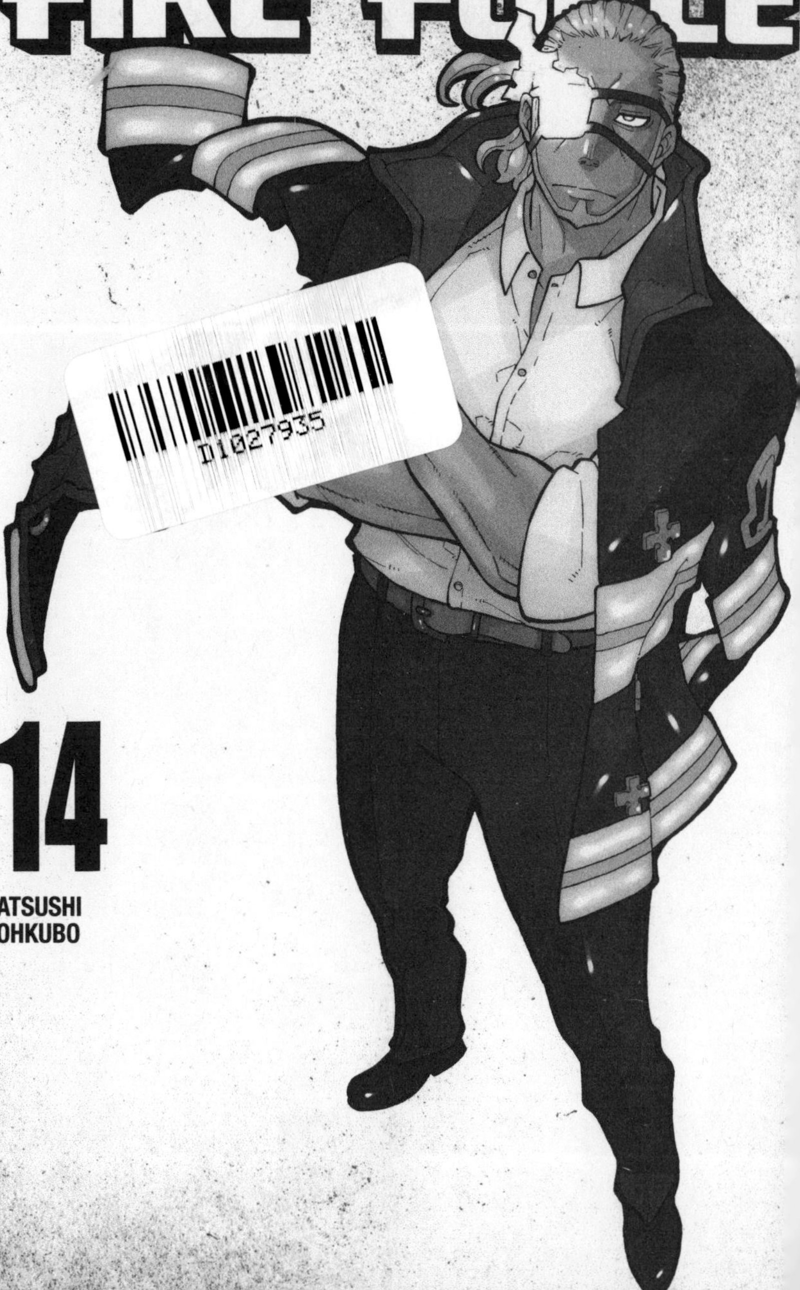

14

ATSUSHI
OHKUBO

world,
adventure,
tragedy....

VOL.14

ATSUSHI OHKUBO

A new
a new
a new

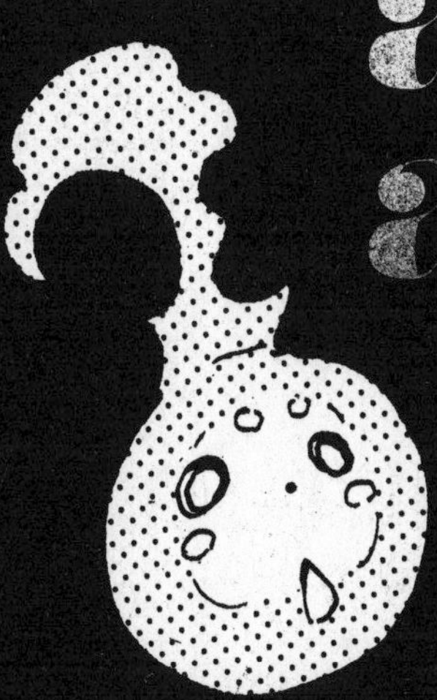

FIRE FORCE

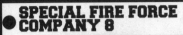

SPECIAL FIRE FORCE COMPANY 8

SECOND CLASS FIRE SOLDIER
(THIRD GENERATION PYROKINETIC)

ARTHUR BOYLE

Trained at the academy with Shinra. He follows his own personal code of chivalry as the self-proclaimed Knight King. He's a blockhead who is bad at mental exercise. But girls love him. He creates a fire sword with a blade that can cut through most anything. He's a weirdo who grows stronger the more delusional he gets. A guard (Knight) in Operation Chinese Landing.

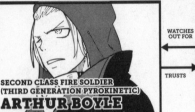

CAPTAIN
(NON-POWERED)

AKITARU ŌBI

The caring leader of the newly established Company 8. His goal is to investigate the other companies and uncover the truth about spontaneous human combustion. He has no powers, but uses his finely honed muscles as a weapon in a battle style that makes him worthy of the Captain title. A man of character, respected even in other companies.

WATCHES OUT FOR

TRUSTS

IDIOT!!

WATCHES OUT FOR

TRUSTS

STRONG BOND

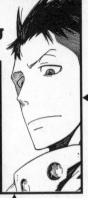

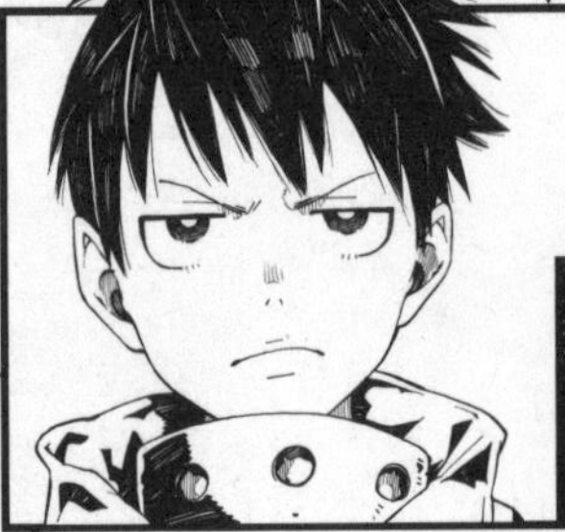

SECOND CLASS FIRE SOLDIER
(THIRD GENERATION PYROKINETIC)

SHINRA KUSAKABE

The bizarre smile that shows on his face when he gets nervous has earned him the derisive nickname of "devil," but he dreams of becoming a hero who saves people from spontaneous combustion! His weapon is a fiery kick. He seems to have a special flame called the Adolla Burst. A guard (Hero) in Operation Chinese Landing.

A NICE GIRL

LOOKS AWESOME ON THE JOB

A TOUGH BUT WEIRD LADY

HANG IN THERE, ROOKIE!

TERRIFIED

STRICT DISCIPLINARIAN

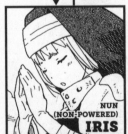

NUN
(NON-POWERED)

IRIS

A sister of the Holy Sol Temple, her prayers are an indispensable part of extinguishing Infernals. Personality-wise, she is no less than an angel. Her boobs are big. Very big. She demonstrated incredible resilience when facing the Infernal hordes.

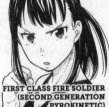

FIRST CLASS FIRE SOLDIER
(SECOND GENERATION PYROKINETIC)

MAKI OZE

A former member of the military, she is an excellent fighter who controls fire. She's a cool lady, but is mad about love stories, and her beauty is overshadowed by her "head full of flowers and wedding bells." She's friendly, but goes berserk when anyone comments on her muscles. Powerful enough to control a firestorm.

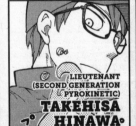

LIEUTENANT
(SECOND GENERATION PYROKINETIC)

TAKEHISA HINAWA

A dry, unemotional ex-military man, whose stern discipline is feared among the new recruits. He helped Ōbi to found Company 8. He never allows the soldiers to play with fire. He is currently working with Karim and the other lieutenants to vanquish demon Infernals.

THE GIRLS' CLUB

RESPECTS

SOLDIERS FROM EACH COMPANY

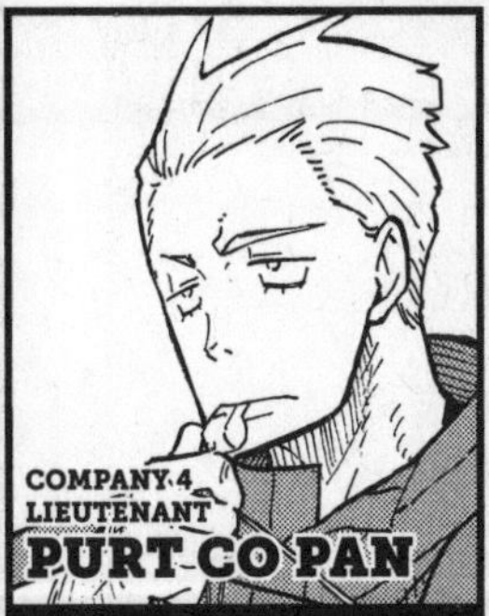

COMPANY 4 LIEUTENANT

PURT CO PAN

An instructor from Shinra's time at the Academy. Specializes in status enhancements. Commander of Operation Chinese Landing.

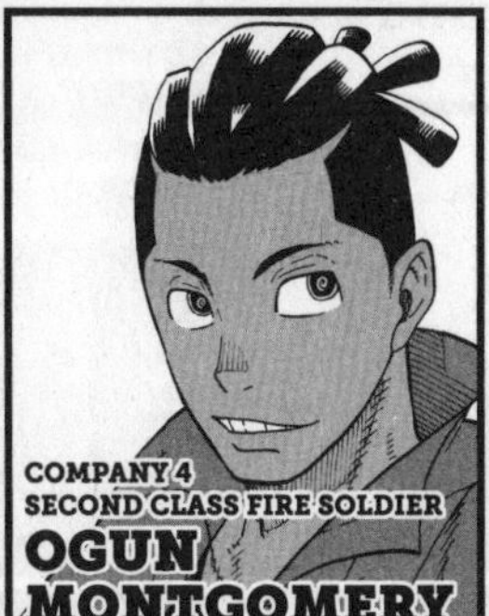

COMPANY 4 SECOND CLASS FIRE SOLDIER

OGUN MONTGOMERY

Classmate from Shinra and Arthur's time at the Academy, and top of the class. Group Leader in Operation Chinese Landing.

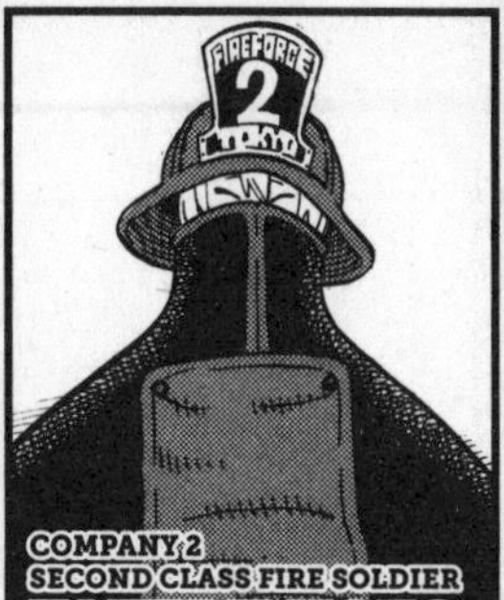

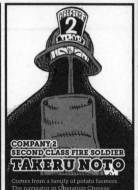

COMPANY 2 SECOND CLASS FIRE SOLDIER

TAKERU NOTO

Comes from a family of potato farmers. The navigator in Operation Chinese Landing.

TALKING MOLE & CROW

Former residents of the Oasis who were chased out by the sudden appearance of a mysterious band of ne'er-do-wells. Volunteered to guide the expedition to the Oasis.

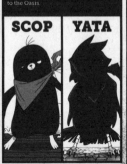

SCOP

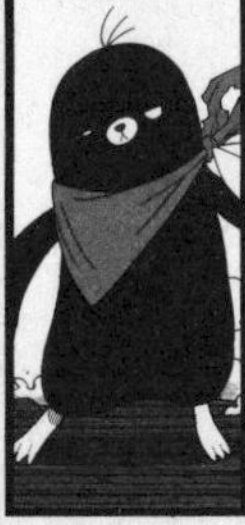

YATA

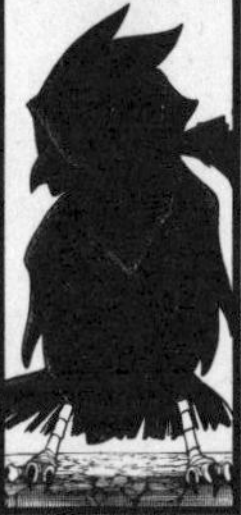

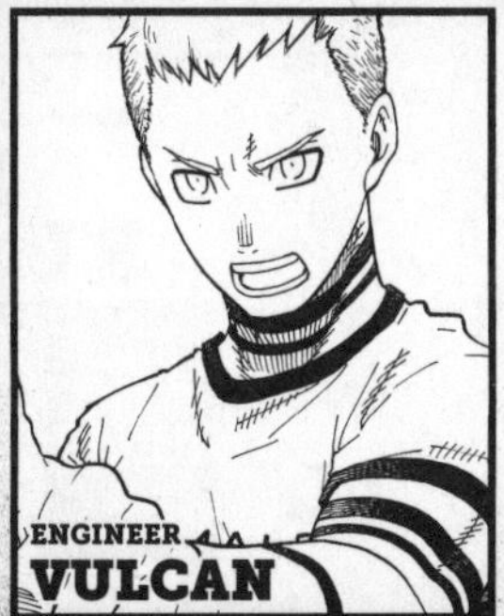

ENGINEER

VULCAN

The greatest engineer of the day, renowned as the God of Fire and the Forge. The weapons he created have increased Company 8's powers immensely. His excessively rock-and-roll designs are Ôbi-approved!

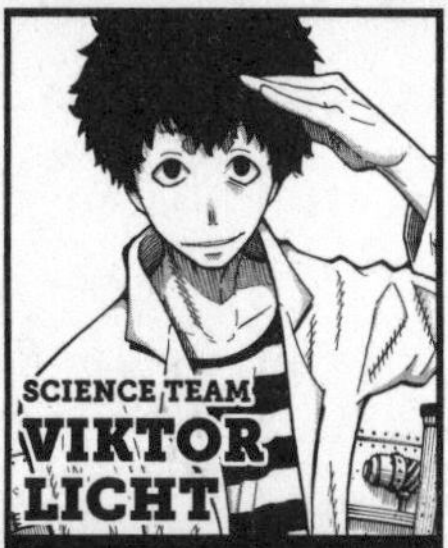

SCIENCE TEAM

VIKTOR LICHT

A suspicious genius deployed from Haijima Industries to fill the vacancy in Company 8's science department. Works to analyze the scenes of fires. Investigator in Operation Chinese Landing.

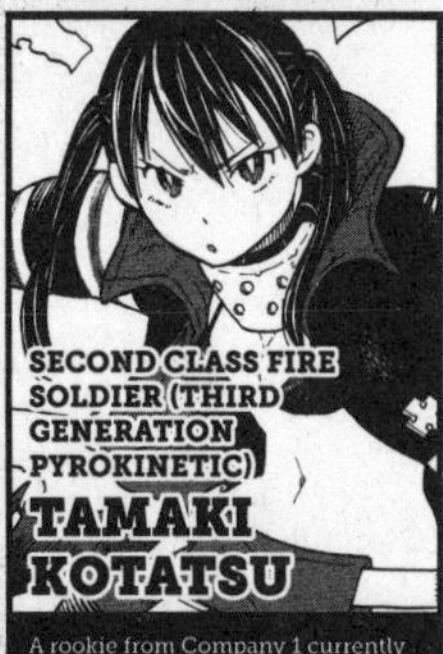

SECOND CLASS FIRE SOLDIER (THIRD GENERATION PYROKINETIC)

TAMAKI KOTATSU

A rookie from Company 1 currently in Company 8's care. Although she has a "lucky lecher lure" condition, she nevertheless has a pure heart. Prayer-giver in Operation Chinese Landing.

SUMMARY...

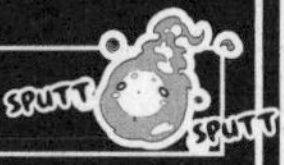
SPUTT
SPUTT

Shinra and six other members of the Special Fire Force have been chosen for Operation Chinese Landing. They head for the Spatial Tear to the northwest of Xinqing Dao, but on their way they meet the mole Scop and other animals who have been chased out of the Oasis. Scop guides the team to his former home, in the heart of which stands the Tabernacle—an edifice identical to Amaterasu, the keystone of the Tokyo Empire. What is the true nature of this Tabernacle? And what is the connection between the Adolla Burst and the Great Cataclysm of 250 years ago?!

FIRE FORCE 14

CONTENTS

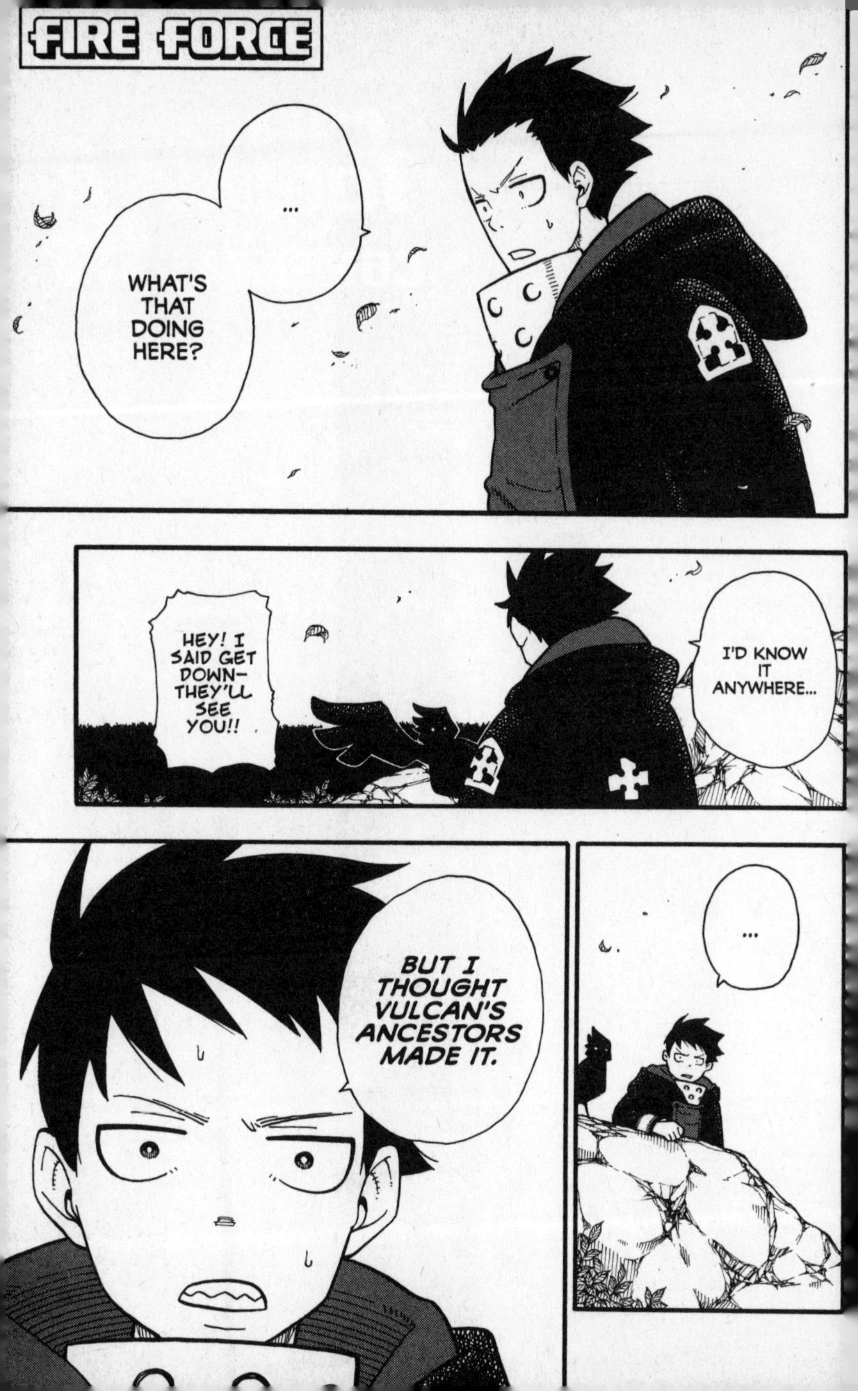
...
WHAT'S THAT DOING HERE?
I'D KNOW IT ANYWHERE...
HEY! I SAID GET DOWN—THEY'LL SEE YOU!!
...
BUT I THOUGHT VULCAN'S ANCESTORS MADE IT.

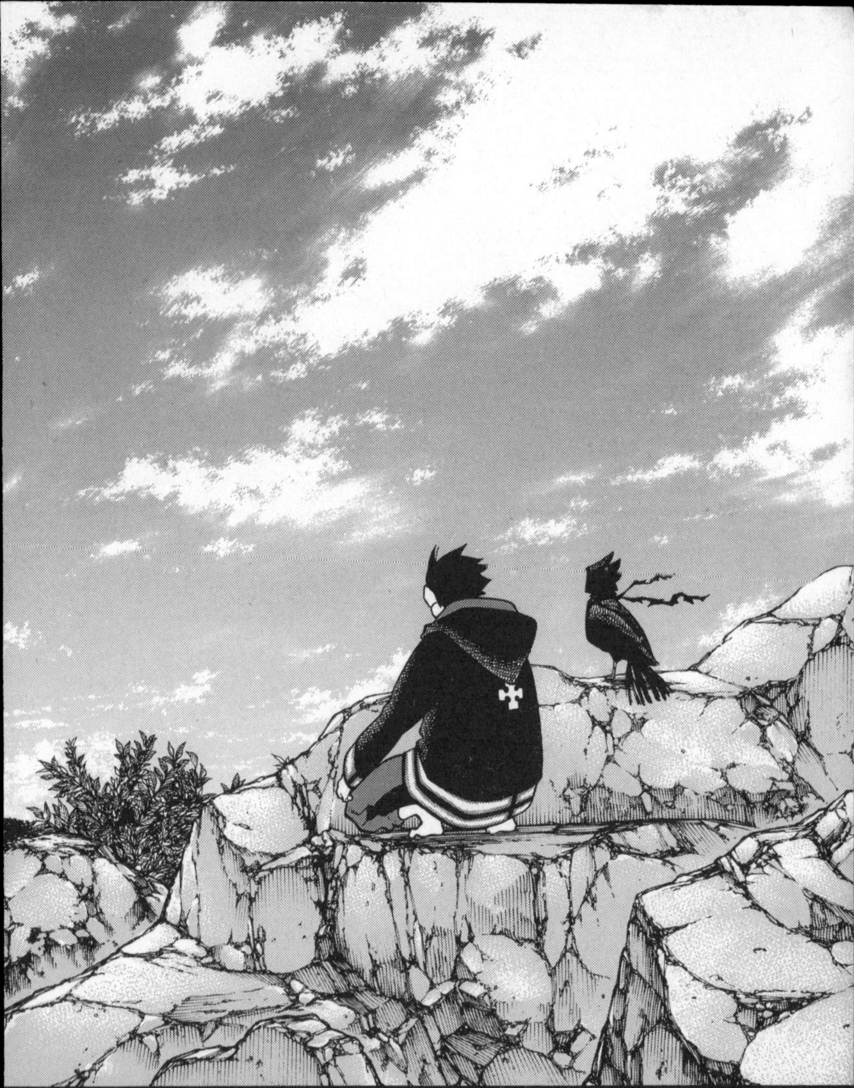

THE OASIS

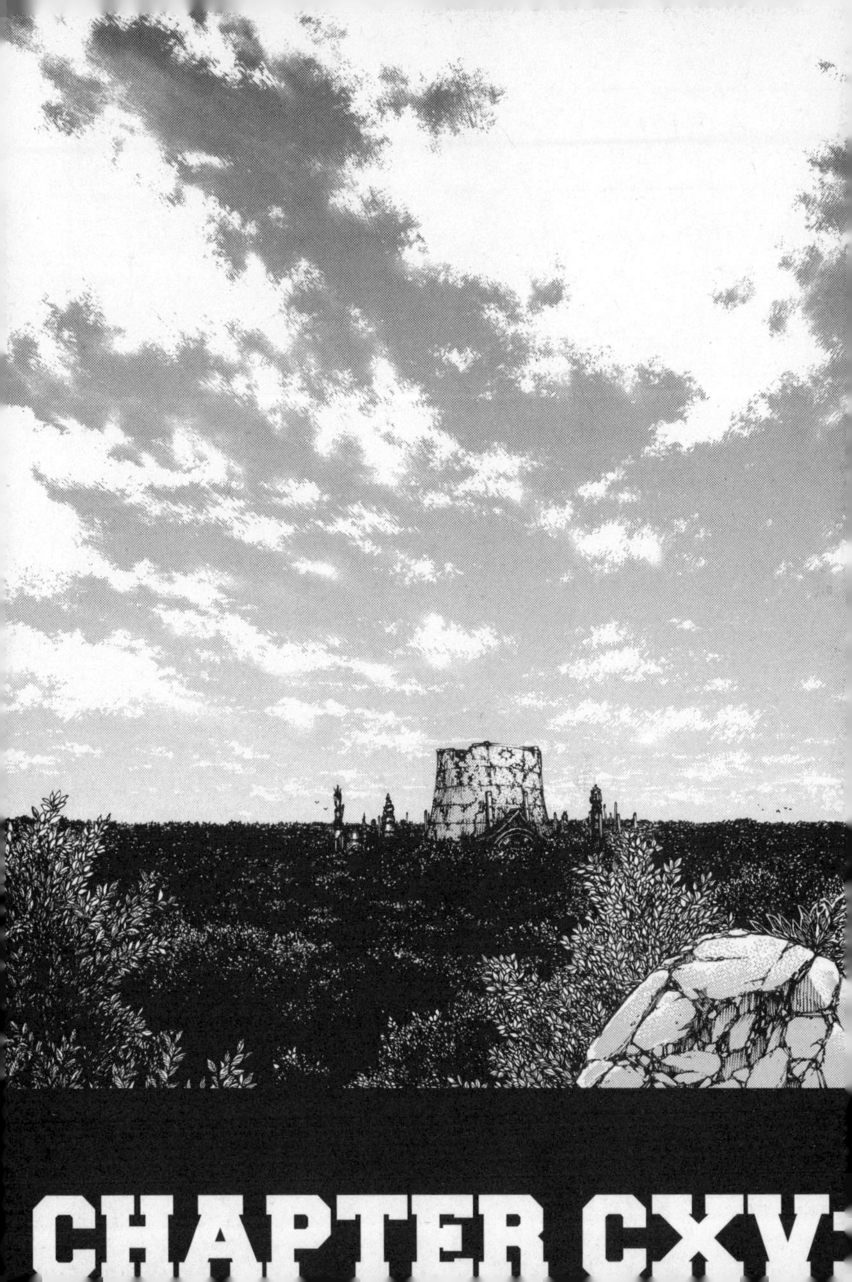

CHAPTER CXV:

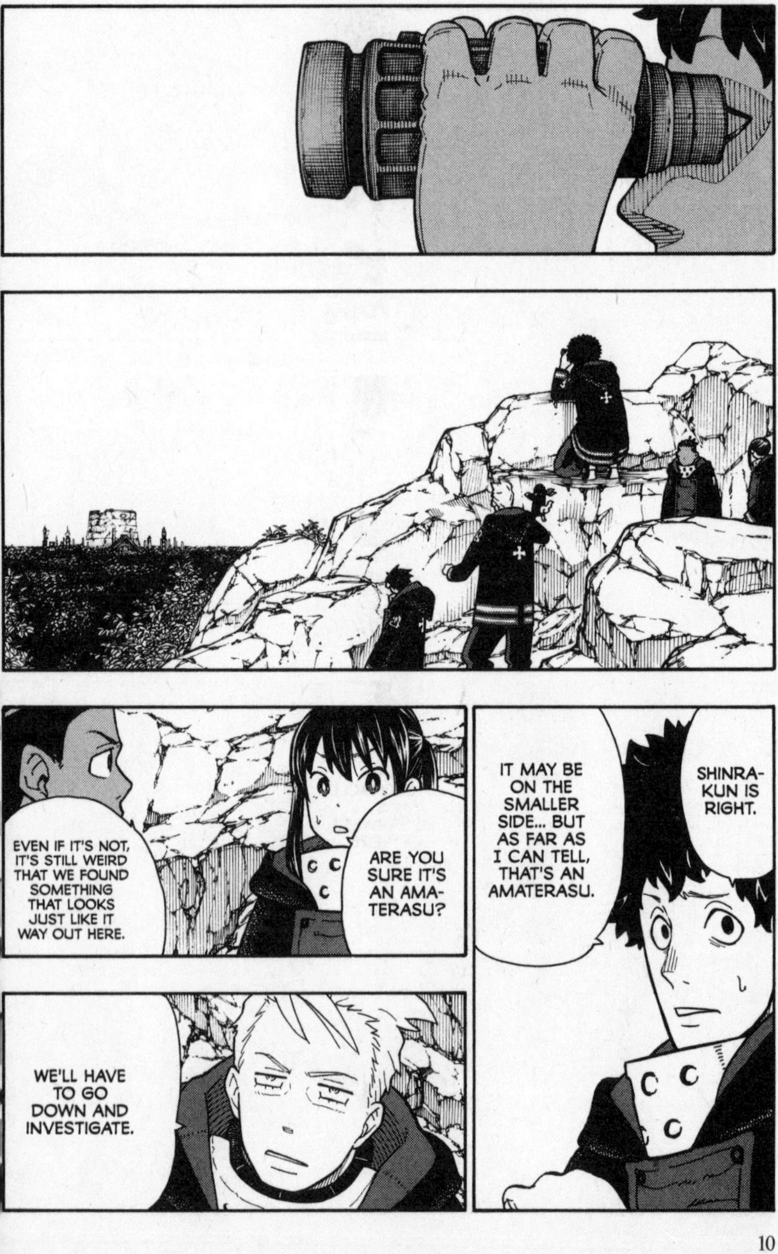
SHINRA-KUN IS RIGHT.
IT MAY BE ON THE SMALLER SIDE... BUT AS FAR AS I CAN TELL, THAT'S AN AMATERASU.
ARE YOU SURE IT'S AN AMA-TERASU?
EVEN IF IT'S NOT, IT'S STILL WEIRD THAT WE FOUND SOMETHING THAT LOOKS JUST LIKE IT WAY OUT HERE.
WE'LL HAVE TO GO DOWN AND INVESTIGATE.

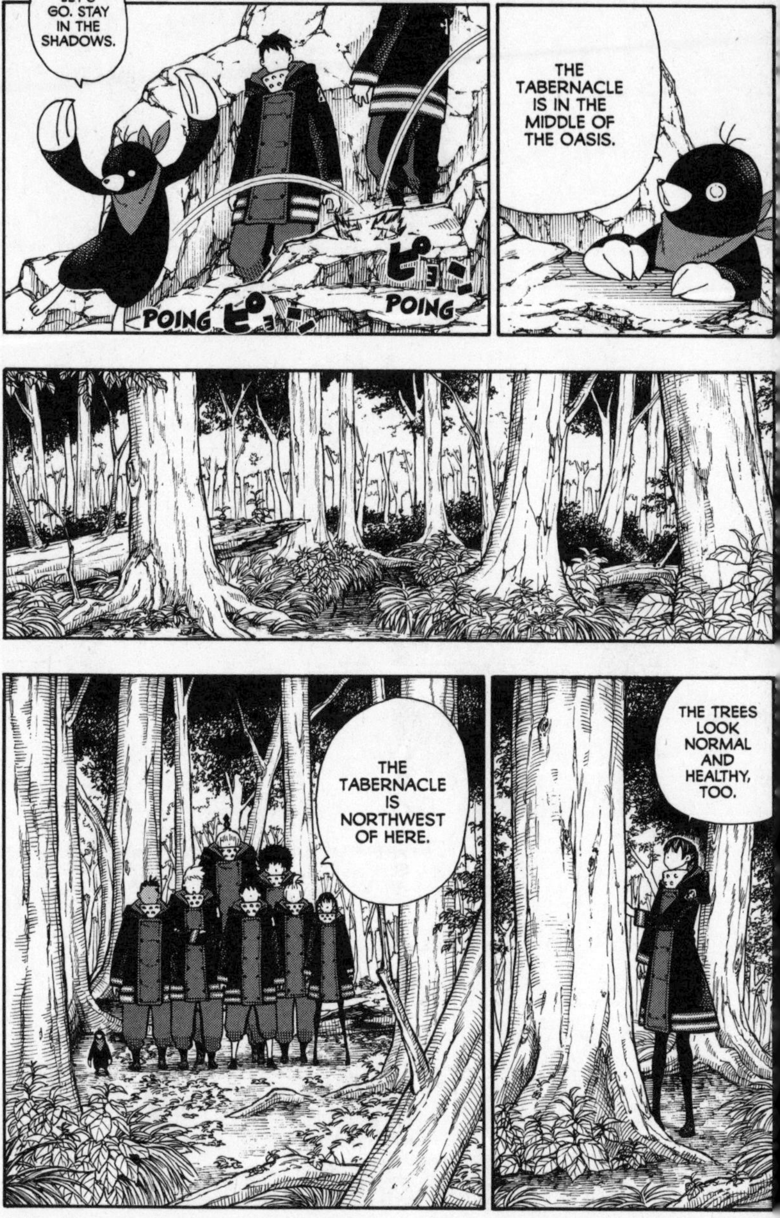
THE TABERNACLE IS IN THE MIDDLE OF THE OASIS.
LET'S GO. STAY IN THE SHADOWS.
POING
POING
THE TREES LOOK NORMAL AND HEALTHY, TOO.
THE TABERNACLE IS NORTHWEST OF HERE.

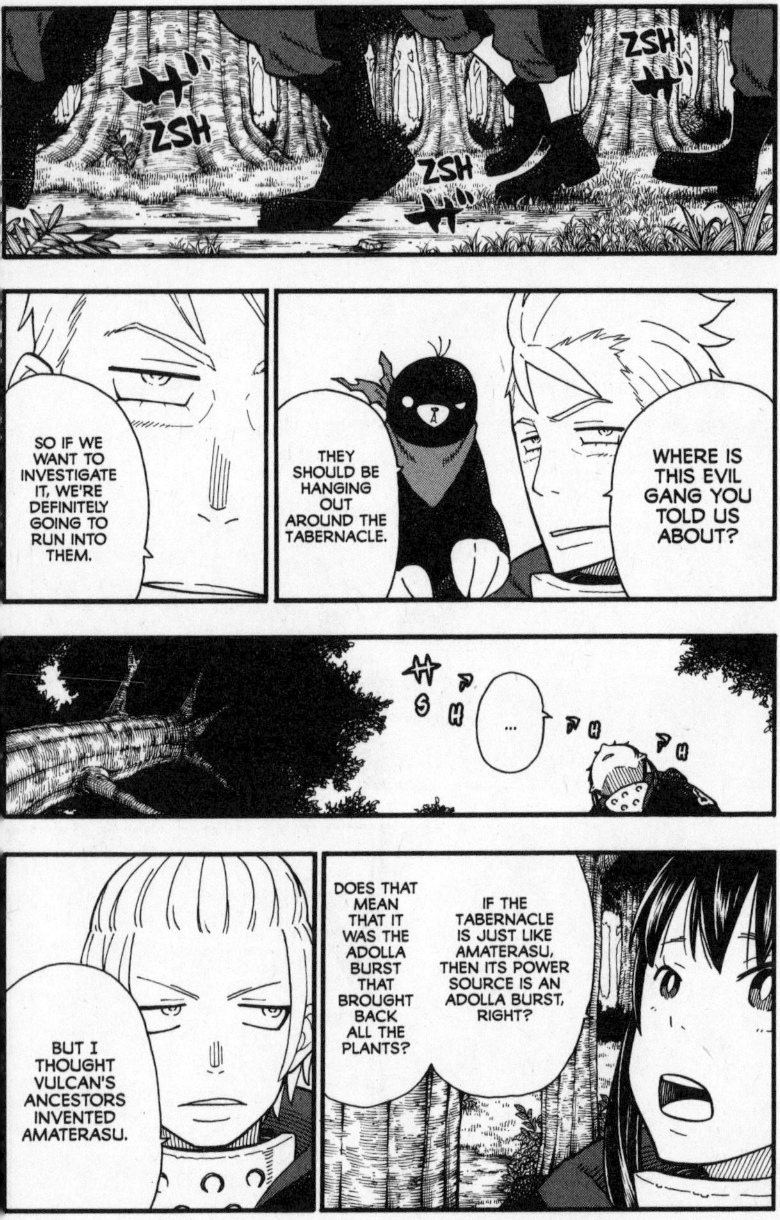
ZSH
ZSH
ZSH
WHERE IS THIS EVIL GANG YOU TOLD US ABOUT?
THEY SHOULD BE HANGING OUT AROUND THE TABERNACLE.
SO IF WE WANT TO INVESTIGATE IT, WE'RE DEFINITELY GOING TO RUN INTO THEM.
...
IF THE TABERNACLE IS JUST LIKE AMATERASU, THEN ITS POWER SOURCE IS AN ADOLLA BURST, RIGHT?
DOES THAT MEAN THAT IT WAS THE ADOLLA BURST THAT BROUGHT BACK ALL THE PLANTS?
BUT I THOUGHT VULCAN'S ANCESTORS INVENTED AMATERASU.

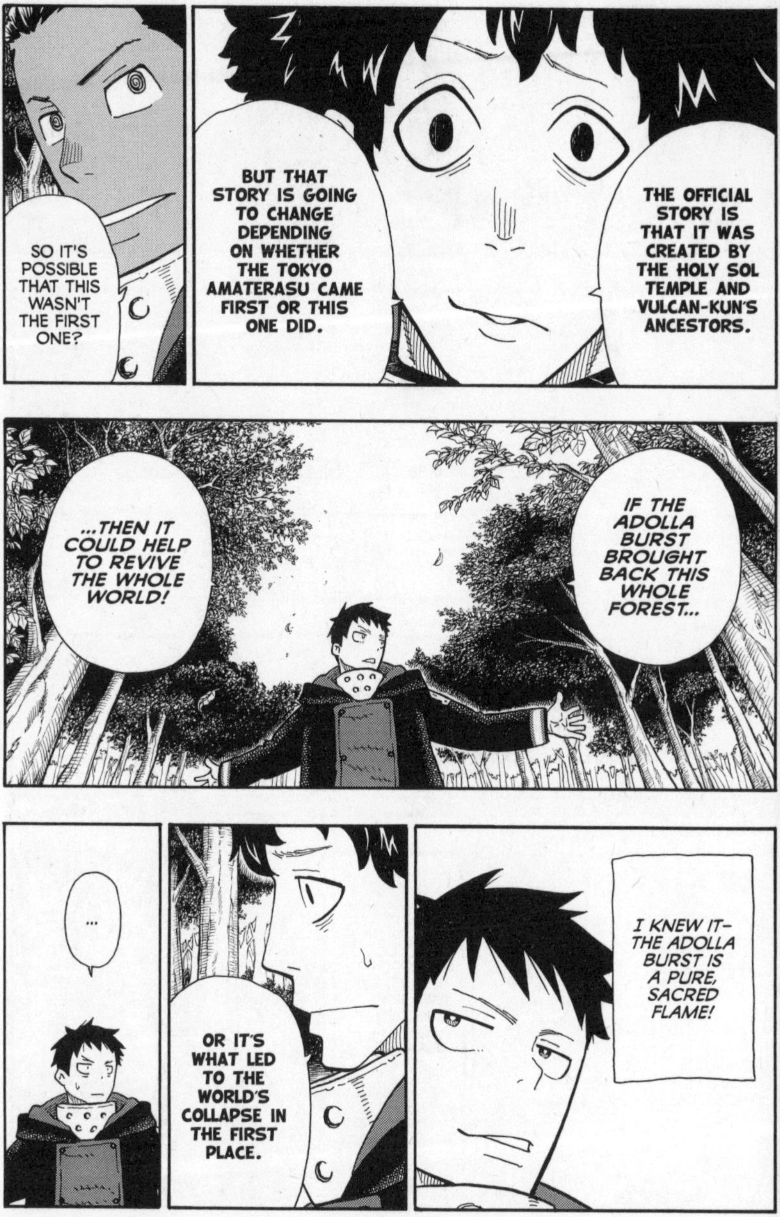
THE OFFICIAL STORY IS THAT IT WAS CREATED BY THE HOLY SOL TEMPLE AND VULCAN-KUN'S ANCESTORS.
BUT THAT STORY IS GOING TO CHANGE DEPENDING ON WHETHER THE TOKYO AMATERASU CAME FIRST OR THIS ONE DID.
SO IT'S POSSIBLE THAT THIS WASN'T THE FIRST ONE?
IF THE ADOLLA BURST BROUGHT BACK THIS WHOLE FOREST...
...THEN IT COULD HELP TO REVIVE THE WHOLE WORLD!
I KNEW IT–THE ADOLLA BURST IS A PURE, SACRED FLAME!
OR IT'S WHAT LED TO THE WORLD'S COLLAPSE IN THE FIRST PLACE.
...

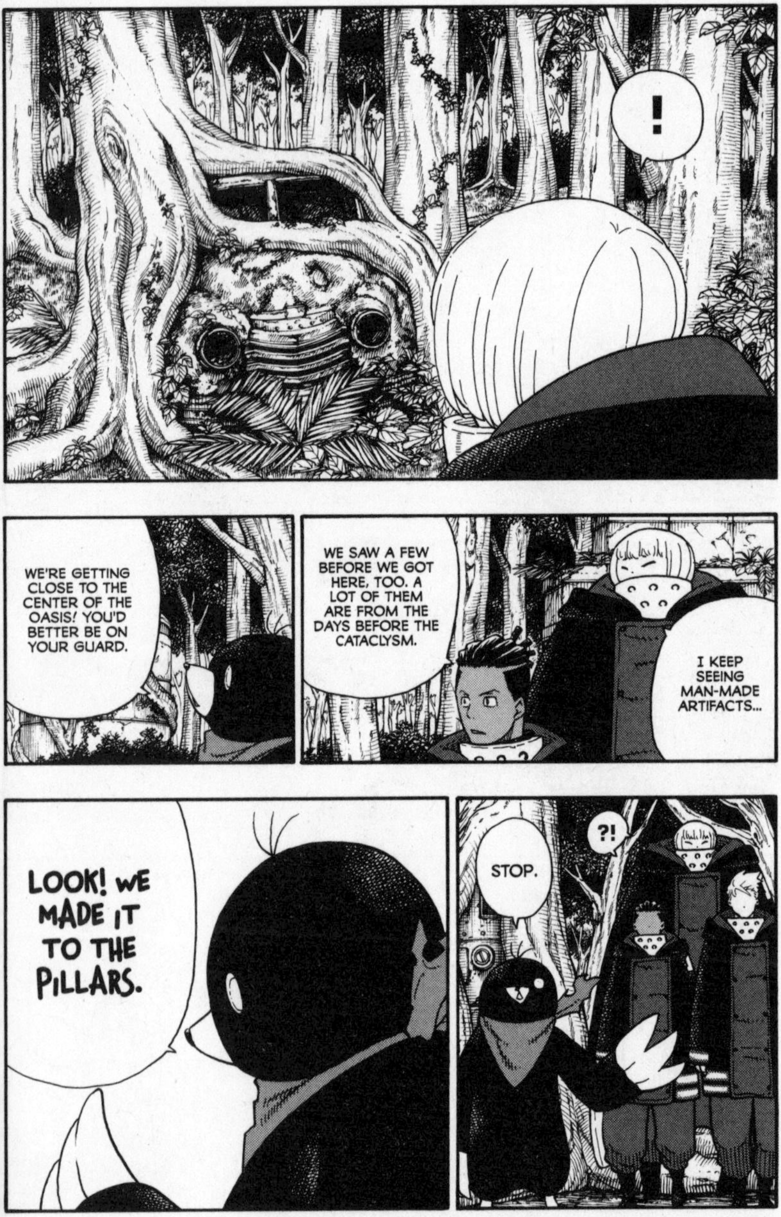
!
I KEEP SEEING MAN-MADE ARTIFACTS...
WE SAW A FEW BEFORE WE GOT HERE, TOO. A LOT OF THEM ARE FROM THE DAYS BEFORE THE CATACLYSM.
WE'RE GETTING CLOSE TO THE CENTER OF THE OASIS! YOU'D BETTER BE ON YOUR GUARD.
STOP.
?!
LOOK! WE MADE IT TO THE PILLARS.

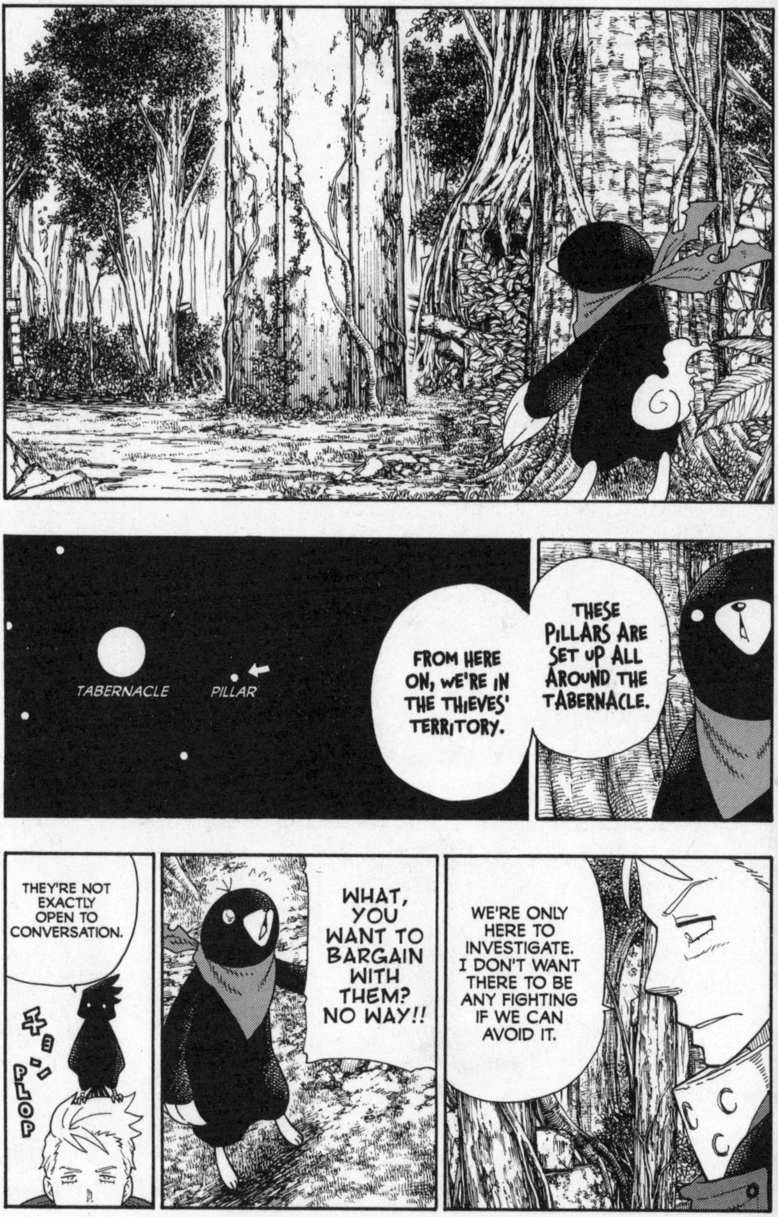
THESE PILLARS ARE SET UP ALL AROUND THE TABERNACLE.
FROM HERE ON, WE'RE IN THE THIEVES' TERRITORY.
TABERNACLE
PILLAR
WE'RE ONLY HERE TO INVESTIGATE. I DON'T WANT THERE TO BE ANY FIGHTING IF WE CAN AVOID IT.
WHAT, YOU WANT TO BARGAIN WITH THEM? NO WAY!!
THEY'RE NOT EXACTLY OPEN TO CONVERSATION.
PLOP

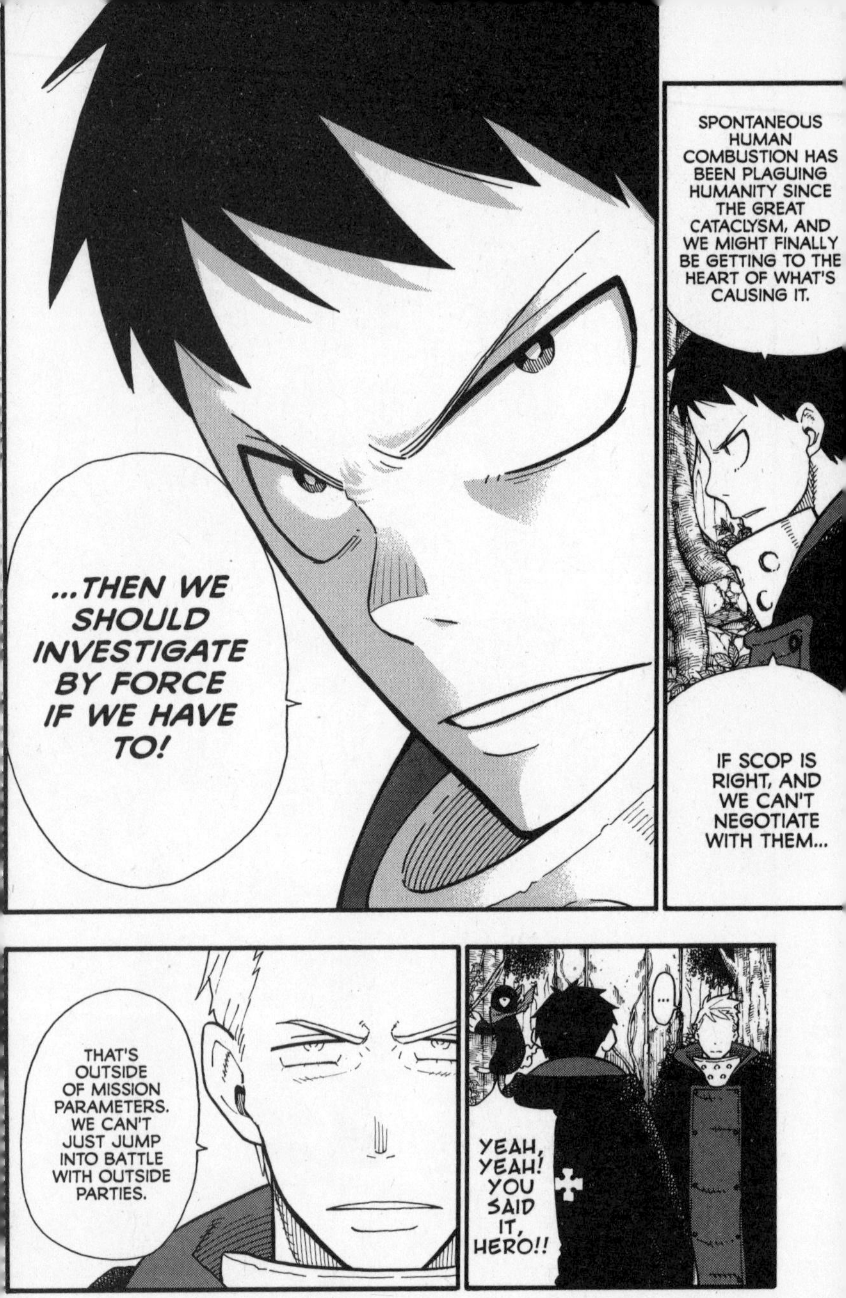
SPONTANEOUS HUMAN COMBUSTION HAS BEEN PLAGUING HUMANITY SINCE THE GREAT CATACLYSM, AND WE MIGHT FINALLY BE GETTING TO THE HEART OF WHAT'S CAUSING IT.
IF SCOP IS RIGHT, AND WE CAN'T NEGOTIATE WITH THEM...
...THEN WE SHOULD INVESTIGATE BY FORCE IF WE HAVE TO!
...
YEAH, YEAH! YOU SAID IT, HERO!!
THAT'S OUTSIDE OF MISSION PARAMETERS. WE CAN'T JUST JUMP INTO BATTLE WITH OUTSIDE PARTIES.

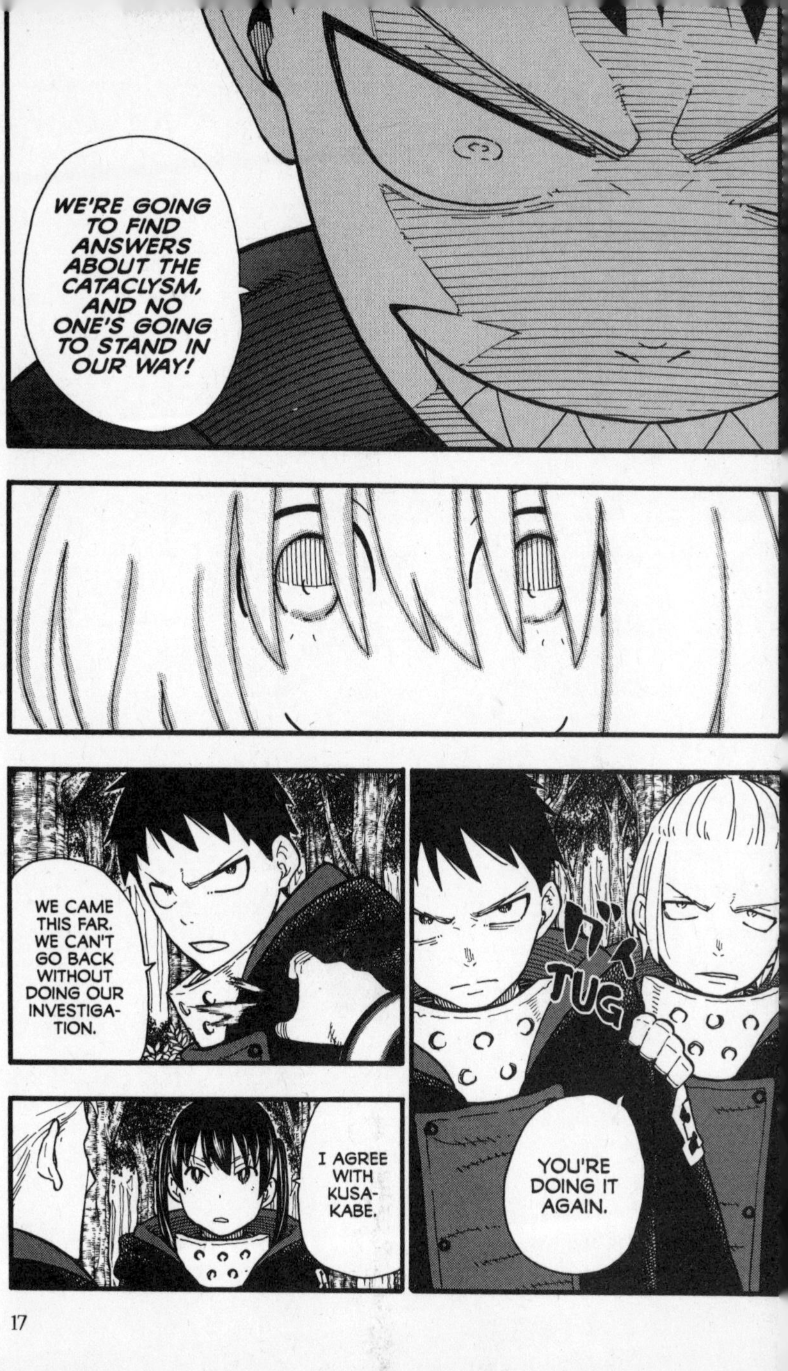
WE'RE GOING TO FIND ANSWERS ABOUT THE CATACLYSM, AND NO ONE'S GOING TO STAND IN OUR WAY!
TUG
YOU'RE DOING IT AGAIN.
WE CAME THIS FAR. WE CAN'T GO BACK WITHOUT DOING OUR INVESTIGA-TION.
I AGREE WITH KUSA-KABE.

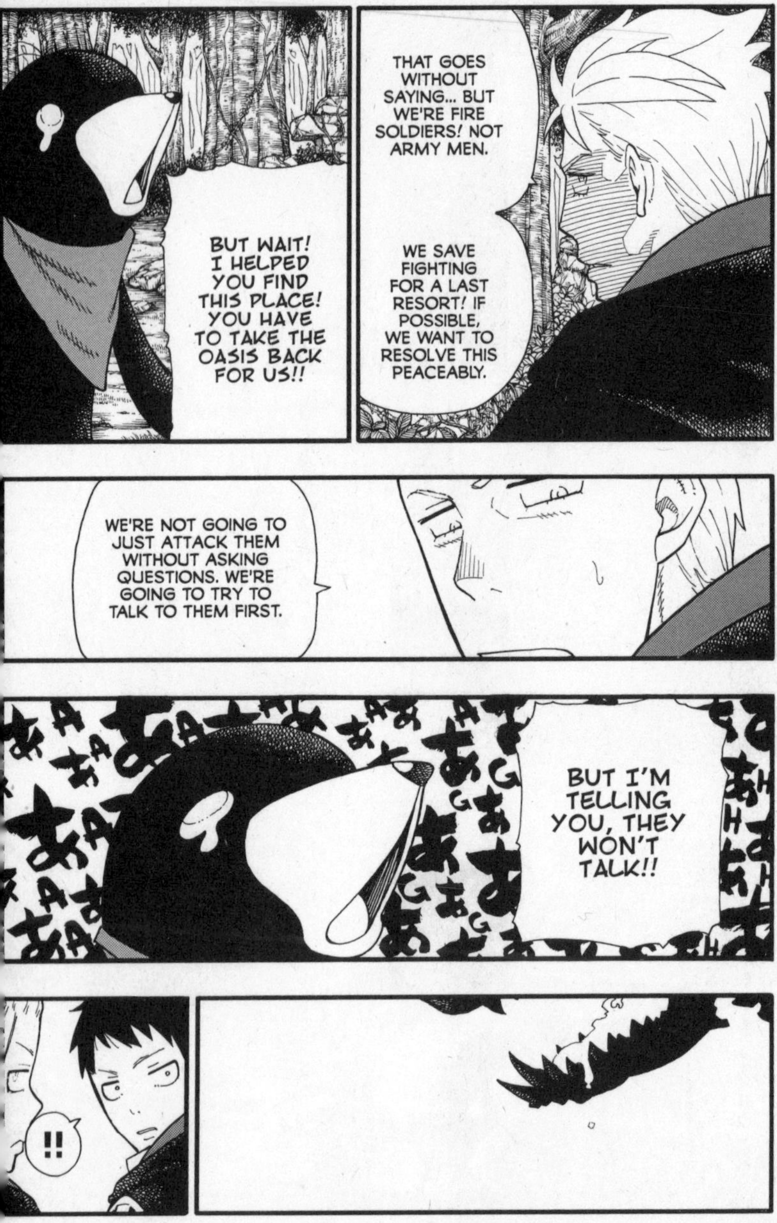
THAT GOES WITHOUT SAYING... BUT WE'RE FIRE SOLDIERS! NOT ARMY MEN.
WE SAVE FIGHTING FOR A LAST RESORT! IF POSSIBLE, WE WANT TO RESOLVE THIS PEACEABLY.
BUT WAIT! I HELPED YOU FIND THIS PLACE! YOU HAVE TO TAKE THE OASIS BACK FOR US!!
WE'RE NOT GOING TO JUST ATTACK THEM WITHOUT ASKING QUESTIONS. WE'RE GOING TO TRY TO TALK TO THEM FIRST.
BUT I'M TELLING YOU, THEY WON'T TALK!!
!!

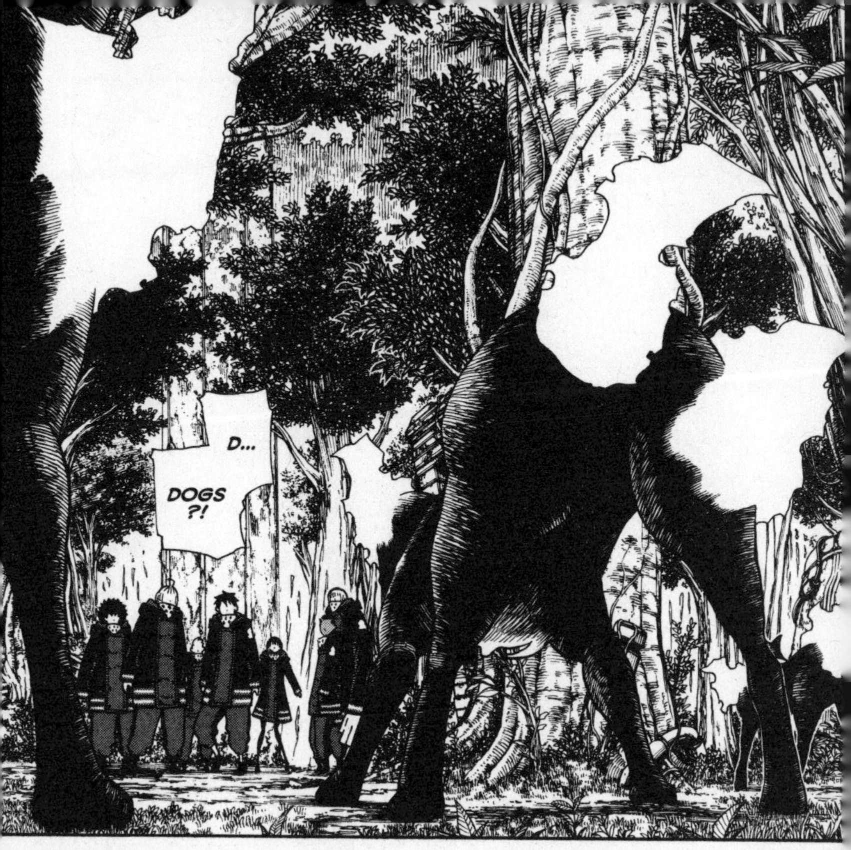
D...
DOGS ?!
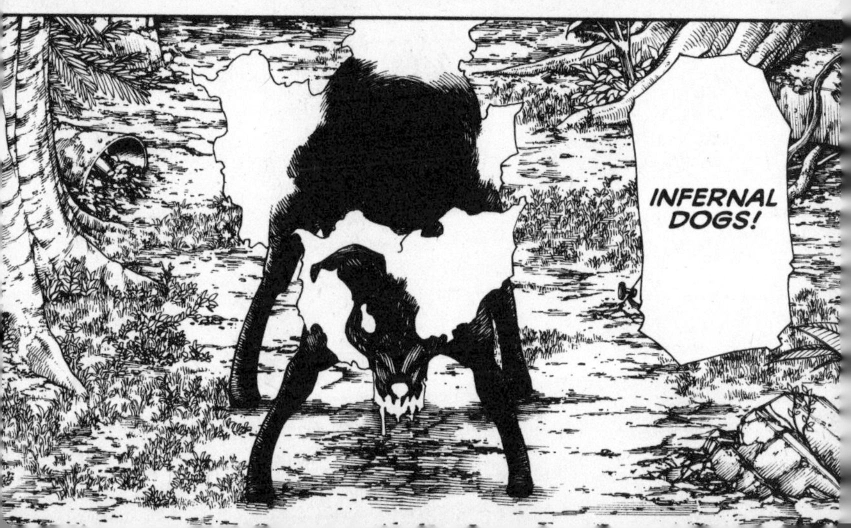
INFERNAL DOGS!

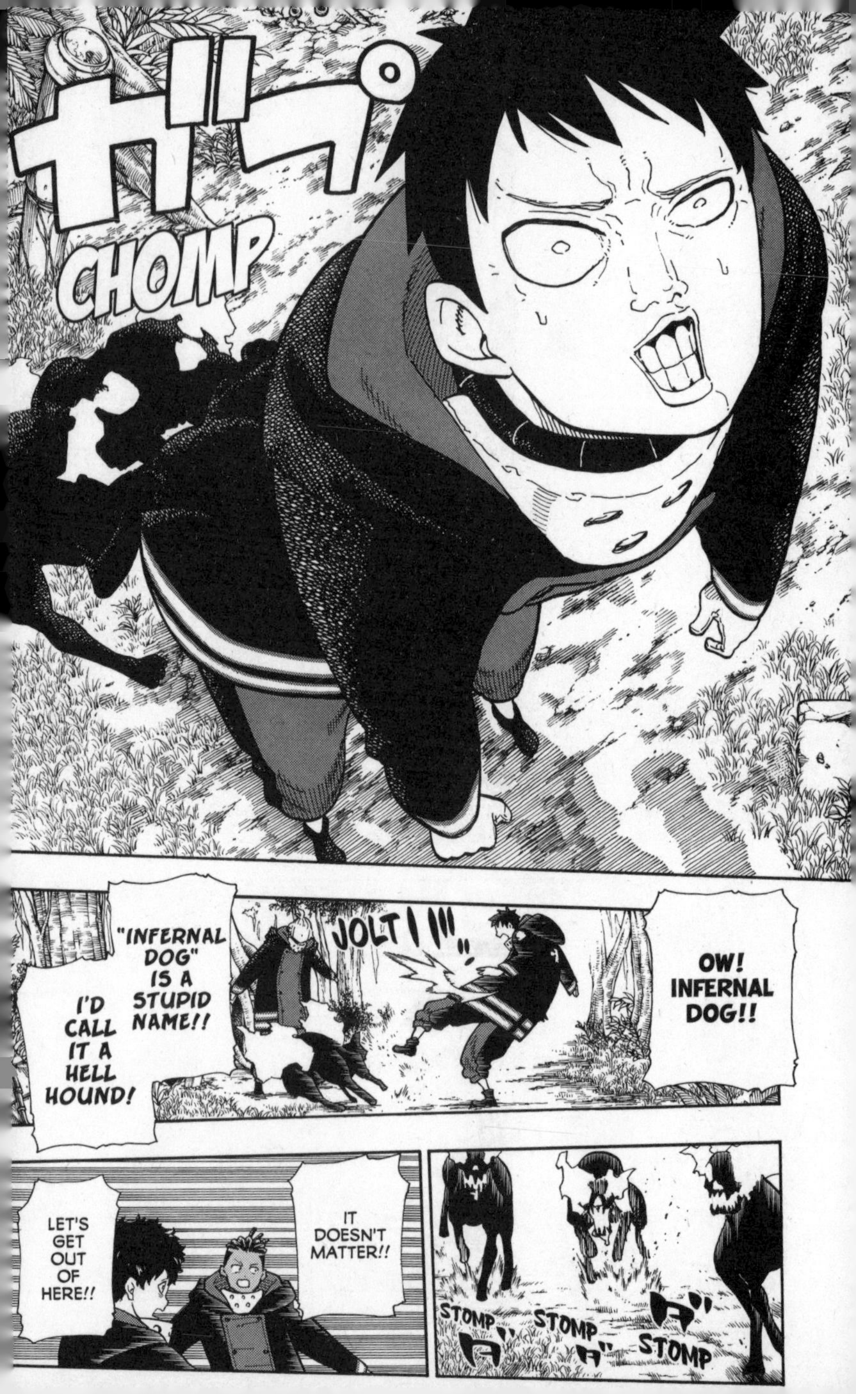
ガプ
CHOMP
OW! INFERNAL DOG!!
JOLT
"INFERNAL DOG" IS A STUPID NAME!!
I'D CALL IT A HELL HOUND!
STOMP
STOMP
STOMP
IT DOESN'T MATTER!!
LET'S GET OUT OF HERE!!

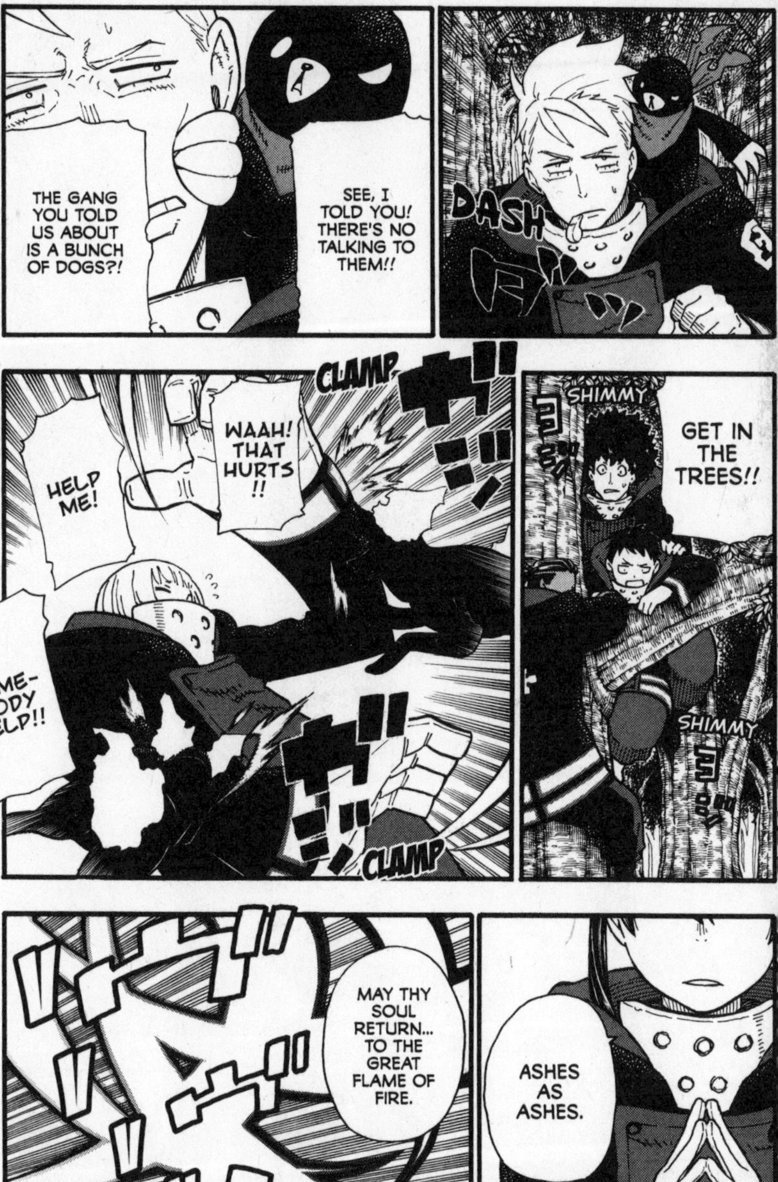

DASH
SEE, I TOLD YOU! THERE'S NO TALKING TO THEM!!
THE GANG YOU TOLD US ABOUT IS A BUNCH OF DOGS?!
GET IN THE TREES!!
SHIMMY
SHIMMY
CLAMP
WAAH! THAT HURTS!!
HELP ME!
SOME-BODY HELP!!
CLAMP
ASHES AS ASHES.
MAY THY SOUL RETURN... TO THE GREAT FLAME OF FIRE.

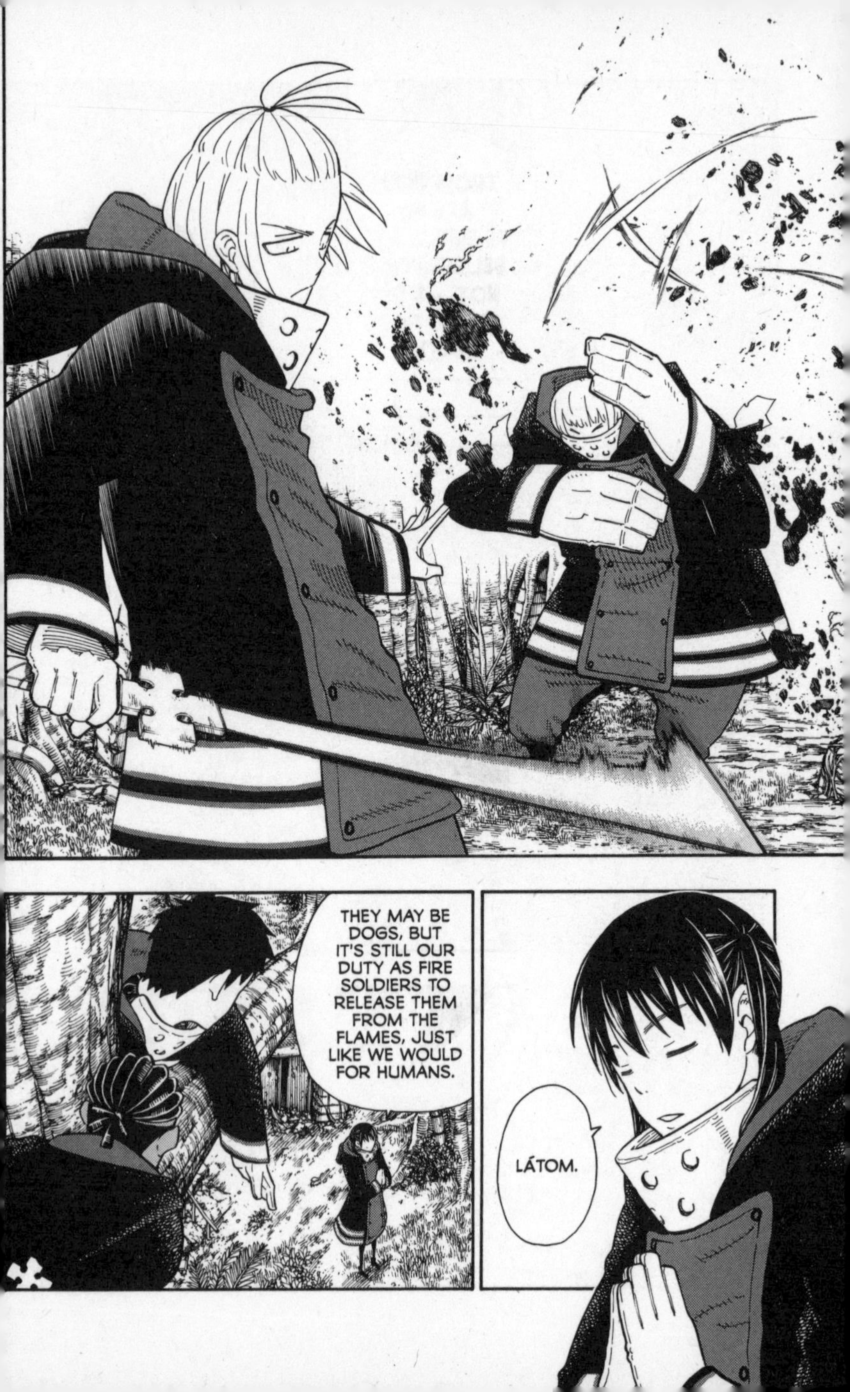
LÁTOM.
THEY MAY BE DOGS, BUT IT'S STILL OUR DUTY AS FIRE SOLDIERS TO RELEASE THEM FROM THE FLAMES, JUST LIKE WE WOULD FOR HUMANS.

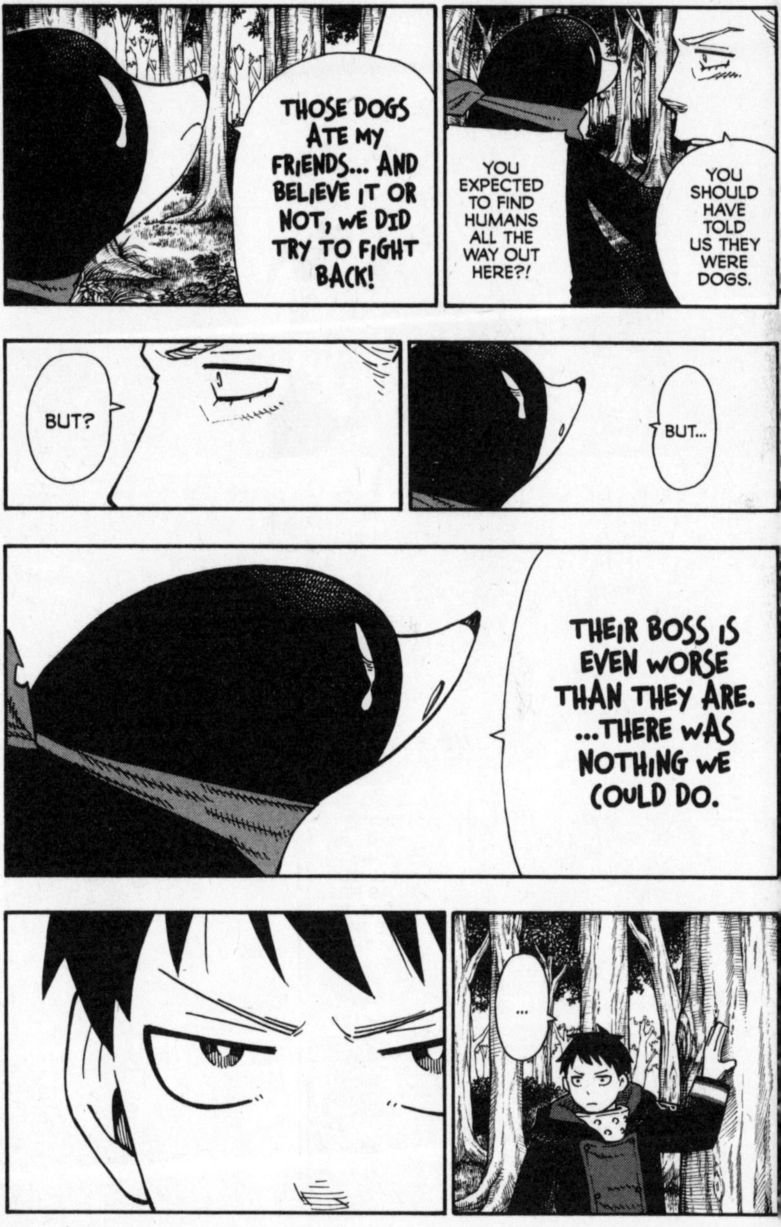
YOU SHOULD HAVE TOLD US THEY WERE DOGS.
YOU EXPECTED TO FIND HUMANS ALL THE WAY OUT HERE?!
THOSE DOGS ATE MY FRIENDS... AND BELIEVE IT OR NOT, WE DID TRY TO FIGHT BACK!
BUT...
BUT?
THEIR BOSS IS EVEN WORSE THAN THEY ARE. ...THERE WAS NOTHING WE COULD DO.
...

"PROTECT THE FOREST."

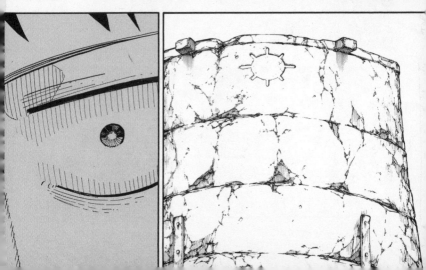

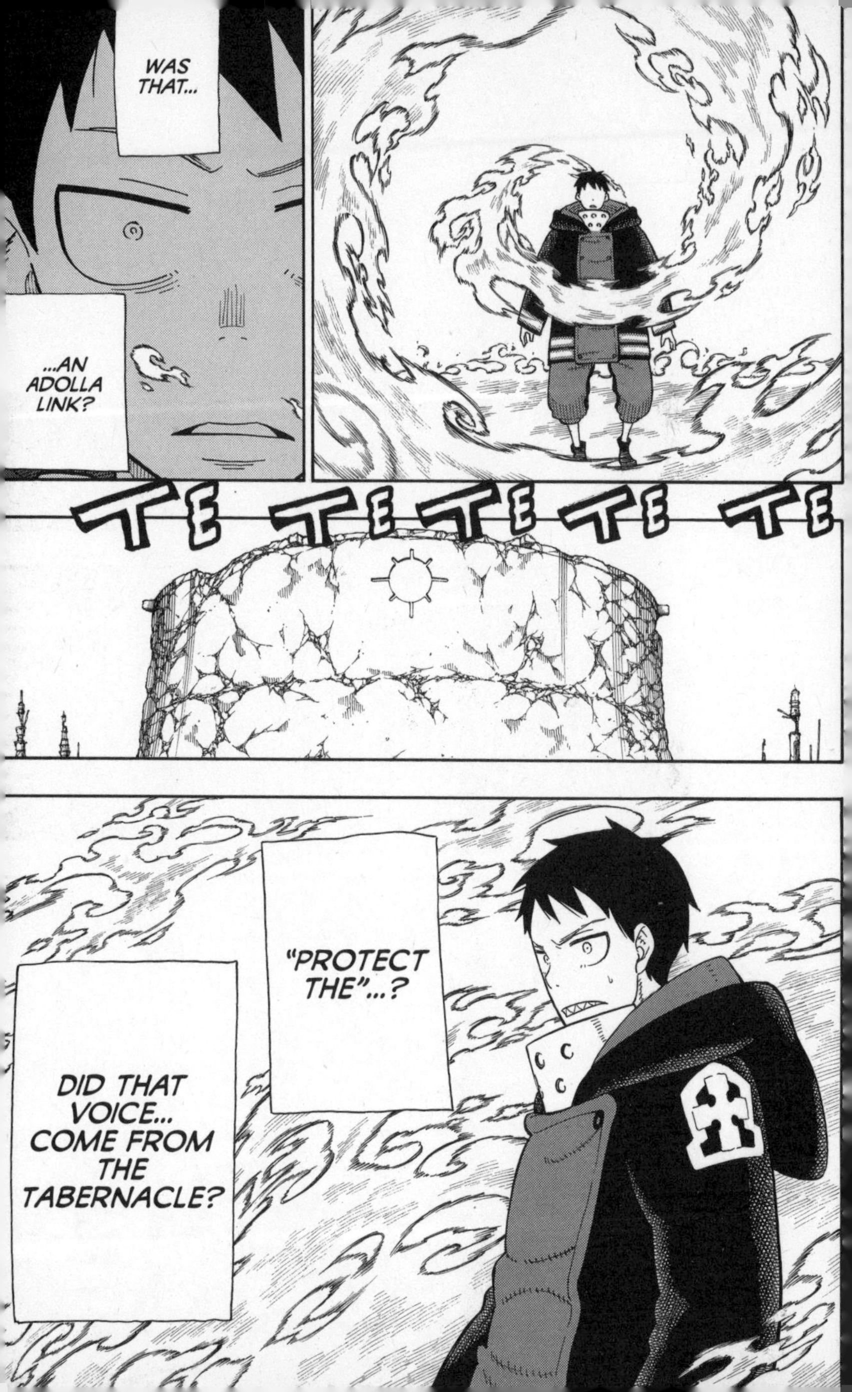
WAS THAT...
...AN ADOLLA LINK?
TE TE TE TE TE
"PROTECT THE"...?
DID THAT VOICE... COME FROM THE TABERNACLE?

FIRE FORCE

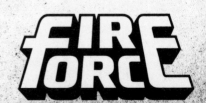

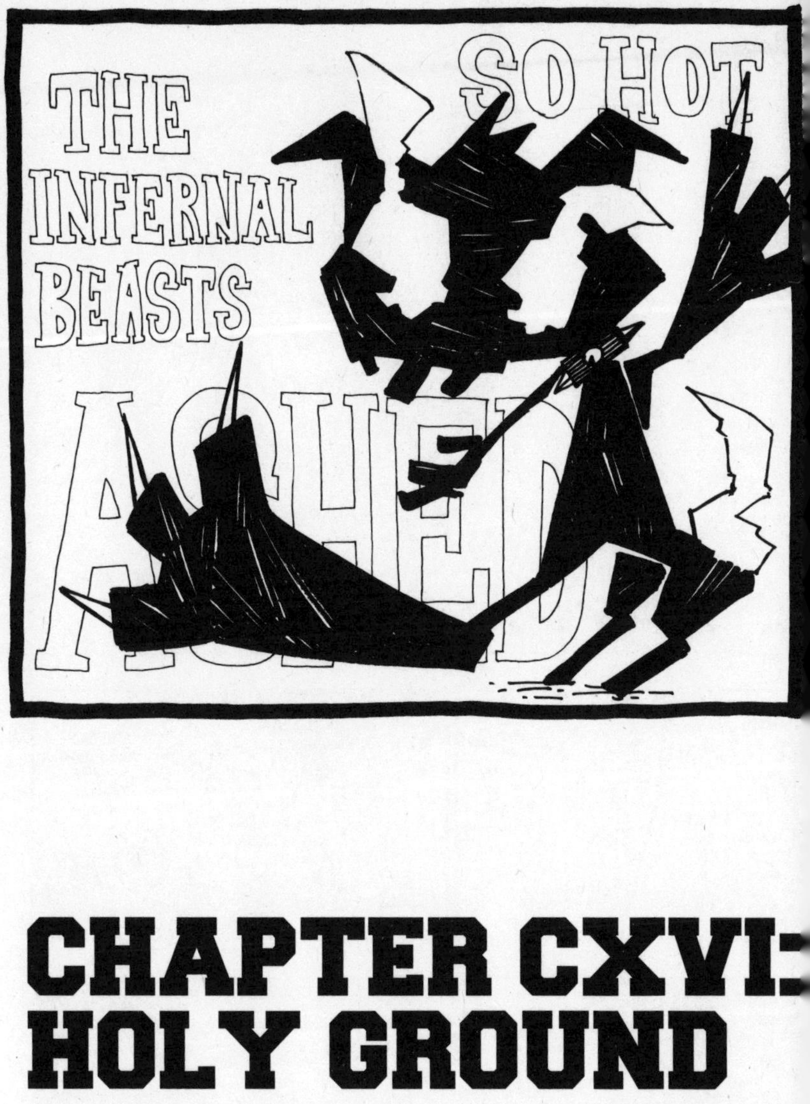
THE INFERNAL BEASTS
SO HOT

CHAPTER CXVI: HOLY GROUND

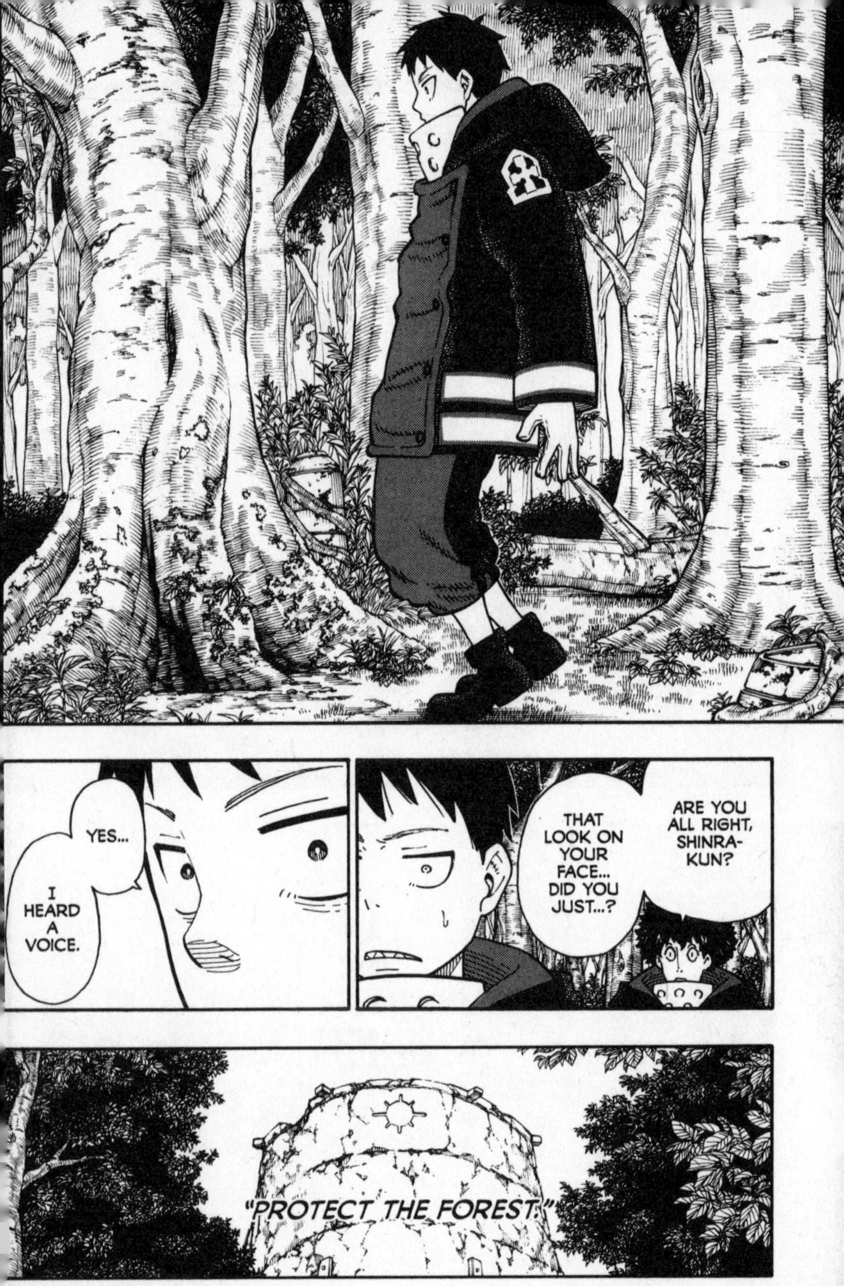
ARE YOU ALL RIGHT, SHINRA-KUN?
THAT LOOK ON YOUR FACE... DID YOU JUST...?
YES...
I HEARD A VOICE.
"PROTECT THE FOREST."

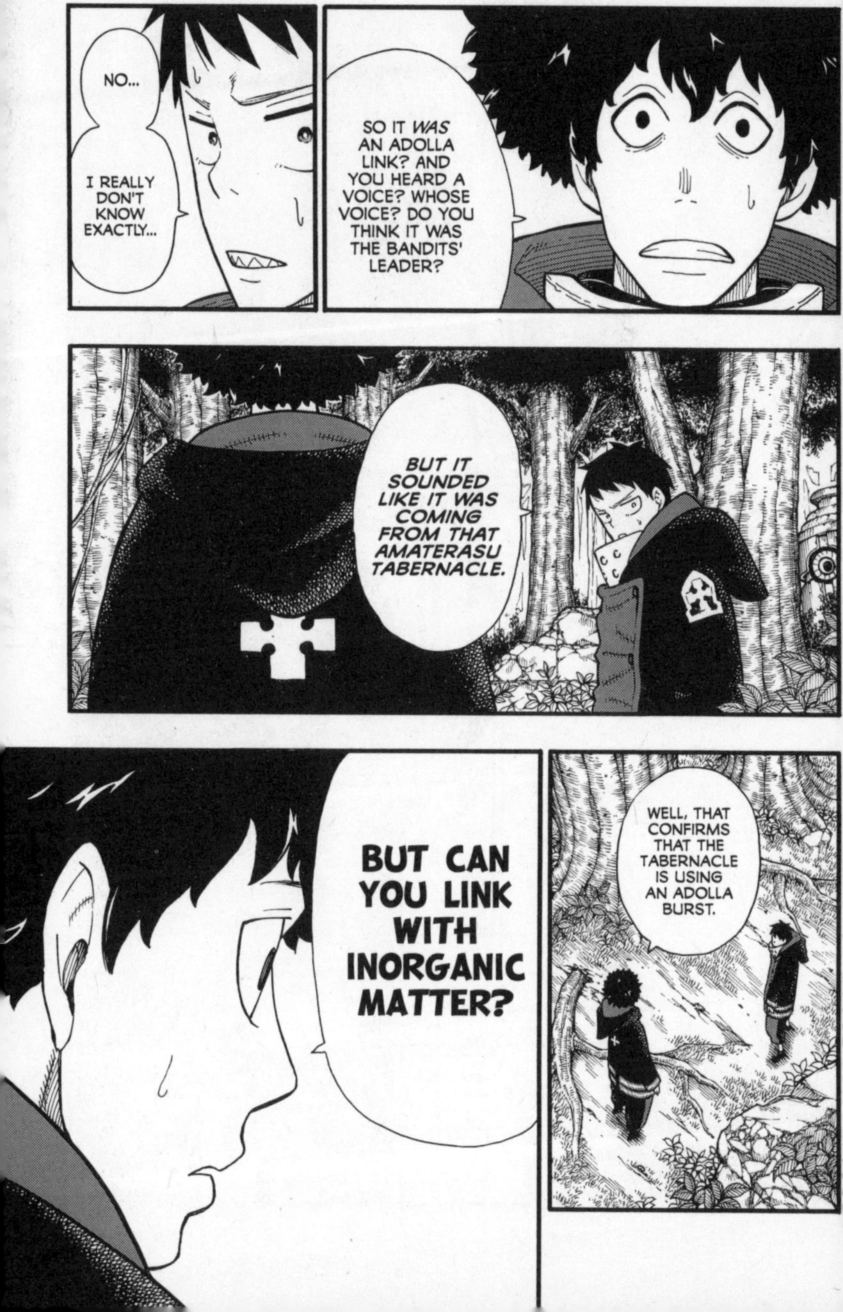
SO IT *WAS* AN ADOLLA LINK? AND YOU HEARD A VOICE? WHOSE VOICE? DO YOU THINK IT WAS THE BANDITS' LEADER?
NO...
I REALLY DON'T KNOW EXACTLY...
BUT IT SOUNDED LIKE IT WAS COMING FROM THAT AMATERASU TABERNACLE.
WELL, THAT CONFIRMS THAT THE TABERNACLE IS USING AN ADOLLA BURST.
BUT CAN YOU LINK WITH INORGANIC MATTER?

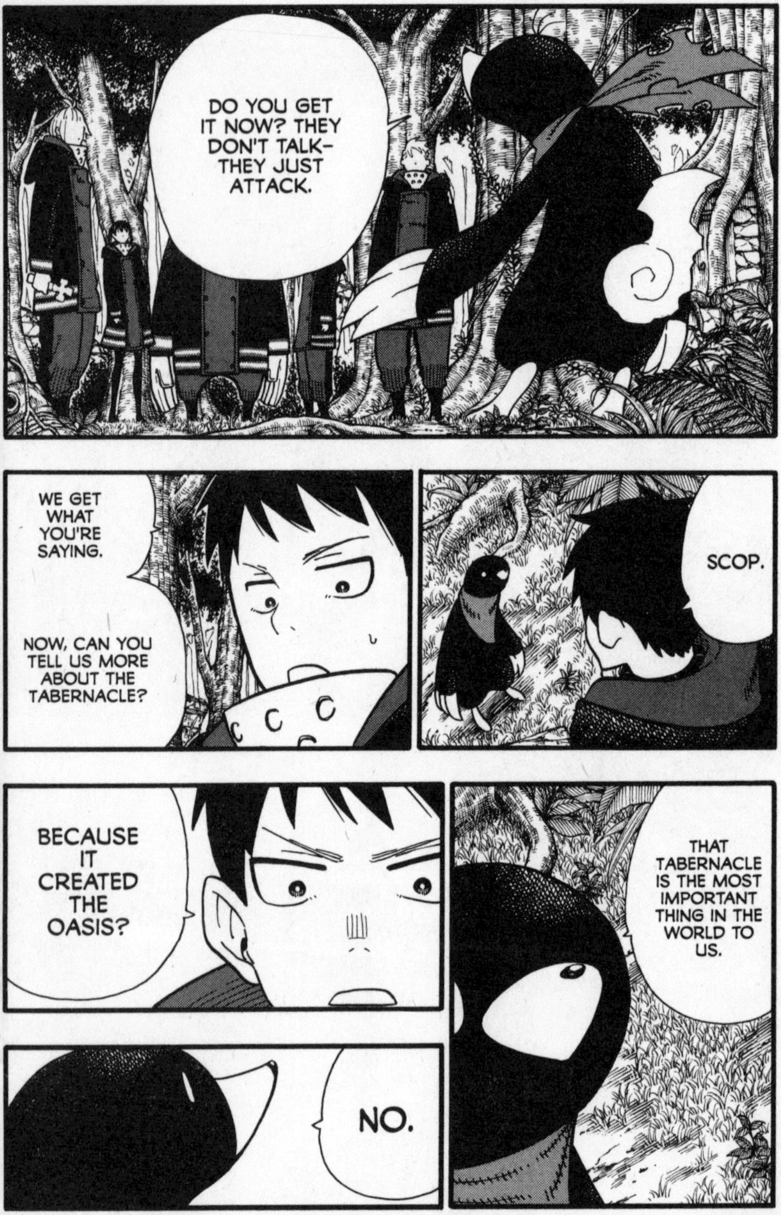
DO YOU GET IT NOW? THEY DON'T TALK–THEY JUST ATTACK.
SCOP.
WE GET WHAT YOU'RE SAYING.
NOW, CAN YOU TELL US MORE ABOUT THE TABERNACLE?
THAT TABERNACLE IS THE MOST IMPORTANT THING IN THE WORLD TO US.
BECAUSE IT CREATED THE OASIS?
NO.

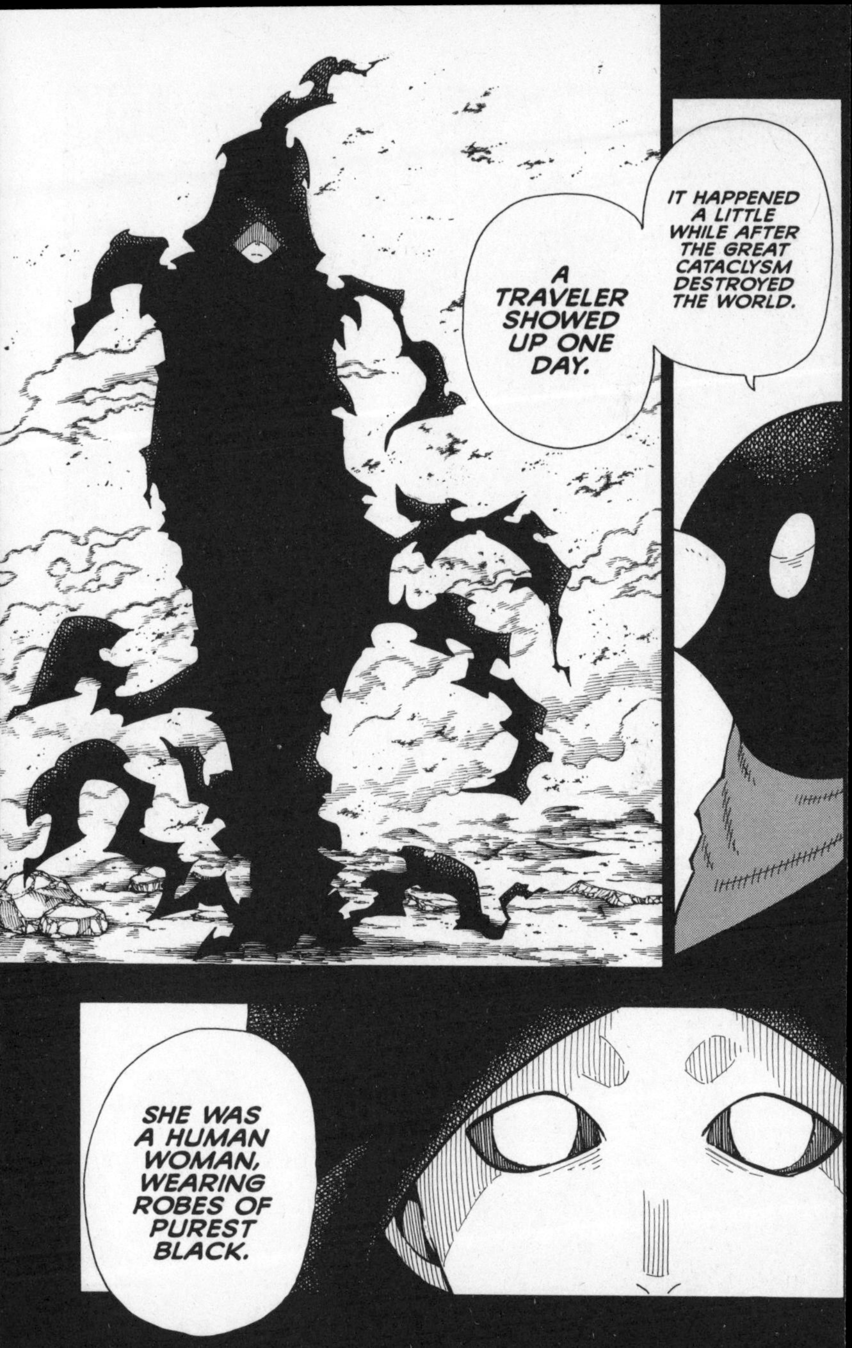
IT HAPPENED A LITTLE WHILE AFTER THE GREAT CATACLYSM DESTROYED THE WORLD.
A TRAVELER SHOWED UP ONE DAY.
SHE WAS A HUMAN WOMAN, WEARING ROBES OF PUREST BLACK.

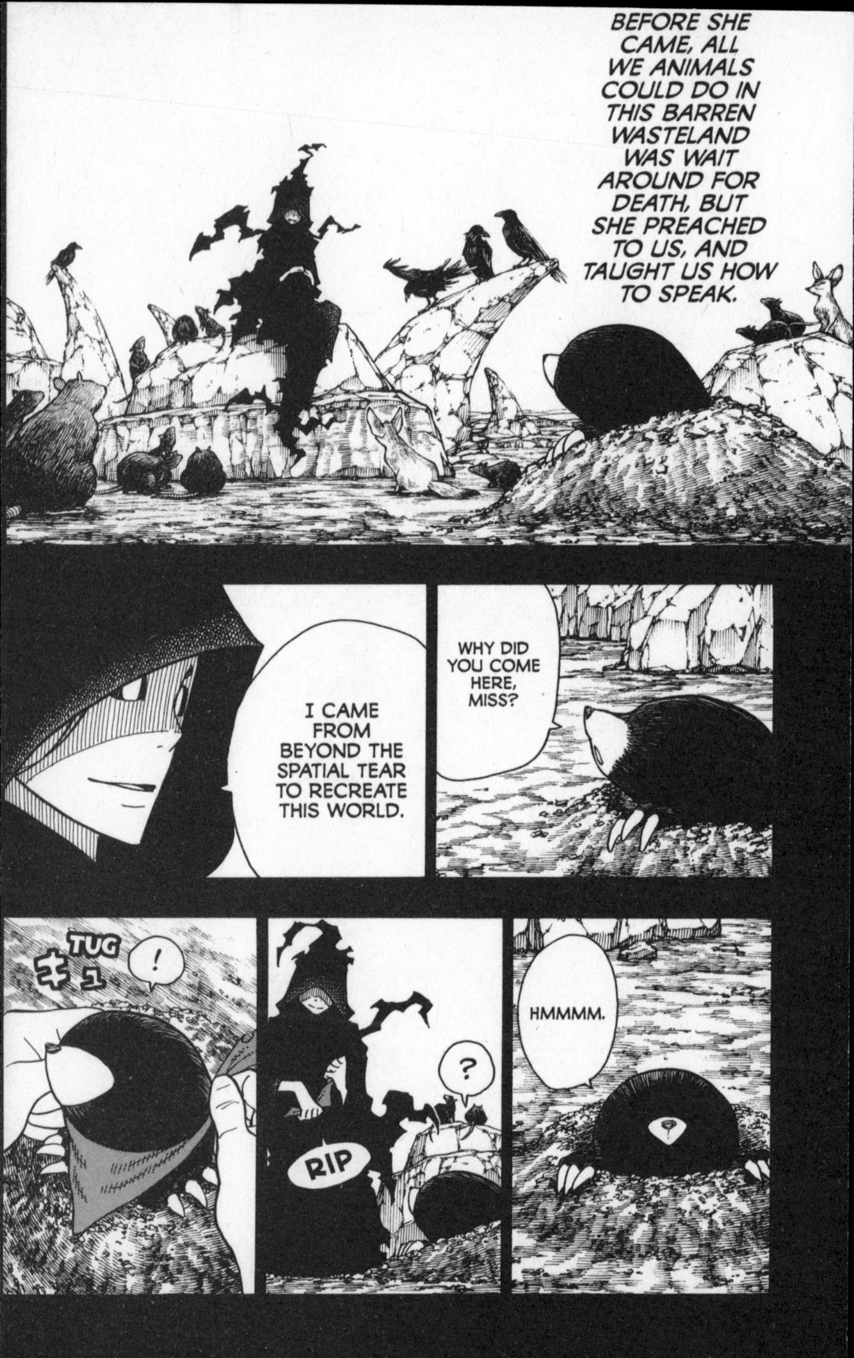
BEFORE SHE CAME, ALL WE ANIMALS COULD DO IN THIS BARREN WASTELAND WAS WAIT AROUND FOR DEATH, BUT SHE PREACHED TO US, AND TAUGHT US HOW TO SPEAK.
WHY DID YOU COME HERE, MISS?
I CAME FROM BEYOND THE SPATIAL TEAR TO RECREATE THIS WORLD.
HMMMM.
?
RIP
TUG
キュ
!

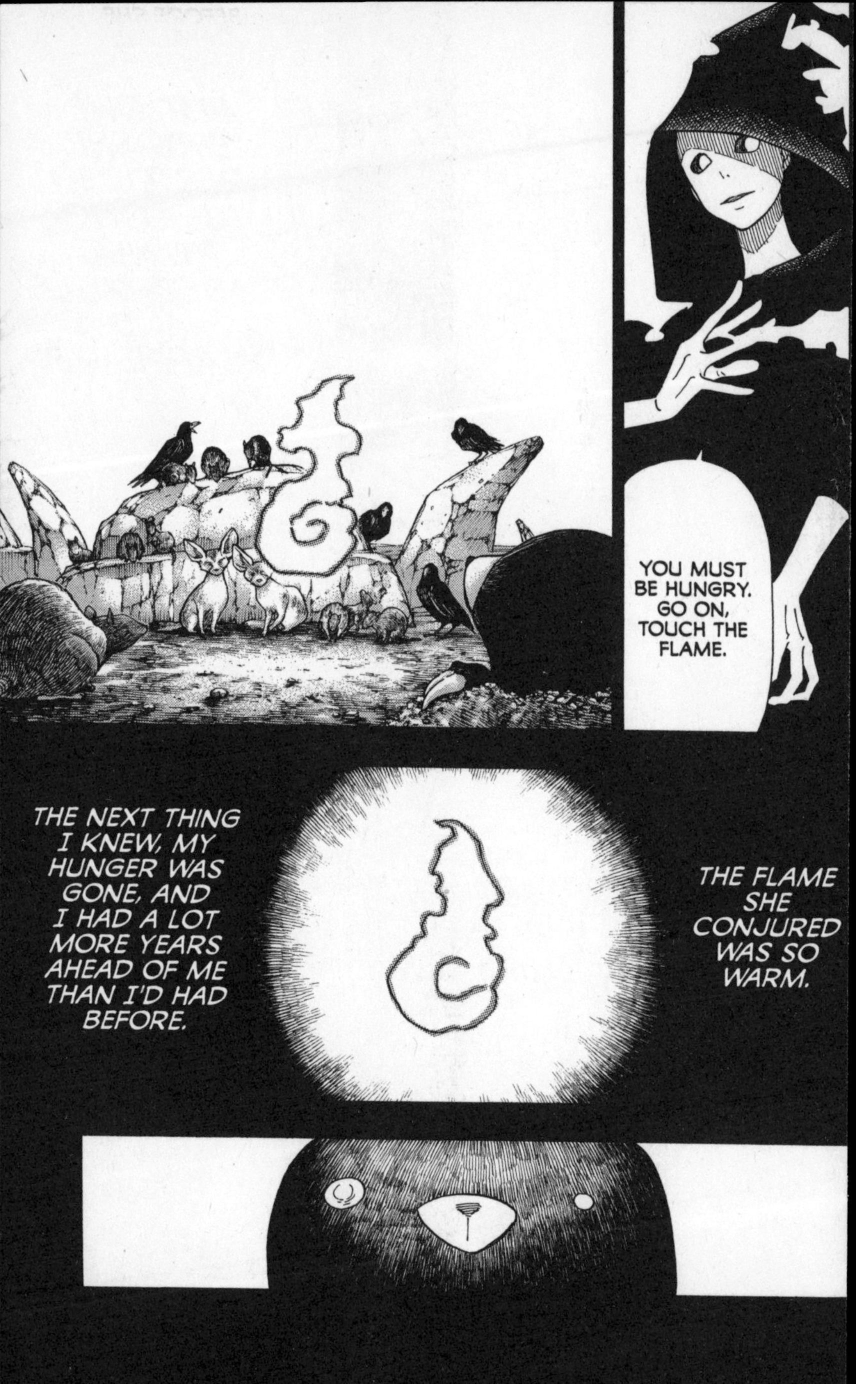
YOU MUST BE HUNGRY. GO ON, TOUCH THE FLAME.
THE FLAME SHE CONJURED WAS SO WARM.
THE NEXT THING I KNEW, MY HUNGER WAS GONE, AND I HAD A LOT MORE YEARS AHEAD OF ME THAN I'D HAD BEFORE.

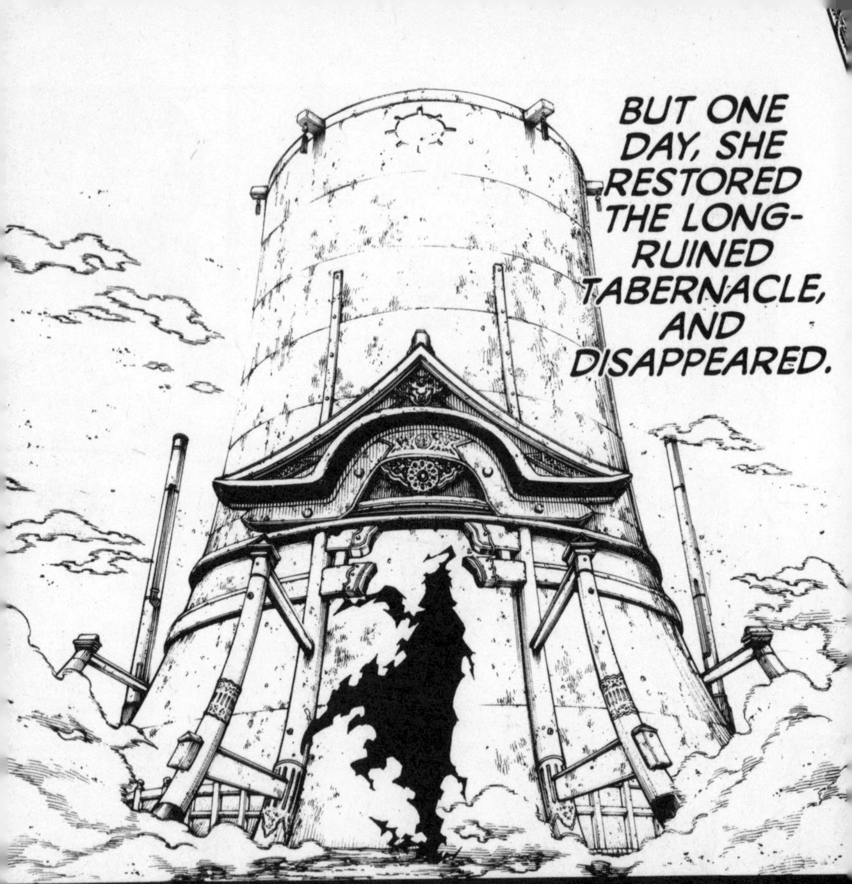
BUT ONE DAY, SHE RESTORED THE LONG-RUINED TABERNACLE, AND DISAPPEARED.
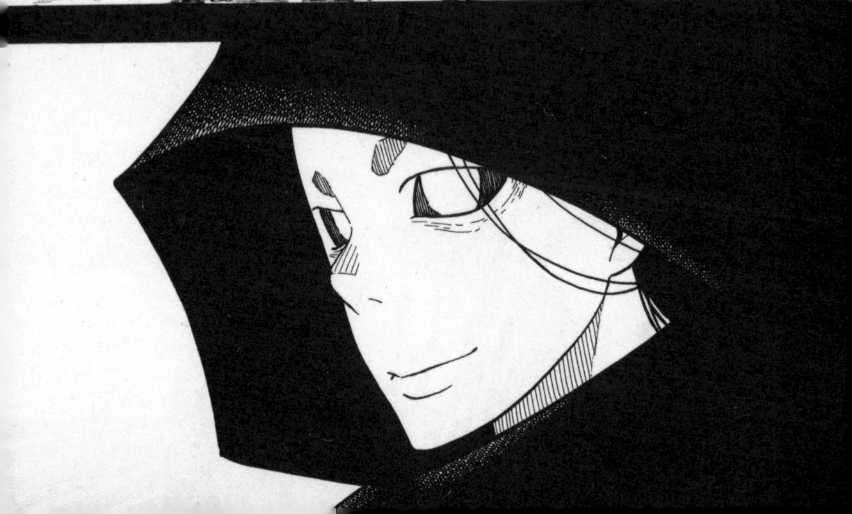

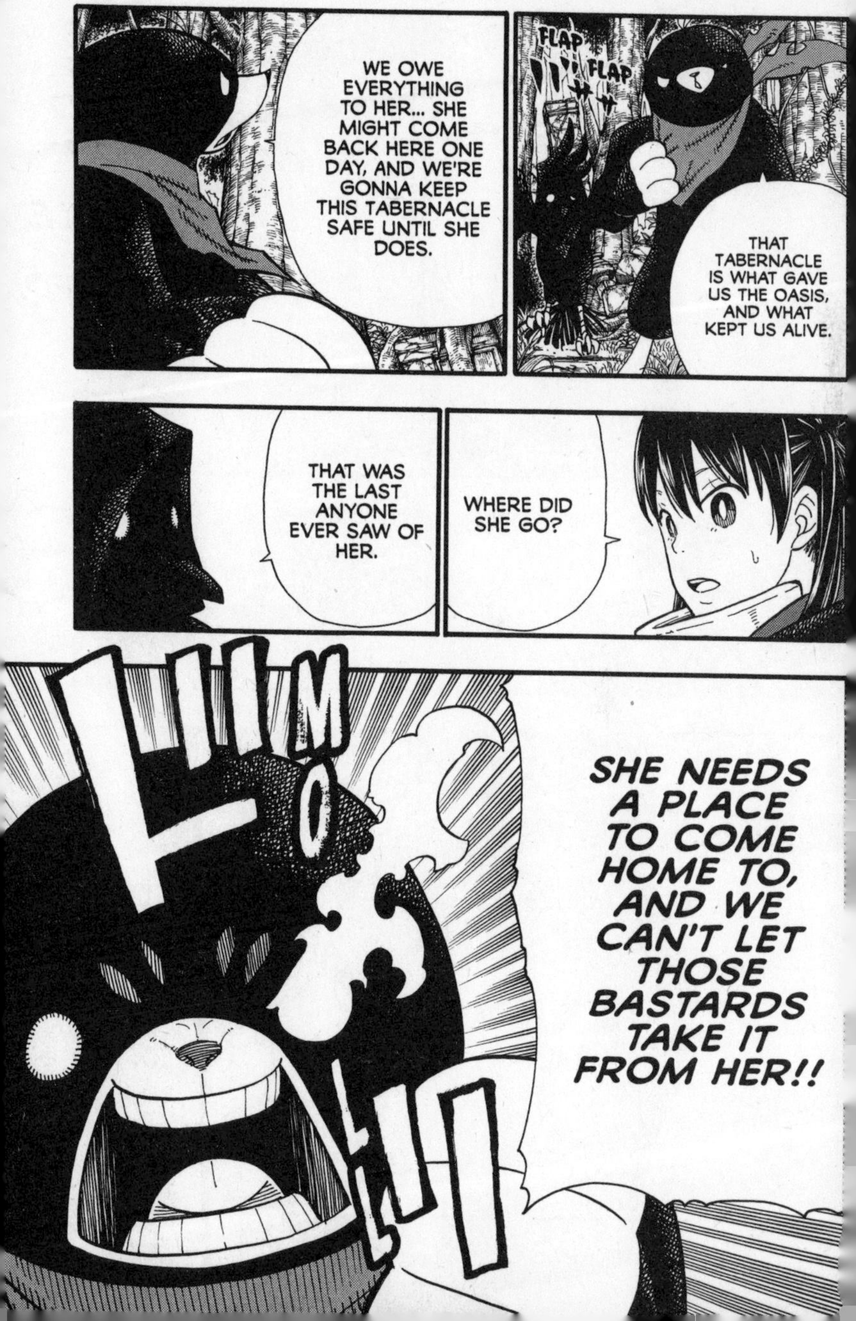
FLAP
FLAP
THAT TABERNACLE IS WHAT GAVE US THE OASIS, AND WHAT KEPT US ALIVE.
WE OWE EVERYTHING TO HER... SHE MIGHT COME BACK HERE ONE DAY, AND WE'RE GONNA KEEP THIS TABERNACLE SAFE UNTIL SHE DOES.
WHERE DID SHE GO?
THAT WAS THE LAST ANYONE EVER SAW OF HER.
SHE NEEDS A PLACE TO COME HOME TO, AND WE CAN'T LET THOSE BASTARDS TAKE IT FROM HER!!

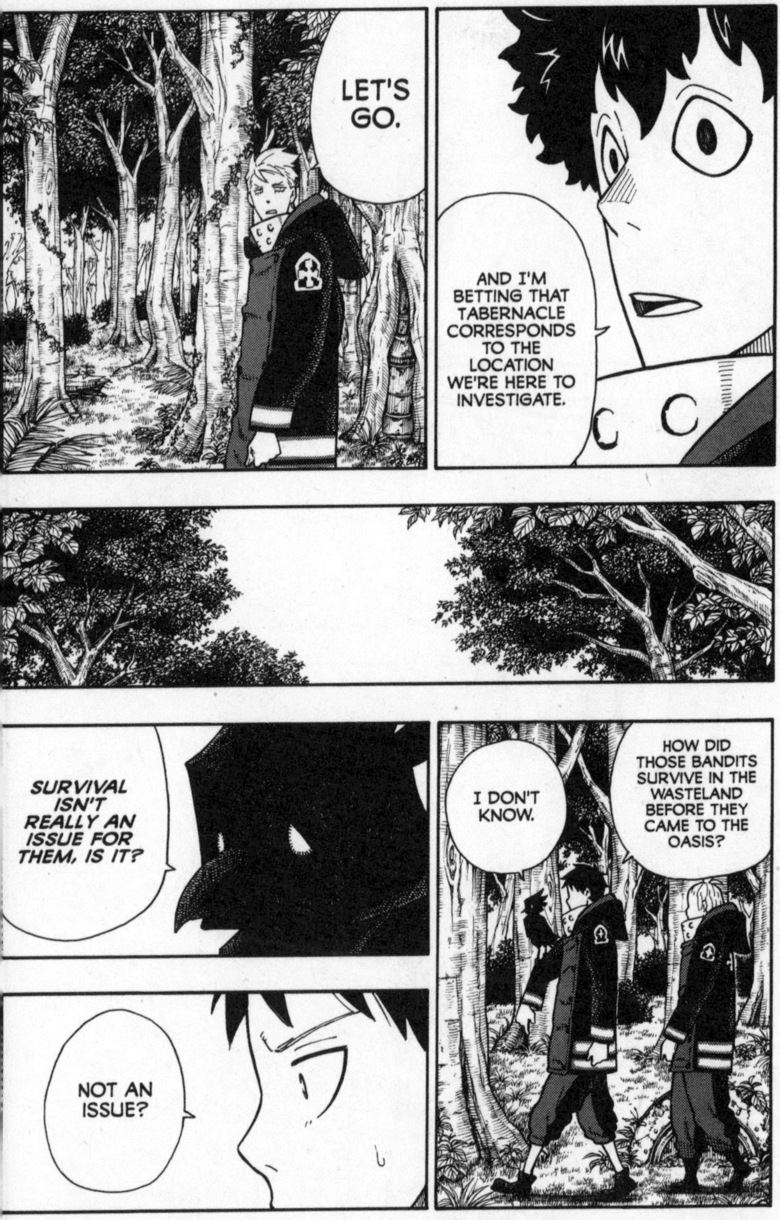
AND I'M BETTING THAT TABERNACLE CORRESPONDS TO THE LOCATION WE'RE HERE TO INVESTIGATE.
LET'S GO.
HOW DID THOSE BANDITS SURVIVE IN THE WASTELAND BEFORE THEY CAME TO THE OASIS?
I DON'T KNOW.
SURVIVAL ISN'T REALLY AN ISSUE FOR THEM, IS IT?
NOT AN ISSUE?

THERE! I SEE ONE!

!!

EX-HUMAN.

A HUMAN?!

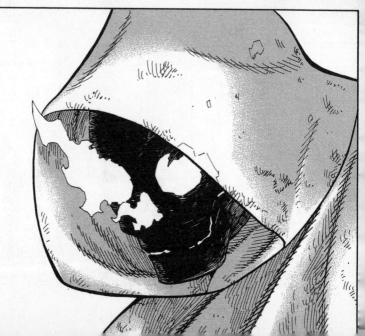

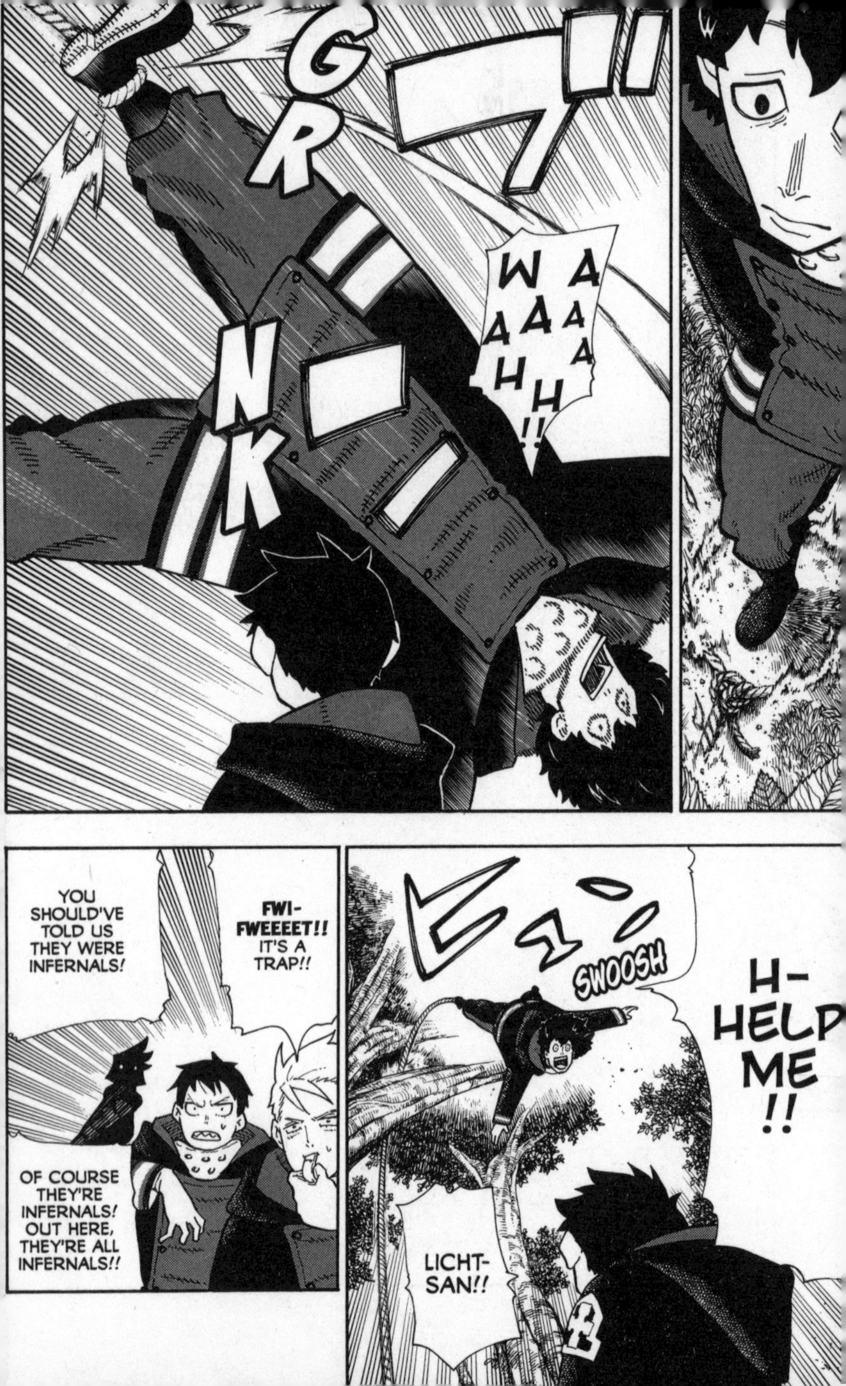
GRNK
WAAAAAAH!!
H-HELP ME!!
SWOOSH
LICHT-SAN!!
FWI-FWEEEEET!! IT'S A TRAP!!
YOU SHOULD'VE TOLD US THEY WERE INFERNALS!
OF COURSE THEY'RE INFERNALS! OUT HERE, THEY'RE ALL INFERNALS!!

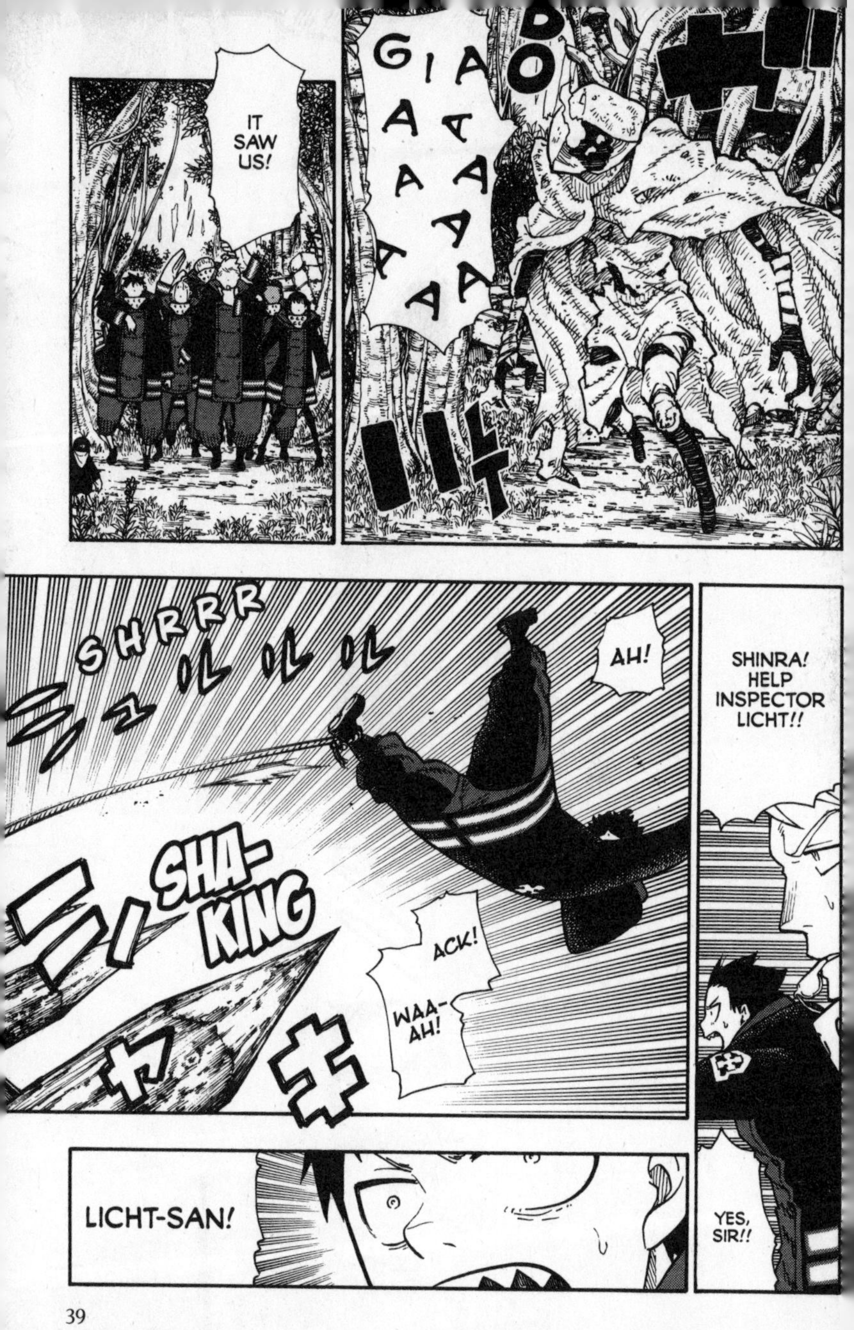
GIAAAAAAAAAA
DO
IT SAW US!
SHINRA! HELP INSPECTOR LICHT!!
YES, SIR!!
AH!
SHRRR
SHA-KING
ACK!
WAA-AH!
LICHT-SAN!

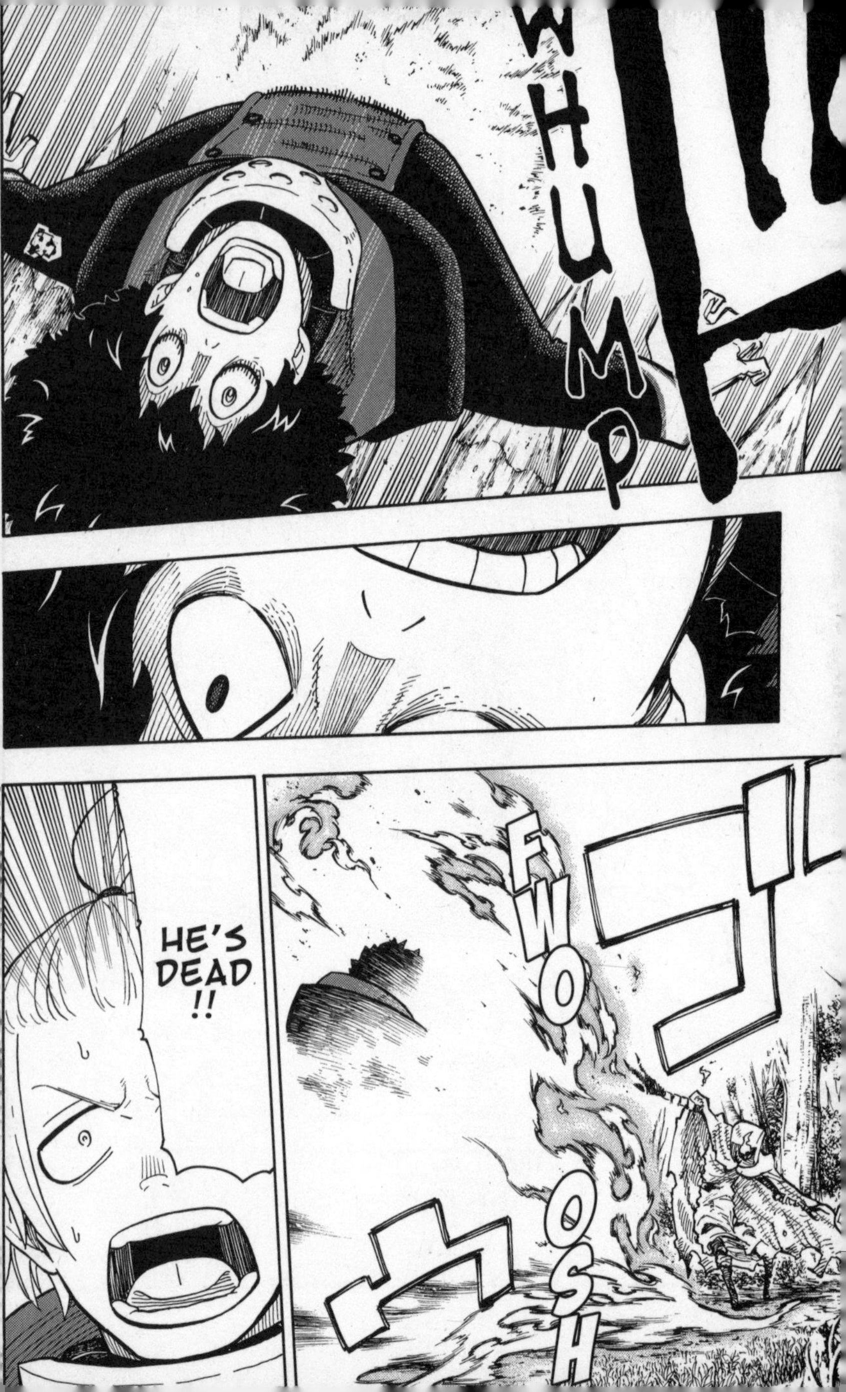
WHUMP
FWOOSH
HE'S DEAD !!

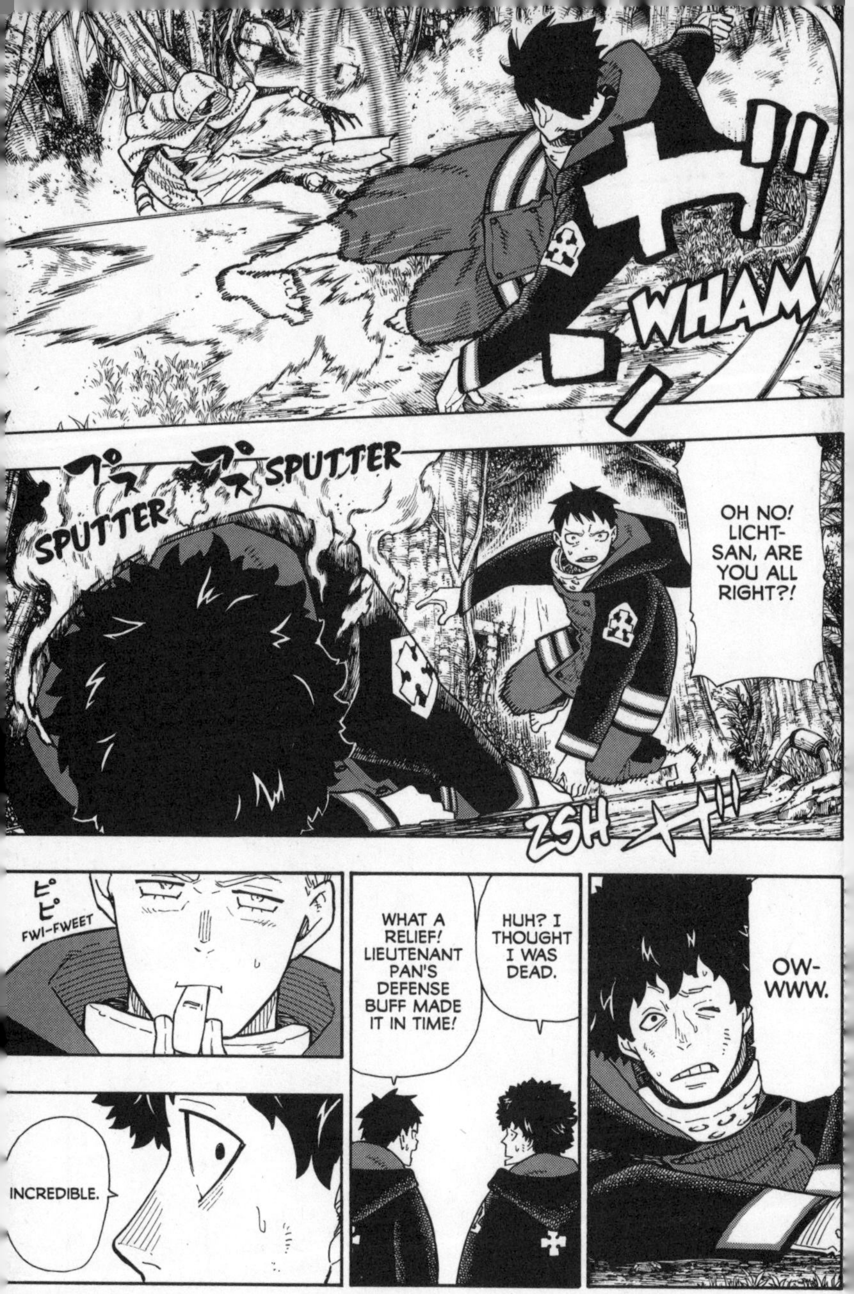
WHAM
プス プス
SPUTTER SPUTTER
OH NO! LICHT-SAN, ARE YOU ALL RIGHT?!
ZSH
OW-WWW.
HUH? I THOUGHT I WAS DEAD.
WHAT A RELIEF! LIEUTENANT PAN'S DEFENSE BUFF MADE IT IN TIME!
ピピ
FWI-FWEET
INCREDIBLE.

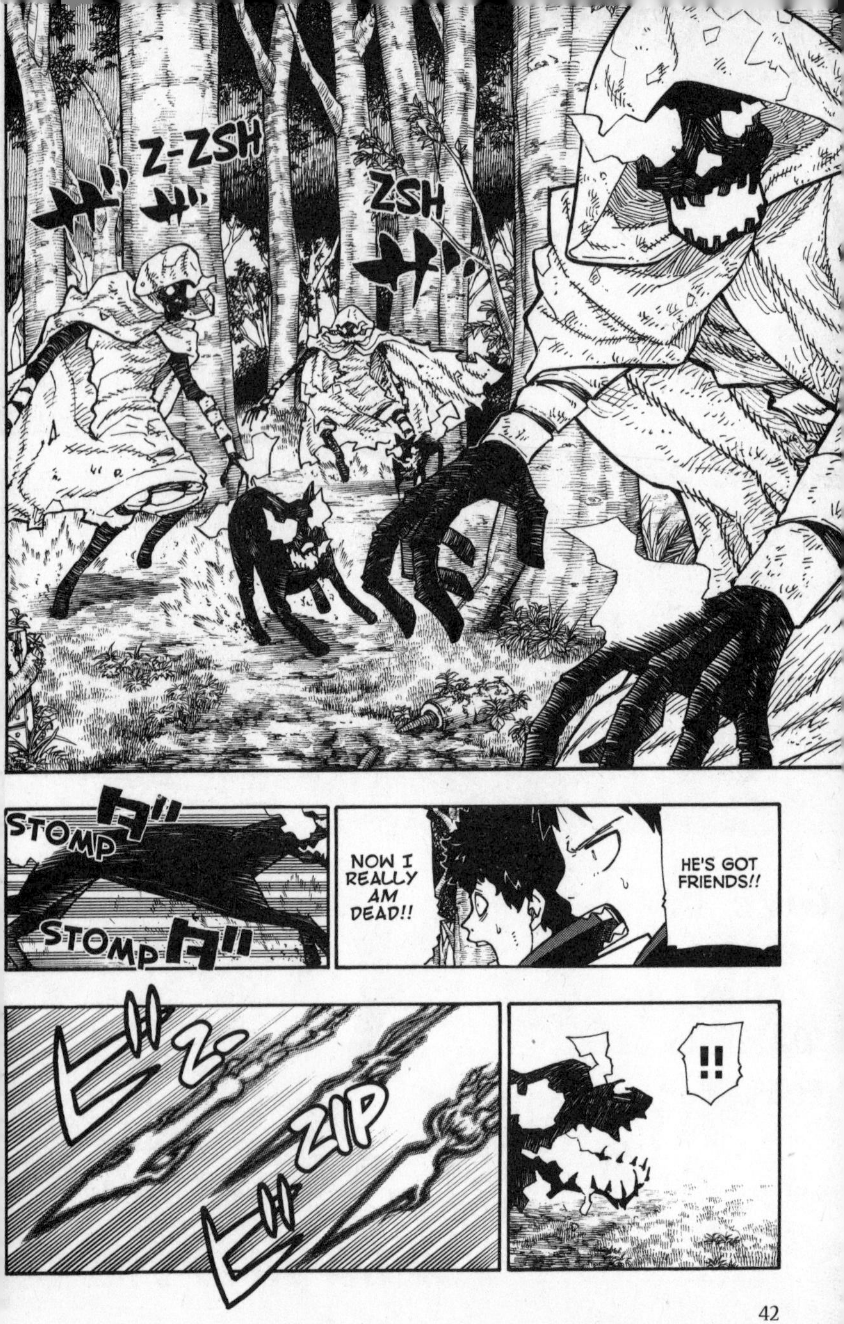
ZSH
Z-ZSH
HE'S GOT FRIENDS!!
NOW I REALLY AM DEAD!!
STOMP
STOMP
!!
Z-
ZIP

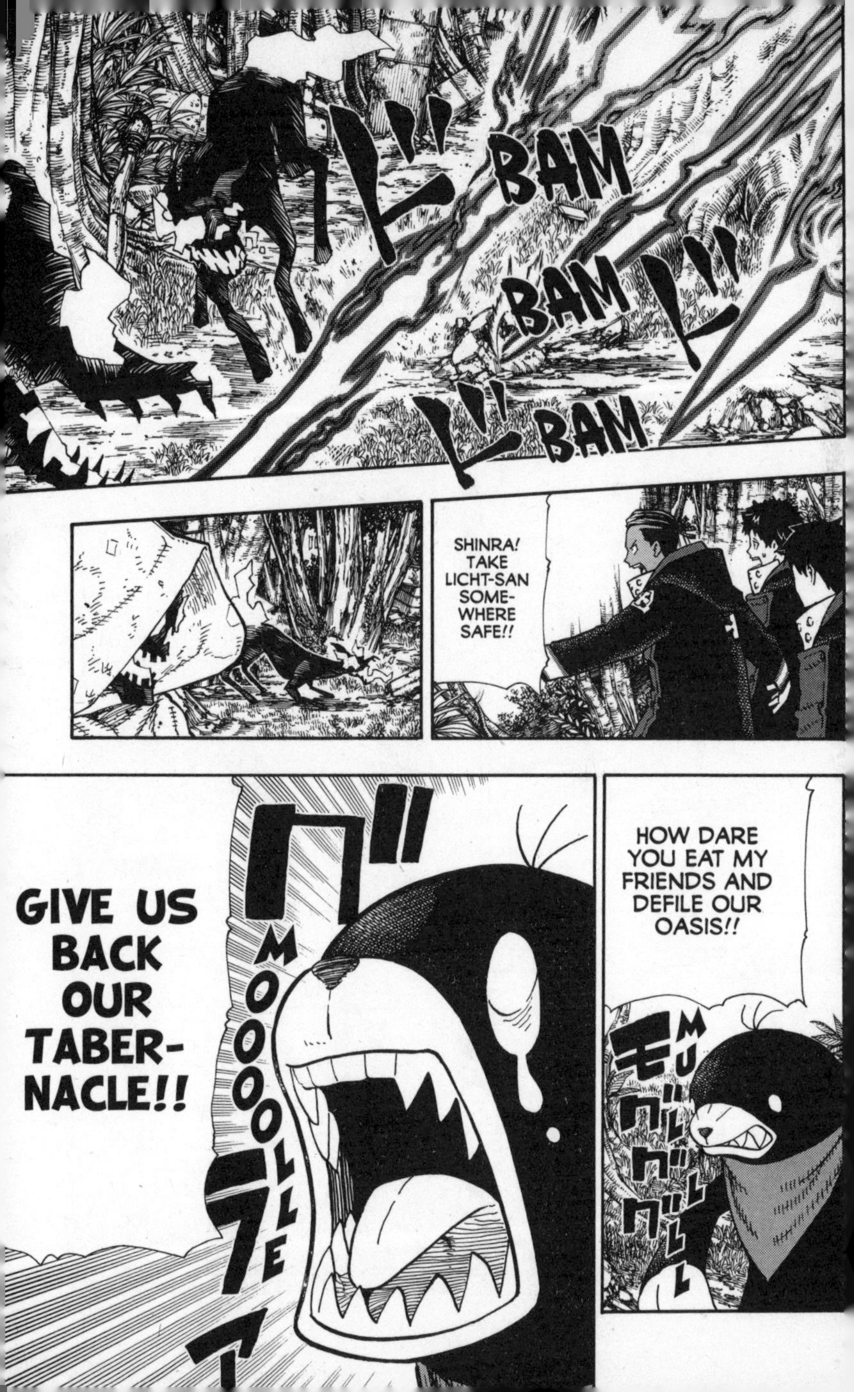
BAM
BAM
BAM
SHINRA! TAKE LICHT-SAN SOME-WHERE SAFE!!
HOW DARE YOU EAT MY FRIENDS AND DEFILE OUR OASIS!!
MULLLL
GIVE US BACK OUR TABER-NACLE!!
MOOOOOLLE

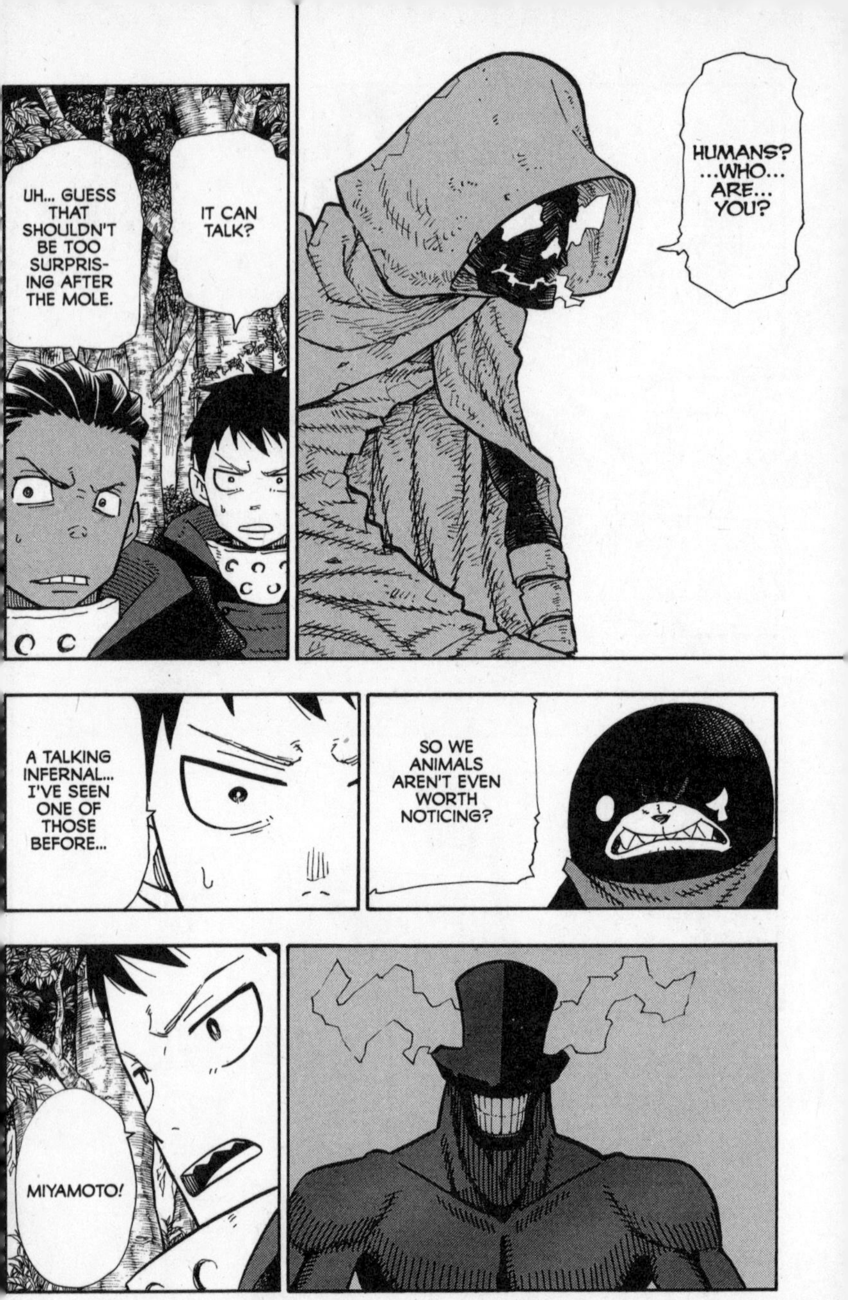
HUMANS? ...WHO... ARE... YOU?
IT CAN TALK?
UH... GUESS THAT SHOULDN'T BE TOO SURPRISING AFTER THE MOLE.
SO WE ANIMALS AREN'T EVEN WORTH NOTICING?
A TALKING INFERNAL... I'VE SEEN ONE OF THOSE BEFORE...
MIYAMOTO!

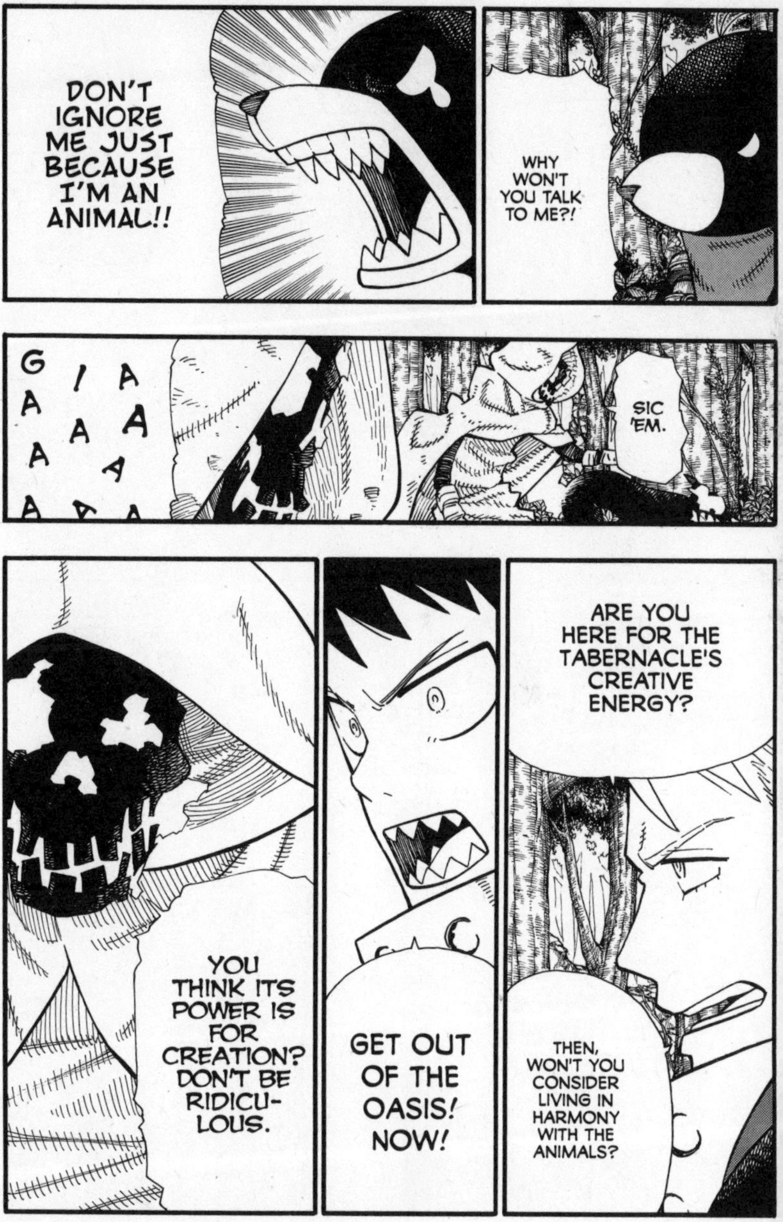
WHY WON'T YOU TALK TO ME?!
DON'T IGNORE ME JUST BECAUSE I'M AN ANIMAL!!
SIC 'EM.
GIAAAAAAAAA
ARE YOU HERE FOR THE TABERNACLE'S CREATIVE ENERGY?
THEN, WON'T YOU CONSIDER LIVING IN HARMONY WITH THE ANIMALS?
GET OUT OF THE OASIS! NOW!
YOU THINK ITS POWER IS FOR CREATION? DON'T BE RIDICU-LOUS.

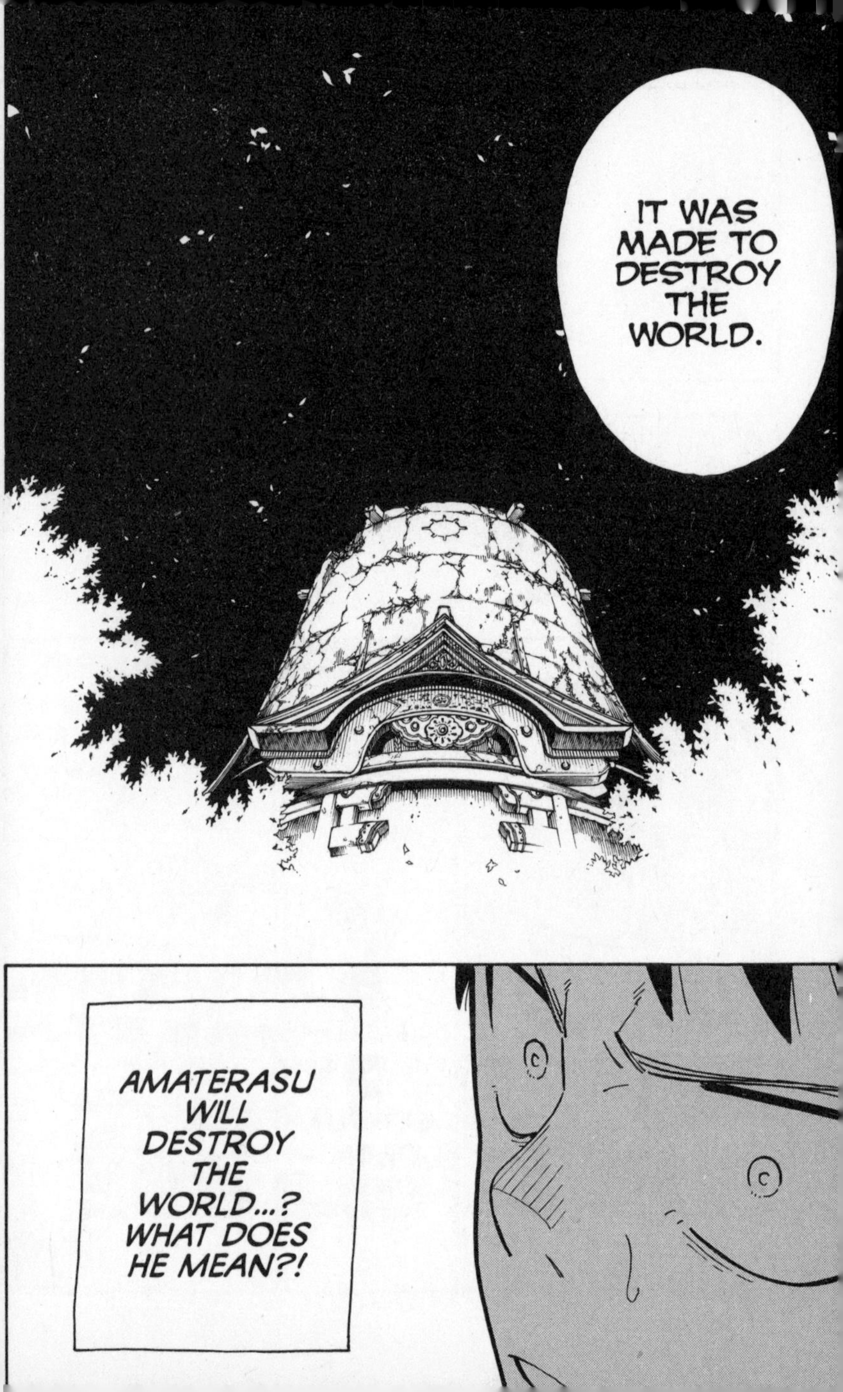
IT WAS MADE TO DESTROY THE WORLD.
AMATERASU WILL DESTROY THE WORLD...? WHAT DOES HE MEAN?!

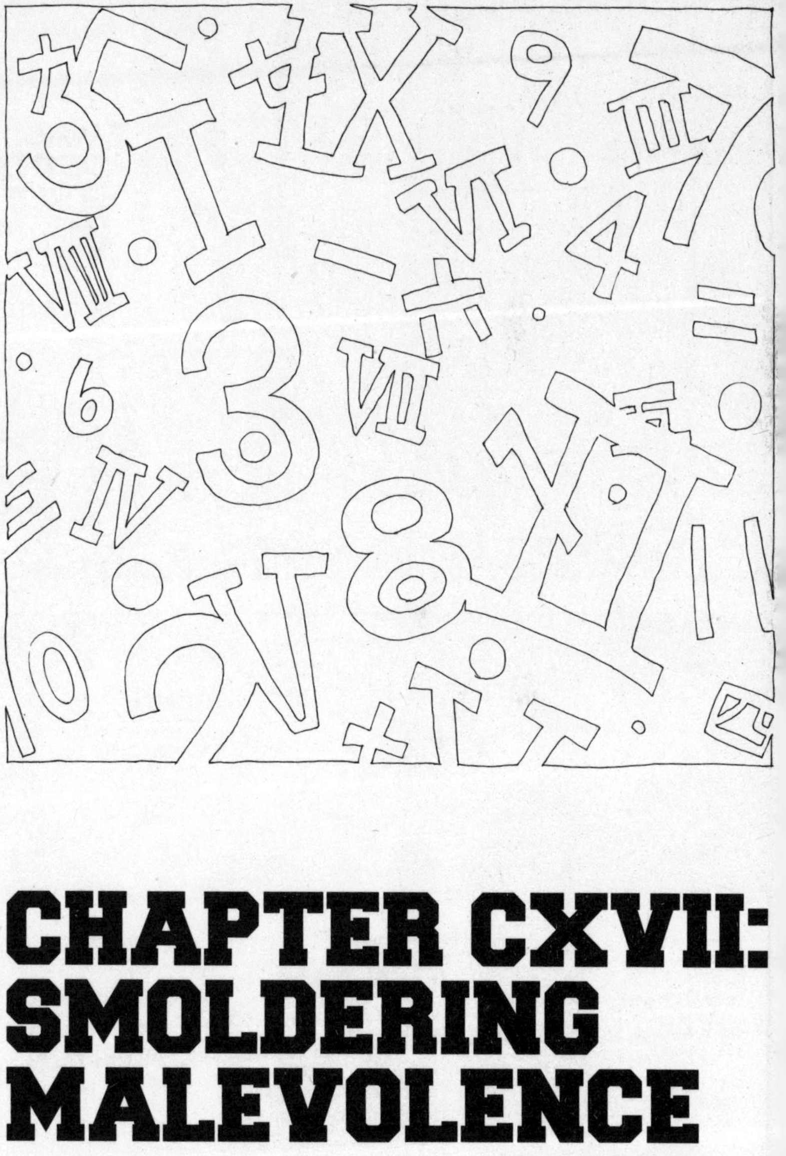

CHAPTER CXVII: SMOLDERING MALEVOLENCE

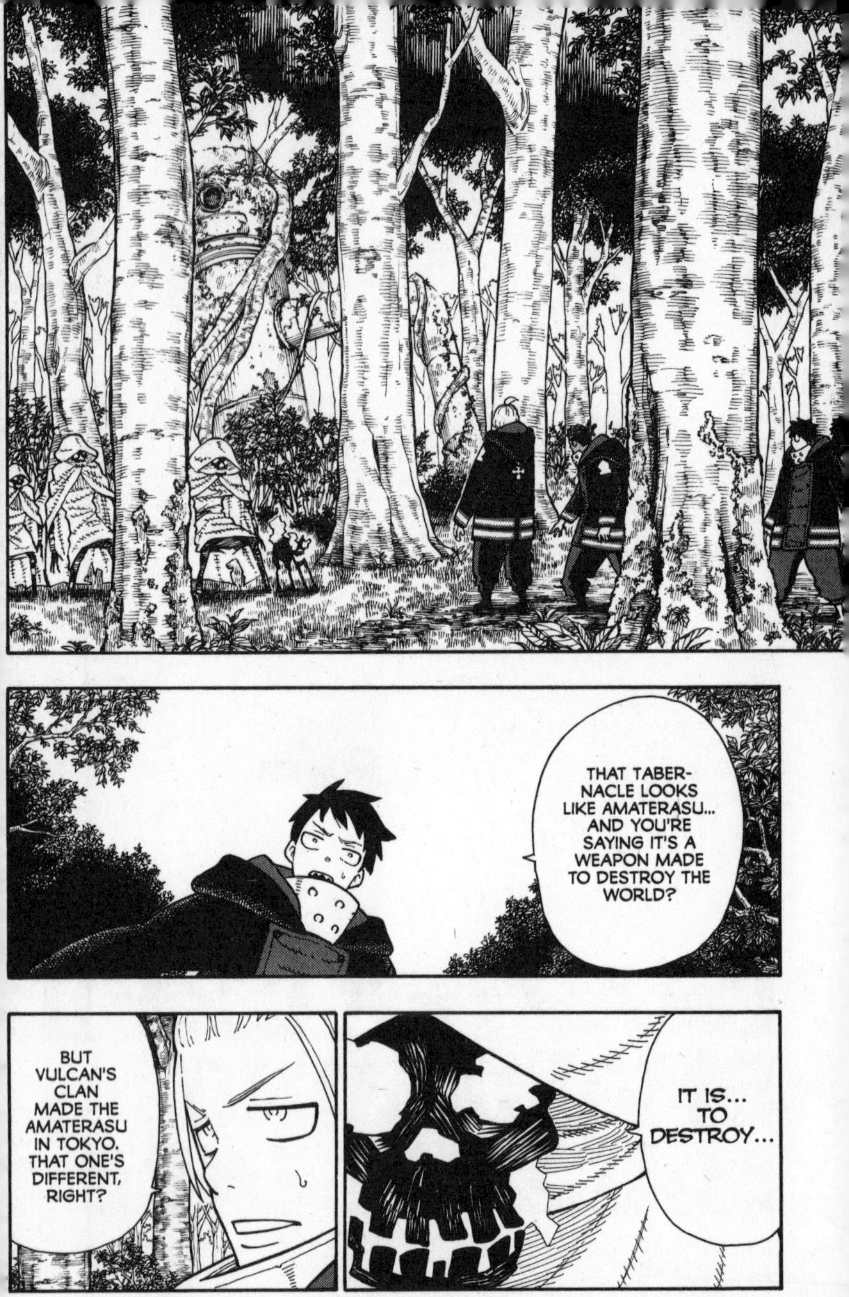
THAT TABER-NACLE LOOKS LIKE AMATERASU... AND YOU'RE SAYING IT'S A WEAPON MADE TO DESTROY THE WORLD?
IT IS... TO DESTROY...
BUT VULCAN'S CLAN MADE THE AMATERASU IN TOKYO. THAT ONE'S DIFFERENT, RIGHT?

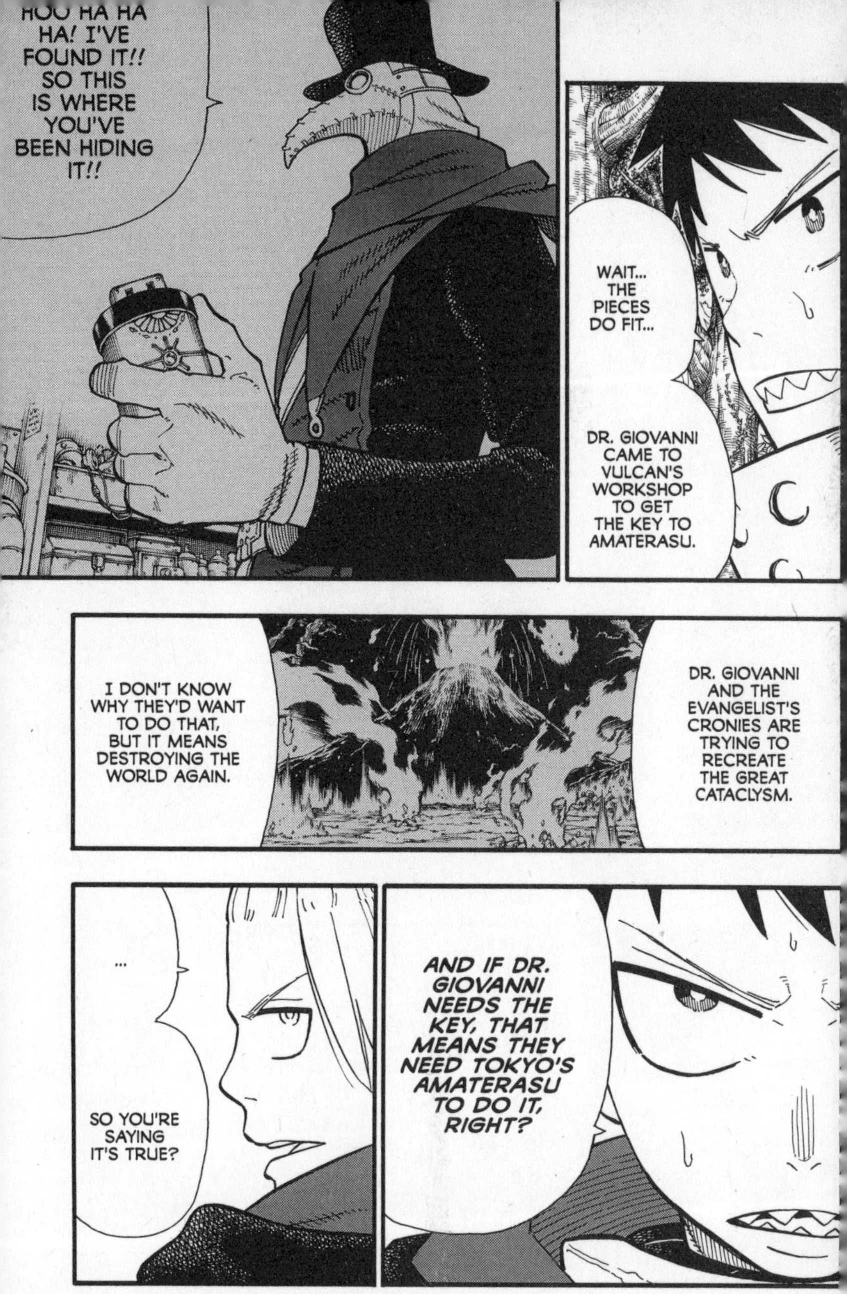
WAIT... THE PIECES DO FIT...
DR. GIOVANNI CAME TO VULCAN'S WORKSHOP TO GET THE KEY TO AMATERASU.
HOO HA HA HA! I'VE FOUND IT!! SO THIS IS WHERE YOU'VE BEEN HIDING IT!!
DR. GIOVANNI AND THE EVANGELIST'S CRONIES ARE TRYING TO RECREATE THE GREAT CATACLYSM.
I DON'T KNOW WHY THEY'D WANT TO DO THAT, BUT IT MEANS DESTROYING THE WORLD AGAIN.
AND IF DR. GIOVANNI NEEDS THE KEY, THAT MEANS THEY NEED TOKYO'S AMATERASU TO DO IT, RIGHT?
...
SO YOU'RE SAYING IT'S TRUE?

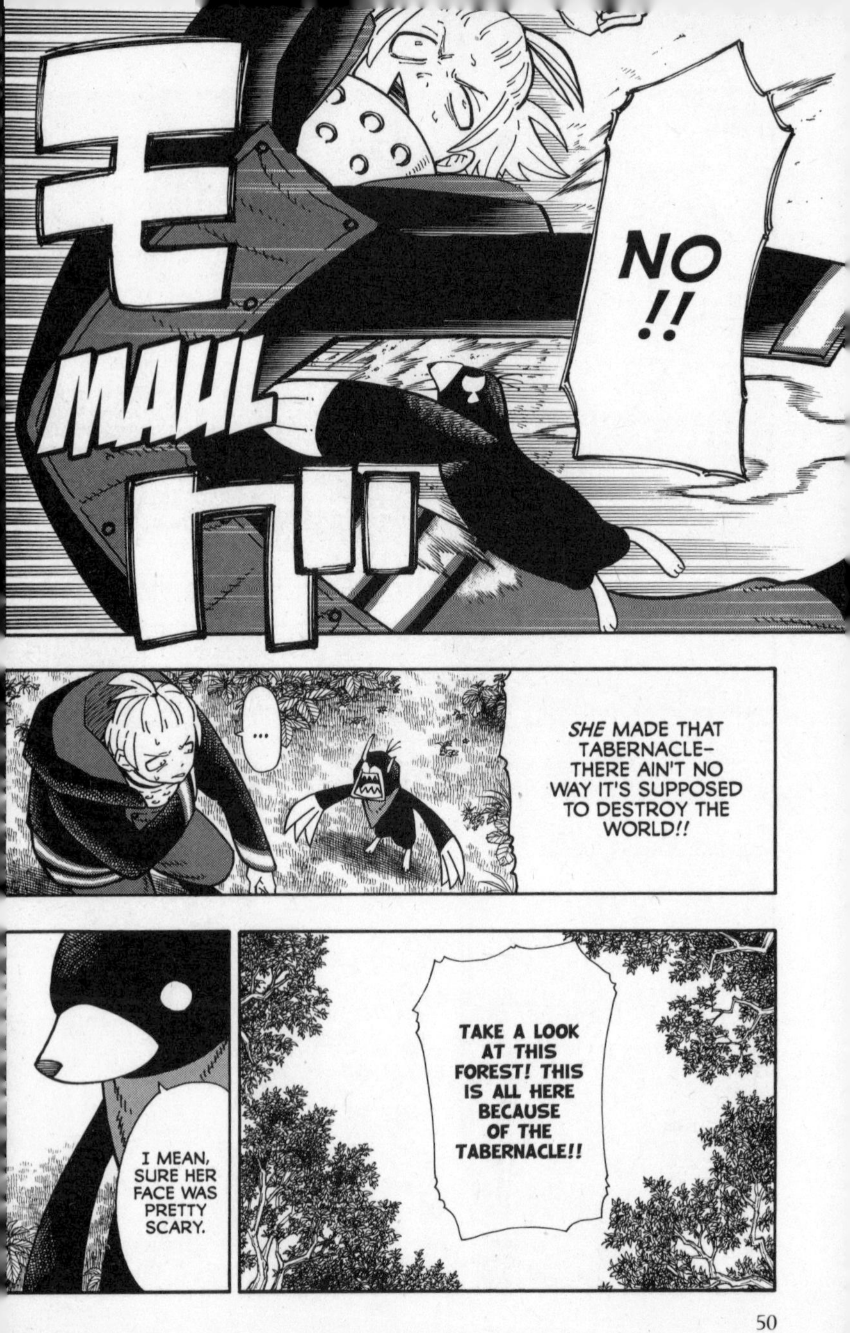
NO!!
MAUL
SHE MADE THAT TABERNACLE– THERE AIN'T NO WAY IT'S SUPPOSED TO DESTROY THE WORLD!!
...
TAKE A LOOK AT THIS FOREST! THIS IS ALL HERE BECAUSE OF THE TABERNACLE!!
I MEAN, SURE HER FACE WAS PRETTY SCARY.

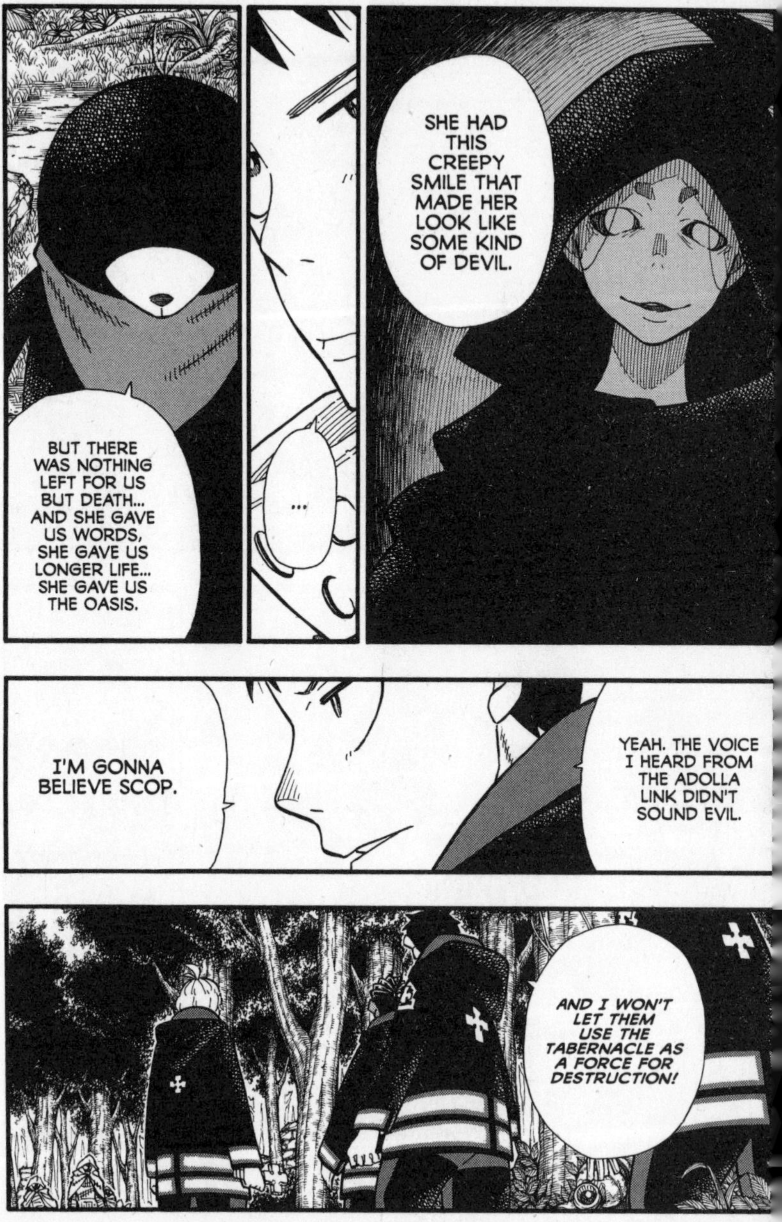
SHE HAD THIS CREEPY SMILE THAT MADE HER LOOK LIKE SOME KIND OF DEVIL.
...
BUT THERE WAS NOTHING LEFT FOR US BUT DEATH... AND SHE GAVE US WORDS, SHE GAVE US LONGER LIFE... SHE GAVE US THE OASIS.
YEAH. THE VOICE I HEARD FROM THE ADOLLA LINK DIDN'T SOUND EVIL.
I'M GONNA BELIEVE SCOP.
AND I WON'T LET THEM USE THE TABERNACLE AS A FORCE FOR DESTRUCTION!

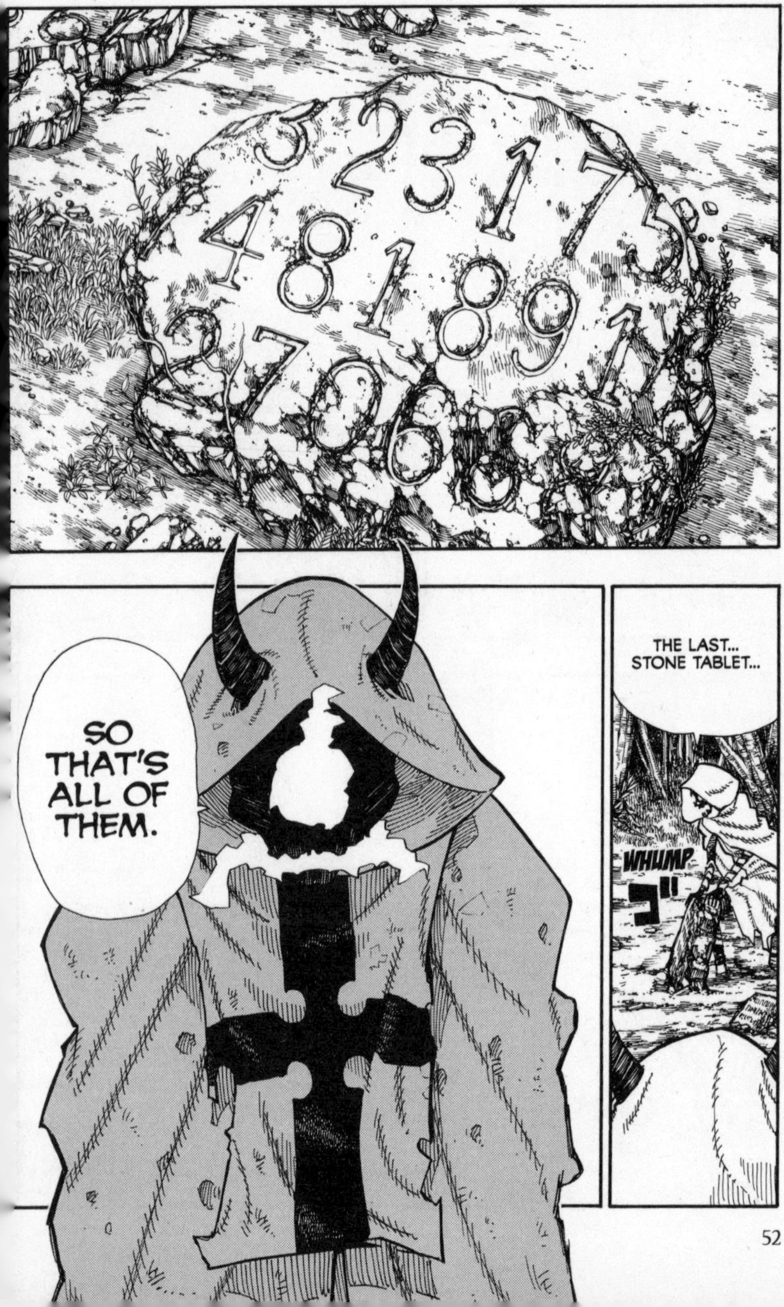
THE LAST... STONE TABLET...
WHUMP
ゴ
SO THAT'S ALL OF THEM.

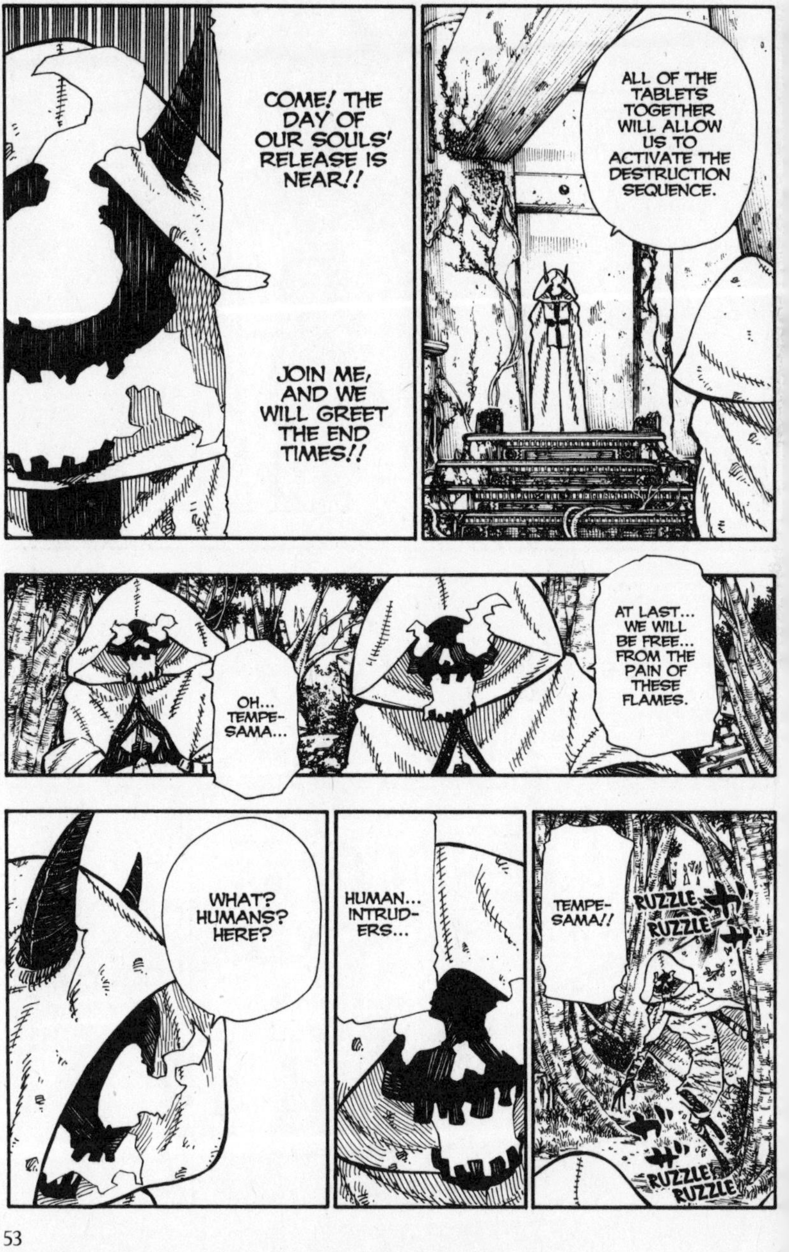
ALL OF THE TABLETS TOGETHER WILL ALLOW US TO ACTIVATE THE DESTRUCTION SEQUENCE.
COME! THE DAY OF OUR SOULS' RELEASE IS NEAR!!
JOIN ME, AND WE WILL GREET THE END TIMES!!
AT LAST... WE WILL BE FREE... FROM THE PAIN OF THESE FLAMES.
OH... TEMPE-SAMA...
TEMPE-SAMA!!
RUZZLE RUZZLE
RUZZLE RUZZLE
HUMAN... INTRUD-ERS...
WHAT? HUMANS? HERE?

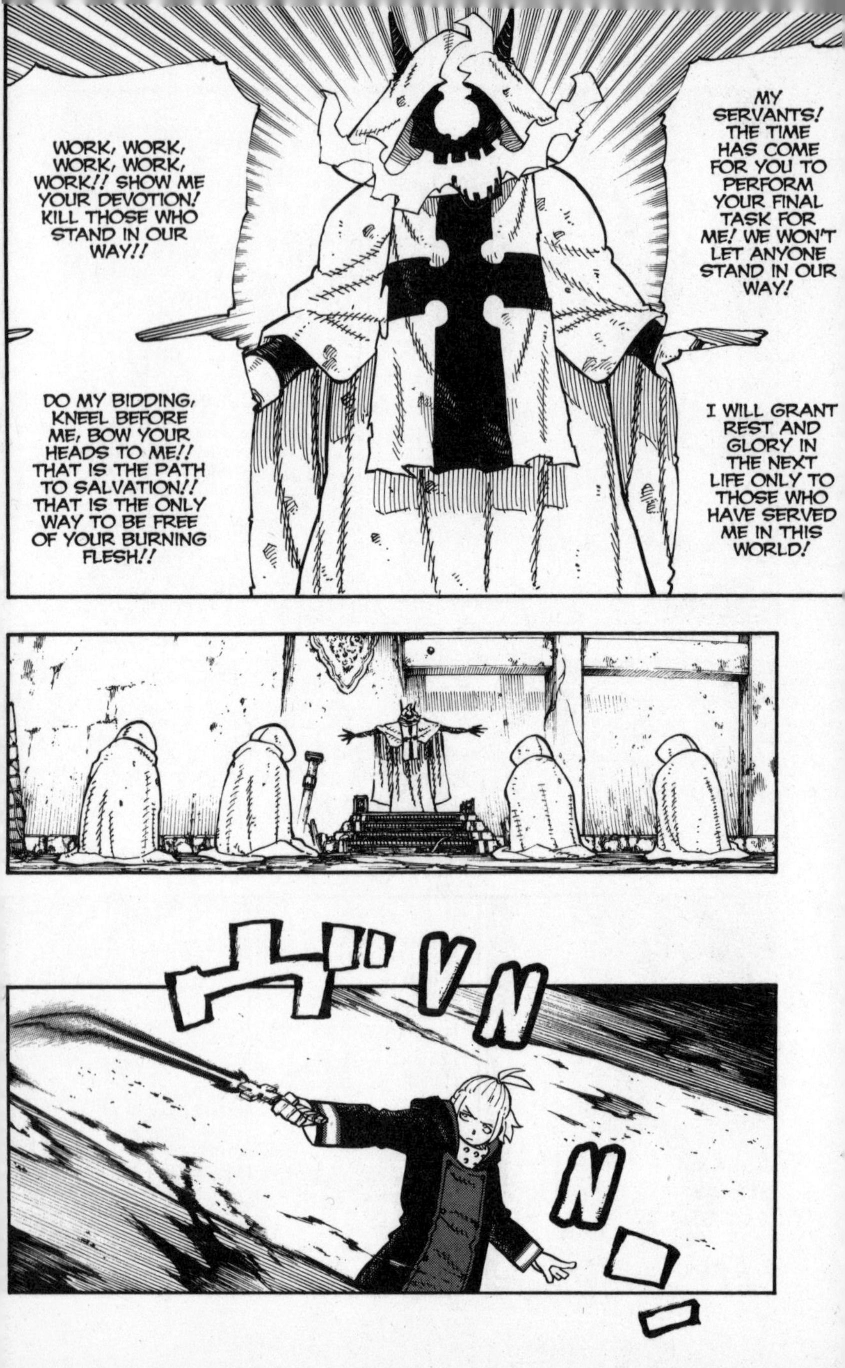
MY SERVANTS! THE TIME HAS COME FOR YOU TO PERFORM YOUR FINAL TASK FOR ME! WE WON'T LET ANYONE STAND IN OUR WAY!
WORK, WORK, WORK, WORK, WORK!! SHOW ME YOUR DEVOTION! KILL THOSE WHO STAND IN OUR WAY!!
I WILL GRANT REST AND GLORY IN THE NEXT LIFE ONLY TO THOSE WHO HAVE SERVED ME IN THIS WORLD!
DO MY BIDDING, KNEEL BEFORE ME, BOW YOUR HEADS TO ME!! THAT IS THE PATH TO SALVATION!! THAT IS THE ONLY WAY TO BE FREE OF YOUR BURNING FLESH!!
VNN

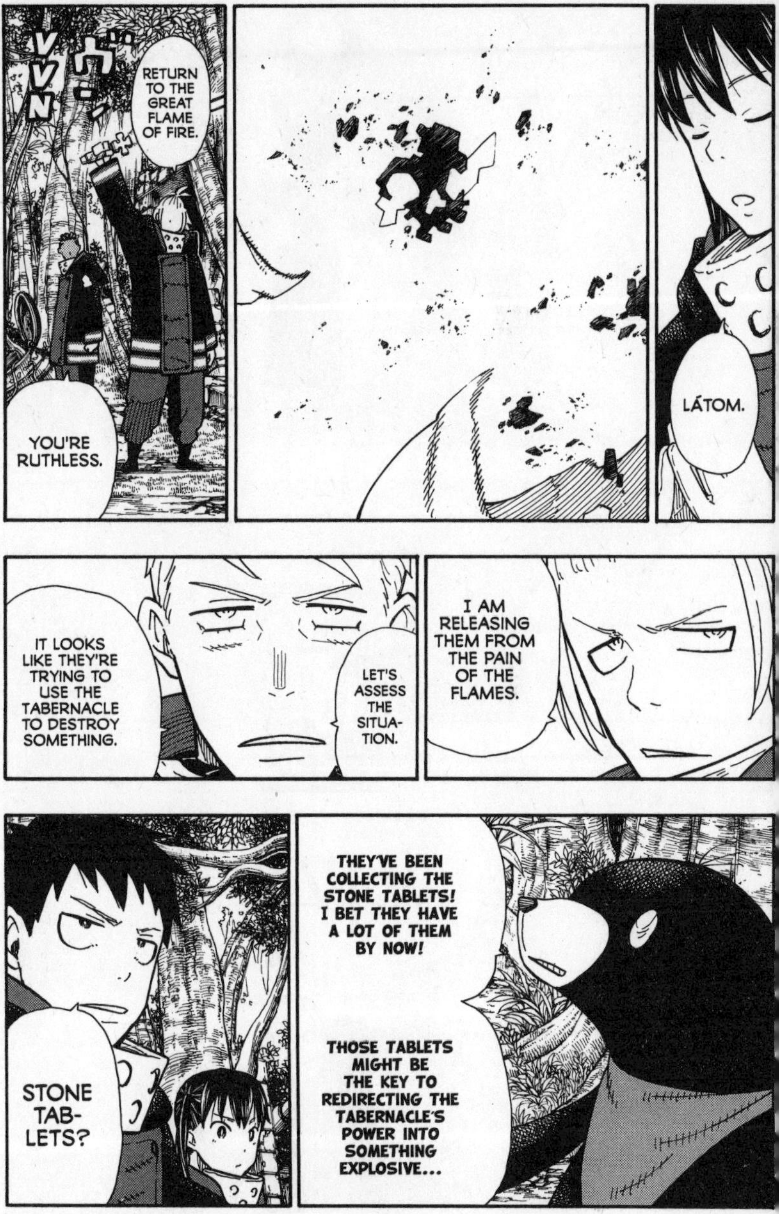
LÁTOM.
RETURN TO THE GREAT FLAME OF FIRE.
VVN
YOU'RE RUTHLESS.
I AM RELEASING THEM FROM THE PAIN OF THE FLAMES.
LET'S ASSESS THE SITUATION.
IT LOOKS LIKE THEY'RE TRYING TO USE THE TABERNACLE TO DESTROY SOMETHING.
THEY'VE BEEN COLLECTING THE STONE TABLETS! I BET THEY HAVE A LOT OF THEM BY NOW!
THOSE TABLETS MIGHT BE THE KEY TO REDIRECTING THE TABERNACLE'S POWER INTO SOMETHING EXPLOSIVE...
STONE TABLETS?

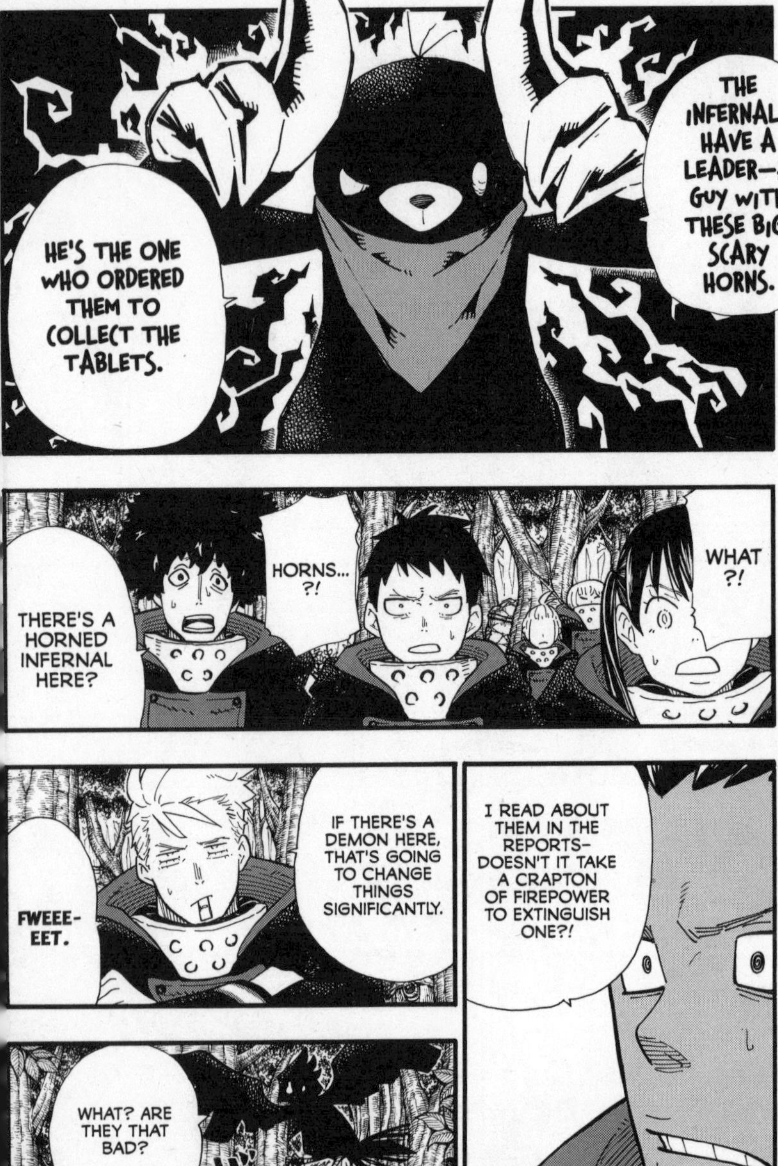
THE INFERNALS HAVE A LEADER—A GUY WITH THESE BIG, SCARY HORNS.
HE'S THE ONE WHO ORDERED THEM TO COLLECT THE TABLETS.
WHAT ?!
HORNS... ?!
THERE'S A HORNED INFERNAL HERE?
I READ ABOUT THEM IN THE REPORTS– DOESN'T IT TAKE A CRAPTON OF FIREPOWER TO EXTINGUISH ONE?!
IF THERE'S A DEMON HERE, THAT'S GOING TO CHANGE THINGS SIGNIFICANTLY.
FWEEE-EET.
WHAT? ARE THEY THAT BAD?
FLAP

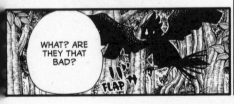

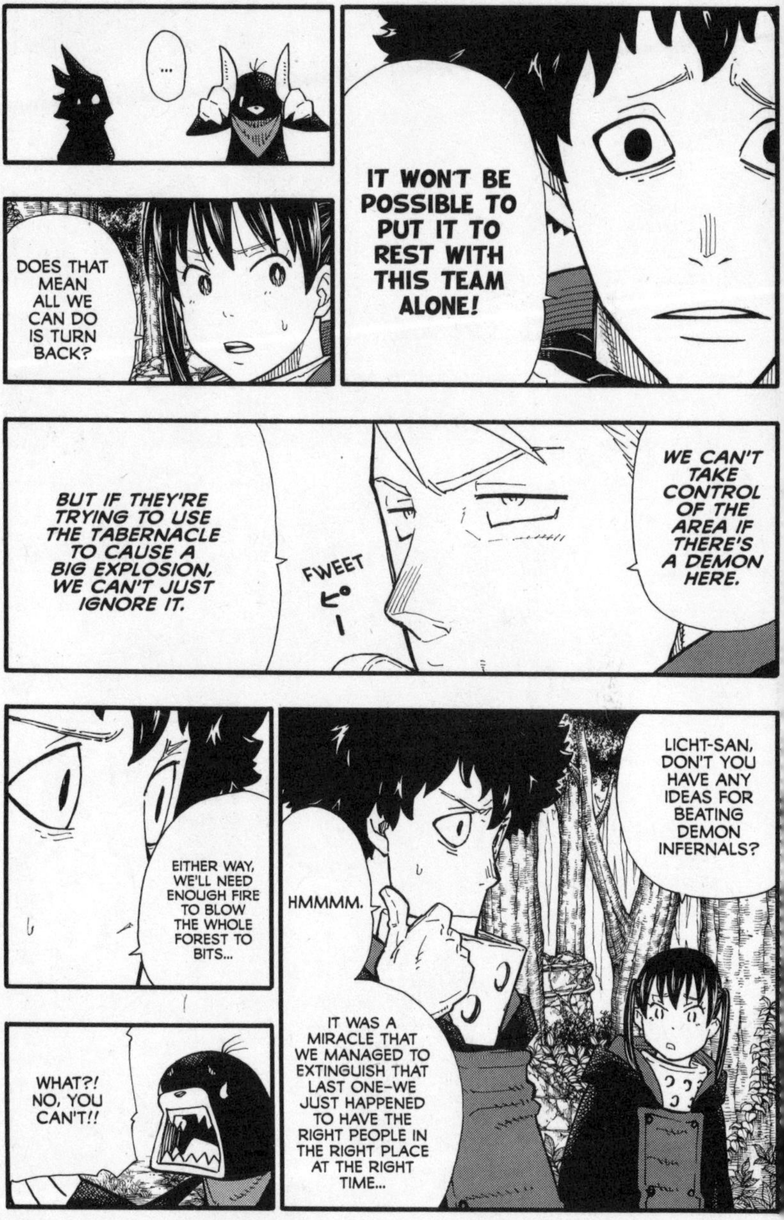
IT WON'T BE POSSIBLE TO PUT IT TO REST WITH THIS TEAM ALONE!
...
DOES THAT MEAN ALL WE CAN DO IS TURN BACK?
WE CAN'T TAKE CONTROL OF THE AREA IF THERE'S A DEMON HERE.
FWEET
ピー
BUT IF THEY'RE TRYING TO USE THE TABERNACLE TO CAUSE A BIG EXPLOSION, WE CAN'T JUST IGNORE IT.
LICHT-SAN, DON'T YOU HAVE ANY IDEAS FOR BEATING DEMON INFERNALS?
HMMMM.
IT WAS A MIRACLE THAT WE MANAGED TO EXTINGUISH THAT LAST ONE—WE JUST HAPPENED TO HAVE THE RIGHT PEOPLE IN THE RIGHT PLACE AT THE RIGHT TIME...
EITHER WAY, WE'LL NEED ENOUGH FIRE TO BLOW THE WHOLE FOREST TO BITS...
WHAT?! NO, YOU CAN'T!!

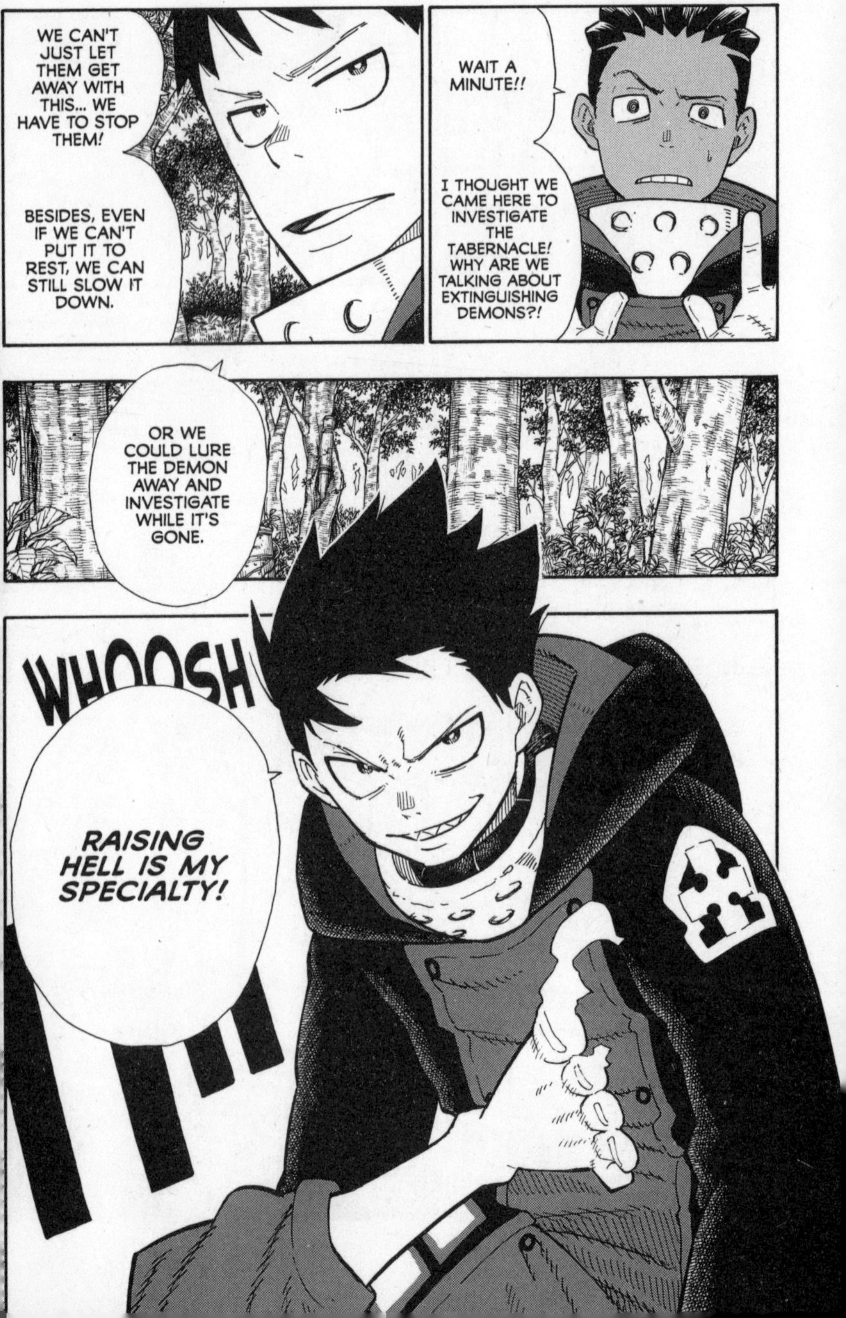
WAIT A MINUTE!!
I THOUGHT WE CAME HERE TO INVESTIGATE THE TABERNACLE! WHY ARE WE TALKING ABOUT EXTINGUISHING DEMONS?!
WE CAN'T JUST LET THEM GET AWAY WITH THIS... WE HAVE TO STOP THEM!
BESIDES, EVEN IF WE CAN'T PUT IT TO REST, WE CAN STILL SLOW IT DOWN.
OR WE COULD LURE THE DEMON AWAY AND INVESTIGATE WHILE IT'S GONE.
WHOOSH
RAISING HELL IS MY SPECIALTY!

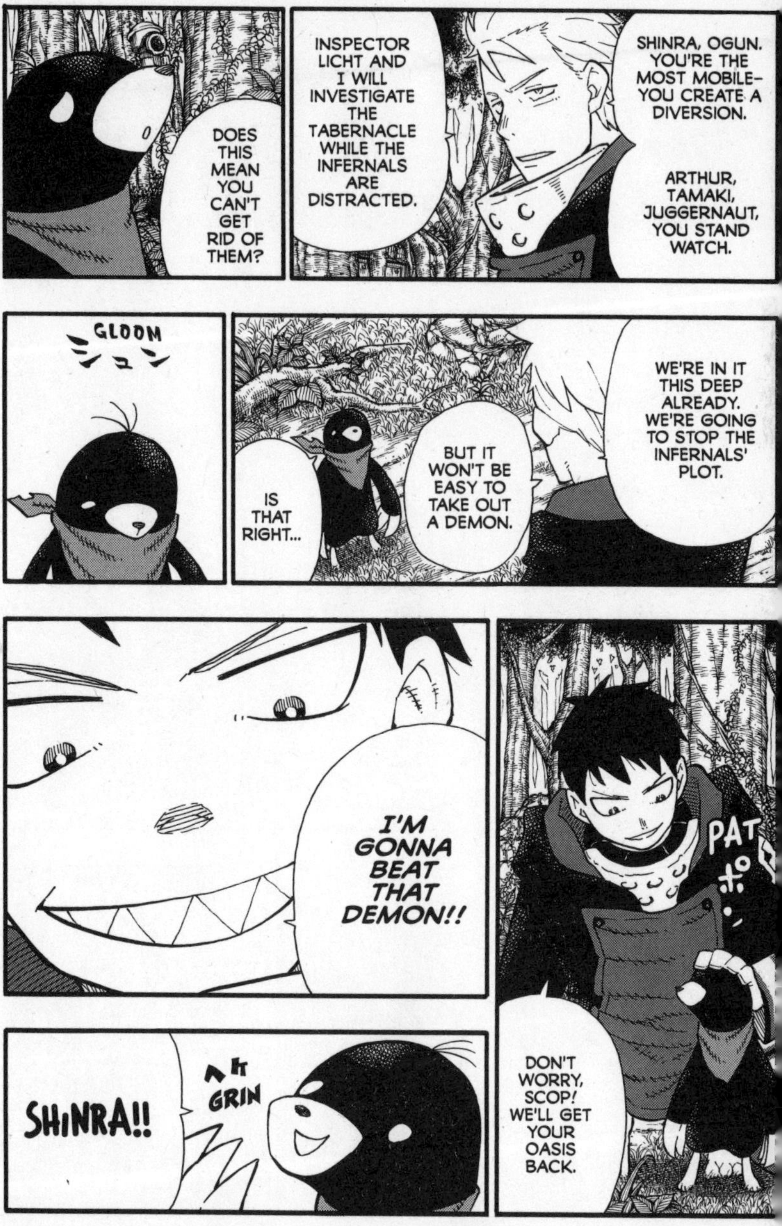
SHINRA, OGUN. YOU'RE THE MOST MOBILE–YOU CREATE A DIVERSION.
ARTHUR, TAMAKI, JUGGERNAUT, YOU STAND WATCH.
INSPECTOR LICHT AND I WILL INVESTIGATE THE TABERNACLE WHILE THE INFERNALS ARE DISTRACTED.
DOES THIS MEAN YOU CAN'T GET RID OF THEM?
WE'RE IN IT THIS DEEP ALREADY. WE'RE GOING TO STOP THE INFERNALS' PLOT.
BUT IT WON'T BE EASY TO TAKE OUT A DEMON.
IS THAT RIGHT...
GLOOM
PAT
DON'T WORRY, SCOP! WE'LL GET YOUR OASIS BACK.
I'M GONNA BEAT THAT DEMON!!
GRIN
SHINRA!!

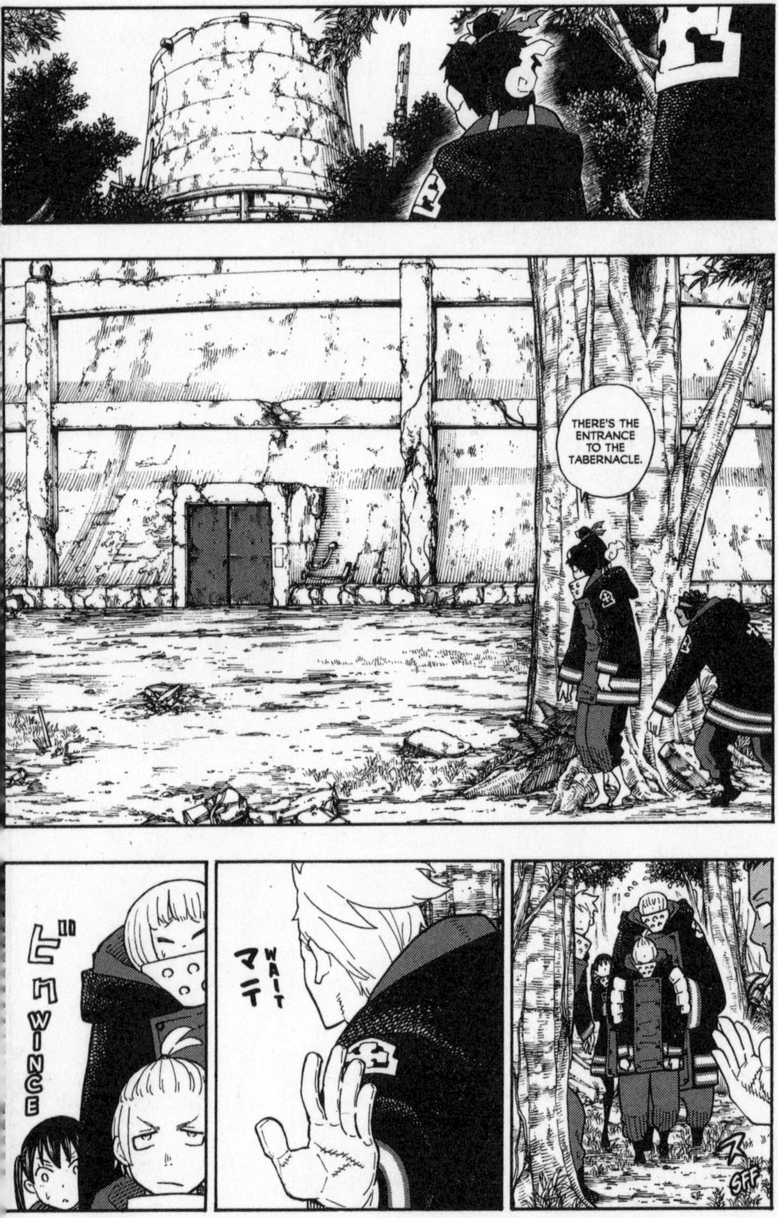
THERE'S THE ENTRANCE TO THE TABERNACLE.
ス
SFF
マテ
WAIT
ビク
WINCE

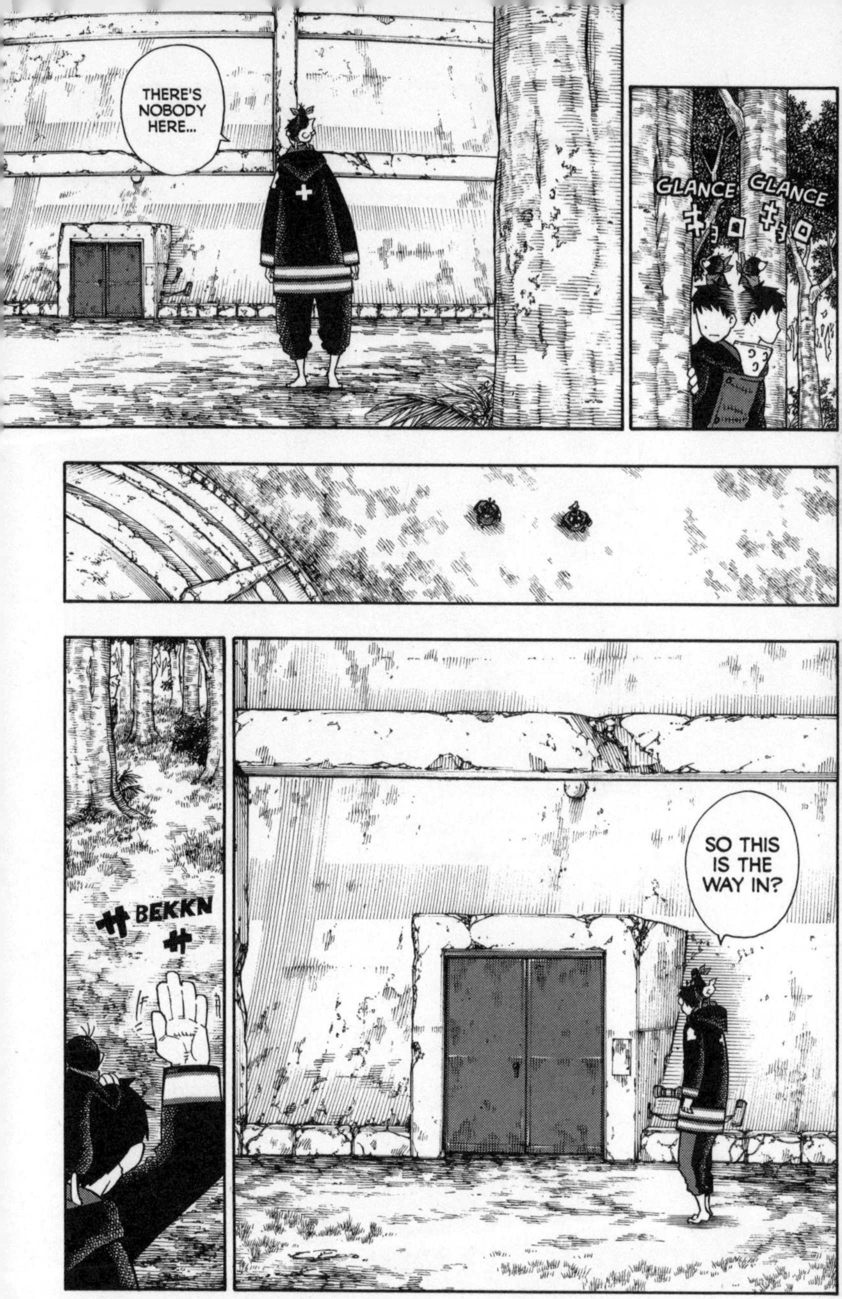
GLANCE GLANCE
キョロキョロ
THERE'S NOBODY HERE...
SO THIS IS THE WAY IN?
BEKKN
ササ

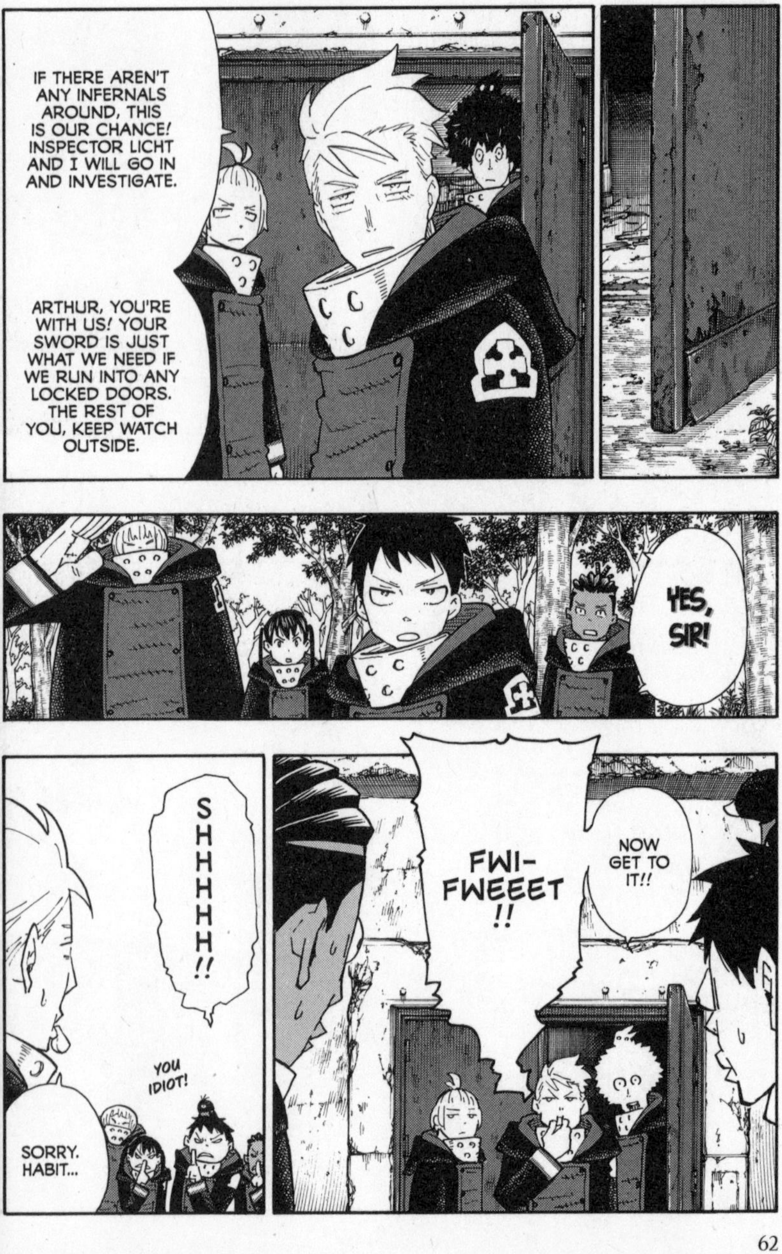
IF THERE AREN'T ANY INFERNALS AROUND, THIS IS OUR CHANCE! INSPECTOR LICHT AND I WILL GO IN AND INVESTIGATE.
ARTHUR, YOU'RE WITH US! YOUR SWORD IS JUST WHAT WE NEED IF WE RUN INTO ANY LOCKED DOORS. THE REST OF YOU, KEEP WATCH OUTSIDE.
YES, SIR!
NOW GET TO IT!!
FWI-FWEEET!!
SHHHHHH!!
YOU IDIOT!
SORRY. HABIT...

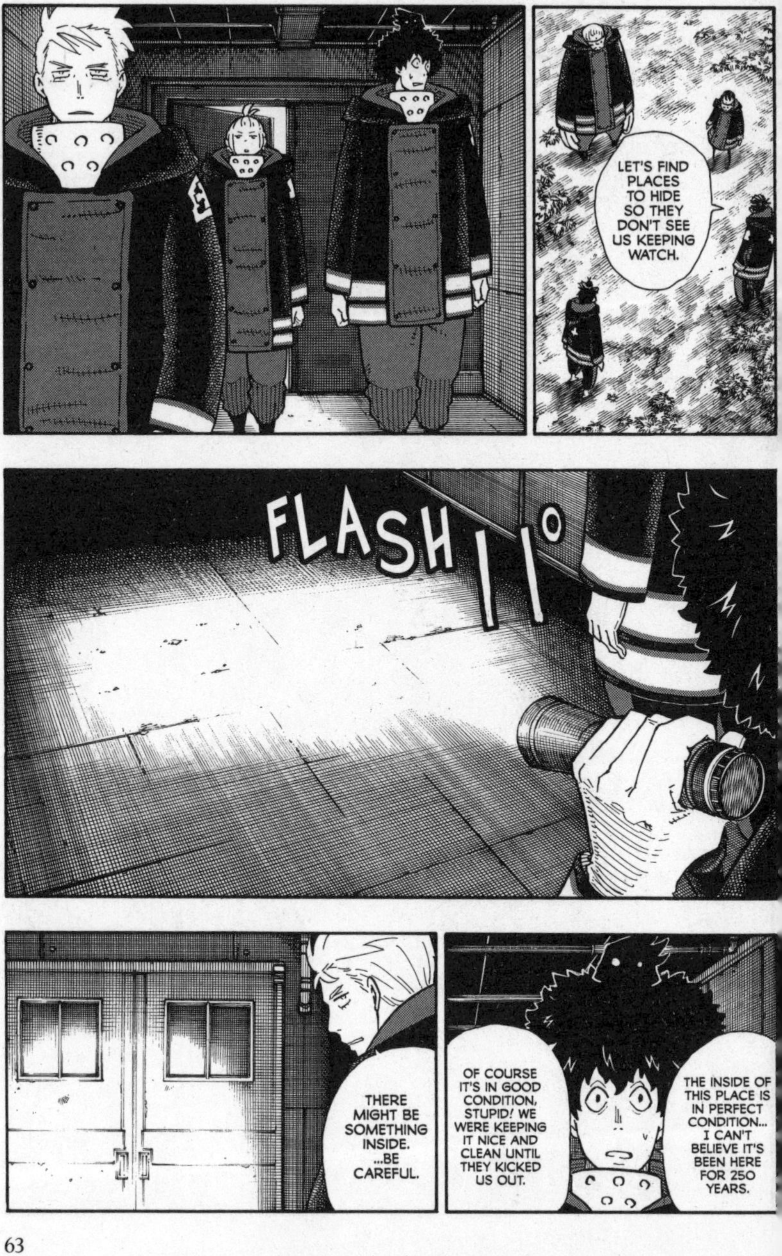
LET'S FIND PLACES TO HIDE SO THEY DON'T SEE US KEEPING WATCH.
FLASH
THE INSIDE OF THIS PLACE IS IN PERFECT CONDITION... I CAN'T BELIEVE IT'S BEEN HERE FOR 250 YEARS.
OF COURSE IT'S IN GOOD CONDITION, STUPID! WE WERE KEEPING IT NICE AND CLEAN UNTIL THEY KICKED US OUT.
THERE MIGHT BE SOMETHING INSIDE. ...BE CAREFUL.

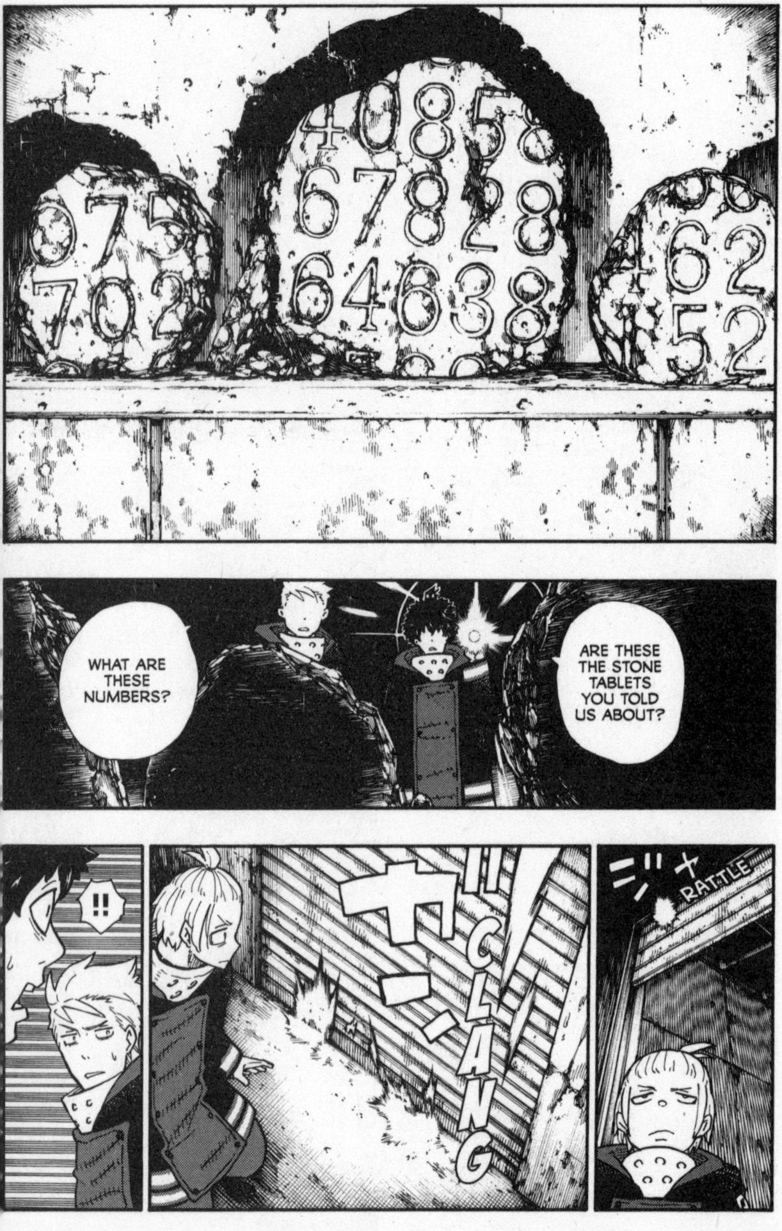
ARE THESE THE STONE TABLETS YOU TOLD US ABOUT?
WHAT ARE THESE NUMBERS?
RATTLE
CLANG
!!

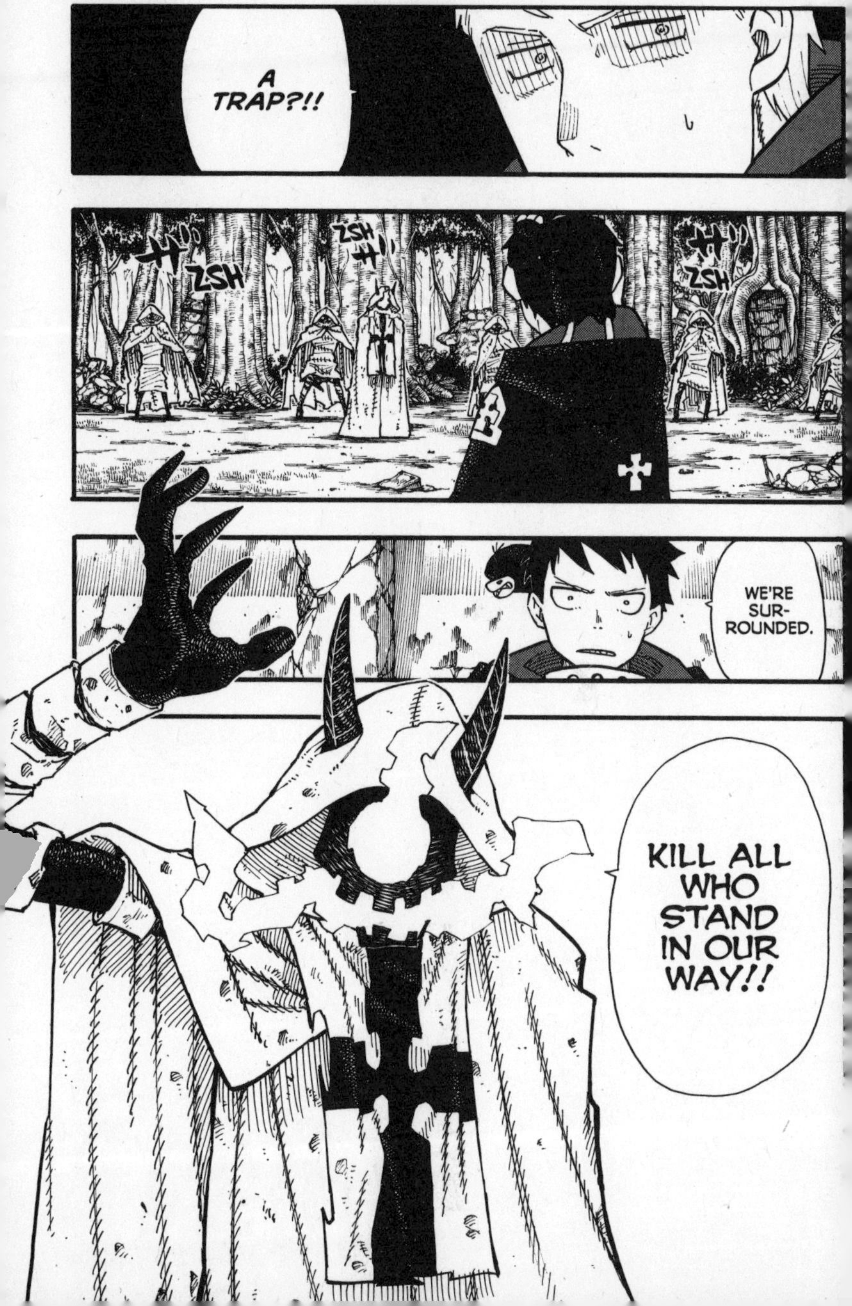
A TRAP?!!
ZSH
ZSH
ZSH
WE'RE SUR-ROUNDED.
KILL ALL WHO STAND IN OUR WAY!!

FIRE FORCE

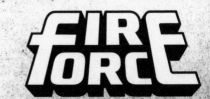

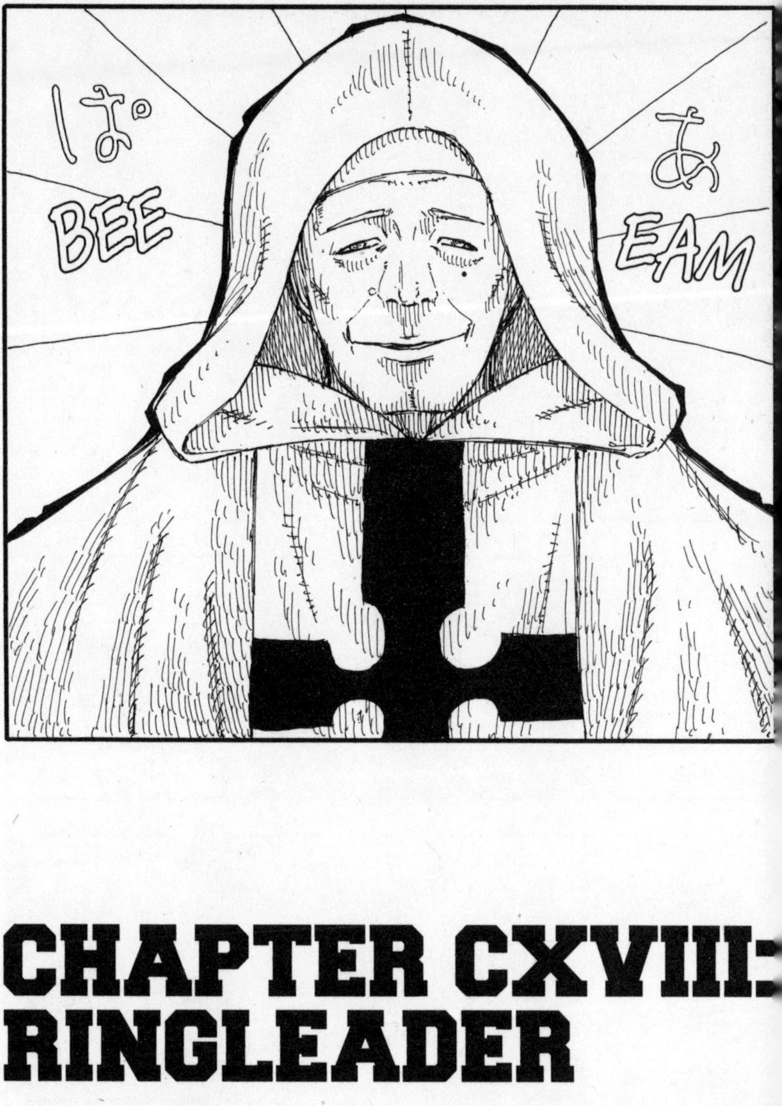
あ
EAM
ば
BEE

CHAPTER CXVIII: RINGLEADER

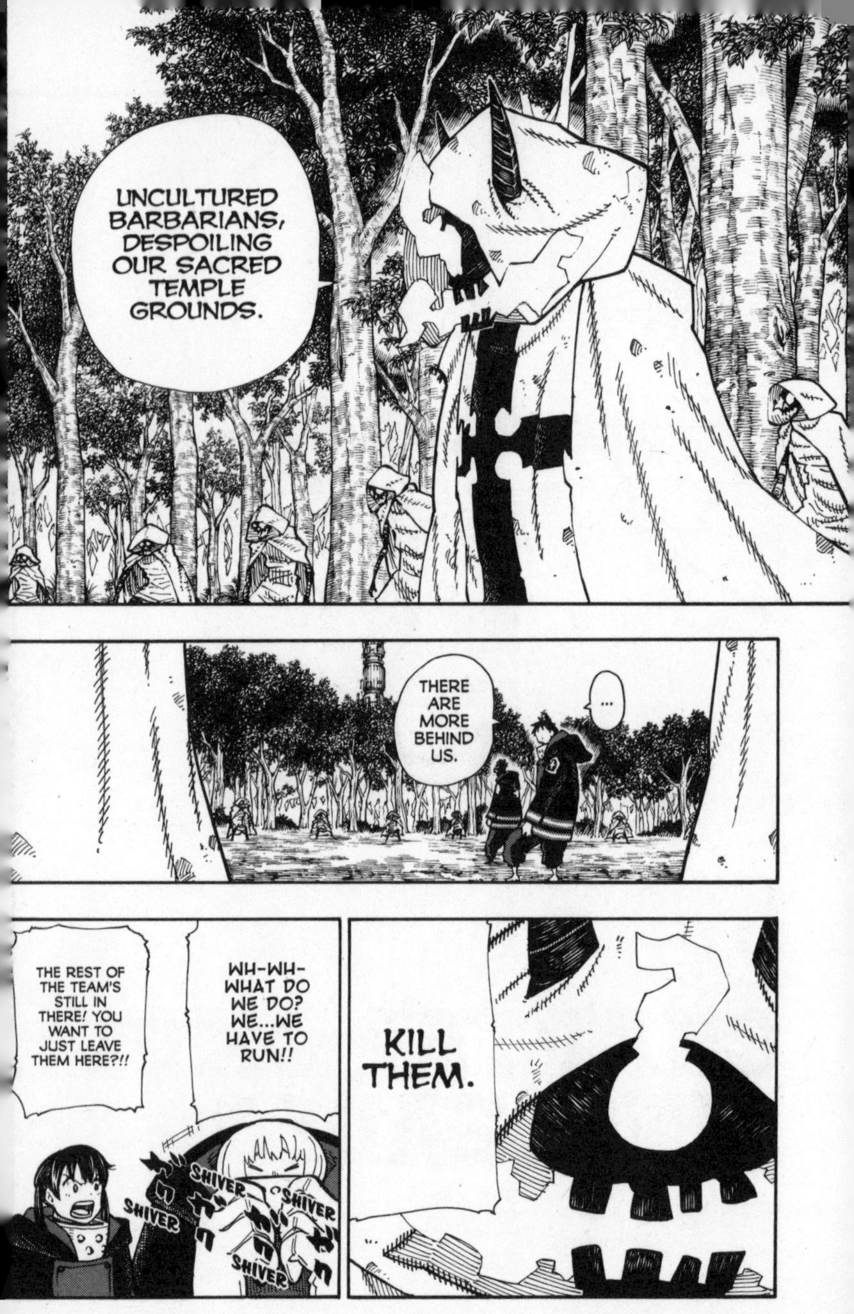
UNCULTURED BARBARIANS, DESPOILING OUR SACRED TEMPLE GROUNDS.
...
THERE ARE MORE BEHIND US.
KILL THEM.
WH-WH-WHAT DO WE DO? WE...WE HAVE TO RUN!!
THE REST OF THE TEAM'S STILL IN THERE! YOU WANT TO JUST LEAVE THEM HERE?!!
SHIVER
SHIVER
SHIVER
SHIVER

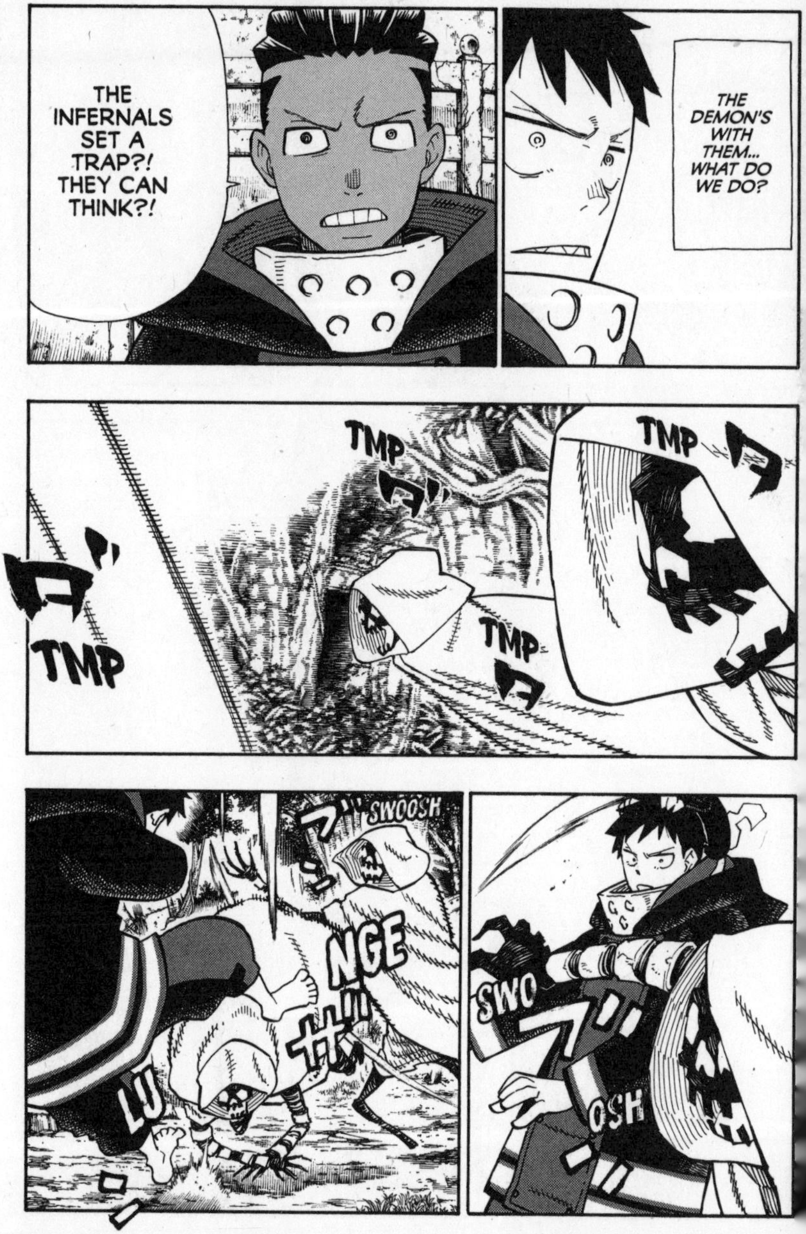
THE DEMON'S WITH THEM... WHAT DO WE DO?
THE INFERNALS SET A TRAP?! THEY CAN THINK?!
TMP
TMP
TMP
TMP
SWO
OSH
SWOOSH
NGE
LU

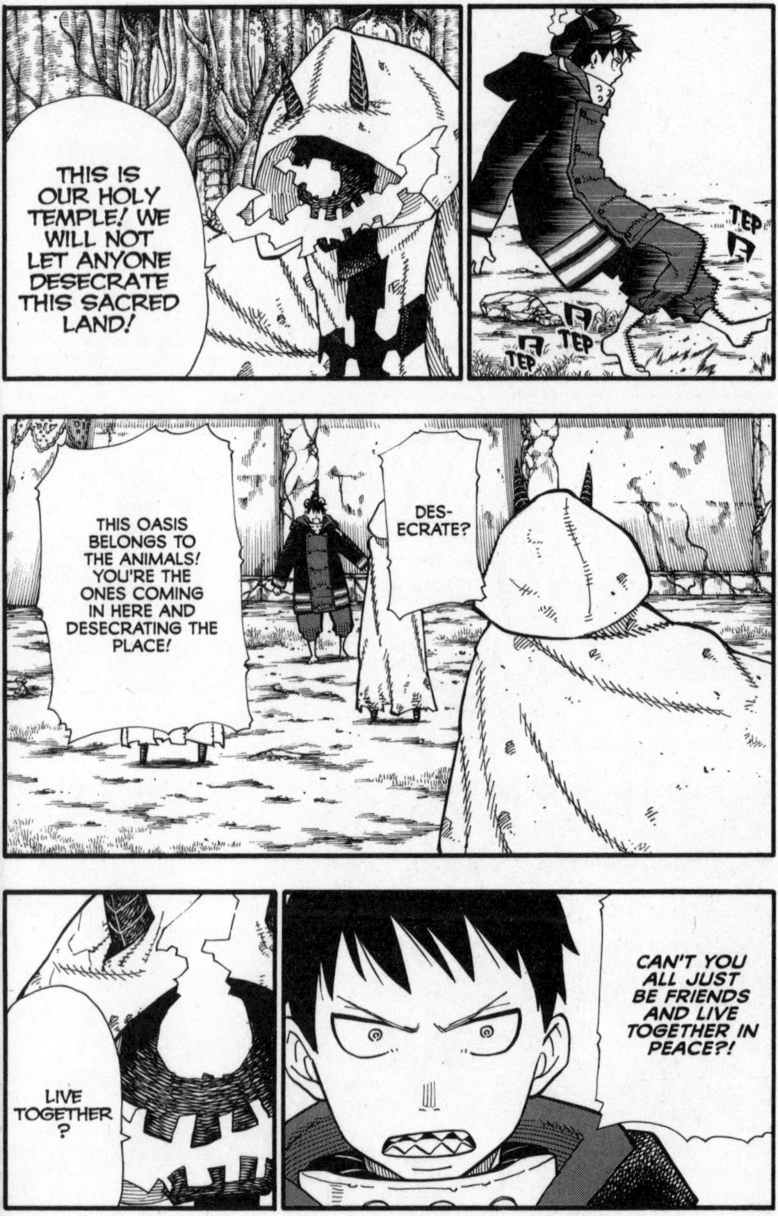
TEP
TEP
TEP
THIS IS OUR HOLY TEMPLE! WE WILL NOT LET ANYONE DESECRATE THIS SACRED LAND!
DES-ECRATE?
THIS OASIS BELONGS TO THE ANIMALS! YOU'RE THE ONES COMING IN HERE AND DESECRATING THE PLACE!
CAN'T YOU ALL JUST BE FRIENDS AND LIVE TOGETHER IN PEACE?!
LIVE TOGETHER?

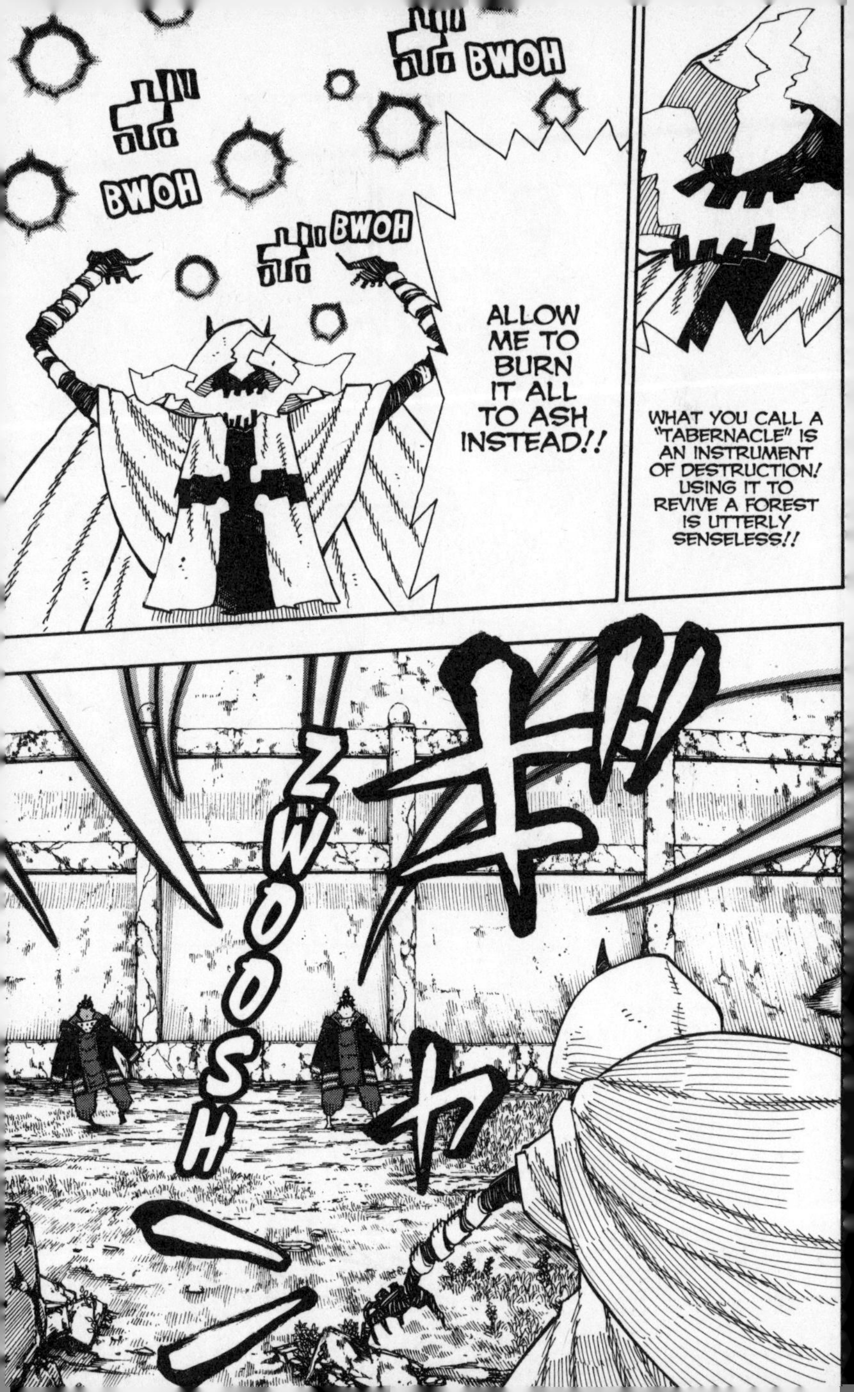
WHAT YOU CALL A "TABERNACLE" IS AN INSTRUMENT OF DESTRUCTION! USING IT TO REVIVE A FOREST IS UTTERLY SENSELESS!!
BWOH
BWOH
BWOH
ALLOW ME TO BURN IT ALL TO ASH INSTEAD!!
ZWOOOSH

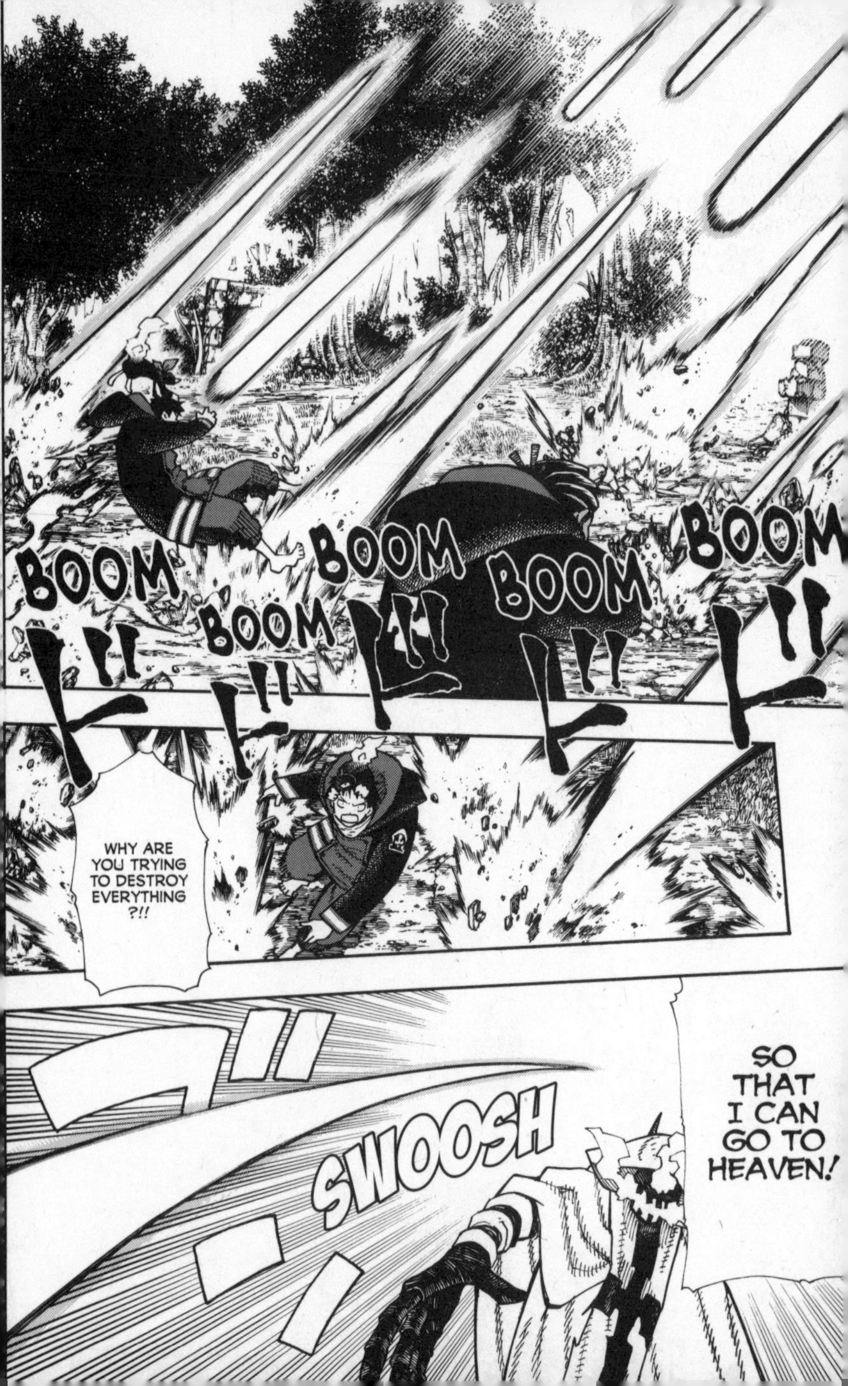
BOOM
ド!!
BOOM
ド!!
BOOM
ド!!
BOOM
ド!!
BOOM
ド!!
WHY ARE YOU TRYING TO DESTROY EVERYTHING?!!
SO THAT I CAN GO TO HEAVEN!
SWOOSH

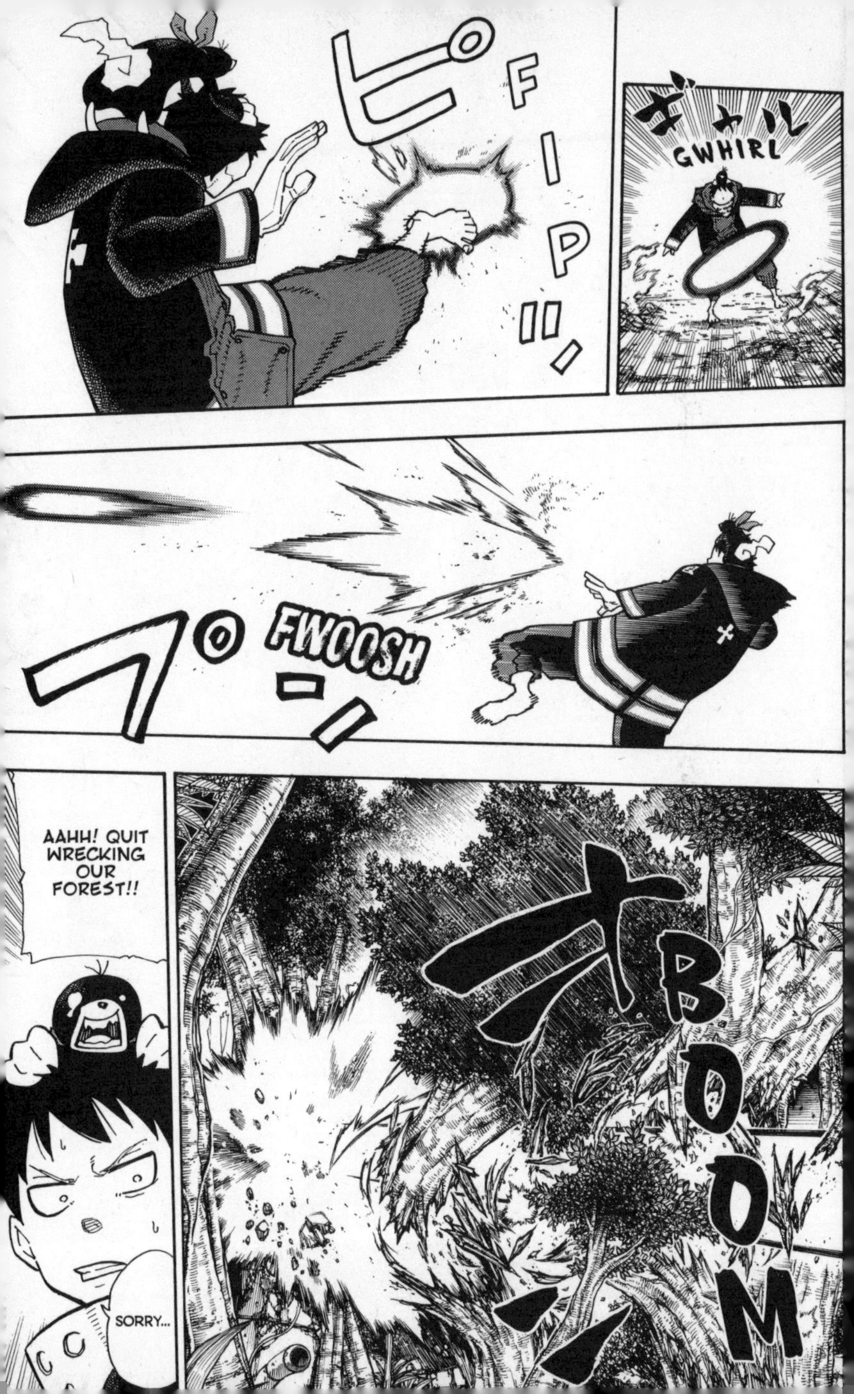
GWHIRL
FIP
FWOOSH
BOOM
AAHH! QUIT WRECKING OUR FOREST!!
SORRY...

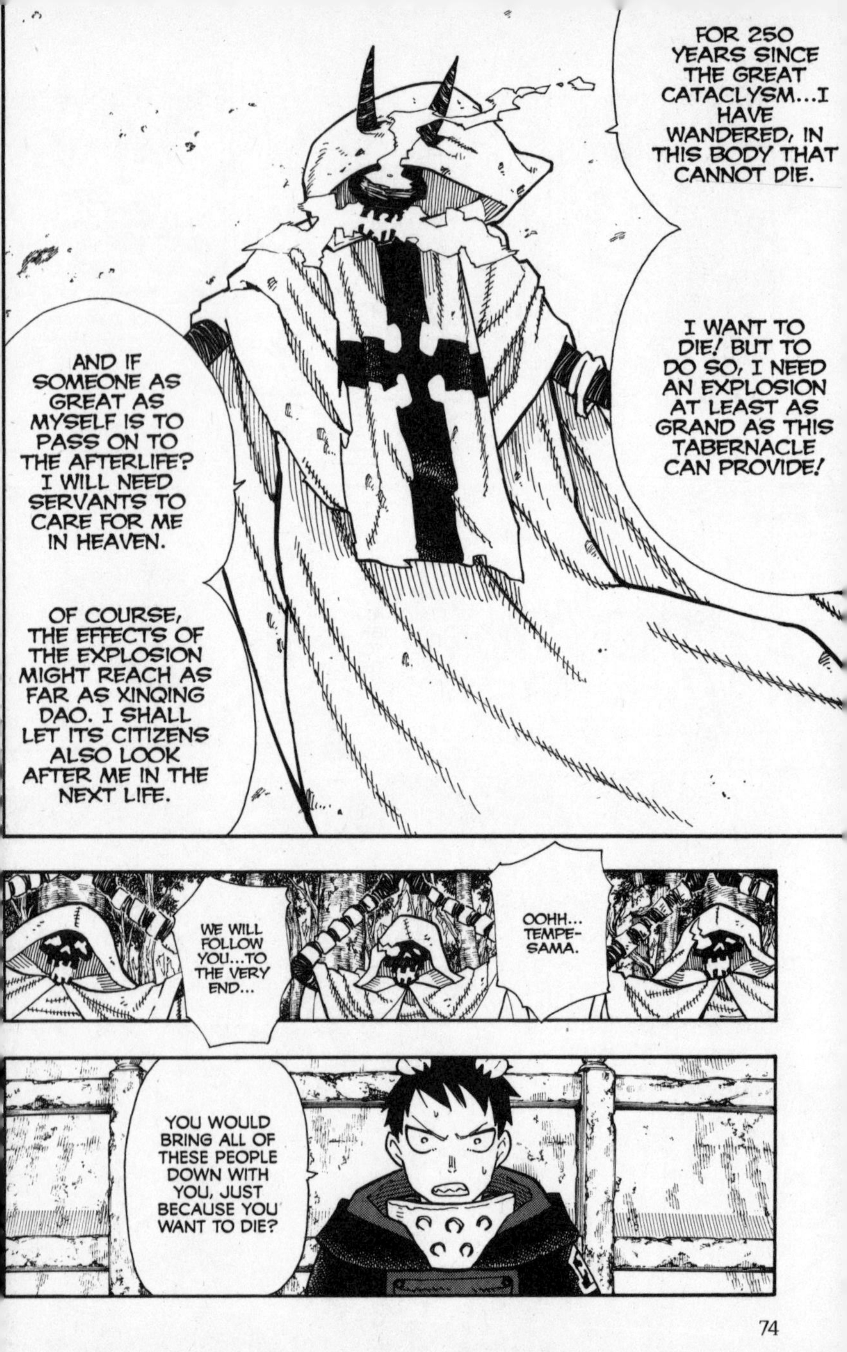
FOR 250 YEARS SINCE THE GREAT CATACLYSM...I HAVE WANDERED, IN THIS BODY THAT CANNOT DIE.
I WANT TO DIE! BUT TO DO SO, I NEED AN EXPLOSION AT LEAST AS GRAND AS THIS TABERNACLE CAN PROVIDE!
AND IF SOMEONE AS GREAT AS MYSELF IS TO PASS ON TO THE AFTERLIFE? I WILL NEED SERVANTS TO CARE FOR ME IN HEAVEN.
OF COURSE, THE EFFECTS OF THE EXPLOSION MIGHT REACH AS FAR AS XINQING DAO. I SHALL LET ITS CITIZENS ALSO LOOK AFTER ME IN THE NEXT LIFE.
OOHH... TEMPE-SAMA.
WE WILL FOLLOW YOU...TO THE VERY END...
YOU WOULD BRING ALL OF THESE PEOPLE DOWN WITH YOU, JUST BECAUSE YOU WANT TO DIE?

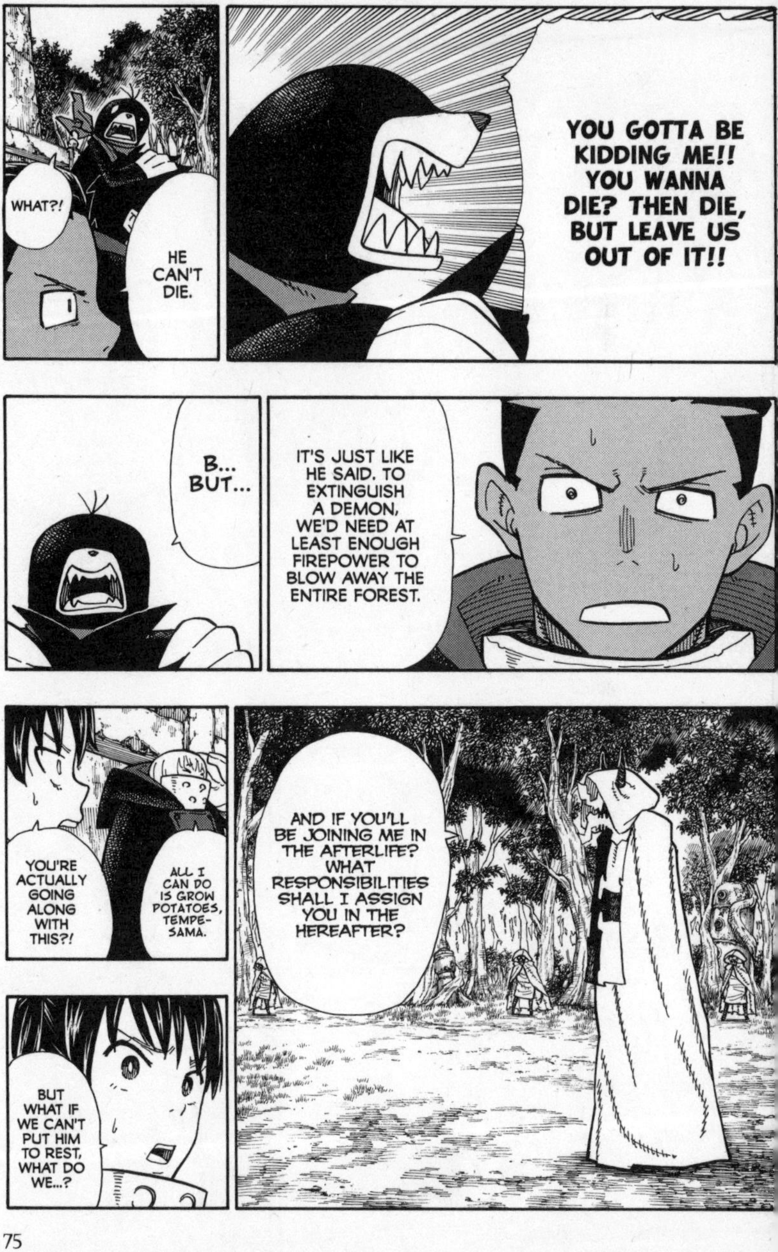
YOU GOTTA BE KIDDING ME!! YOU WANNA DIE? THEN DIE, BUT LEAVE US OUT OF IT!!
HE CAN'T DIE.
WHAT?!
IT'S JUST LIKE HE SAID. TO EXTINGUISH A DEMON, WE'D NEED AT LEAST ENOUGH FIREPOWER TO BLOW AWAY THE ENTIRE FOREST.
B... BUT...
AND IF YOU'LL BE JOINING ME IN THE AFTERLIFE? WHAT RESPONSIBILITIES SHALL I ASSIGN YOU IN THE HEREAFTER?
YOU'RE ACTUALLY GOING ALONG WITH THIS?!
ALL I CAN DO IS GROW POTATOES, TEMPE-SAMA.
BUT WHAT IF WE CAN'T PUT HIM TO REST, WHAT DO WE...?

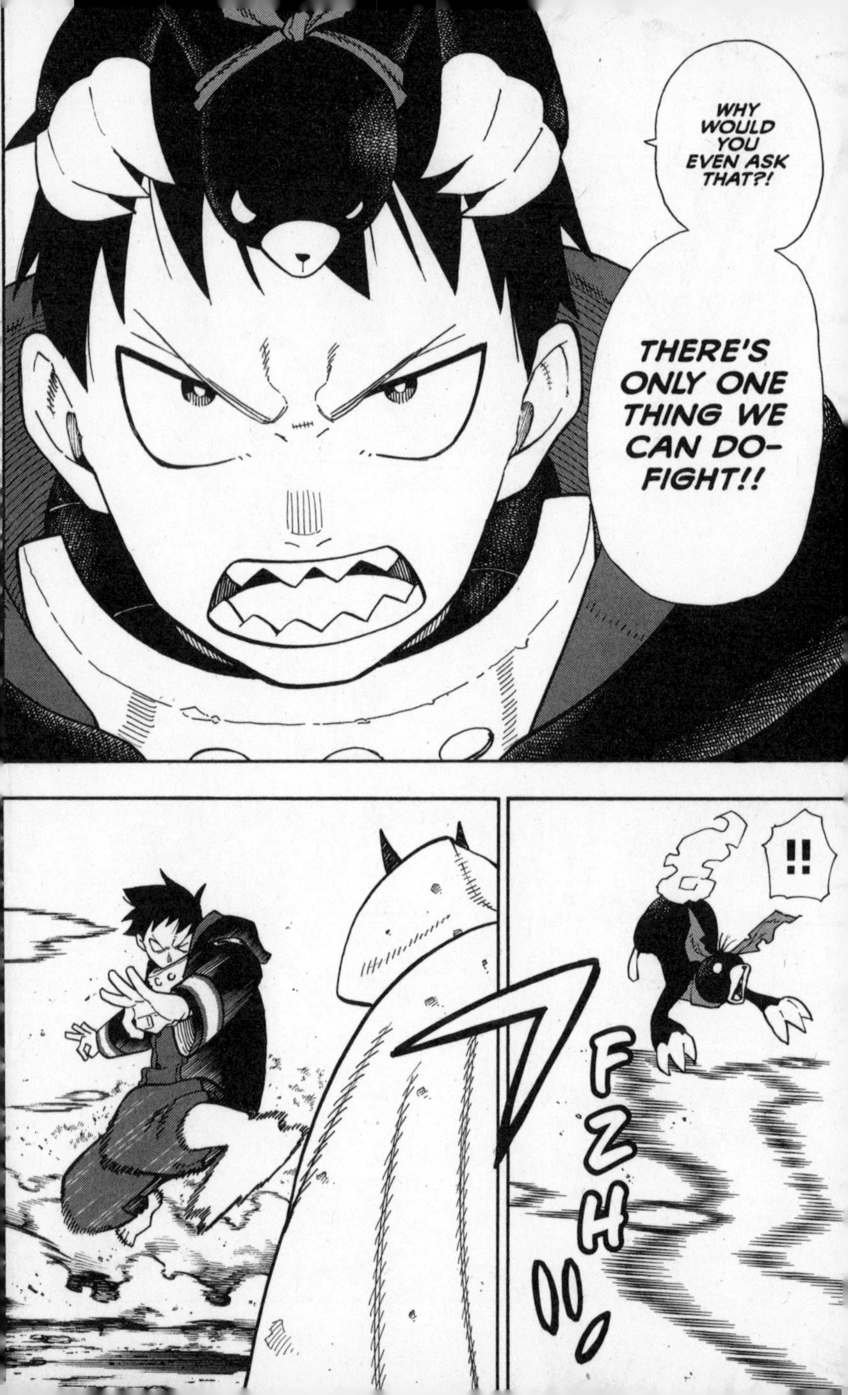
WHY WOULD YOU EVEN ASK THAT?!
THERE'S ONLY ONE THING WE CAN DO- FIGHT!!
!!
FZH

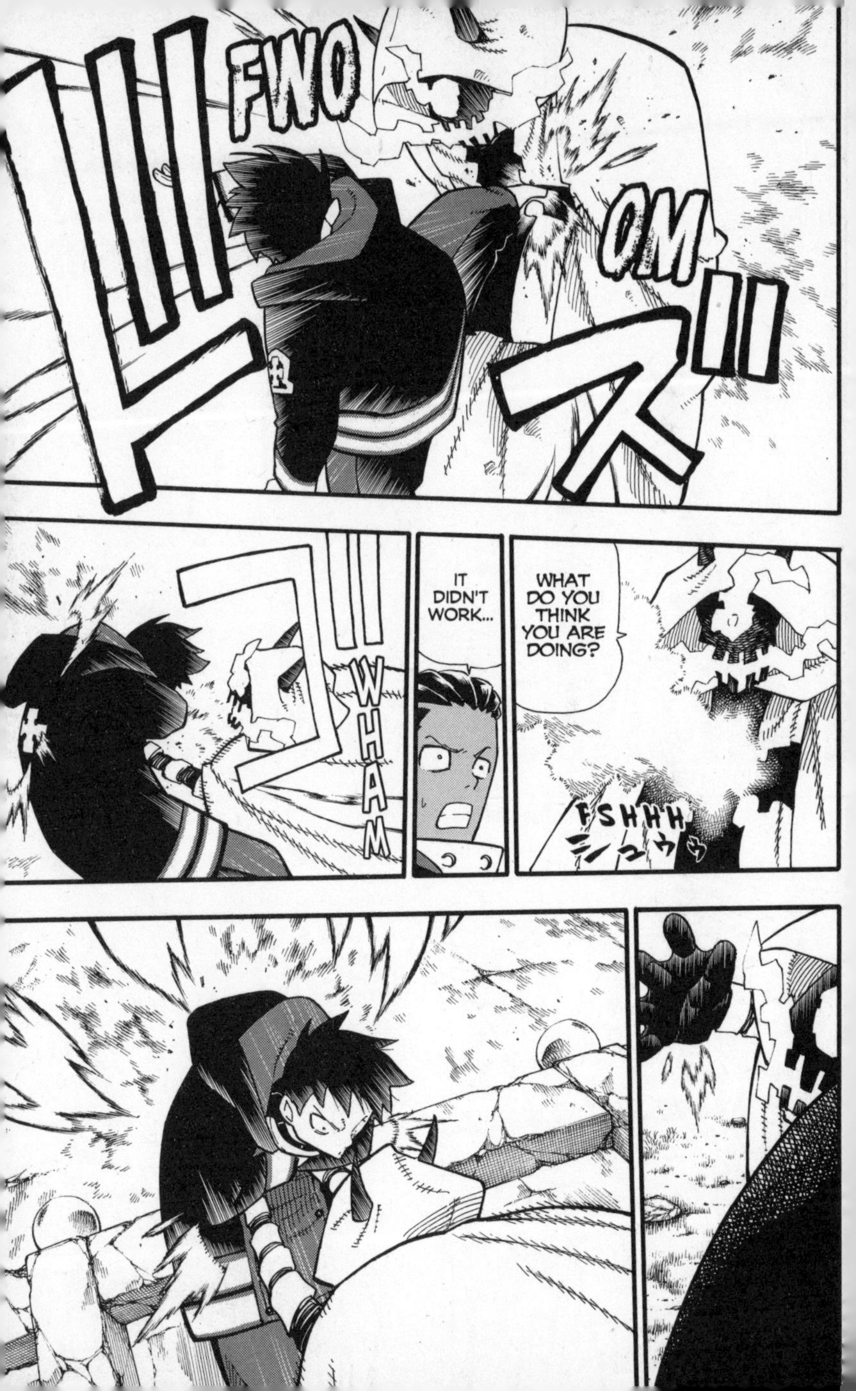
FWO
OM
WHAT DO YOU THINK YOU ARE DOING?
FSHHH
IT DIDN'T WORK...
WHAM

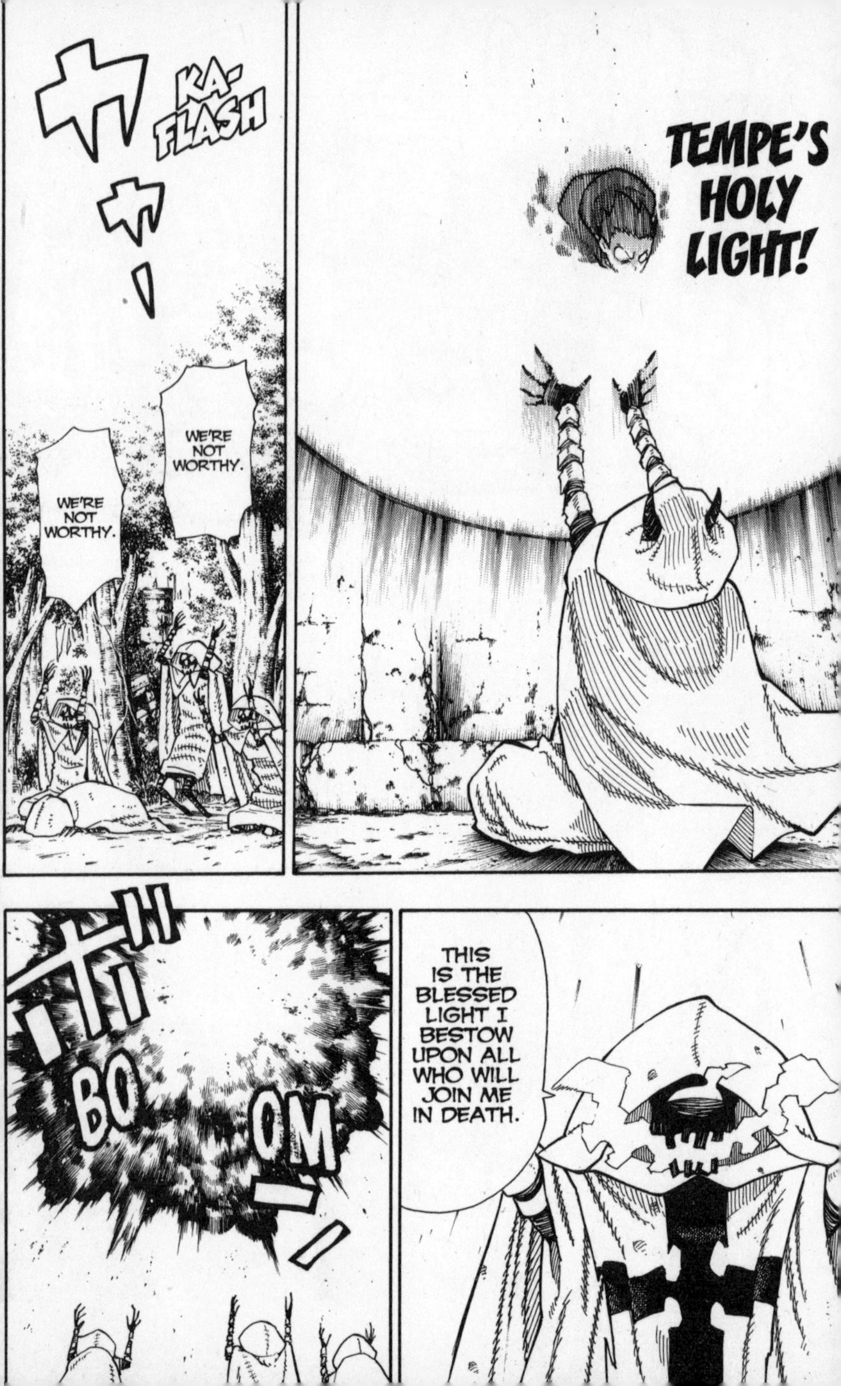
TEMPE'S HOLY LIGHT!
KA-FLASH
WE'RE NOT WORTHY.
WE'RE NOT WORTHY.
THIS IS THE BLESSED LIGHT I BESTOW UPON ALL WHO WILL JOIN ME IN DEATH.
BOOM

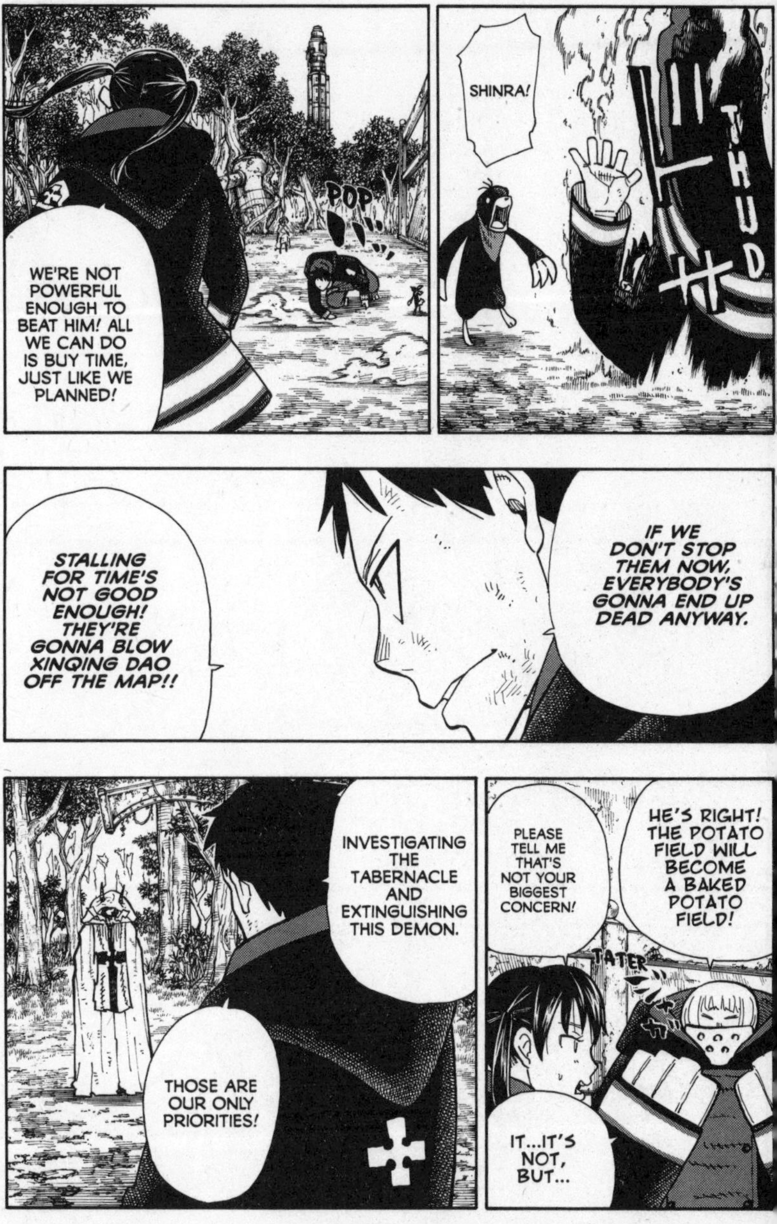
SHINRA!
THUD
POP
WE'RE NOT POWERFUL ENOUGH TO BEAT HIM! ALL WE CAN DO IS BUY TIME, JUST LIKE WE PLANNED!
IF WE DON'T STOP THEM NOW, EVERYBODY'S GONNA END UP DEAD ANYWAY.
STALLING FOR TIME'S NOT GOOD ENOUGH! THEY'RE GONNA BLOW XINQING DAO OFF THE MAP!!
HE'S RIGHT! THE POTATO FIELD WILL BECOME A BAKED POTATO FIELD!
PLEASE TELL ME THAT'S NOT YOUR BIGGEST CONCERN!
TATER
IT...IT'S NOT, BUT...
INVESTIGATING THE TABERNACLE AND EXTINGUISHING THIS DEMON.
THOSE ARE OUR ONLY PRIORITIES!

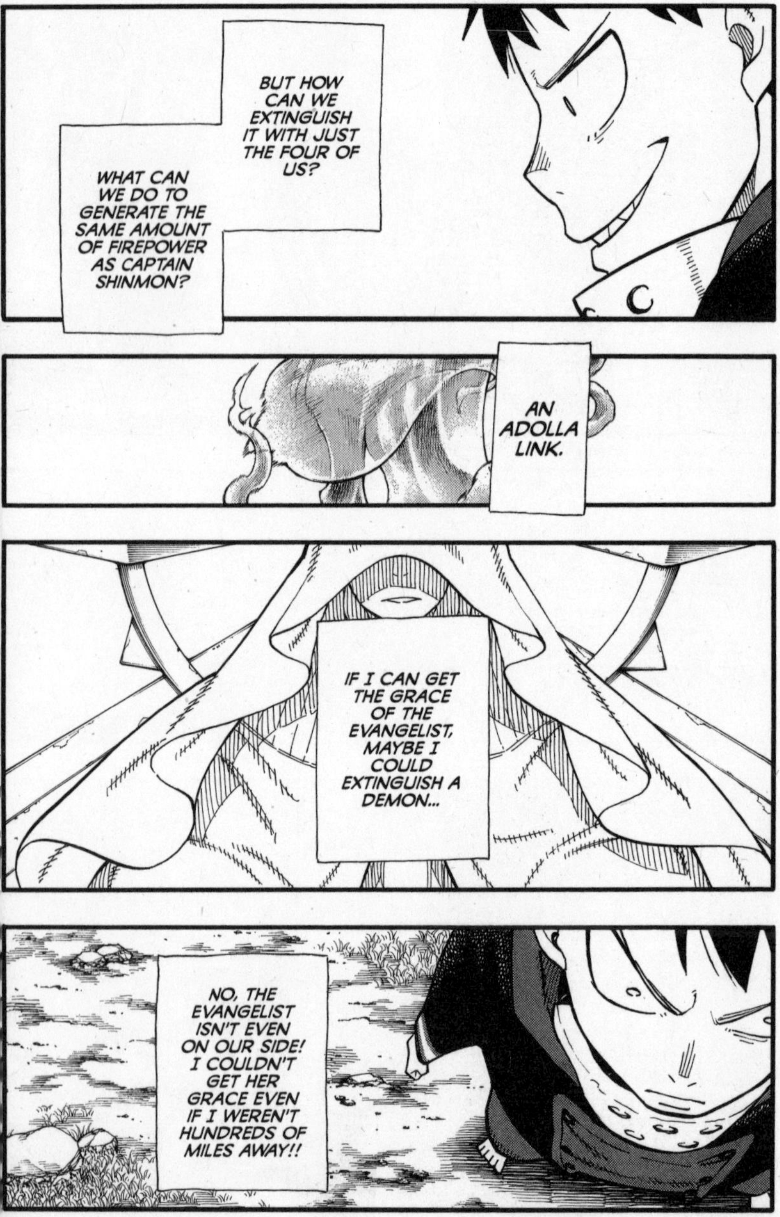
BUT HOW CAN WE EXTINGUISH IT WITH JUST THE FOUR OF US?
WHAT CAN WE DO TO GENERATE THE SAME AMOUNT OF FIREPOWER AS CAPTAIN SHINMON?
AN ADOLLA LINK.
IF I CAN GET THE GRACE OF THE EVANGELIST, MAYBE I COULD EXTINGUISH A DEMON...
NO, THE EVANGELIST ISN'T EVEN ON OUR SIDE! I COULDN'T GET HER GRACE EVEN IF I WEREN'T HUNDREDS OF MILES AWAY!!

WE'LL GIVE IT ALL THE FIREPOWER WE'VE GOT.

RESISTING ME WILL EARN YOU A DEMOTION IN THE AFTERLIFE.

WHEN LIEUTENANT PAN AND THE OTHERS GET BACK OUTSIDE, HE COULD USE SOME ENHANCEMENTS, THEN MAYBE...

WHAT'S WRONG, KUSAKABE?

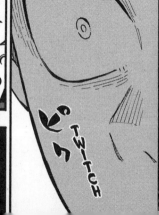

TWITCH

B-DMP

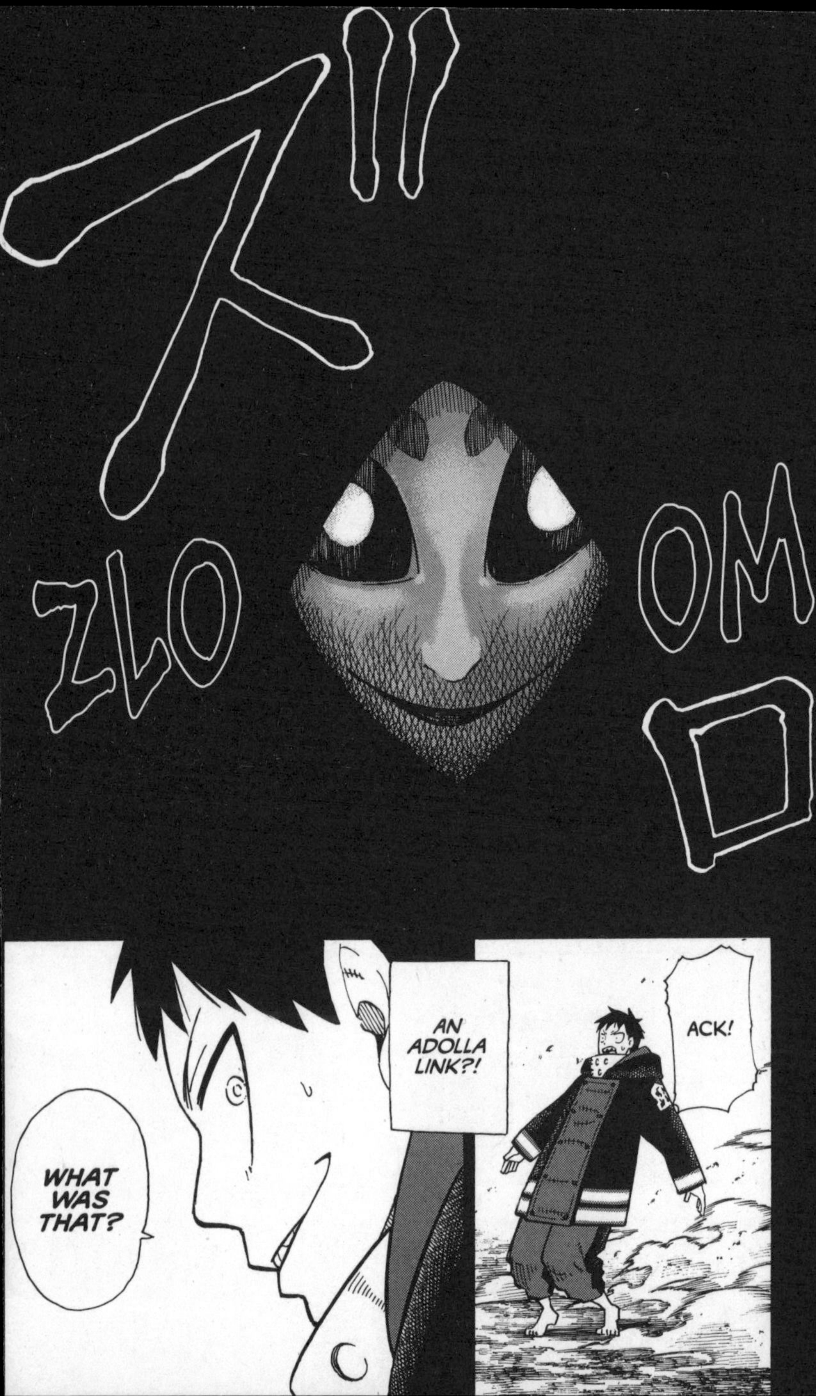
ZLOOM
ACK!
AN ADOLLA LINK?!
WHAT WAS THAT?

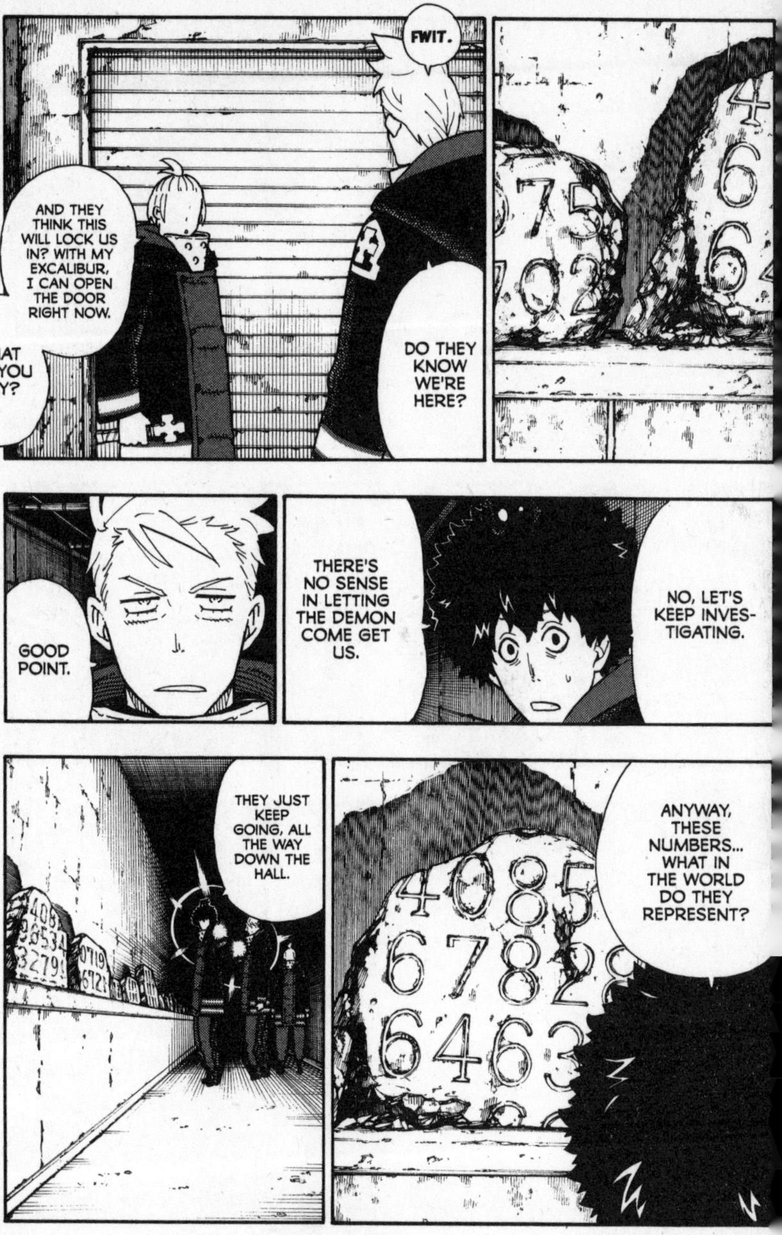
FWIT.
DO THEY KNOW WE'RE HERE?
AND THEY THINK THIS WILL LOCK US IN? WITH MY EXCALIBUR, I CAN OPEN THE DOOR RIGHT NOW.
WHAT DO YOU SAY?
NO, LET'S KEEP INVES-TIGATING.
THERE'S NO SENSE IN LETTING THE DEMON COME GET US.
GOOD POINT.
ANYWAY, THESE NUMBERS... WHAT IN THE WORLD DO THEY REPRESENT?
THEY JUST KEEP GOING, ALL THE WAY DOWN THE HALL.

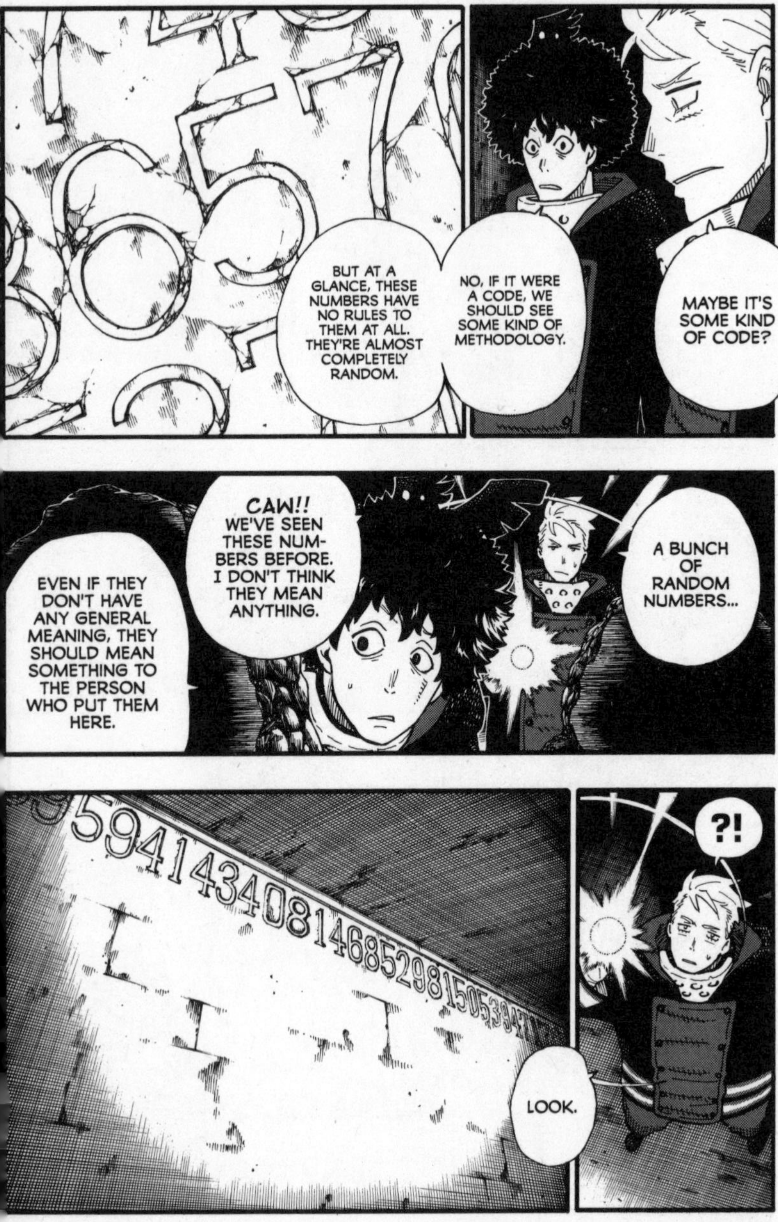
MAYBE IT'S SOME KIND OF CODE?
NO, IF IT WERE A CODE, WE SHOULD SEE SOME KIND OF METHODOLOGY.
BUT AT A GLANCE, THESE NUMBERS HAVE NO RULES TO THEM AT ALL. THEY'RE ALMOST COMPLETELY RANDOM.
A BUNCH OF RANDOM NUMBERS...
CAW!! WE'VE SEEN THESE NUMBERS BEFORE. I DON'T THINK THEY MEAN ANYTHING.
EVEN IF THEY DON'T HAVE ANY GENERAL MEANING, THEY SHOULD MEAN SOMETHING TO THE PERSON WHO PUT THEM HERE.
?!
LOOK.
5941434081468529815053

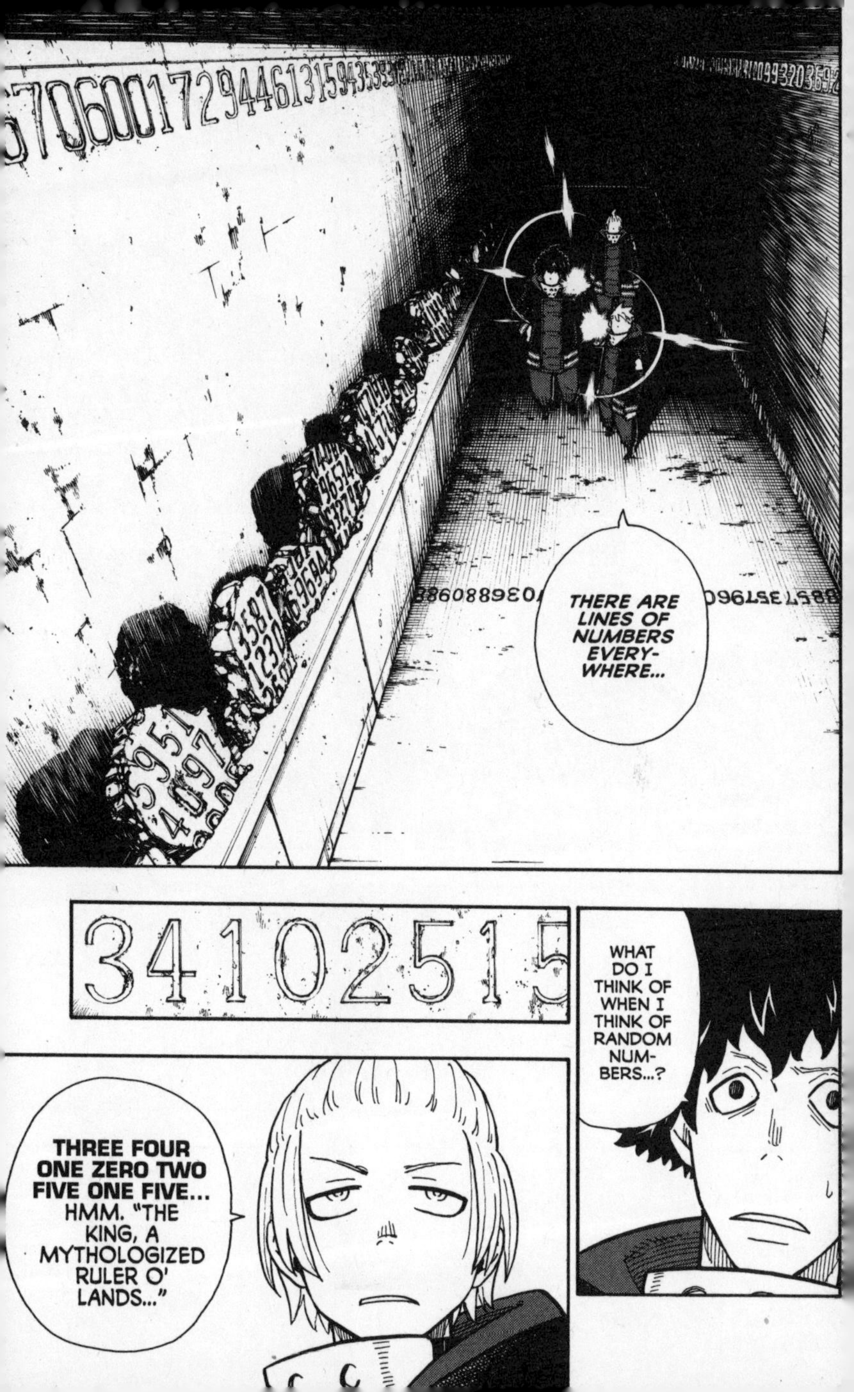
THERE ARE LINES OF NUMBERS EVERY-WHERE...
WHAT DO I THINK OF WHEN I THINK OF RANDOM NUM-BERS...?
34102515
THREE FOUR ONE ZERO TWO FIVE ONE FIVE... HMM. "THE KING, A MYTHOLOGIZED RULER O' LANDS..."

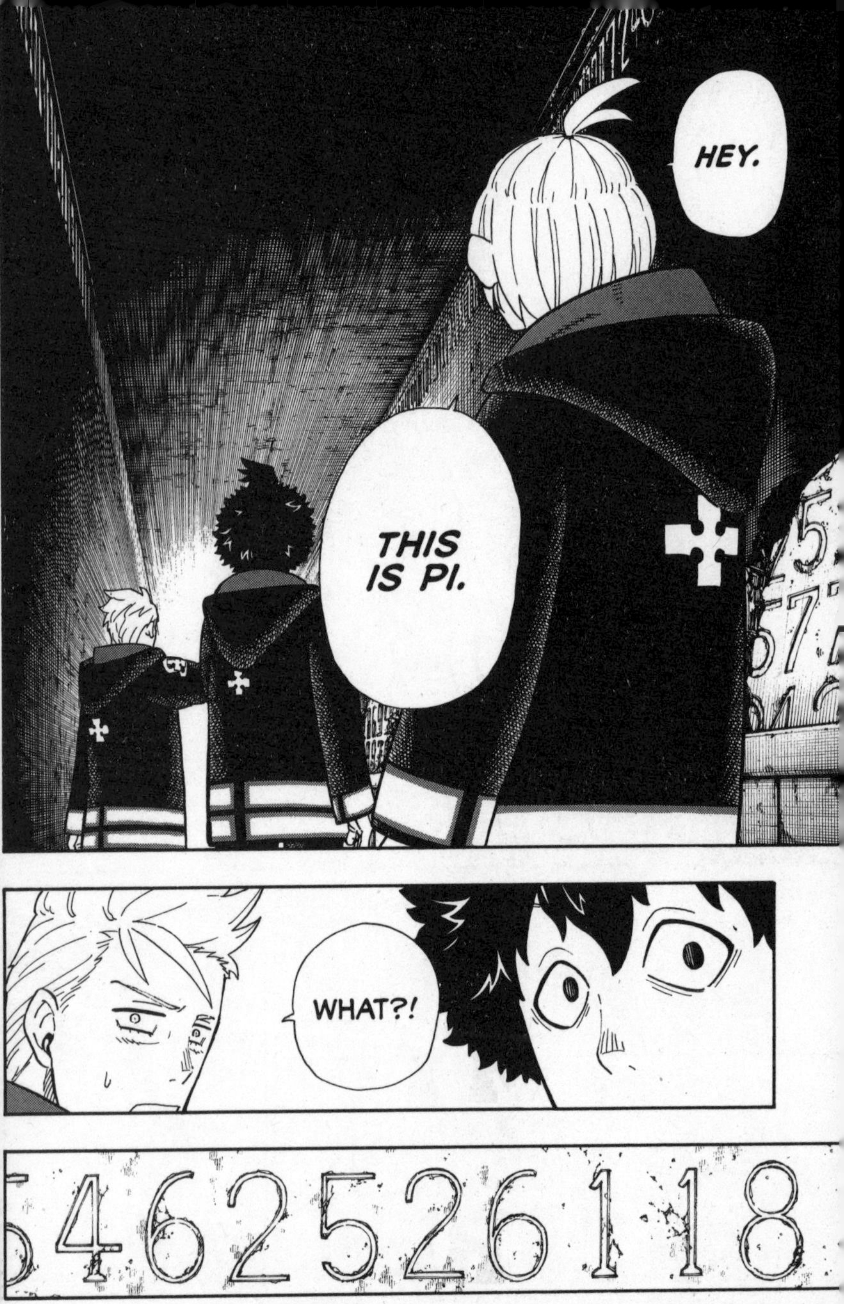
HEY.
THIS IS PI.
WHAT?!
5462526118

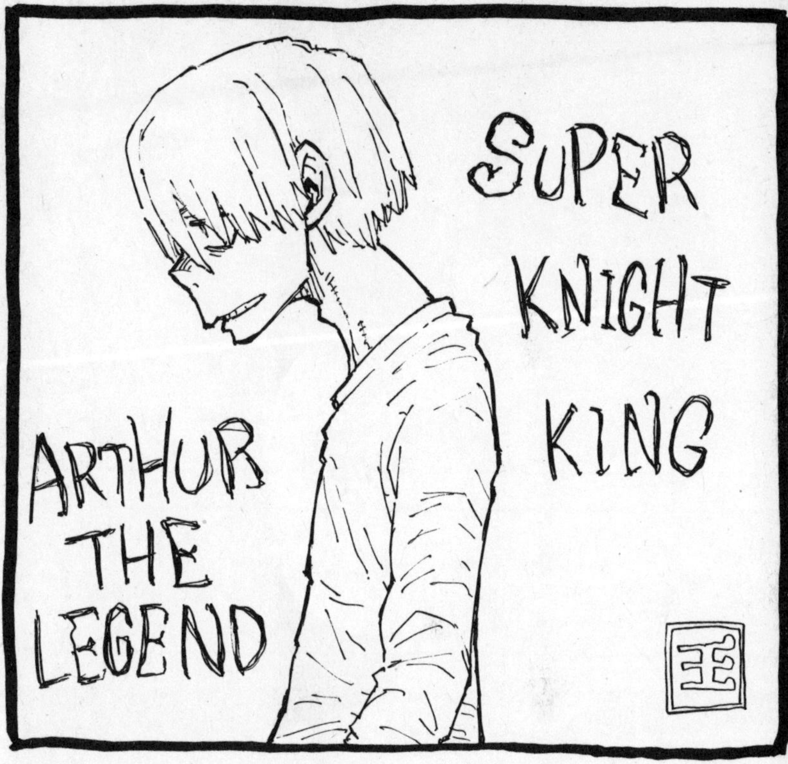
SUPER
KNIGHT
KING
ARTHUR
THE
LEGEND
Stamp: King

CHAPTER CXIX: THE MYSTERY OF THE TABERNACLE

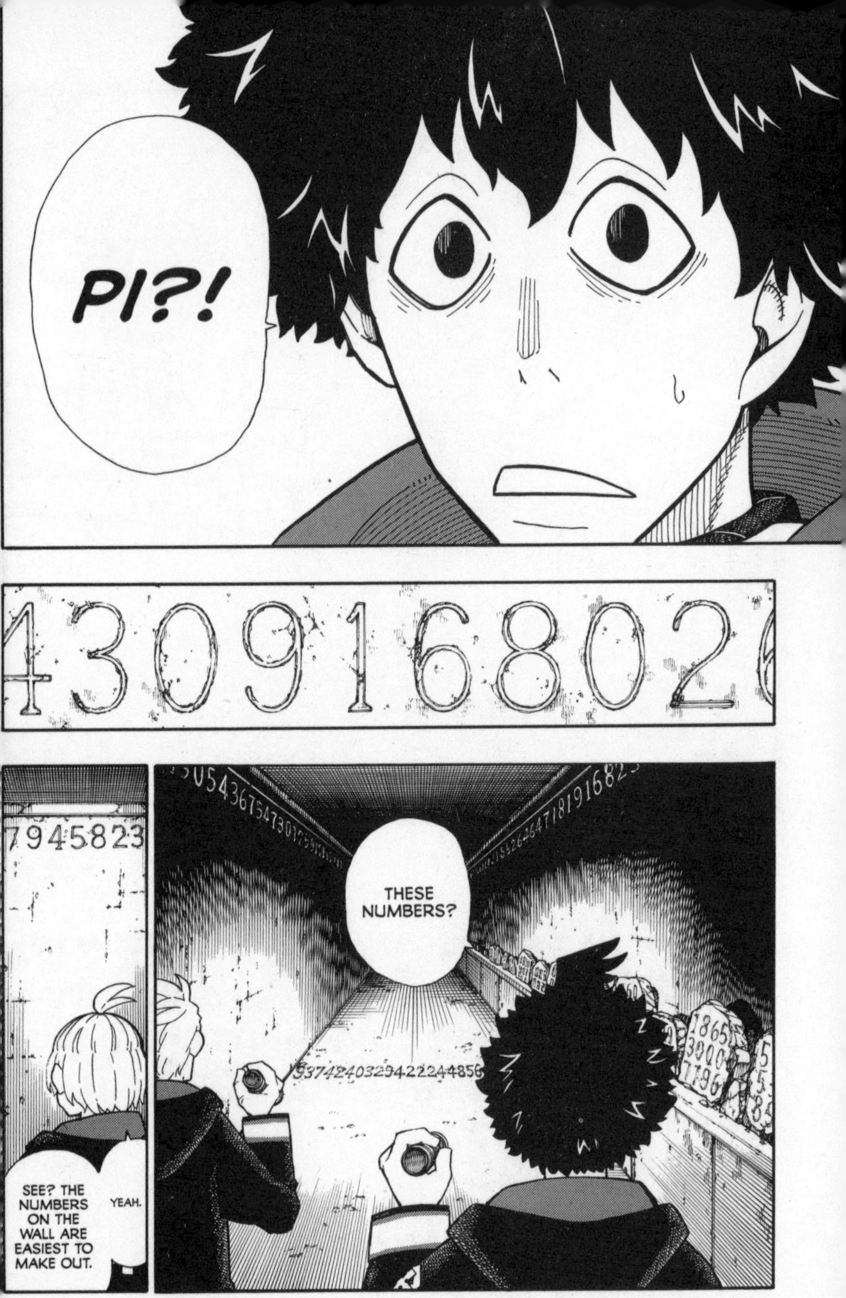
PI?!
THESE NUMBERS?
SEE? THE NUMBERS ON THE WALL ARE EASIEST TO MAKE OUT.
YEAH.

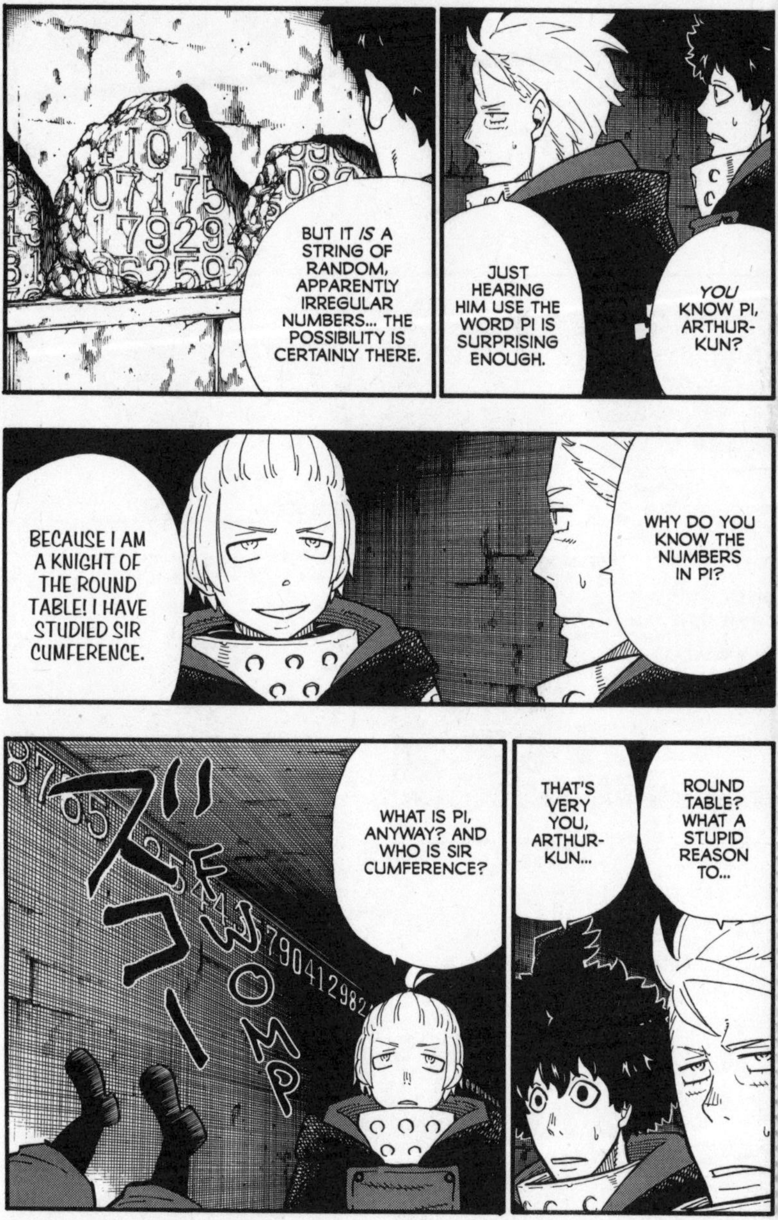
YOU KNOW PI, ARTHUR-KUN?
JUST HEARING HIM USE THE WORD PI IS SURPRISING ENOUGH.
BUT IT *IS* A STRING OF RANDOM, APPARENTLY IRREGULAR NUMBERS... THE POSSIBILITY IS CERTAINLY THERE.
WHY DO YOU KNOW THE NUMBERS IN PI?
BECAUSE I AM A KNIGHT OF THE ROUND TABLE! I HAVE STUDIED SIR CUMFERENCE.
ROUND TABLE? WHAT A STUPID REASON TO...
THAT'S VERY YOU, ARTHUR-KUN...
WHAT IS PI, ANYWAY? AND WHO IS SIR CUMFERENCE?
ズコー
FWOMP

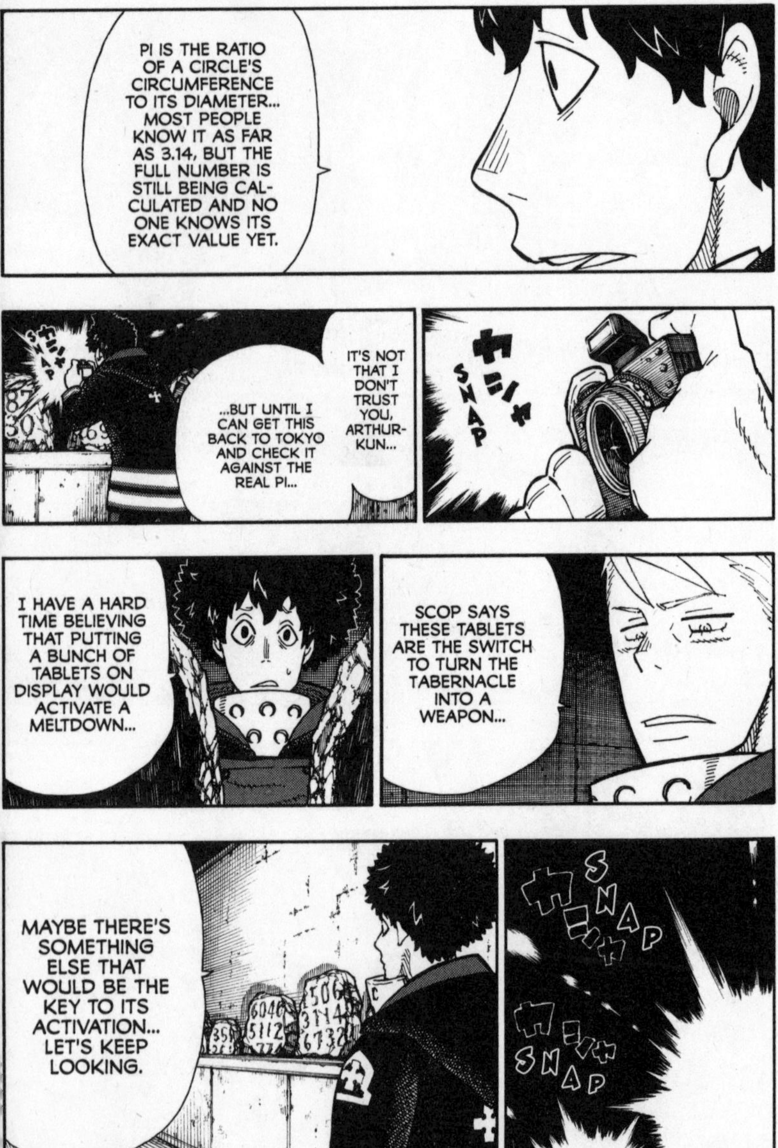
PI IS THE RATIO OF A CIRCLE'S CIRCUMFERENCE TO ITS DIAMETER... MOST PEOPLE KNOW IT AS FAR AS 3.14, BUT THE FULL NUMBER IS STILL BEING CALCULATED AND NO ONE KNOWS ITS EXACT VALUE YET.
SNAP
IT'S NOT THAT I DON'T TRUST YOU, ARTHUR-KUN...
...BUT UNTIL I CAN GET THIS BACK TO TOKYO AND CHECK IT AGAINST THE REAL PI...
SNAP
SCOP SAYS THESE TABLETS ARE THE SWITCH TO TURN THE TABERNACLE INTO A WEAPON...
I HAVE A HARD TIME BELIEVING THAT PUTTING A BUNCH OF TABLETS ON DISPLAY WOULD ACTIVATE A MELTDOWN...
SNAP
SNAP
MAYBE THERE'S SOMETHING ELSE THAT WOULD BE THE KEY TO ITS ACTIVATION... LET'S KEEP LOOKING.

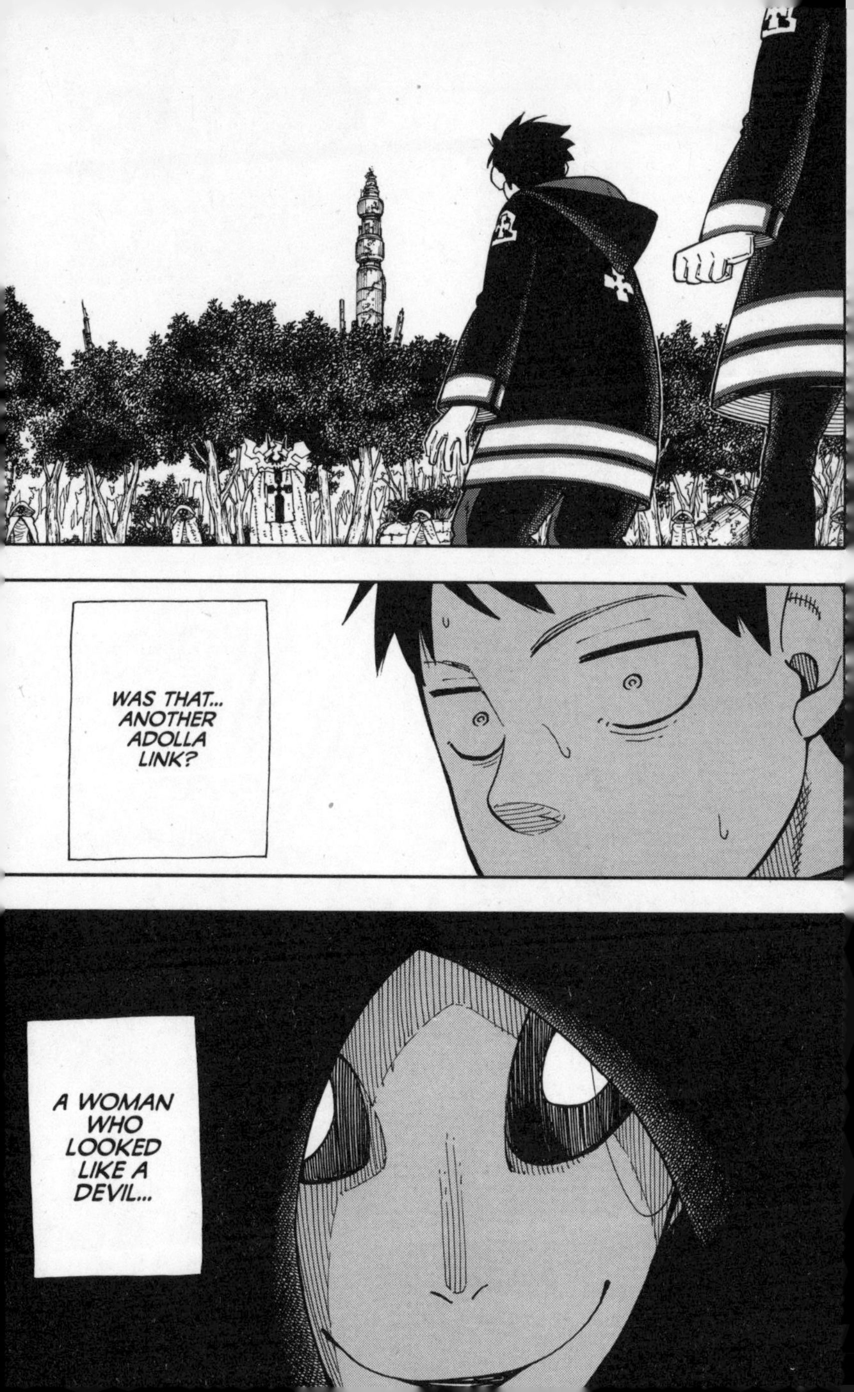
WAS THAT... ANOTHER ADOLLA LINK?
A WOMAN WHO LOOKED LIKE A DEVIL...

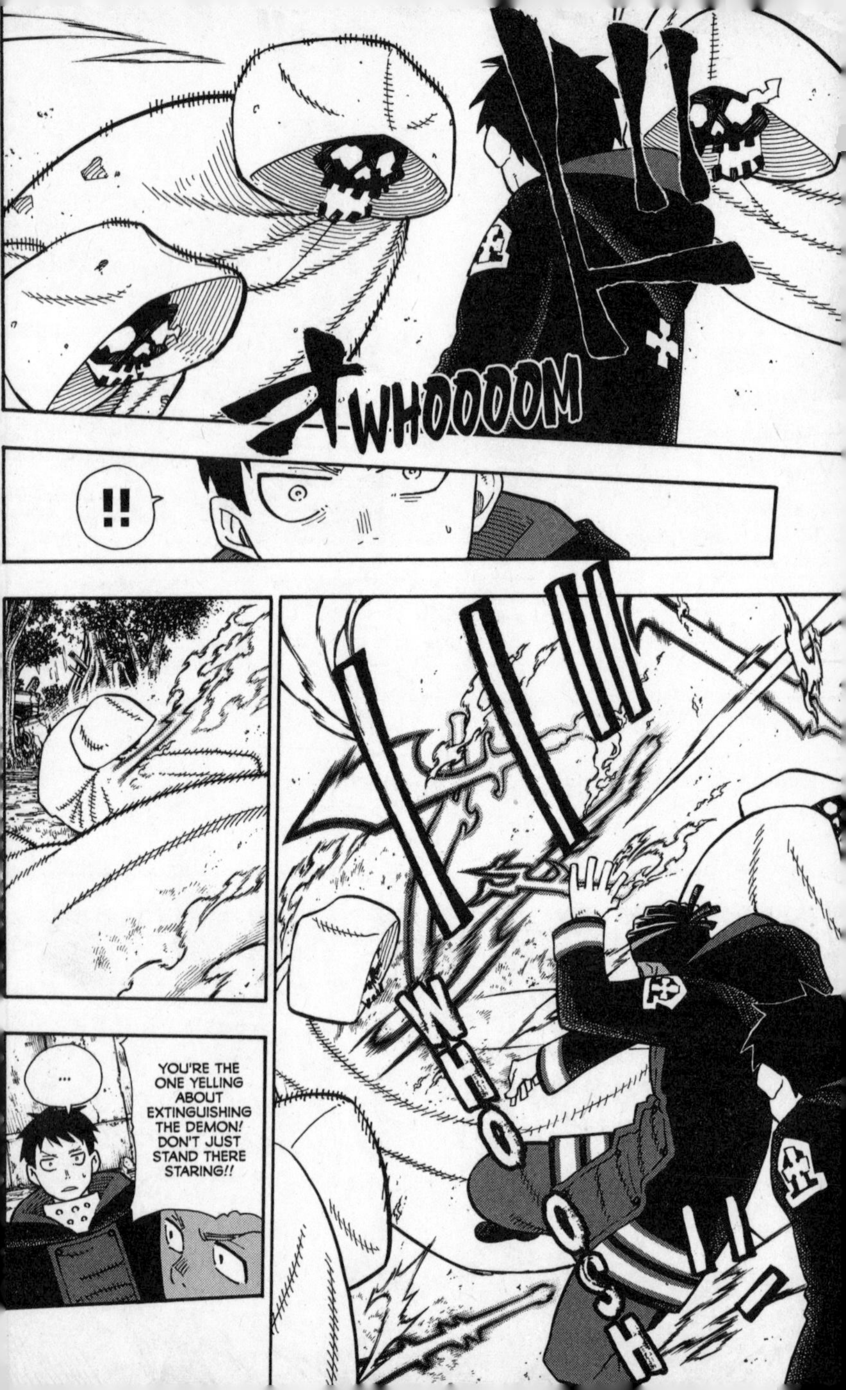
WHOOOOM
!!
WHOOOSH
...
YOU'RE THE ONE YELLING ABOUT EXTINGUISHING THE DEMON! DON'T JUST STAND THERE STARING!!

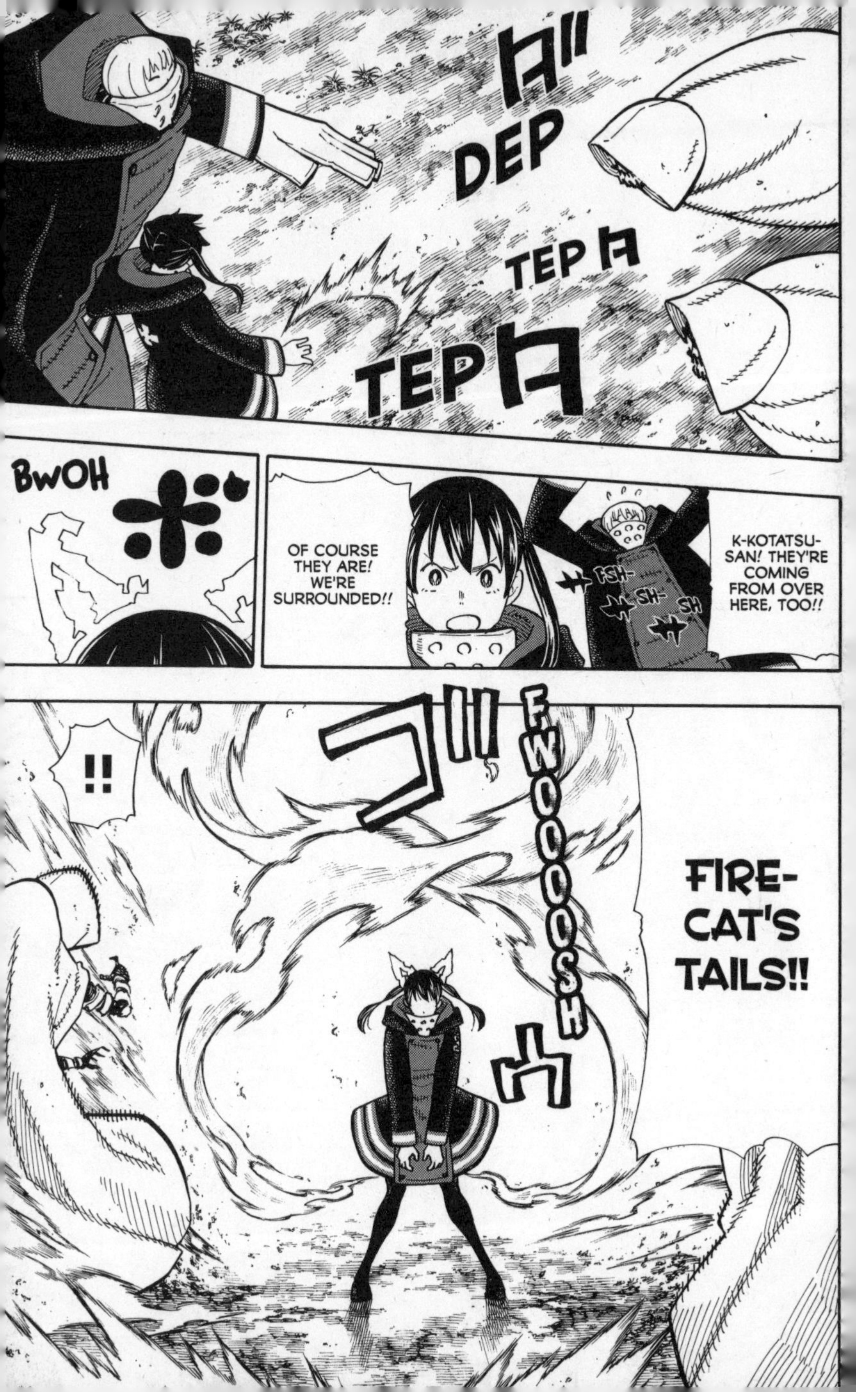
DEP
TEP
TEP
K-KOTATSU-SAN! THEY'RE COMING FROM OVER HERE, TOO!!
FSH-
SH-
SH
OF COURSE THEY ARE! WE'RE SURROUNDED!!
BWOH
FIRE-CAT'S TAILS!!
FWOOOOOSH
!!

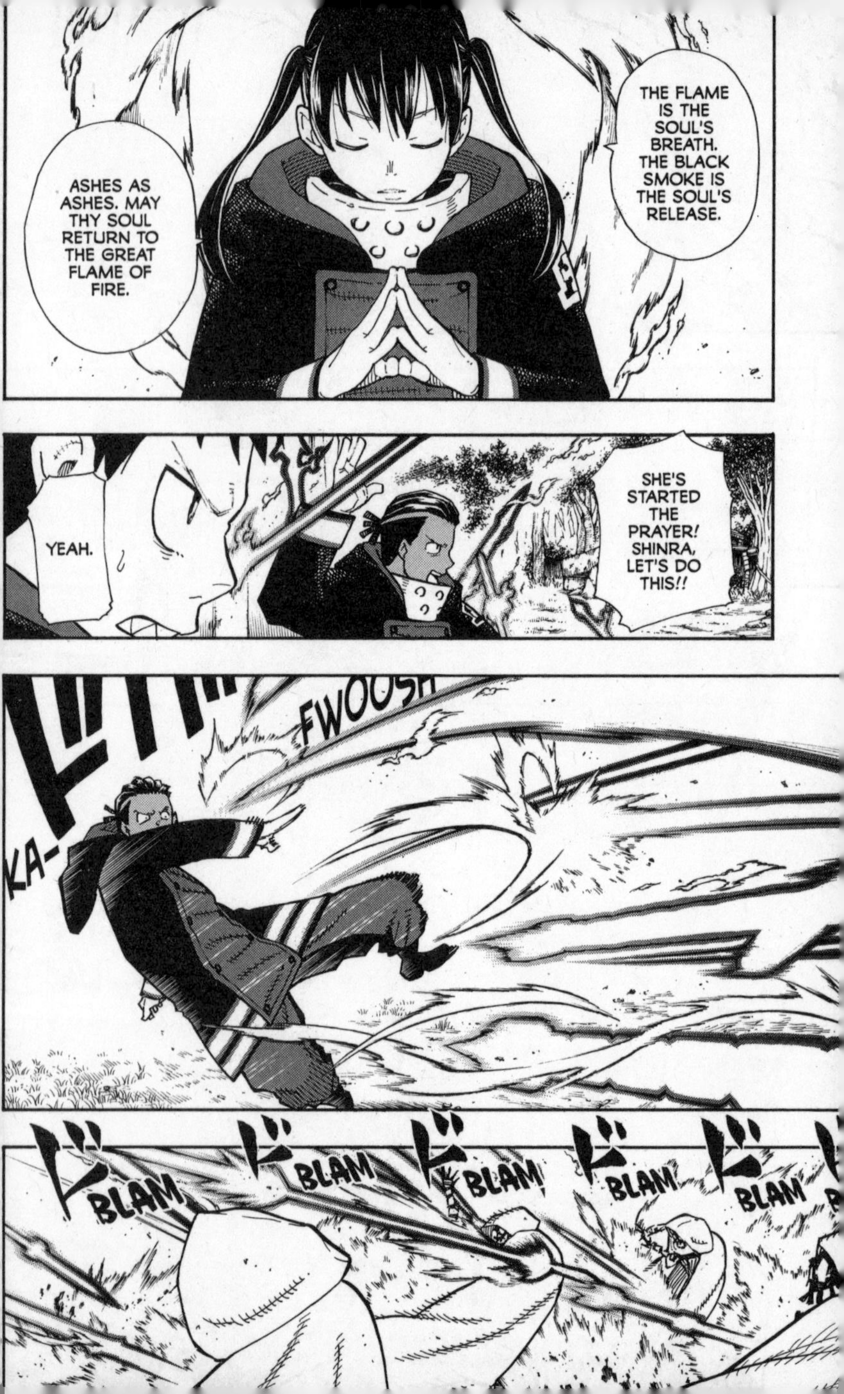

THE FLAME IS THE SOUL'S BREATH. THE BLACK SMOKE IS THE SOUL'S RELEASE.
ASHES AS ASHES. MAY THY SOUL RETURN TO THE GREAT FLAME OF FIRE.
SHE'S STARTED THE PRAYER! SHINRA, LET'S DO THIS!!
YEAH.
FWOOSH
KA-
ド
BLAM
ド
BLAM
ド
BLAM
ド
BLAM
ド
BLAM
ド
BLAM

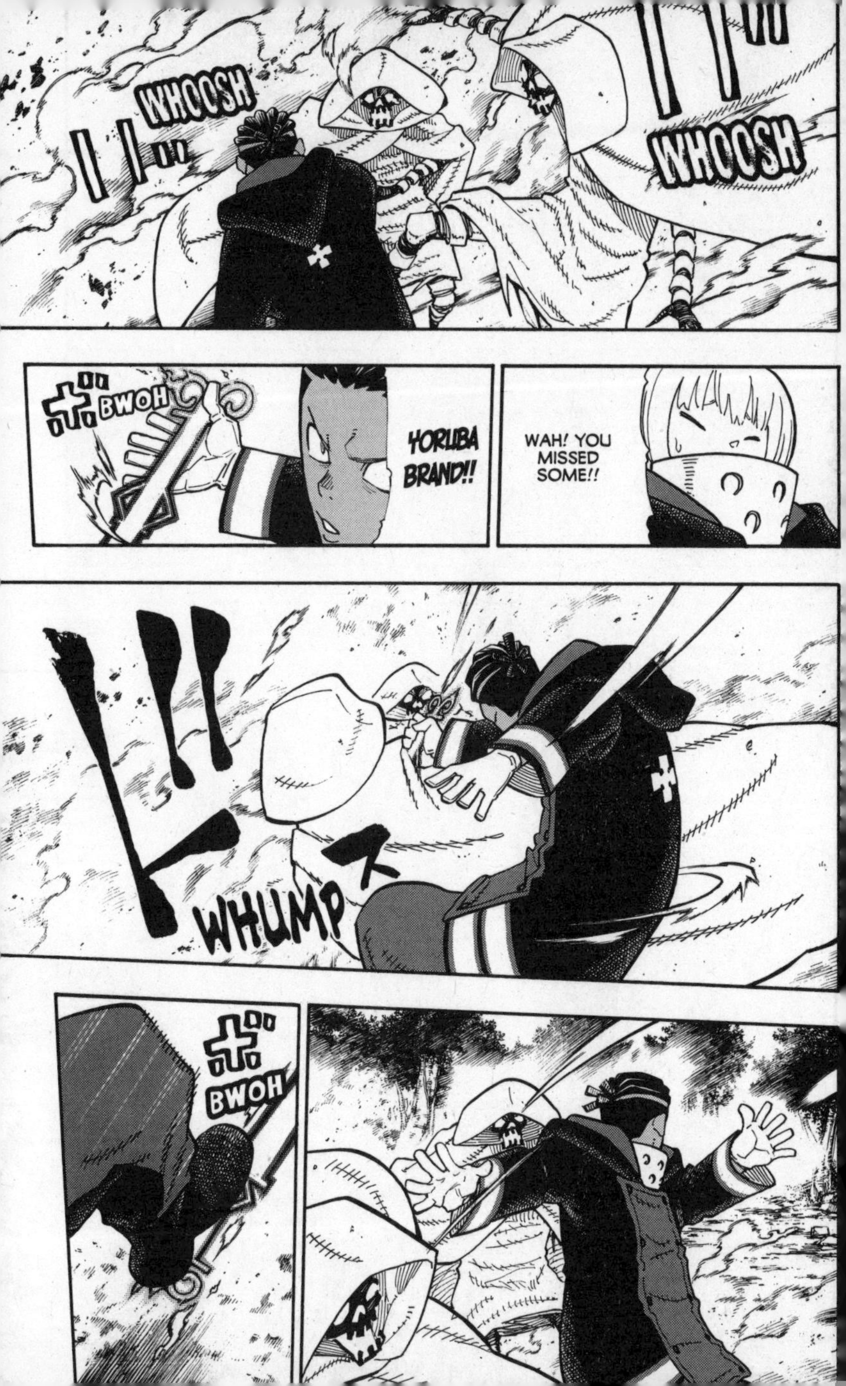
WHOOSH
WHOOSH
WAH! YOU MISSED SOME!!
YORUBA BRAND!!
BWOH
WHUMP
BWOH

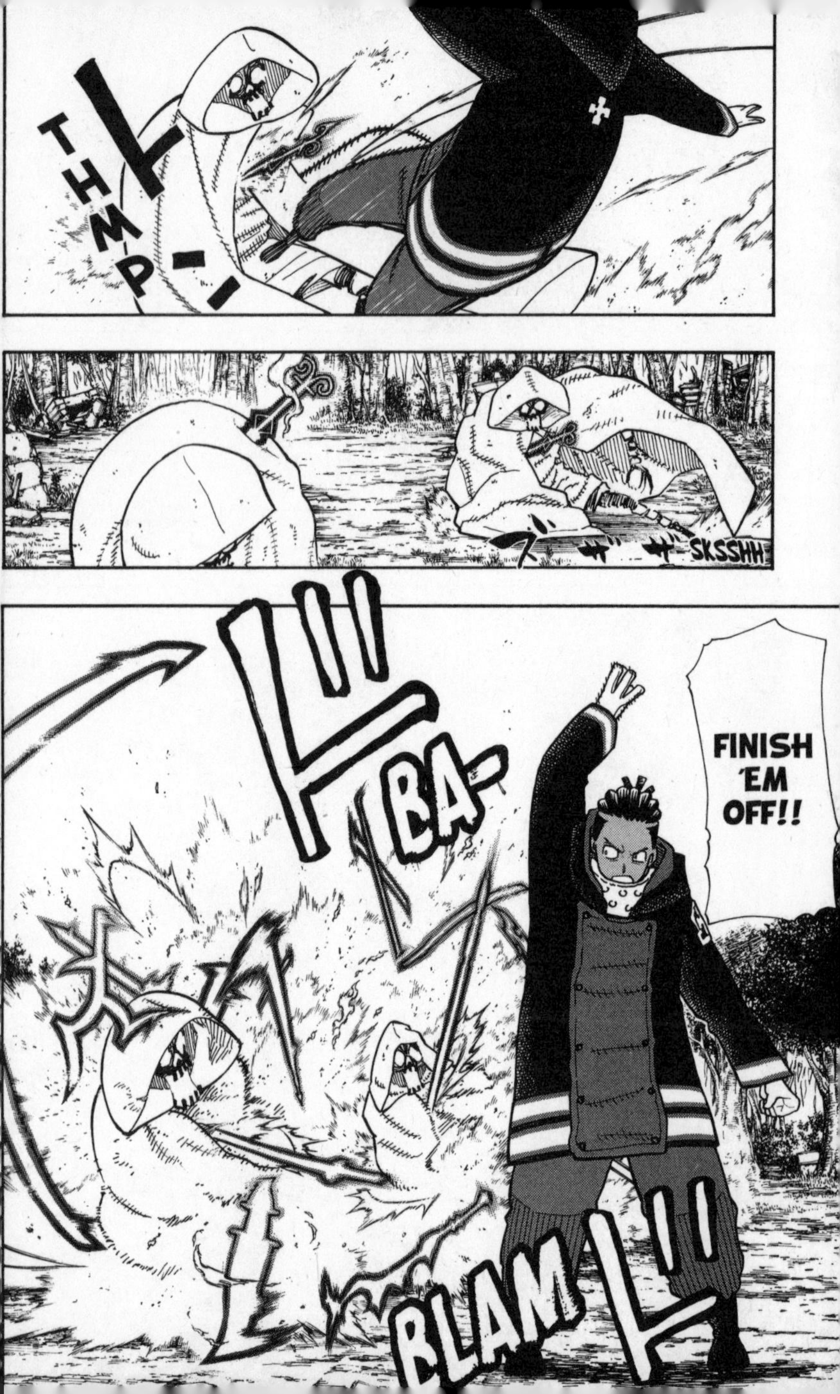
THMP--!
SKSSHH
FINISH 'EM OFF!!
BA-
BLAM!!

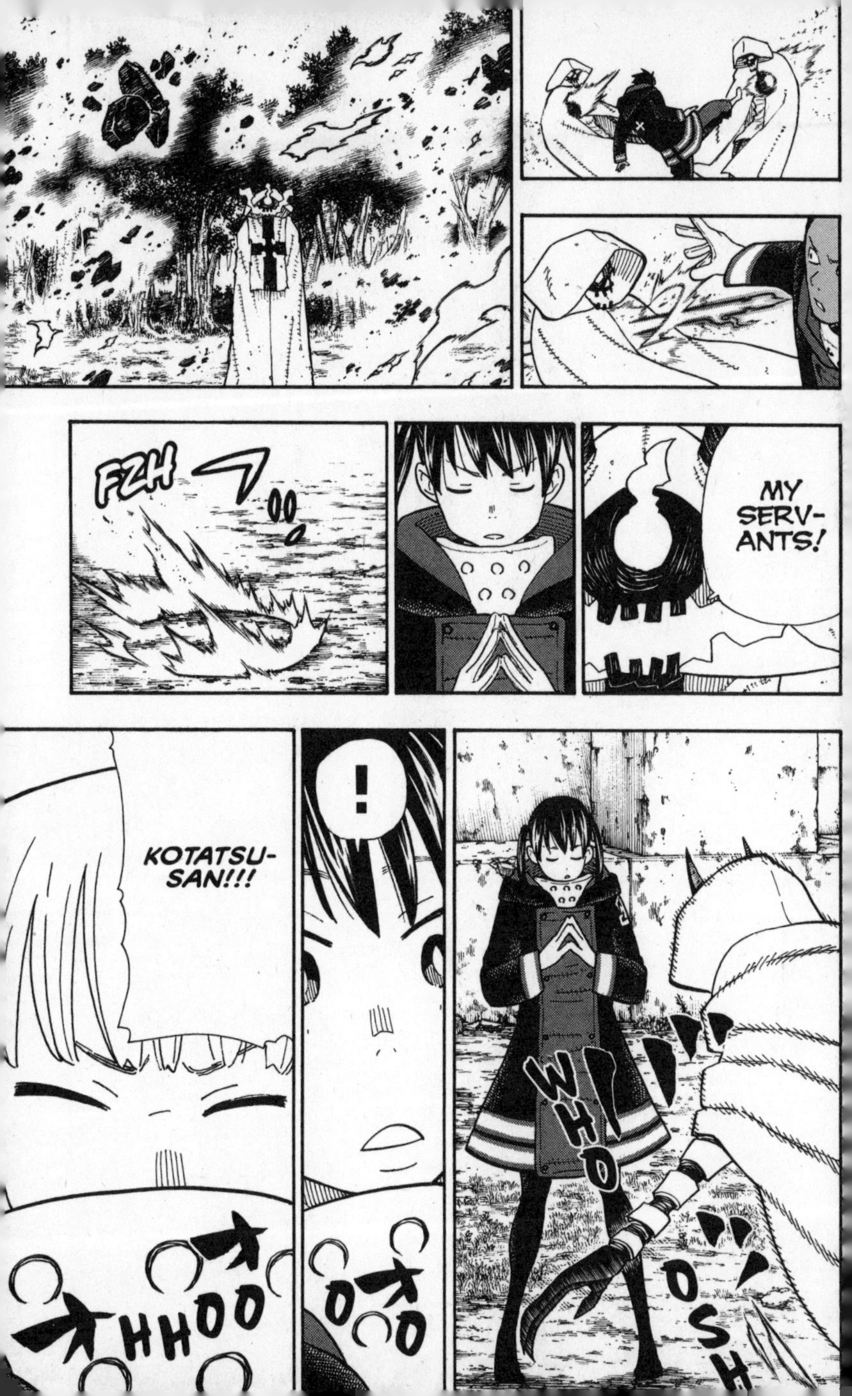
MY SERV-
ANTS!
FZH
WHOOSH
!
KOTATSU-
SAN!!!
HHOO

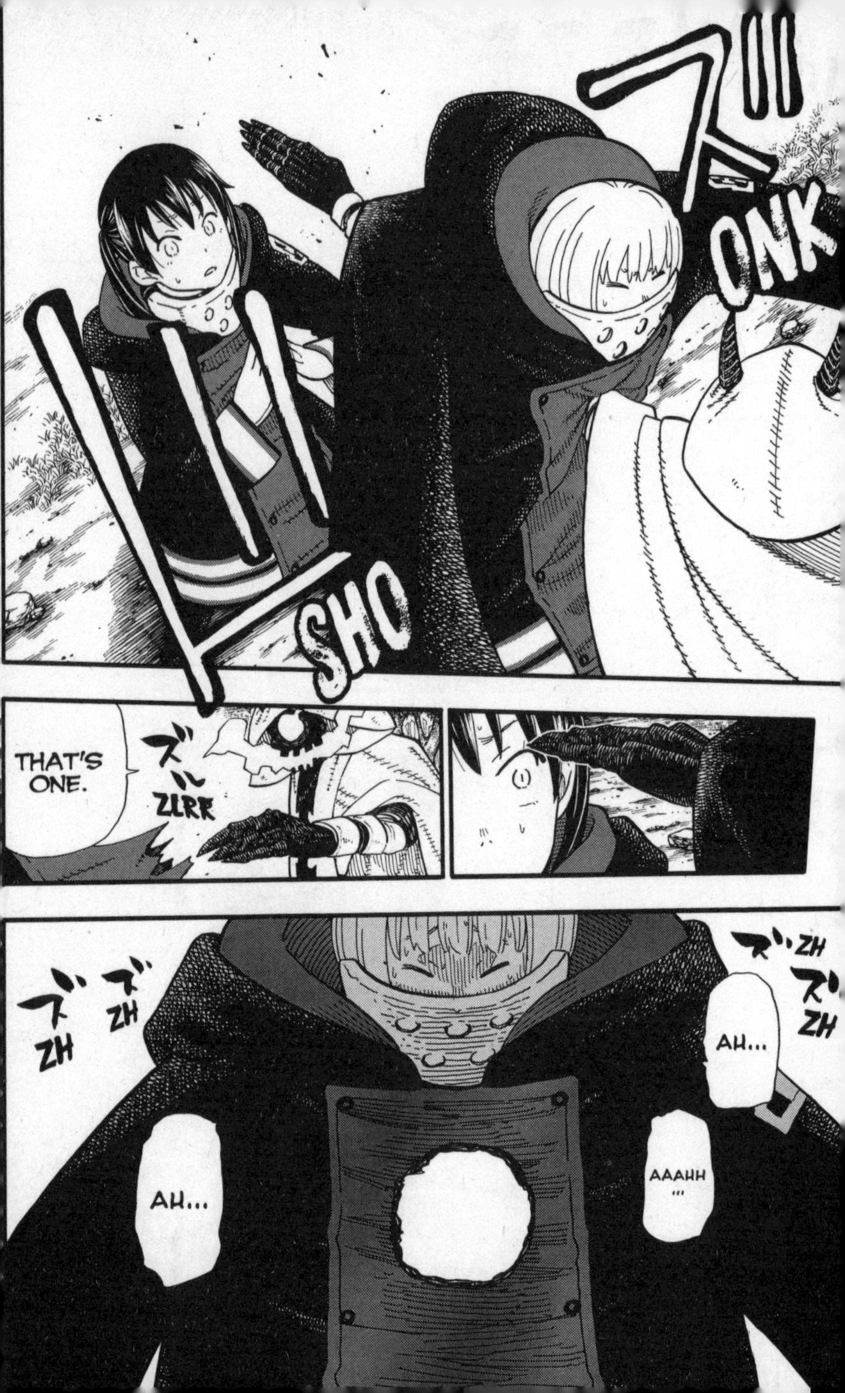

ONK
SHO
ZLRR
THAT'S ONE.
ZH
ZH
AH...
AAAHH...
AH...
ZH
ZH

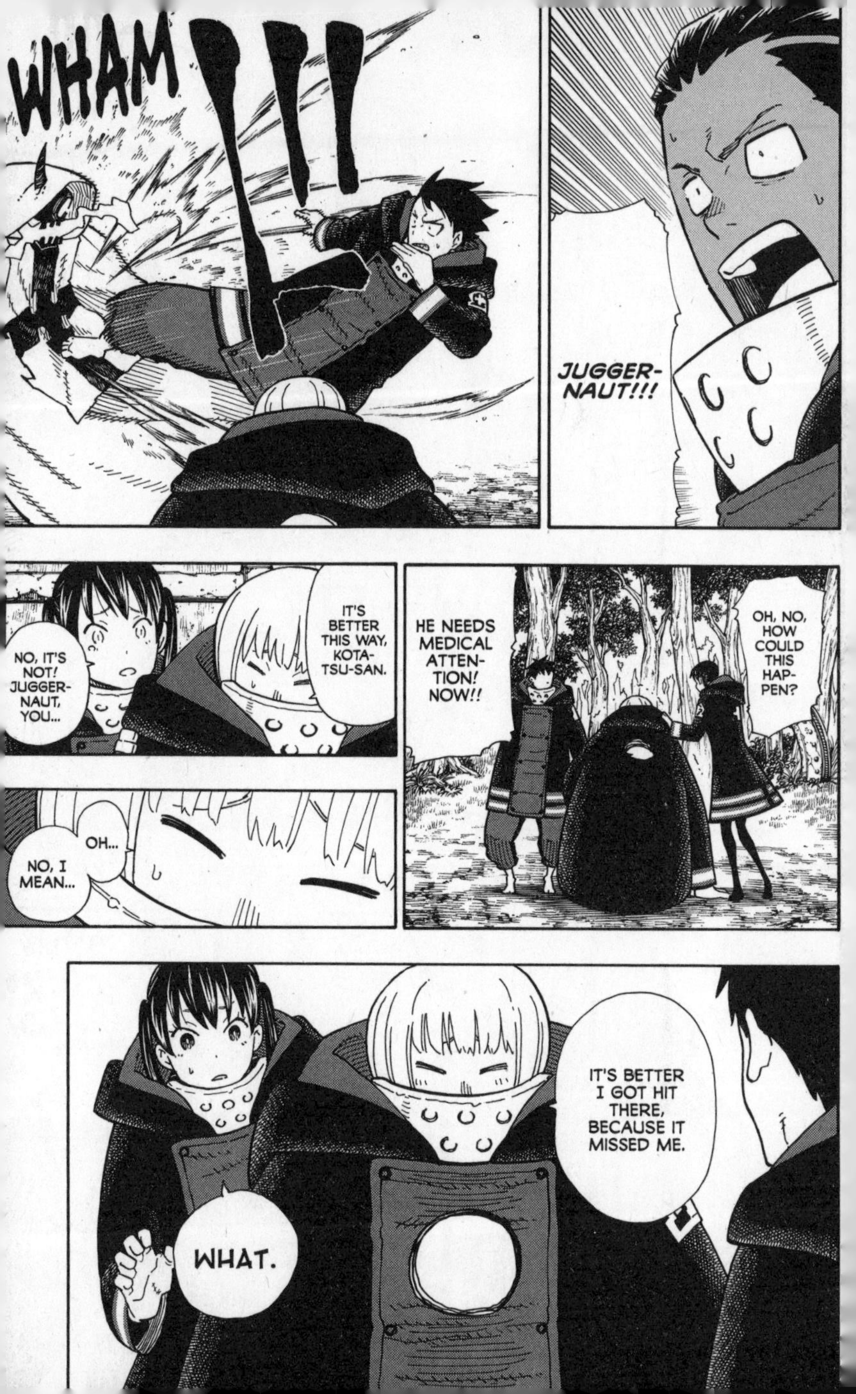

JUGGER-NAUT!!!
WHAM!!!
OH, NO, HOW COULD THIS HAP-PEN?
HE NEEDS MEDICAL ATTEN-TION! NOW!!
IT'S BETTER THIS WAY, KOTA-TSU-SAN.
NO, IT'S NOT! JUGGER-NAUT, YOU...
OH...
NO, I MEAN...
IT'S BETTER I GOT HIT THERE, BECAUSE IT MISSED ME.
WHAT.

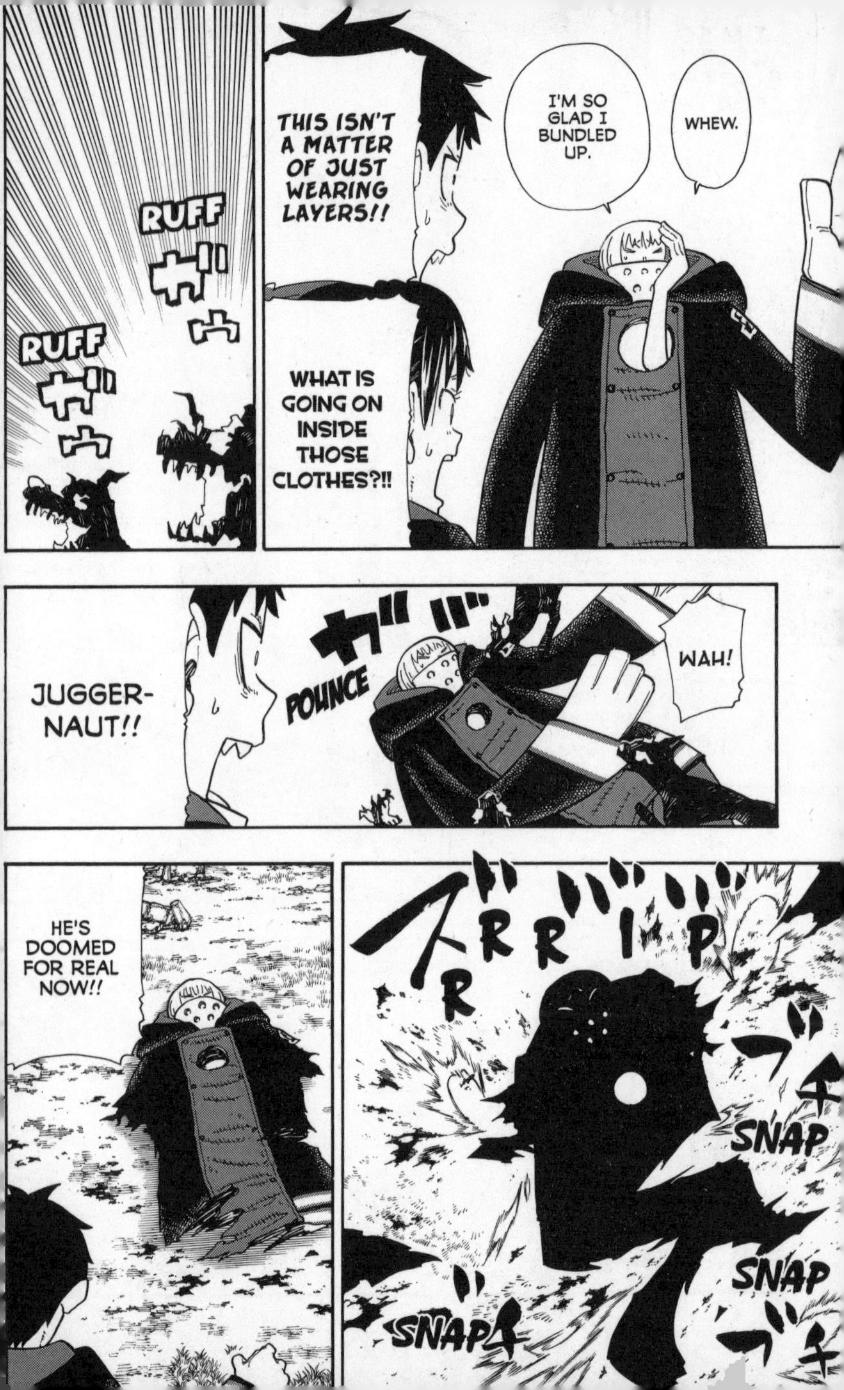
WHEW.
I'M SO GLAD I BUNDLED UP.
THIS ISN'T A MATTER OF JUST WEARING LAYERS!!
WHAT IS GOING ON INSIDE THOSE CLOTHES?!!
RUFF
RUFF
WAH!
POUNCE
JUGGER-NAUT!!
RRRRIP
SNAP
SNAP
SNAP
HE'S DOOMED FOR REAL NOW!!

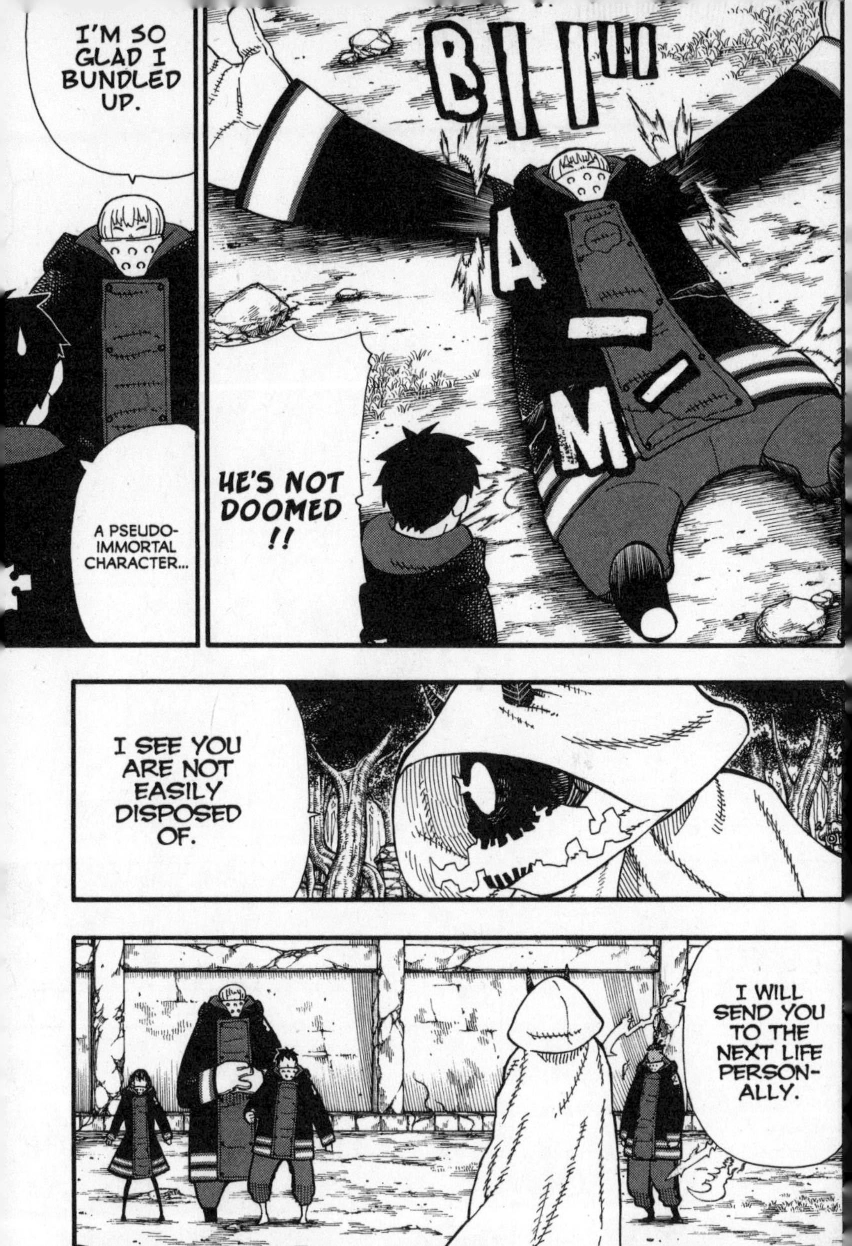
HE'S NOT DOOMED !!
I'M SO GLAD I BUNDLED UP.
A PSEUDO-IMMORTAL CHARACTER...
I SEE YOU ARE NOT EASILY DISPOSED OF.
I WILL SEND YOU TO THE NEXT LIFE PERSON-ALLY.

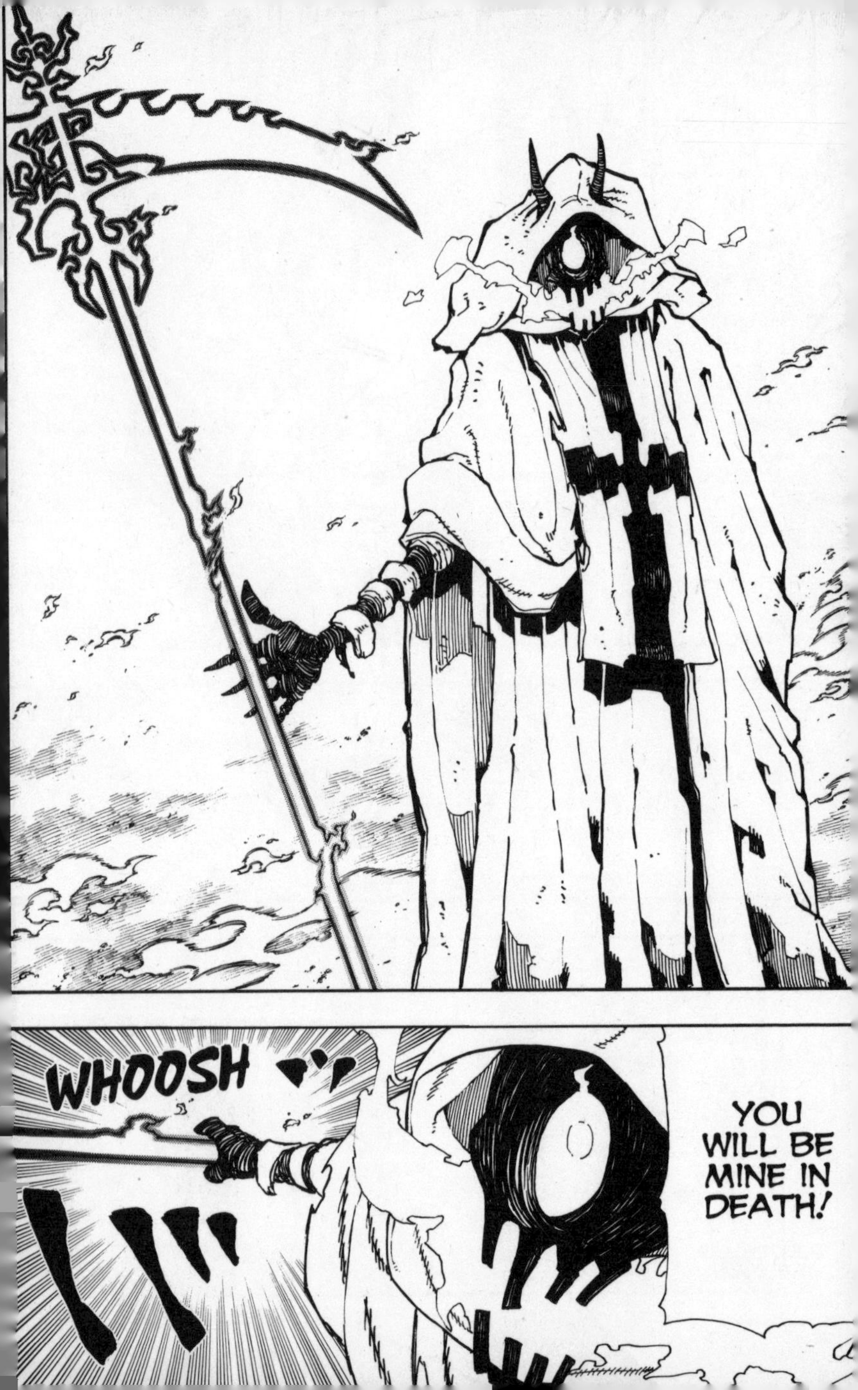
YOU WILL BE MINE IN DEATH!
WHOOSH

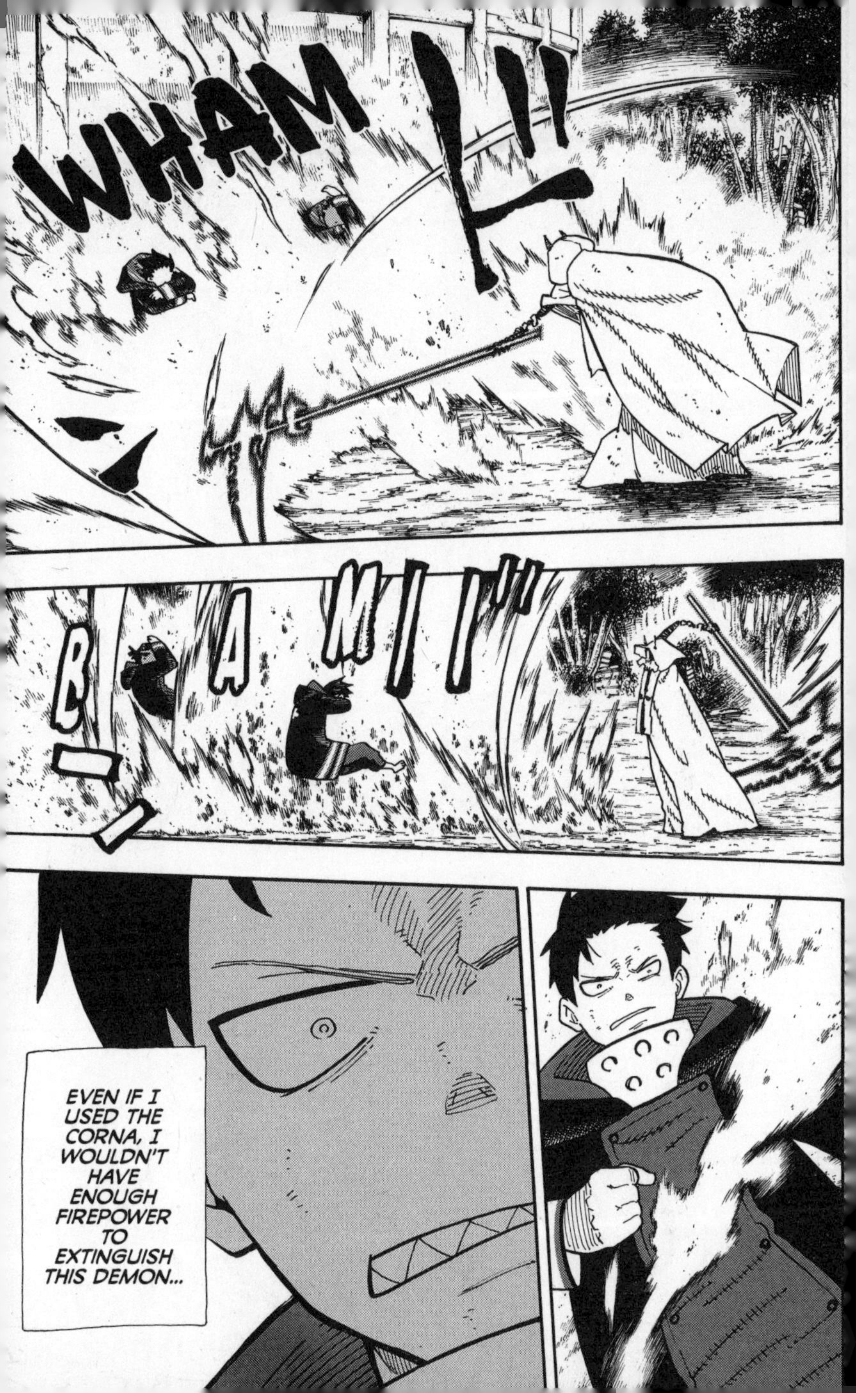
WHAM !!
BAM !!
EVEN IF I USED THE CORNA, I WOULDN'T HAVE ENOUGH FIREPOWER TO EXTINGUISH THIS DEMON...

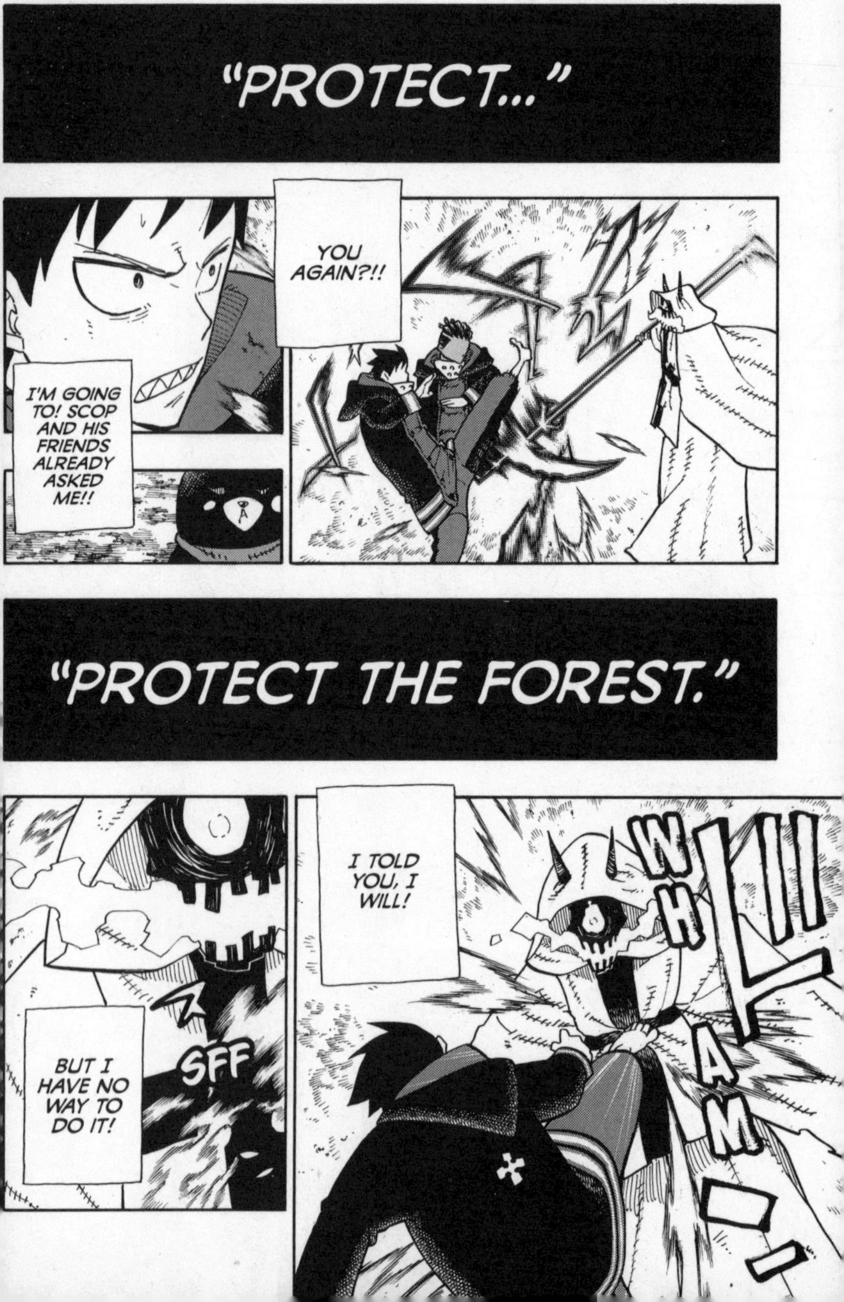
"PROTECT..."
YOU AGAIN?!!
I'M GOING TO! SCOP AND HIS FRIENDS ALREADY ASKED ME!!
"PROTECT THE FOREST."
I TOLD YOU, I WILL!
WHAM!
BUT I HAVE NO WAY TO DO IT!
SFF

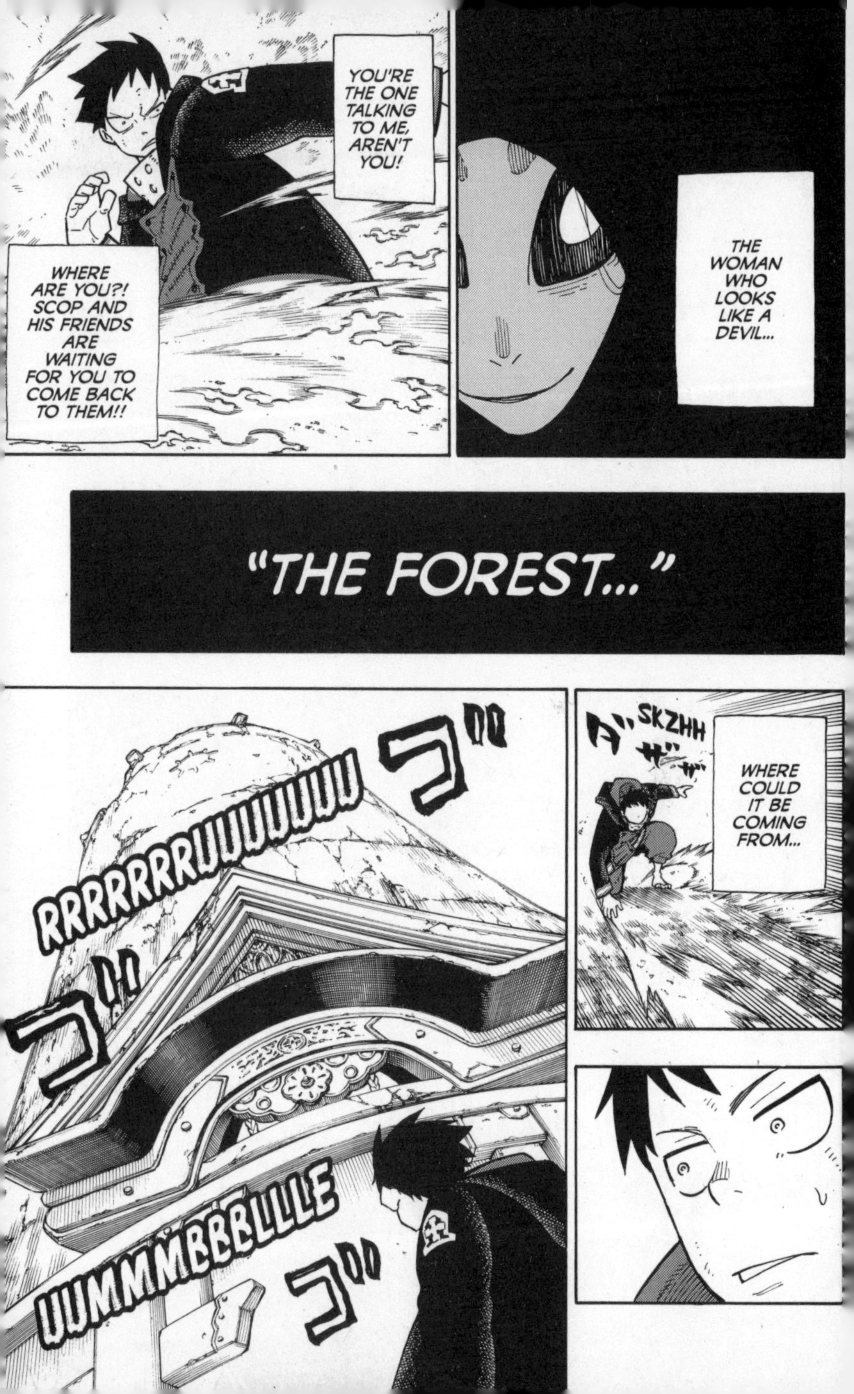
THE WOMAN WHO LOOKS LIKE A DEVIL...
YOU'RE THE ONE TALKING TO ME, AREN'T YOU!
WHERE ARE YOU?! SCOP AND HIS FRIENDS ARE WAITING FOR YOU TO COME BACK TO THEM!!
"THE FOREST..."
SKZHH
WHERE COULD IT BE COMING FROM...
RRRRRRRUUUUUUUU
UUMMMBBBLLLE

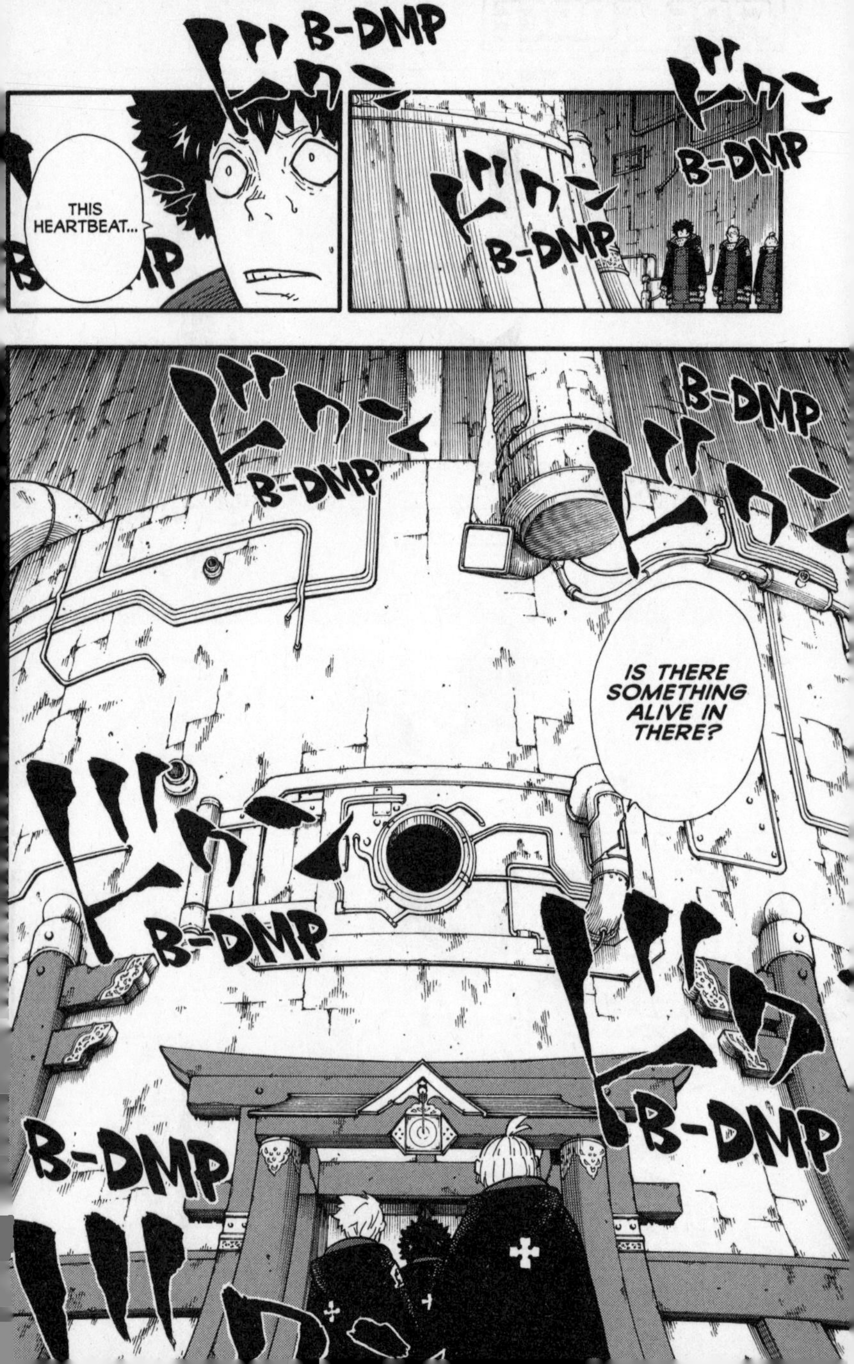
B-DMP
B-DMP
B-DMP
THIS HEARTBEAT...
B-DMP
B-DMP
IS THERE SOMETHING ALIVE IN THERE?
B-DMP
B-DMP
B-DMP

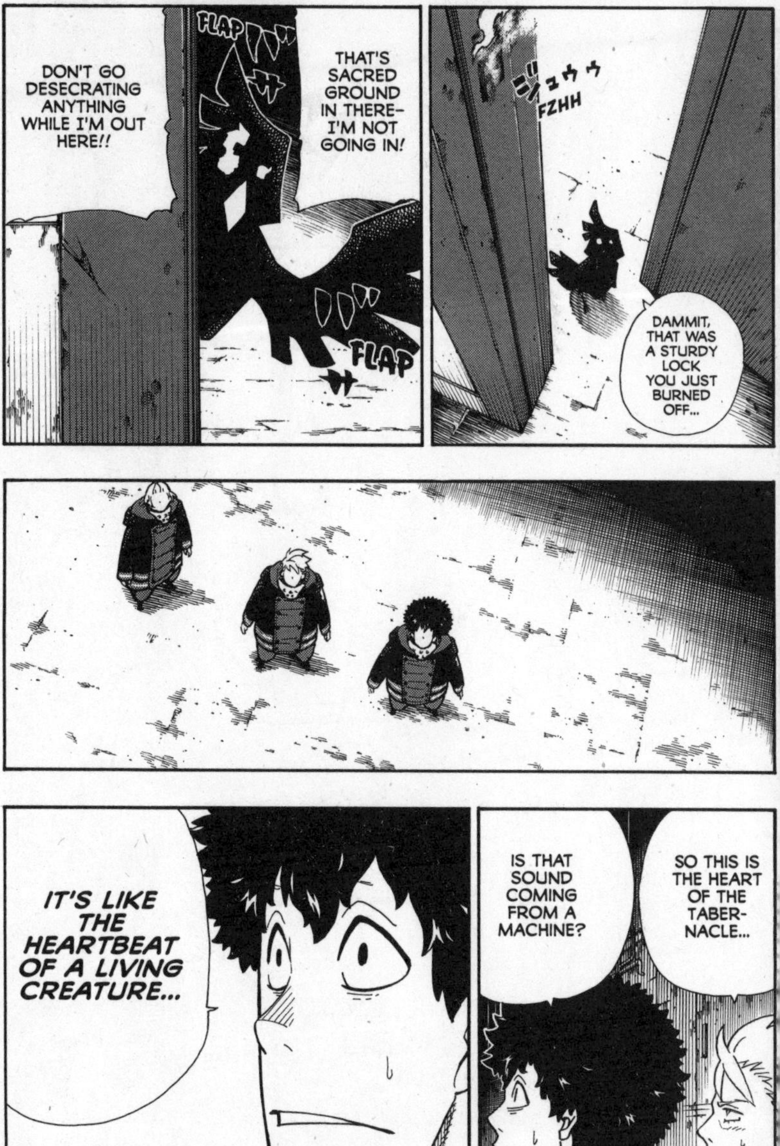
ジュウウ
FZHH
DAMMIT, THAT WAS A STURDY LOCK YOU JUST BURNED OFF...
THAT'S SACRED GROUND IN THERE–I'M NOT GOING IN!
FLAP
DON'T GO DESECRATING ANYTHING WHILE I'M OUT HERE!!
FLAP
SO THIS IS THE HEART OF THE TABERNACLE...
IS THAT SOUND COMING FROM A MACHINE?
IT'S LIKE THE HEARTBEAT OF A LIVING CREATURE...

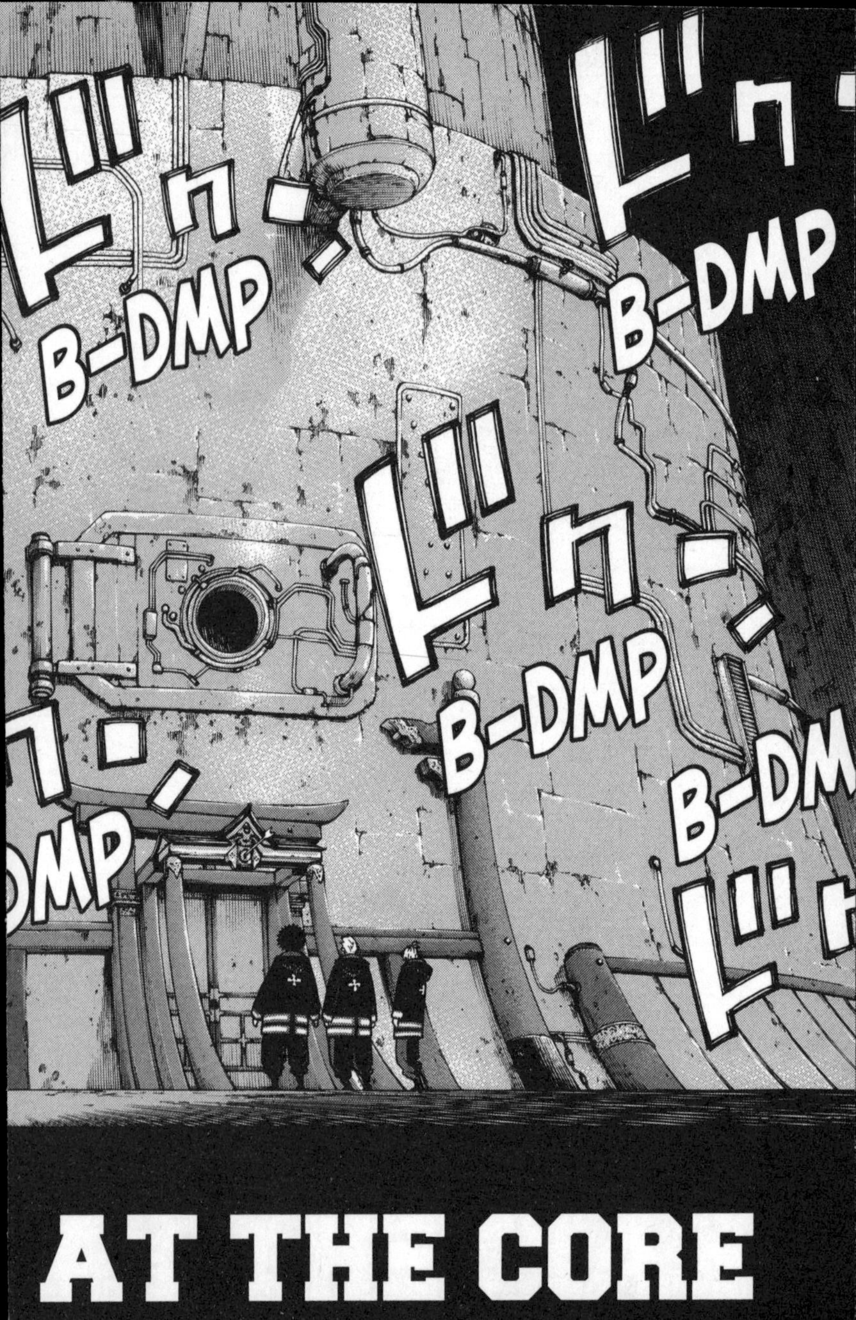
B-DMP
B-DMP
B-DMP
B-DM
DMP

AT THE CORE

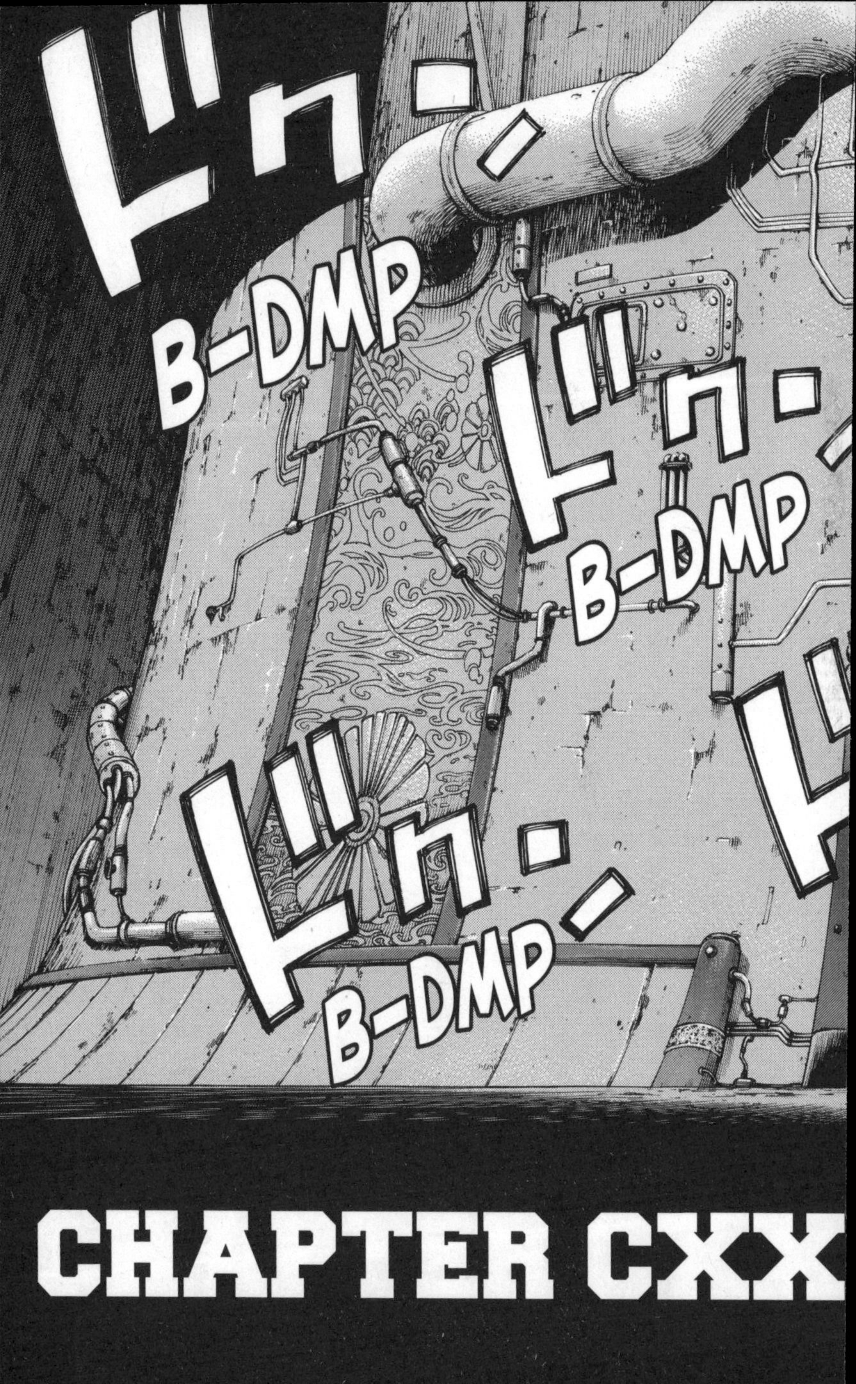
B-DMP
B-DMP
B-DMP

CHAPTER CXX

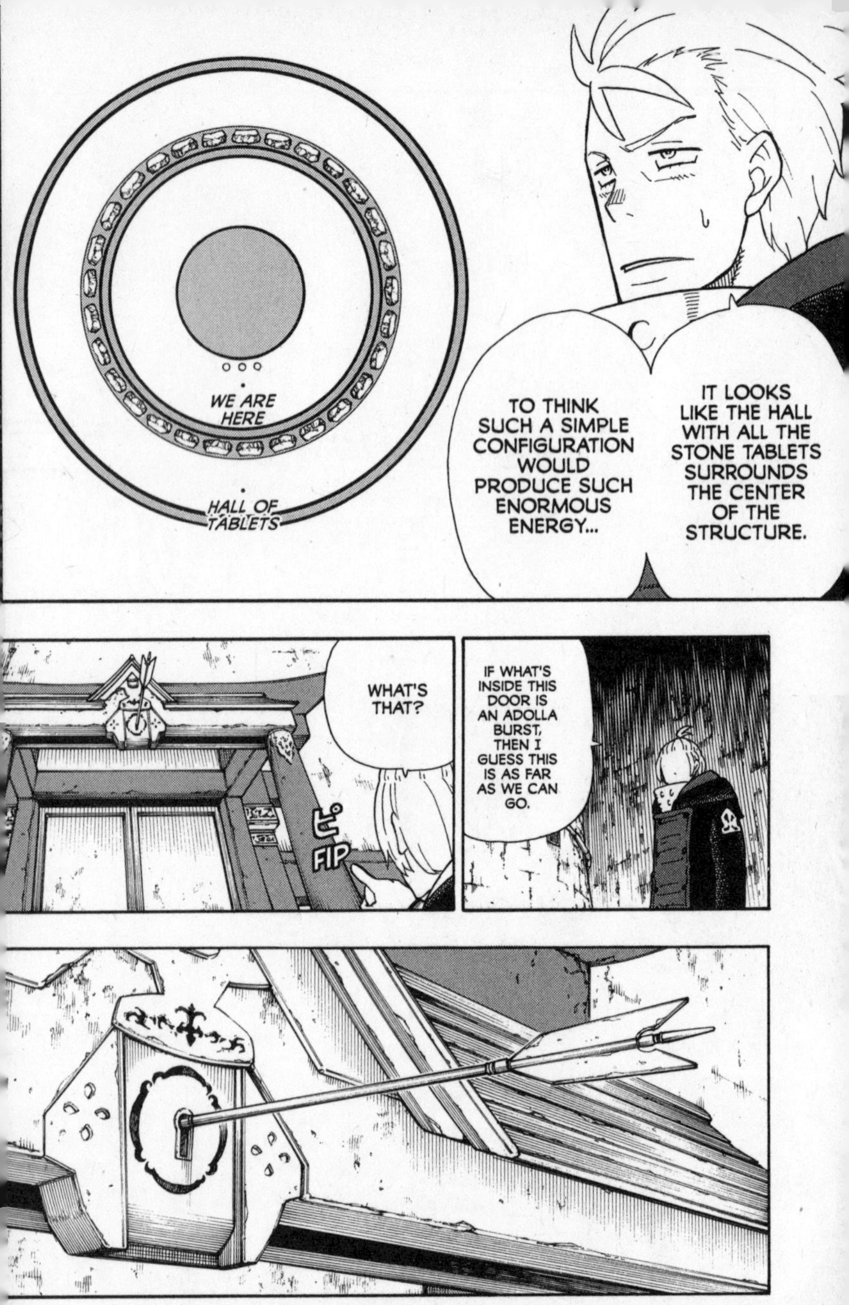
IT LOOKS LIKE THE HALL WITH ALL THE STONE TABLETS SURROUNDS THE CENTER OF THE STRUCTURE.
TO THINK SUCH A SIMPLE CONFIGURATION WOULD PRODUCE SUCH ENORMOUS ENERGY...
WE ARE HERE
HALL OF TABLETS
IF WHAT'S INSIDE THIS DOOR IS AN ADOLLA BURST, THEN I GUESS THIS IS AS FAR AS WE CAN GO.
WHAT'S THAT?
ピ
FIP

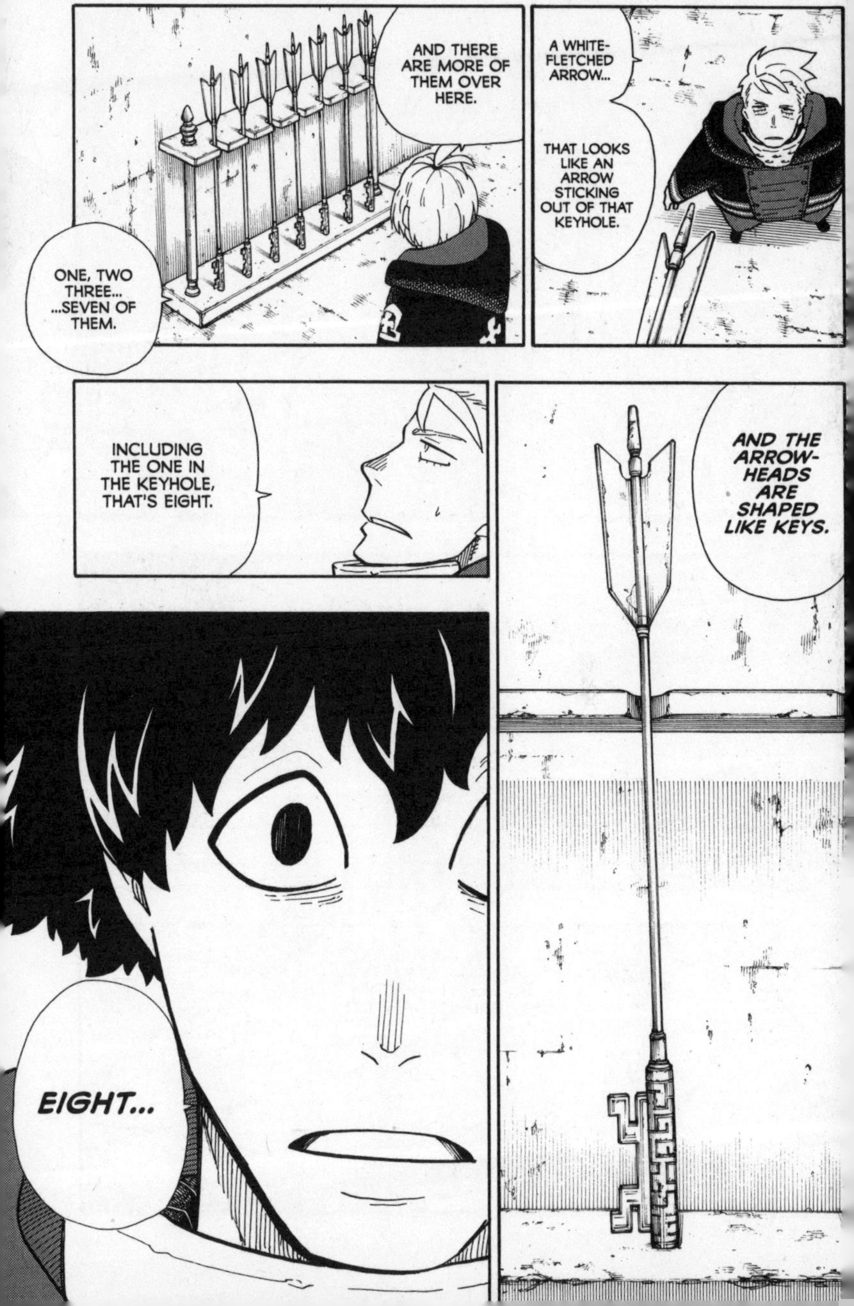
A WHITE-FLETCHED ARROW...
THAT LOOKS LIKE AN ARROW STICKING OUT OF THAT KEYHOLE.
AND THERE ARE MORE OF THEM OVER HERE.
ONE, TWO THREE... ...SEVEN OF THEM.
AND THE ARROW-HEADS ARE SHAPED LIKE KEYS.
INCLUDING THE ONE IN THE KEYHOLE, THAT'S EIGHT.
EIGHT...

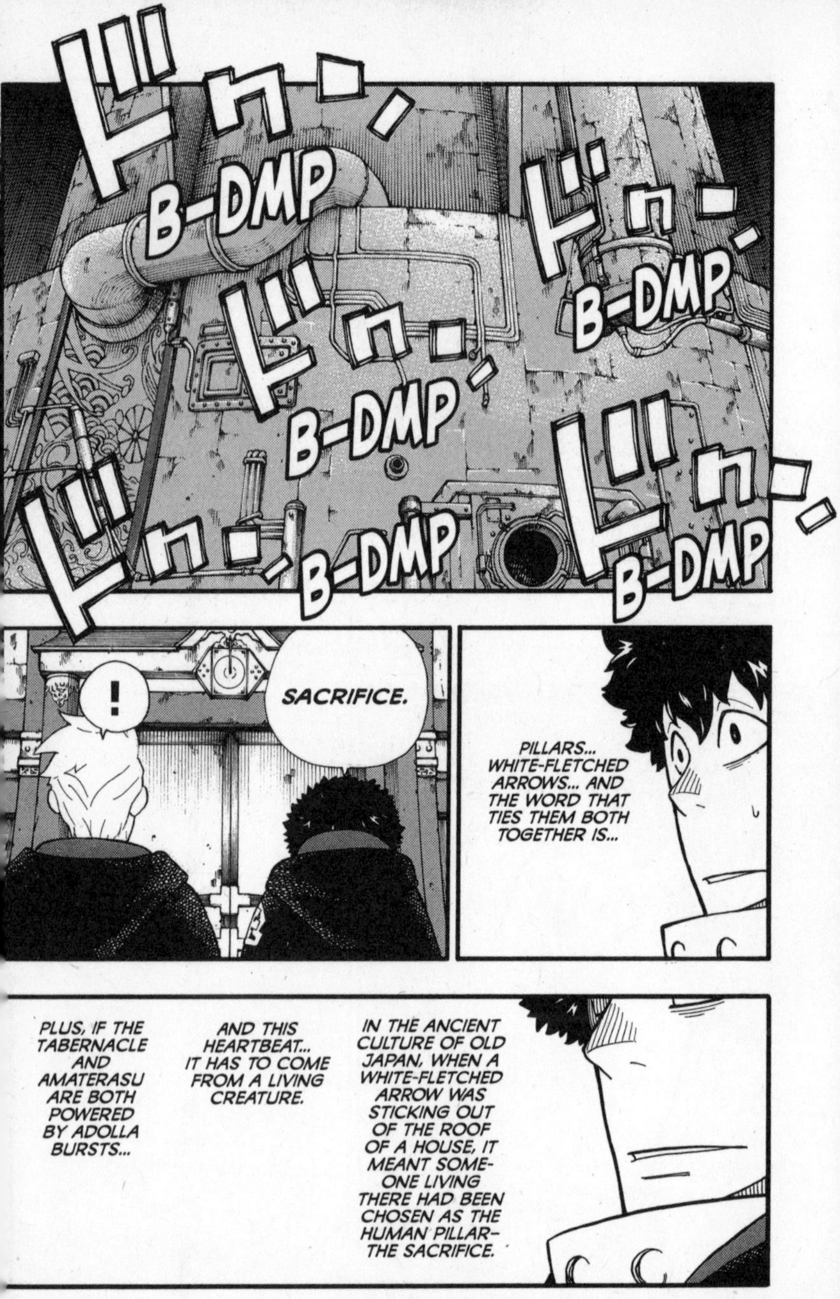
B-DMP
B-DMP
B-DMP
B-DMP
B-DMP
B-DMP
PILLARS... WHITE-FLETCHED ARROWS... AND THE WORD THAT TIES THEM BOTH TOGETHER IS...
!
SACRIFICE.
IN THE ANCIENT CULTURE OF OLD JAPAN, WHEN A WHITE-FLETCHED ARROW WAS STICKING OUT OF THE ROOF OF A HOUSE, IT MEANT SOME-ONE LIVING THERE HAD BEEN CHOSEN AS THE HUMAN PILLAR– THE SACRIFICE.
AND THIS HEARTBEAT... IT HAS TO COME FROM A LIVING CREATURE.
PLUS, IF THE TABERNACLE AND AMATERASU ARE BOTH POWERED BY ADOLLA BURSTS...

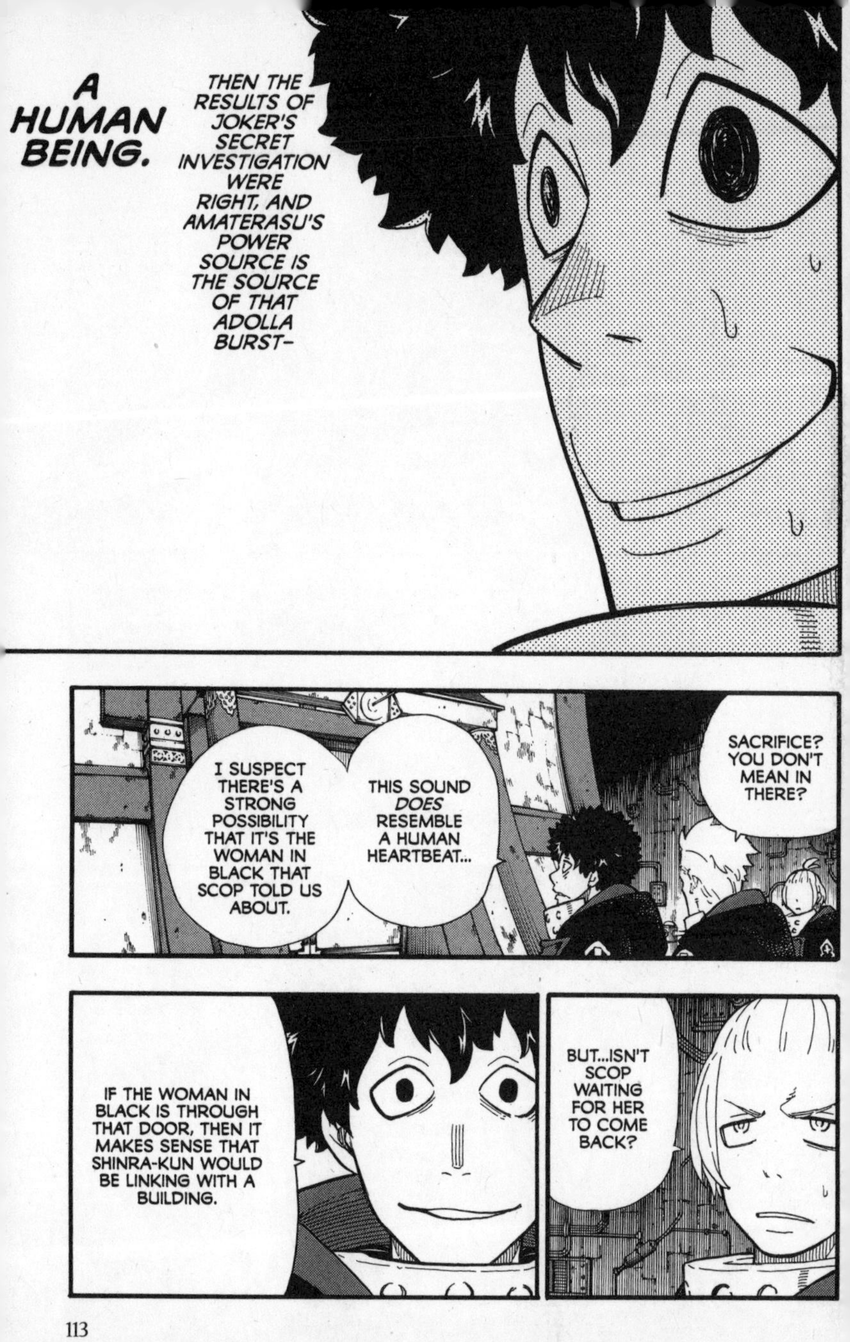
THEN THE RESULTS OF JOKER'S SECRET INVESTIGATION WERE RIGHT, AND AMATERASU'S POWER SOURCE IS THE SOURCE OF THAT ADOLLA BURST-
A HUMAN BEING.
SACRIFICE? YOU DON'T MEAN IN THERE?
THIS SOUND *DOES* RESEMBLE A HUMAN HEARTBEAT...
I SUSPECT THERE'S A STRONG POSSIBILITY THAT IT'S THE WOMAN IN BLACK THAT SCOP TOLD US ABOUT.
BUT...ISN'T SCOP WAITING FOR HER TO COME BACK?
IF THE WOMAN IN BLACK IS THROUGH THAT DOOR, THEN IT MAKES SENSE THAT SHINRA-KUN WOULD BE LINKING WITH A BUILDING.

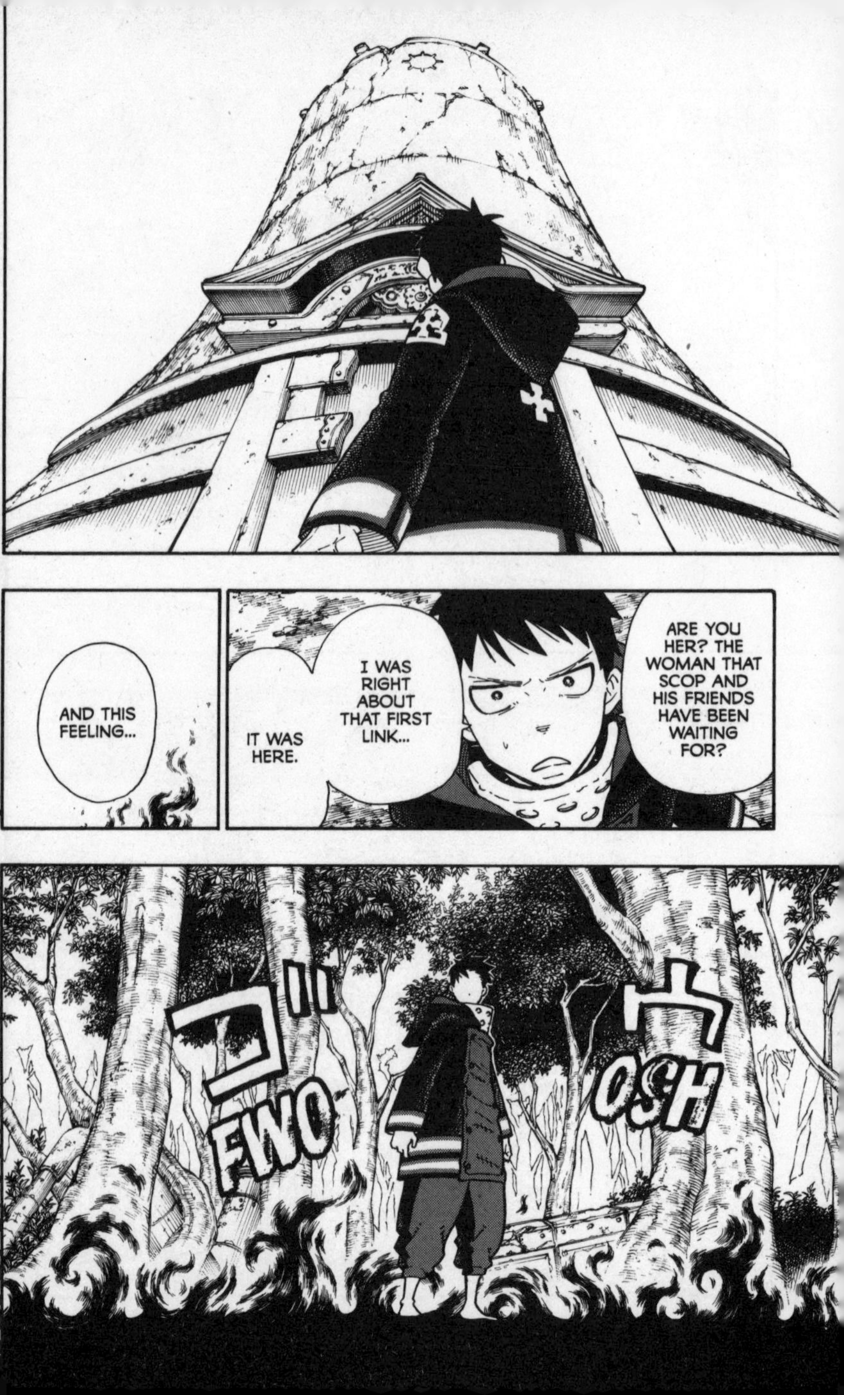
ARE YOU HER? THE WOMAN THAT SCOP AND HIS FRIENDS HAVE BEEN WAITING FOR?
I WAS RIGHT ABOUT THAT FIRST LINK...
IT WAS HERE.
AND THIS FEELING...
ゴ FWO
ウ OSH

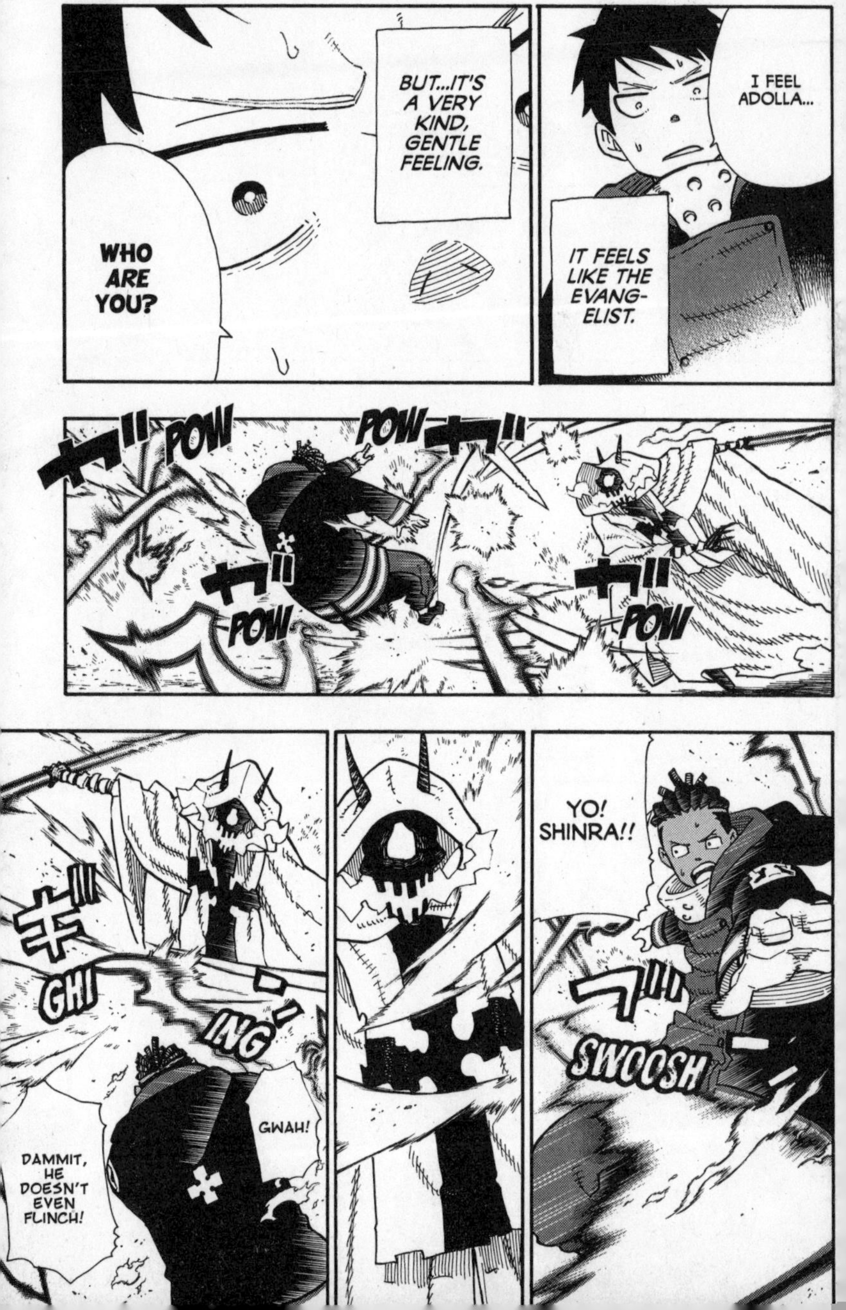
I FEEL ADOLLA...
IT FEELS LIKE THE EVANG-ELIST.
BUT...IT'S A VERY KIND, GENTLE FEELING.
WHO ARE YOU?
POW
POW
POW
POW
YO! SHINRA!!
SWOOSH
GHI
ING
GWAH!
DAMMIT, HE DOESN'T EVEN FLINCH!

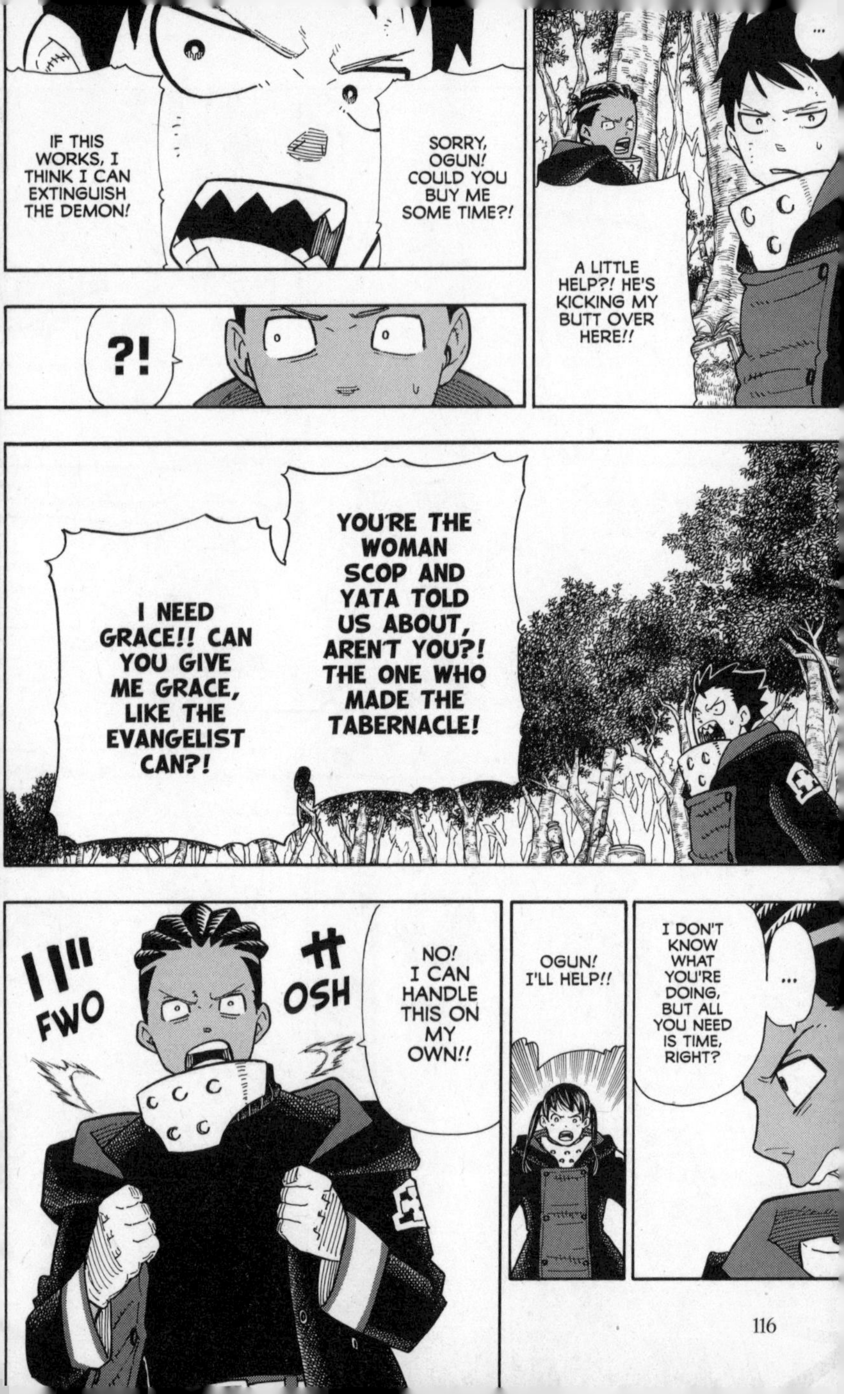
...
A LITTLE HELP?! HE'S KICKING MY BUTT OVER HERE!!
SORRY, OGUN! COULD YOU BUY ME SOME TIME?!
IF THIS WORKS, I THINK I CAN EXTINGUISH THE DEMON!
?!
YOU'RE THE WOMAN SCOP AND YATA TOLD US ABOUT, AREN'T YOU?! THE ONE WHO MADE THE TABERNACLE!
I NEED GRACE!! CAN YOU GIVE ME GRACE, LIKE THE EVANGELIST CAN?!
...
I DON'T KNOW WHAT YOU'RE DOING, BUT ALL YOU NEED IS TIME, RIGHT?
OGUN! I'LL HELP!!
NO! I CAN HANDLE THIS ON MY OWN!!
FWOOSH

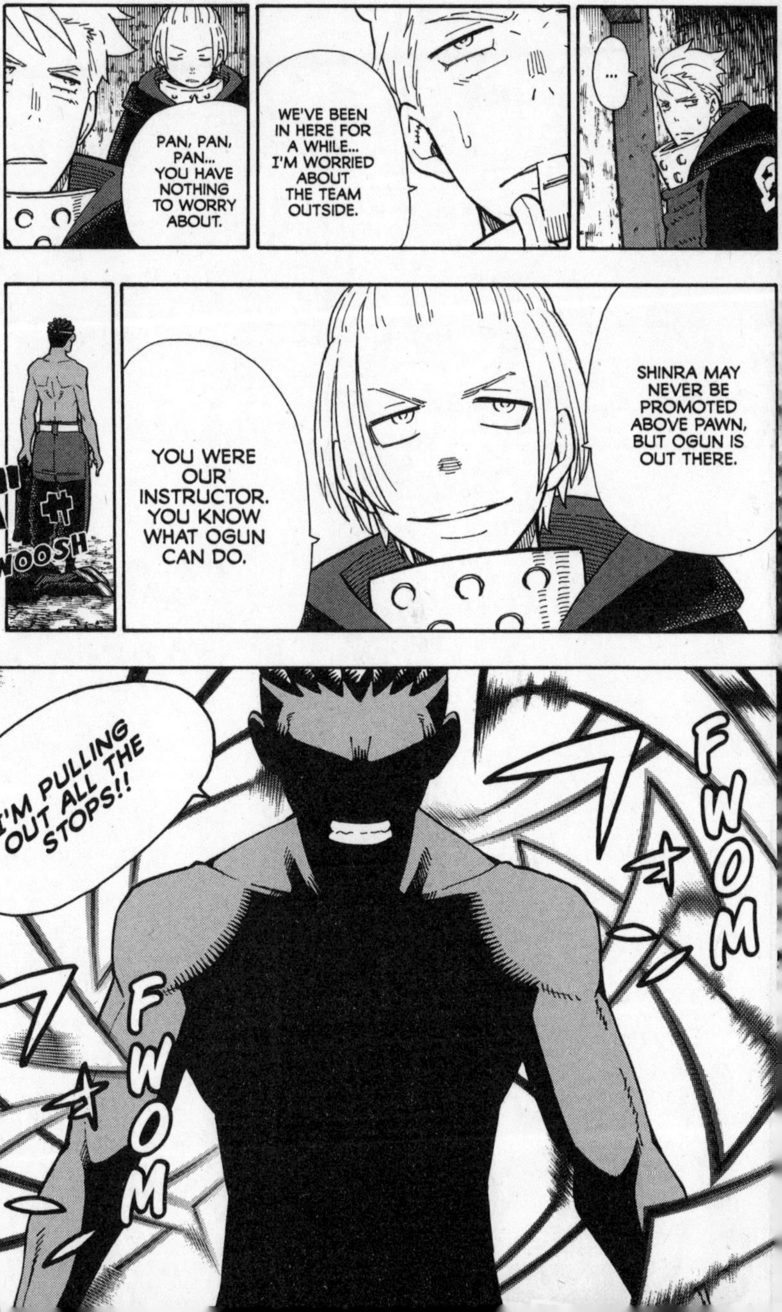
...
WE'VE BEEN IN HERE FOR A WHILE... I'M WORRIED ABOUT THE TEAM OUTSIDE.
PAN, PAN, PAN... YOU HAVE NOTHING TO WORRY ABOUT.
SHINRA MAY NEVER BE PROMOTED ABOVE PAWN, BUT OGUN IS OUT THERE.
YOU WERE OUR INSTRUCTOR. YOU KNOW WHAT OGUN CAN DO.
FWOOSH
FWOM
I'M PULLING OUT ALL THE STOPS!!
FWOM

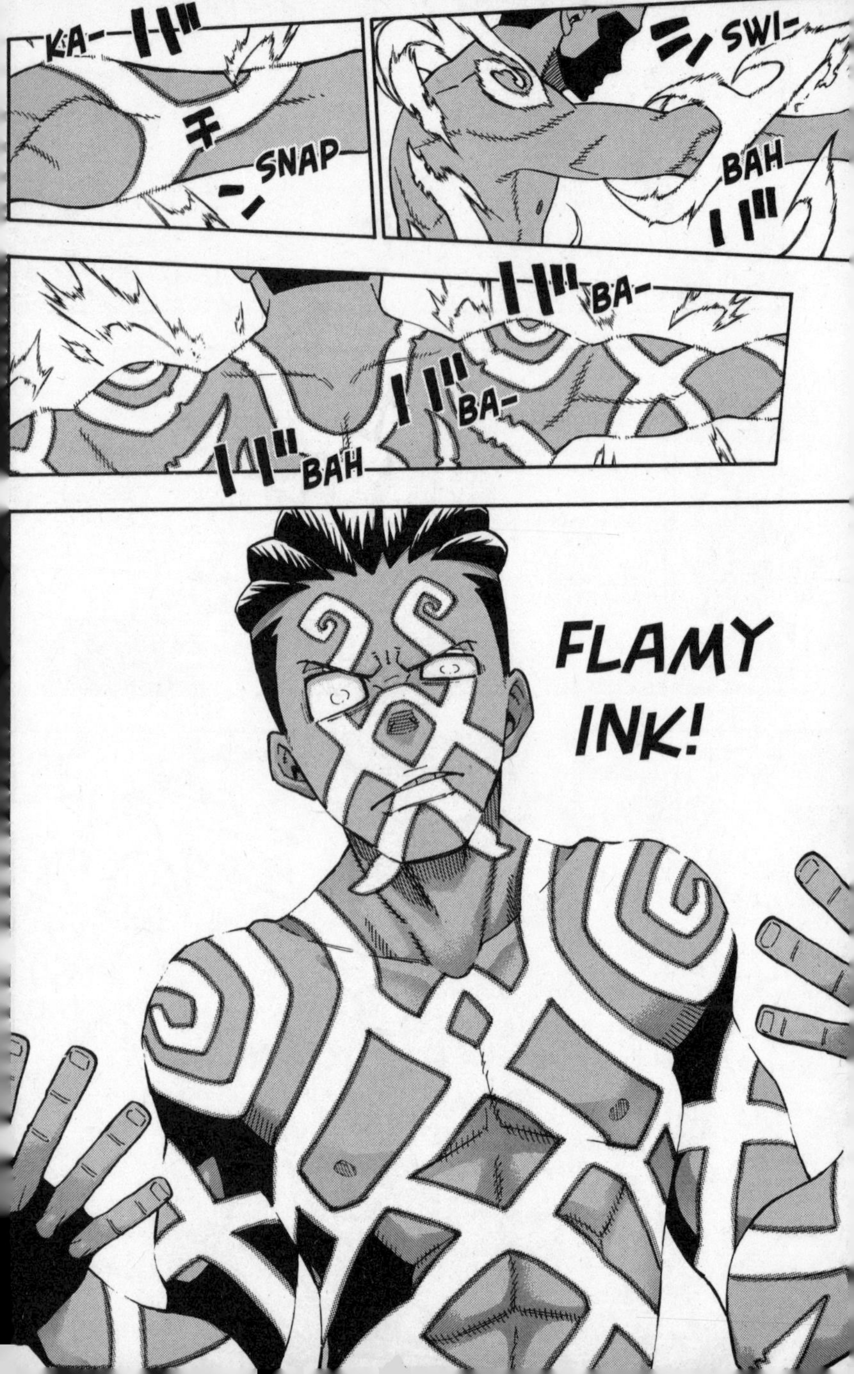
SWI-
BAH
KA-
SNAP
BA-
BA-
BAH
FLAMY INK!

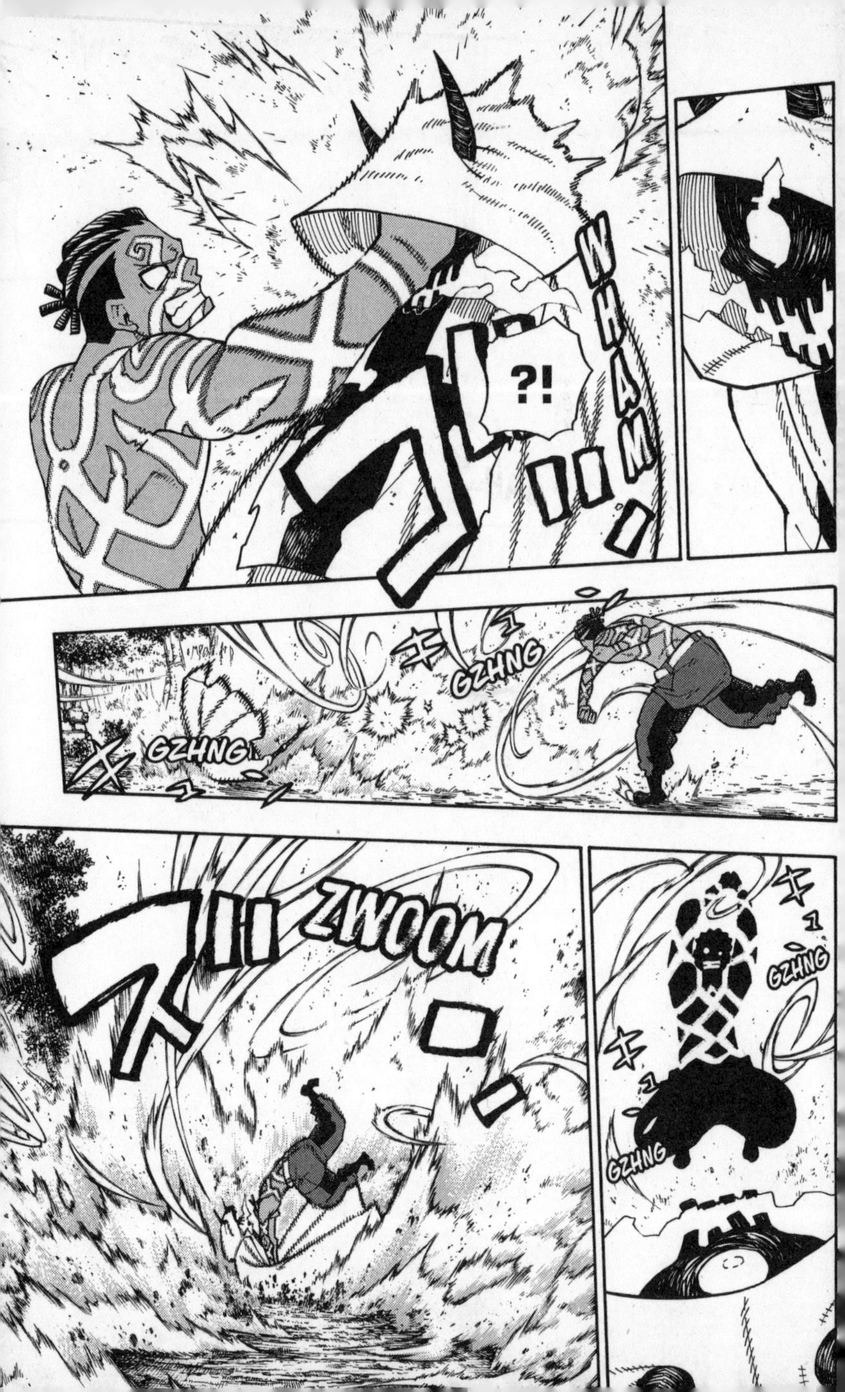
WHAM
?!
GZHNG
GZHNG
GZHNG
GZHNG
ZWOOM

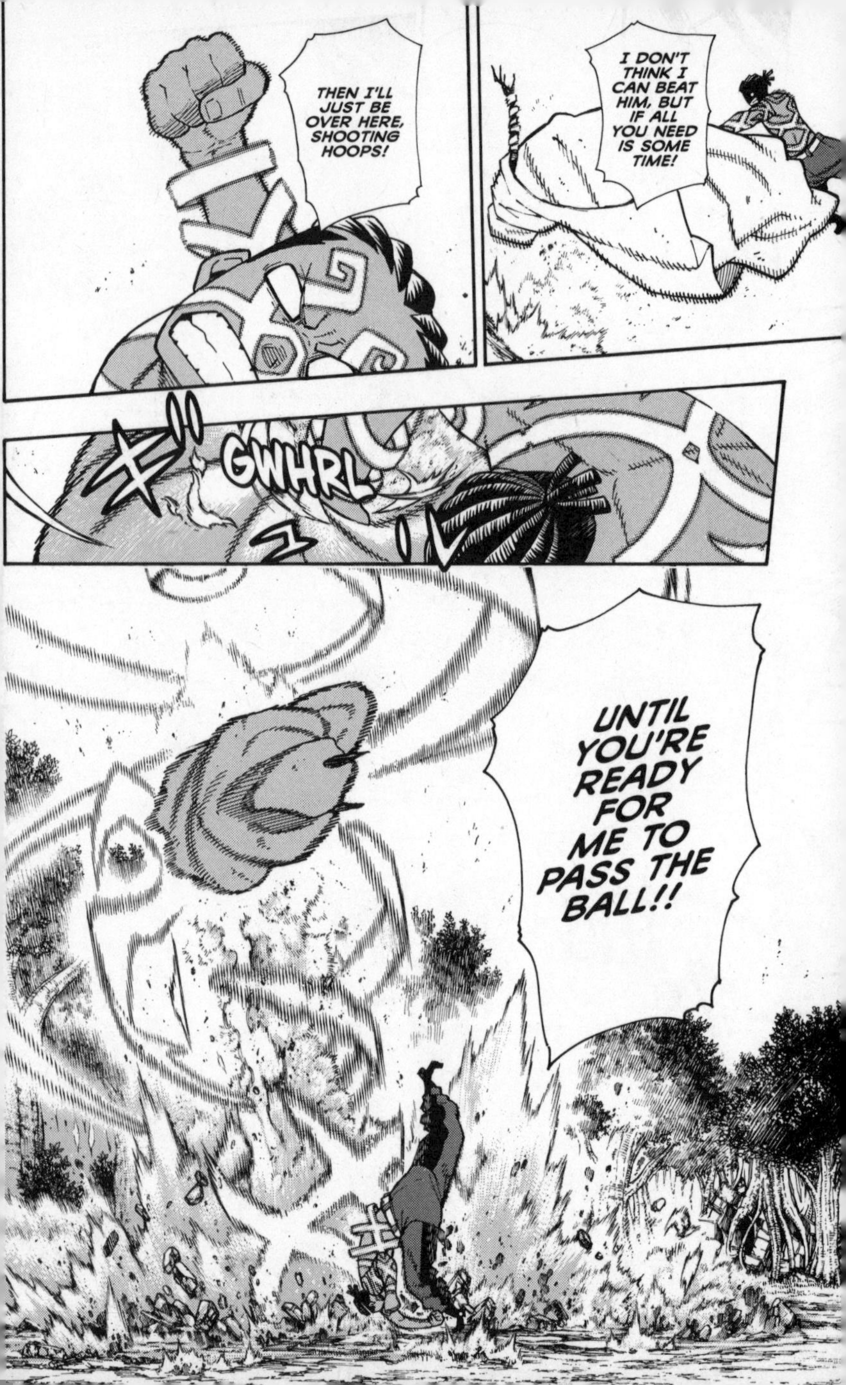
I DON'T THINK I CAN BEAT HIM, BUT IF ALL YOU NEED IS SOME TIME!
THEN I'LL JUST BE OVER HERE, SHOOTING HOOPS!
GWHRL
UNTIL YOU'RE READY FOR ME TO PASS THE BALL!!

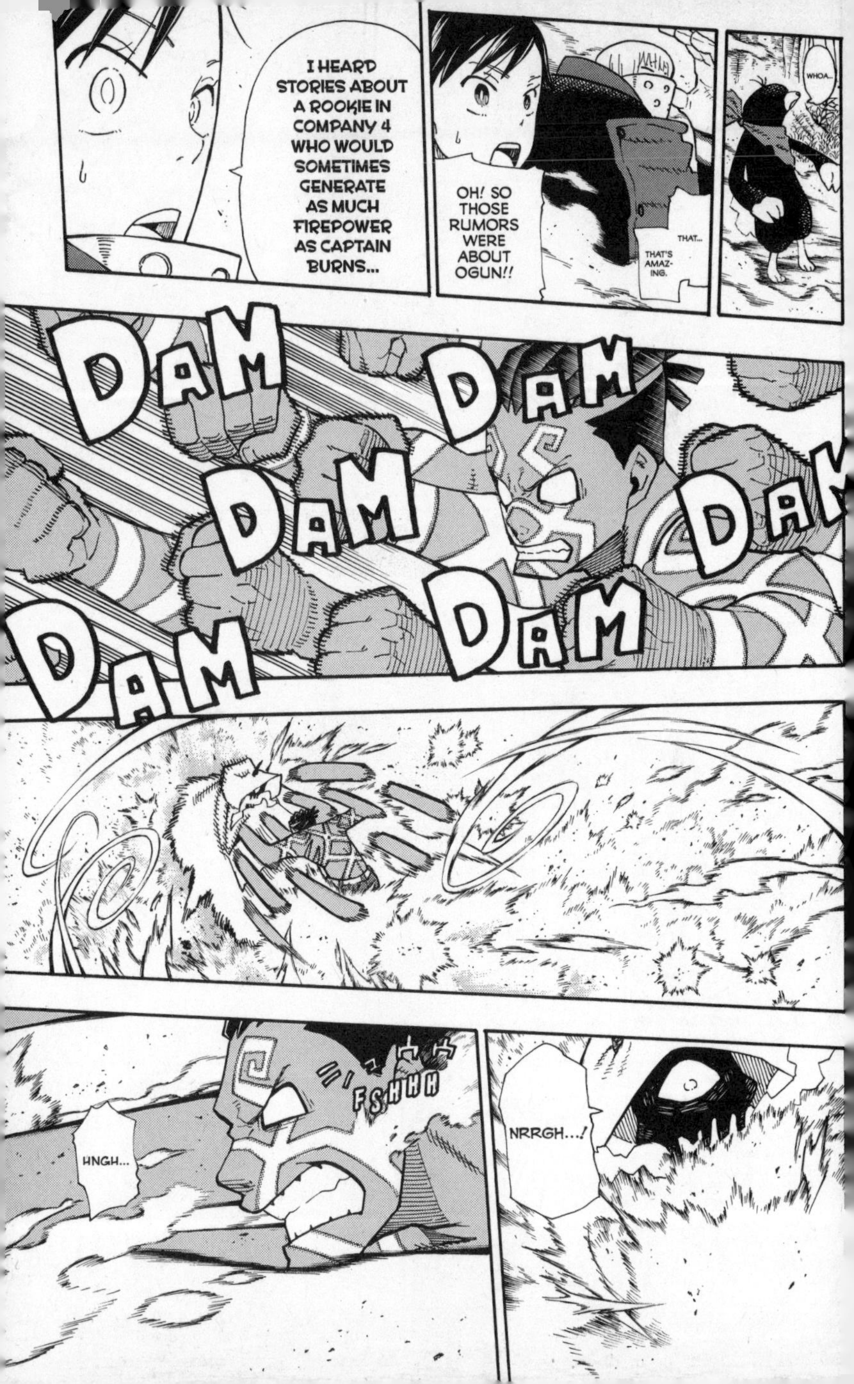

WHOA...
THAT...
THAT'S AMAZ-ING.
OH! SO THOSE RUMORS WERE ABOUT OGUN!!
I HEARD STORIES ABOUT A ROOKIE IN COMPANY 4 WHO WOULD SOMETIMES GENERATE AS MUCH FIREPOWER AS CAPTAIN BURNS...
DAM DAM DAM DAM DAM DAM
NRRGH...!
FSHHH
HNGH...

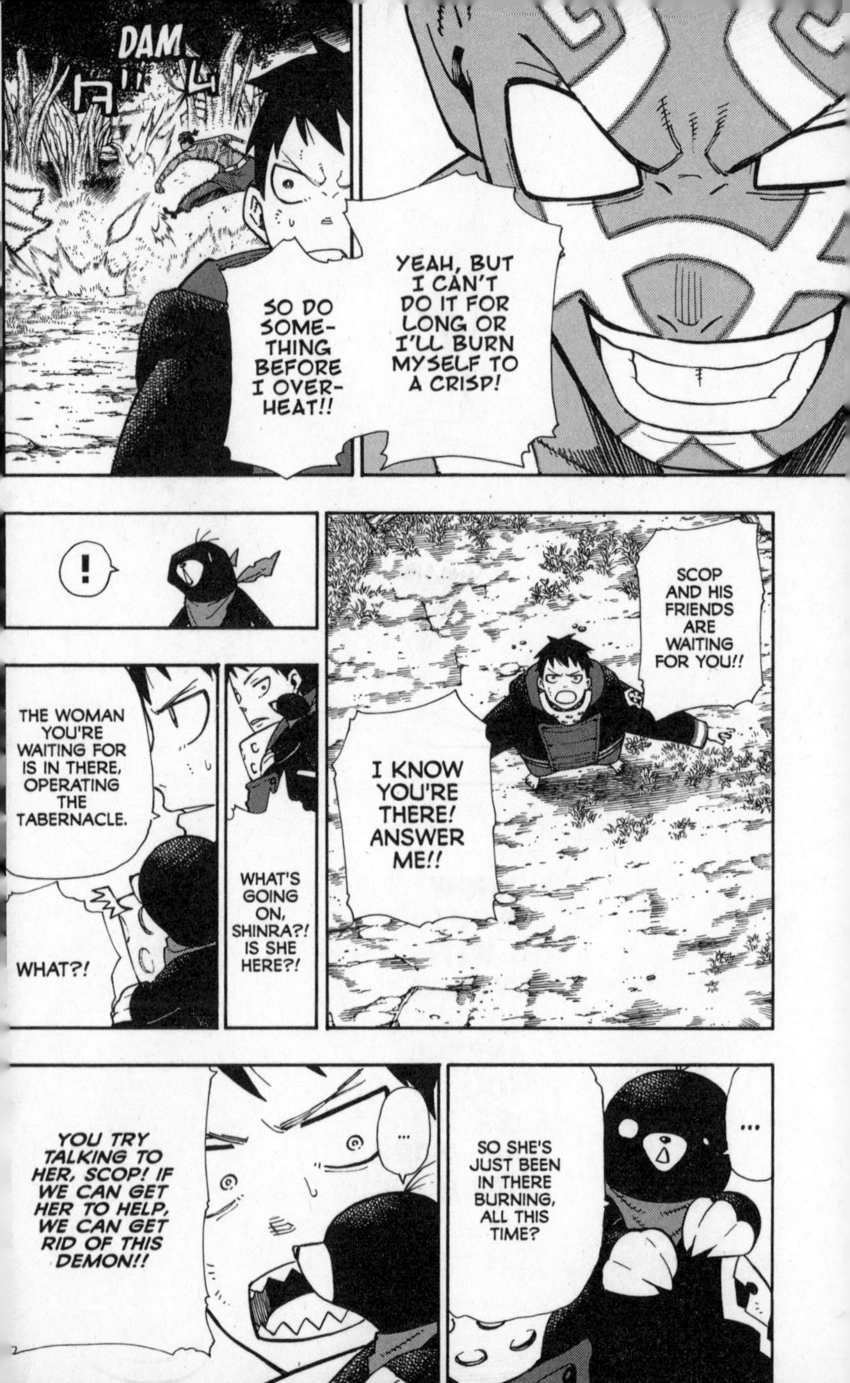
YEAH, BUT I CAN'T DO IT FOR LONG OR I'LL BURN MYSELF TO A CRISP!
DAM
SO DO SOME-THING BEFORE I OVER-HEAT!!
SCOP AND HIS FRIENDS ARE WAITING FOR YOU!!
I KNOW YOU'RE THERE! ANSWER ME!!
!
WHAT'S GOING ON, SHINRA?! IS SHE HERE?!
THE WOMAN YOU'RE WAITING FOR IS IN THERE, OPERATING THE TABERNACLE.
WHAT?!
...
SO SHE'S JUST BEEN IN THERE BURNING, ALL THIS TIME?
...
YOU TRY TALKING TO HER, SCOP! IF WE CAN GET HER TO HELP, WE CAN GET RID OF THIS DEMON!!

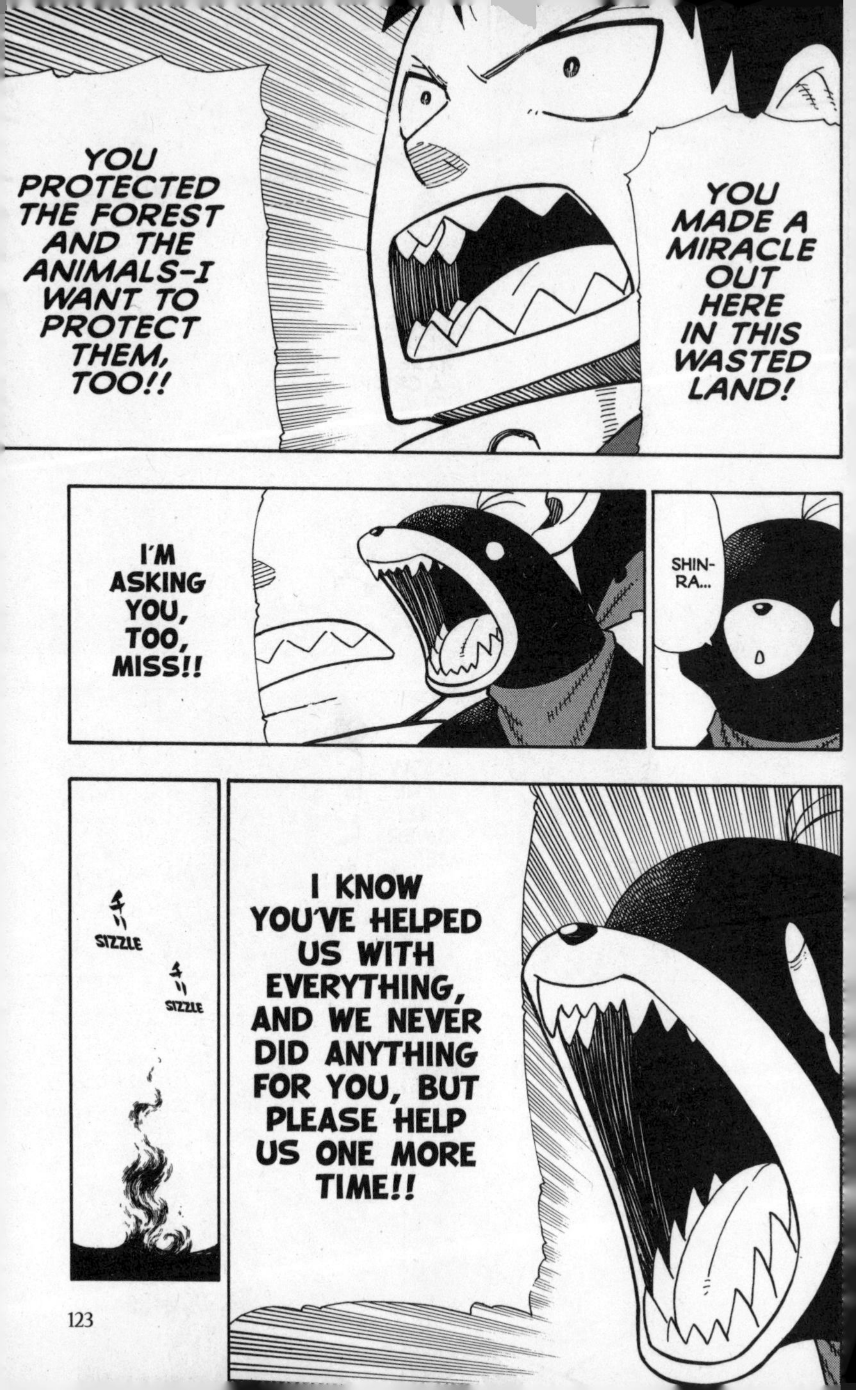
YOU MADE A MIRACLE OUT HERE IN THIS WASTED LAND!
YOU PROTECTED THE FOREST AND THE ANIMALS–I WANT TO PROTECT THEM, TOO!!
SHIN-RA...
I'M ASKING YOU, TOO, MISS!!
I KNOW YOU'VE HELPED US WITH EVERYTHING, AND WE NEVER DID ANYTHING FOR YOU, BUT PLEASE HELP US ONE MORE TIME!!
SIZZLE
SIZZLE

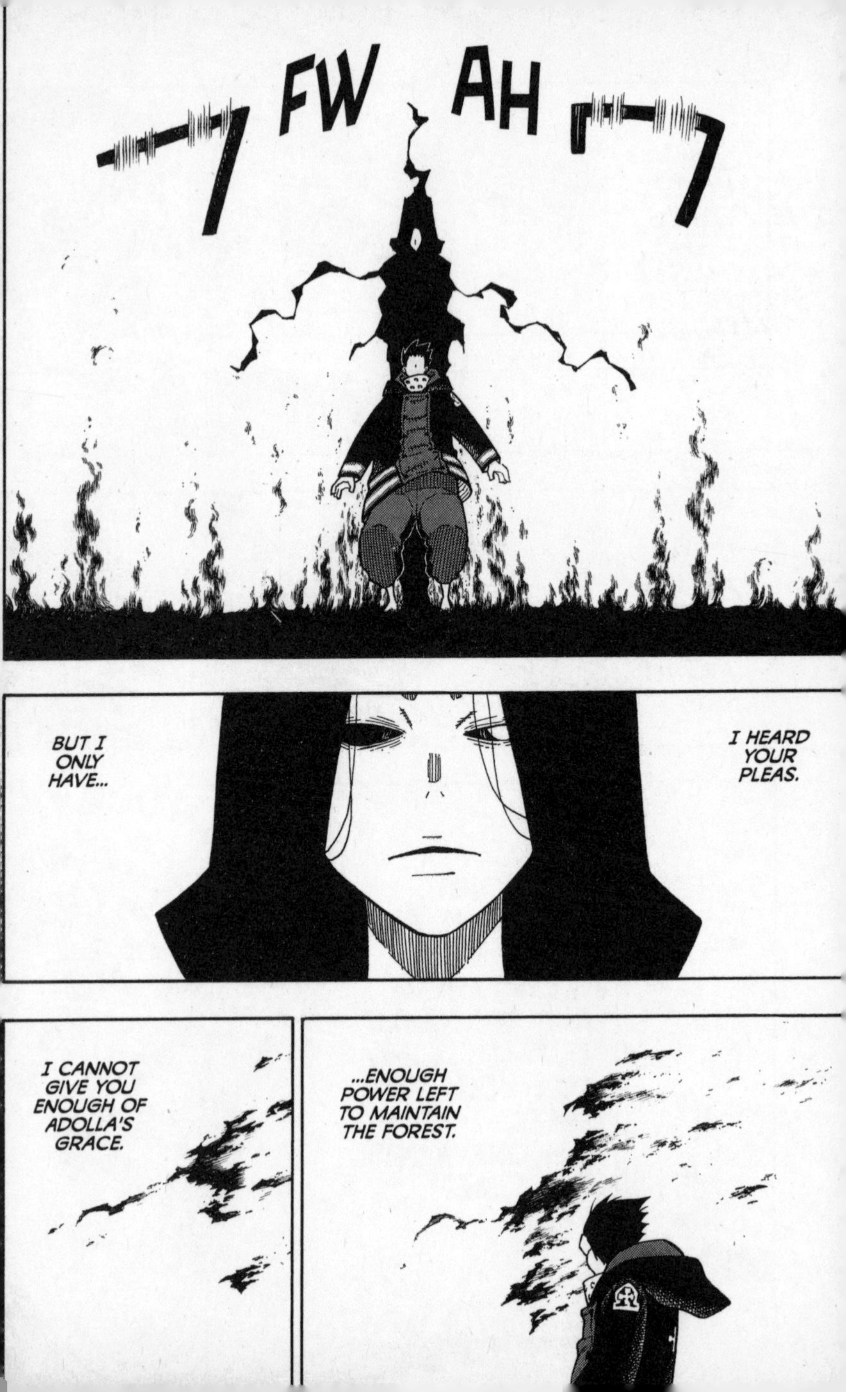
FW AH
I HEARD YOUR PLEAS.
BUT I ONLY HAVE...
...ENOUGH POWER LEFT TO MAINTAIN THE FOREST.
I CANNOT GIVE YOU ENOUGH OF ADOLLA'S GRACE.

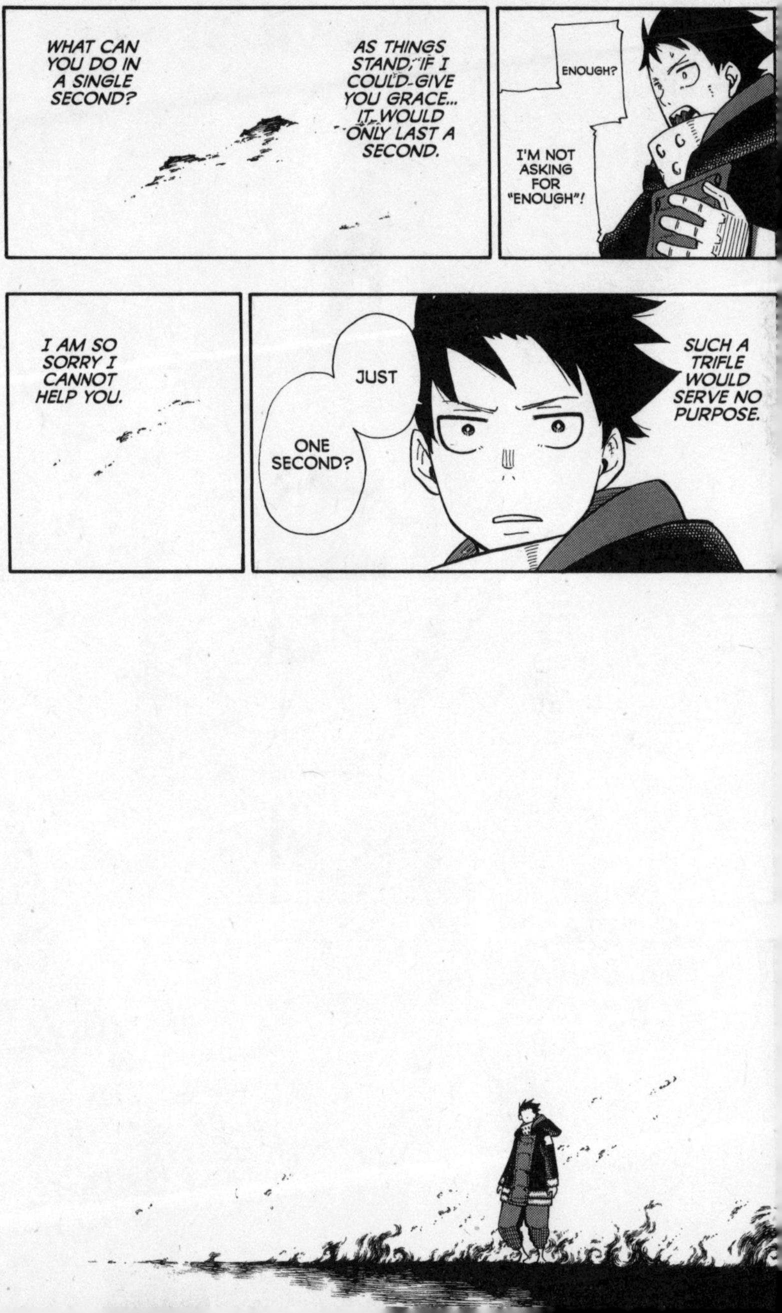
ENOUGH?
I'M NOT ASKING FOR "ENOUGH"!
AS THINGS STAND, IF I COULD GIVE YOU GRACE... IT WOULD ONLY LAST A SECOND.
WHAT CAN YOU DO IN A SINGLE SECOND?
SUCH A TRIFLE WOULD SERVE NO PURPOSE.
JUST ONE SECOND?
I AM SO SORRY I CANNOT HELP YOU.

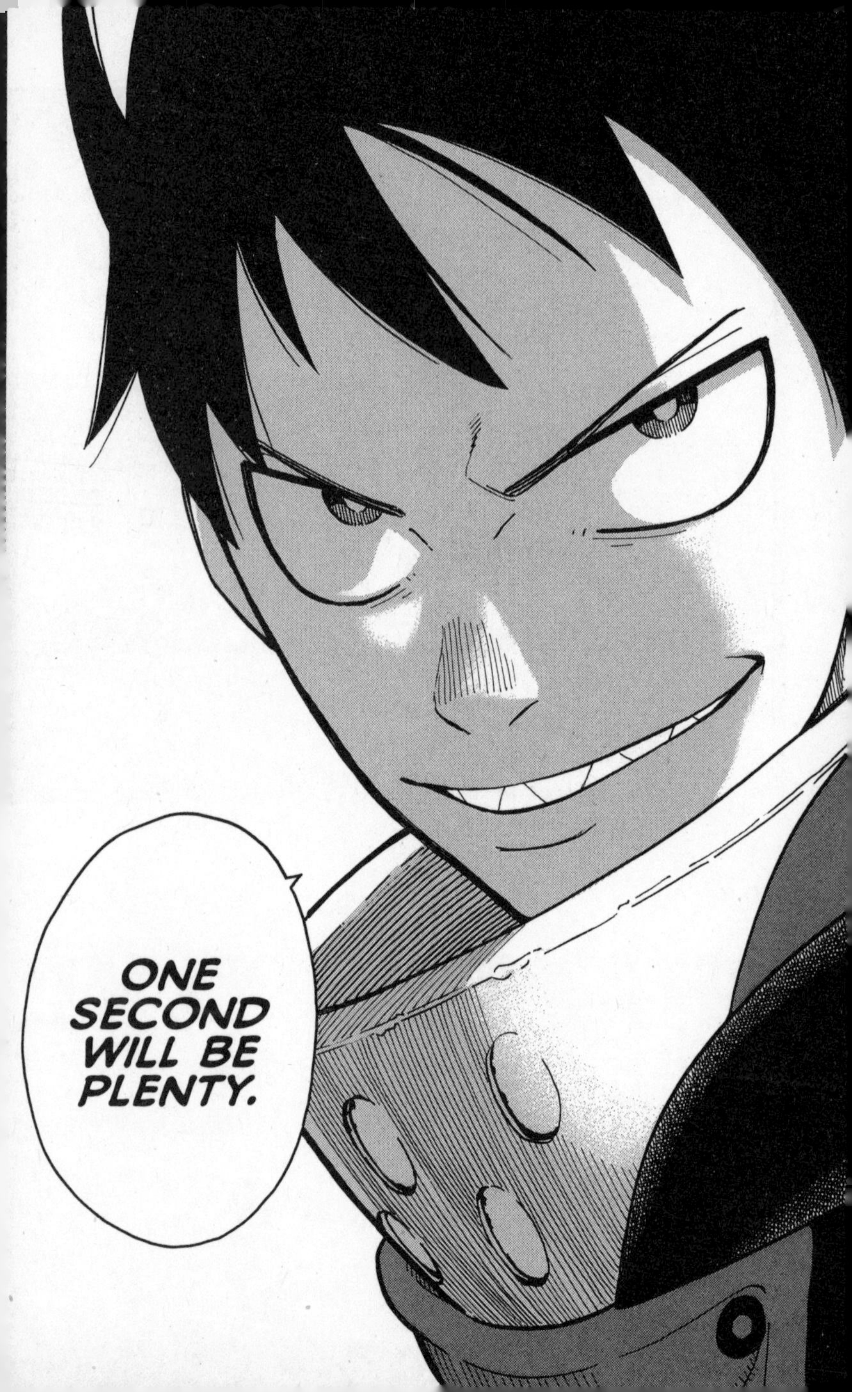
ONE SECOND WILL BE PLENTY.

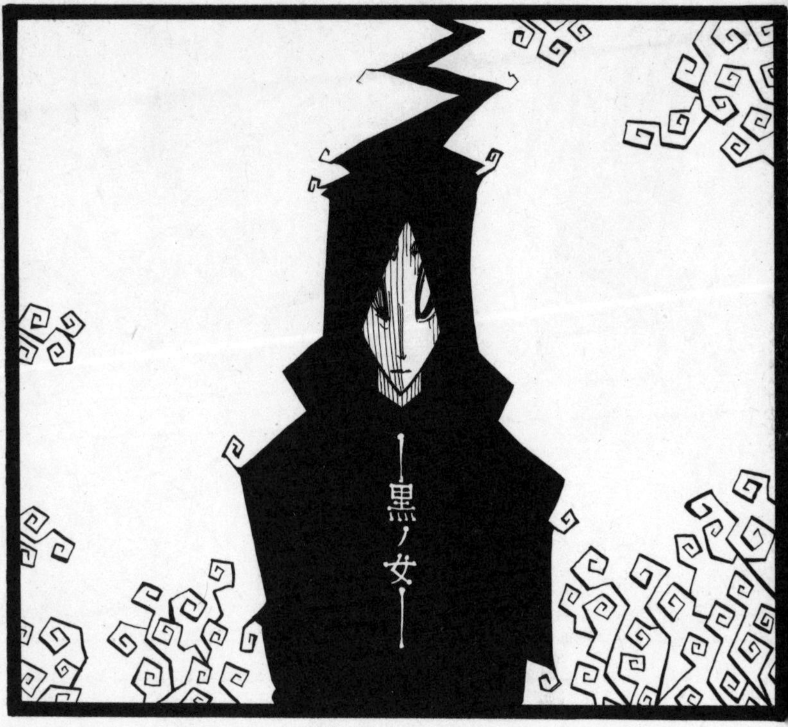
黒ノ女
The Woman in Black

CHAPTER CXXI: 1 SECOND/250 YEARS

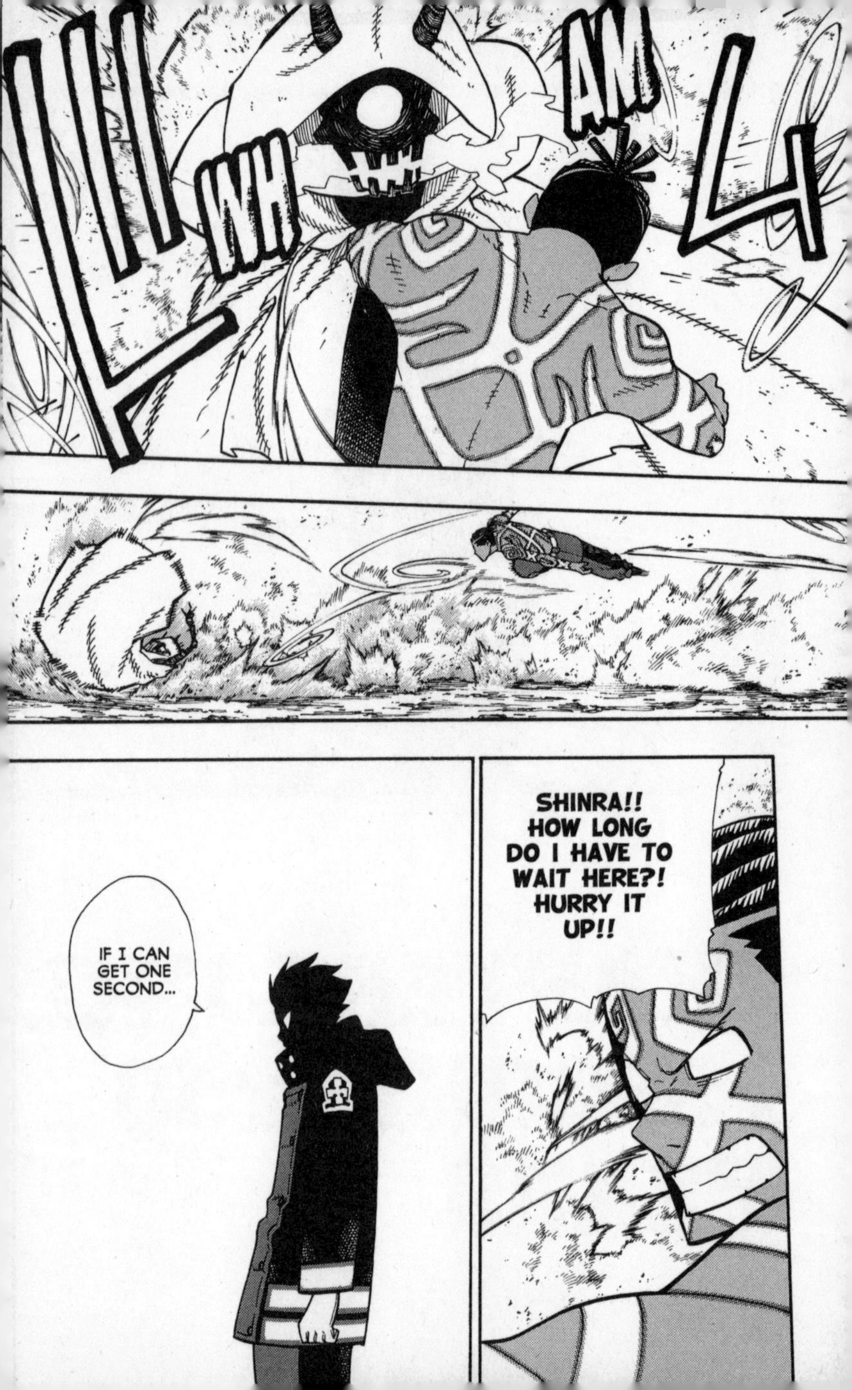
WHAM
SHINRA!! HOW LONG DO I HAVE TO WAIT HERE?! HURRY IT UP!!
IF I CAN GET ONE SECOND...

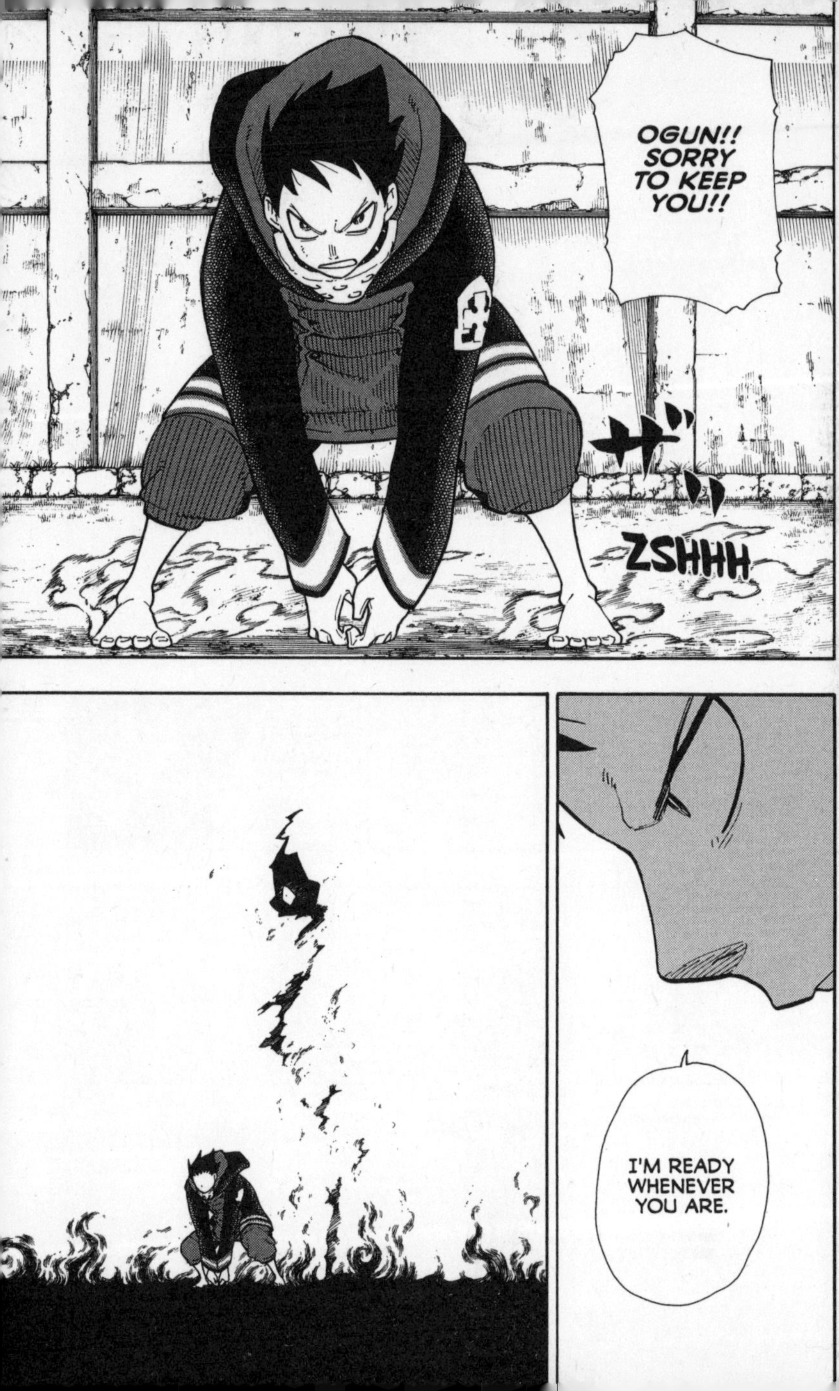
OGUN!! SORRY TO KEEP YOU!!
ザッ
ZSHHH
I'M READY WHENEVER YOU ARE.

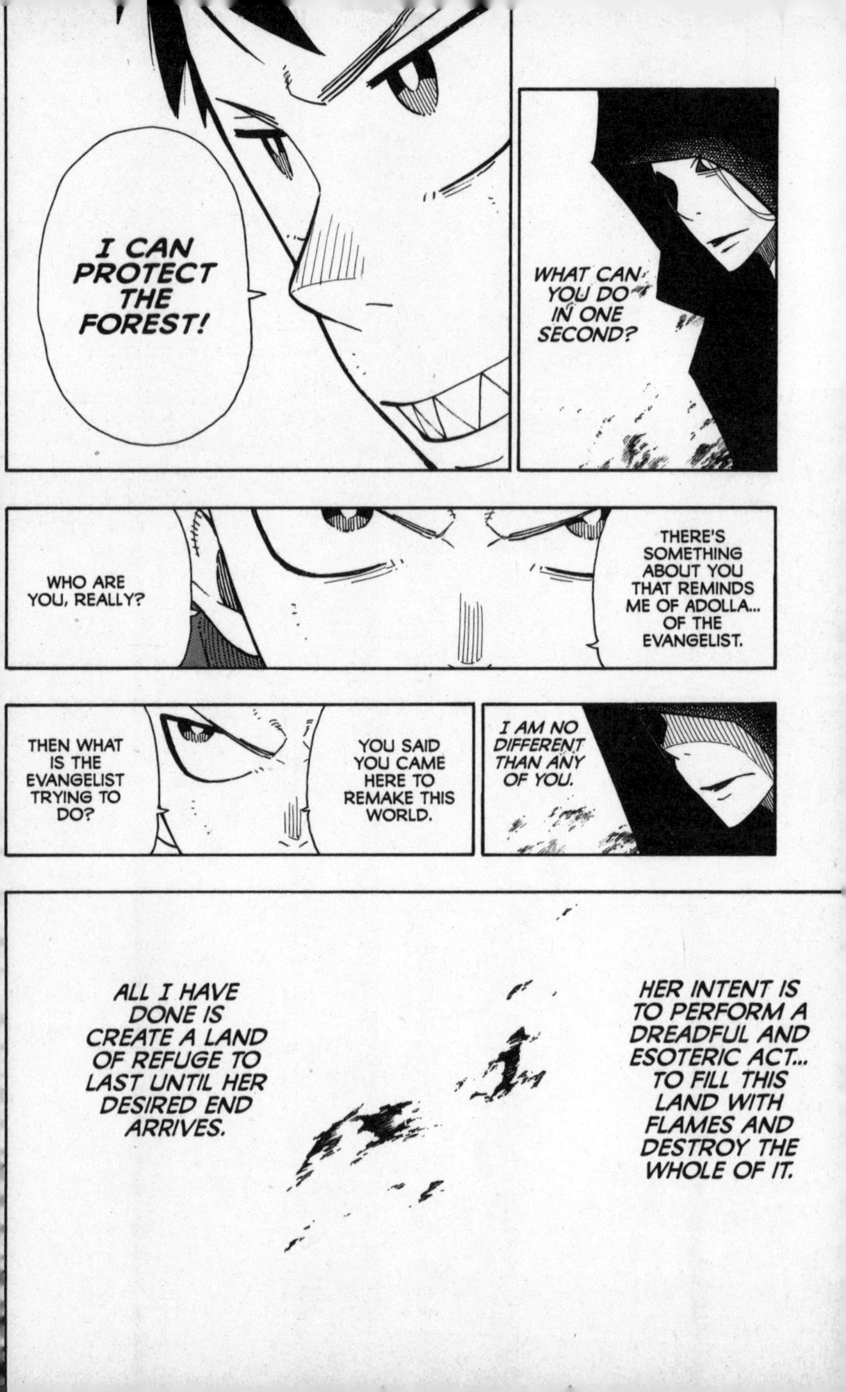
WHAT CAN YOU DO IN ONE SECOND?
I CAN PROTECT THE FOREST!
THERE'S SOMETHING ABOUT YOU THAT REMINDS ME OF ADOLLA... OF THE EVANGELIST.
WHO ARE YOU, REALLY?
I AM NO DIFFERENT THAN ANY OF YOU.
YOU SAID YOU CAME HERE TO REMAKE THIS WORLD.
THEN WHAT IS THE EVANGELIST TRYING TO DO?
HER INTENT IS TO PERFORM A DREADFUL AND ESOTERIC ACT... TO FILL THIS LAND WITH FLAMES AND DESTROY THE WHOLE OF IT.
ALL I HAVE DONE IS CREATE A LAND OF REFUGE TO LAST UNTIL HER DESIRED END ARRIVES.

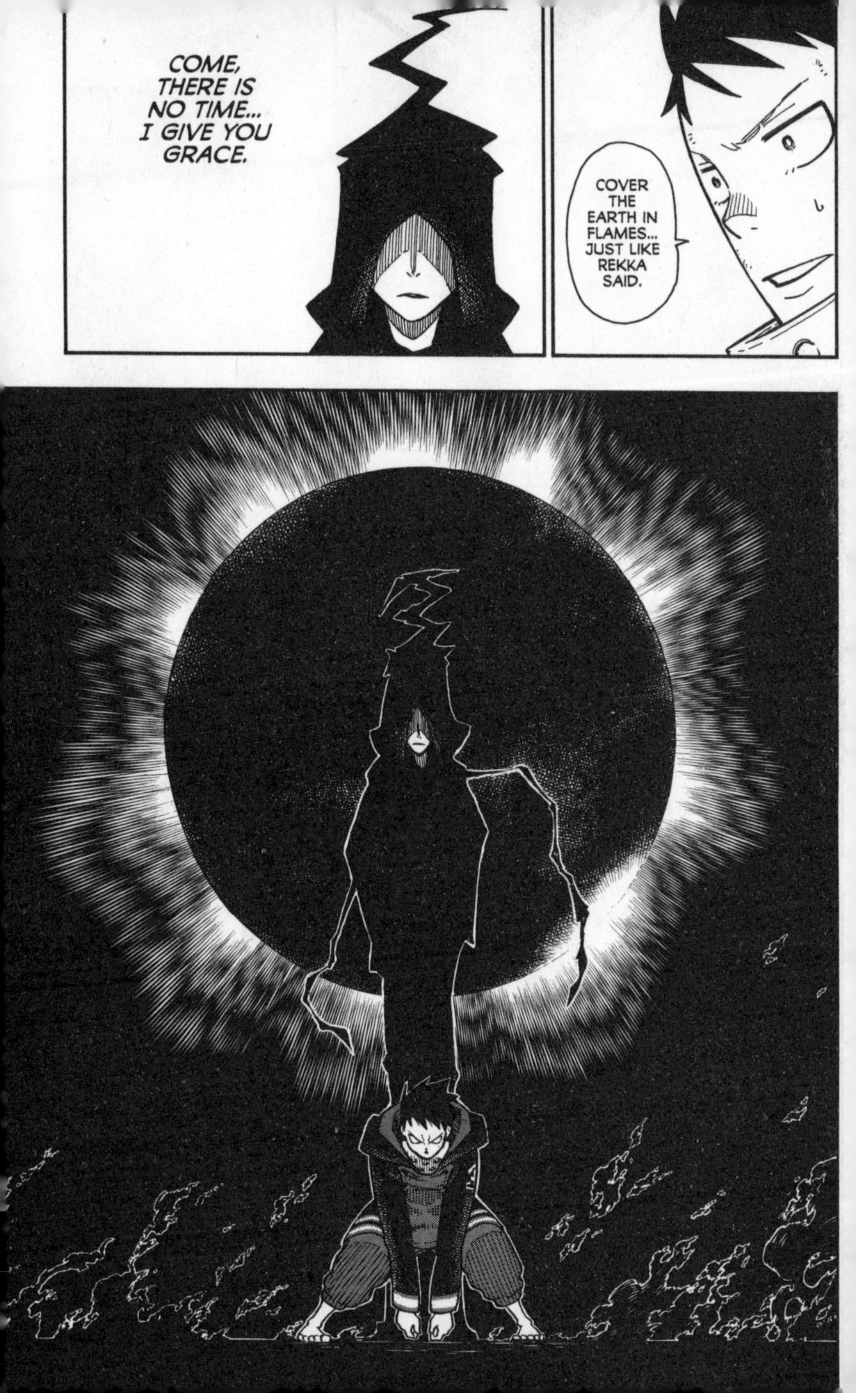
COVER THE EARTH IN FLAMES... JUST LIKE REKKA SAID.
COME, THERE IS NO TIME... I GIVE YOU GRACE.

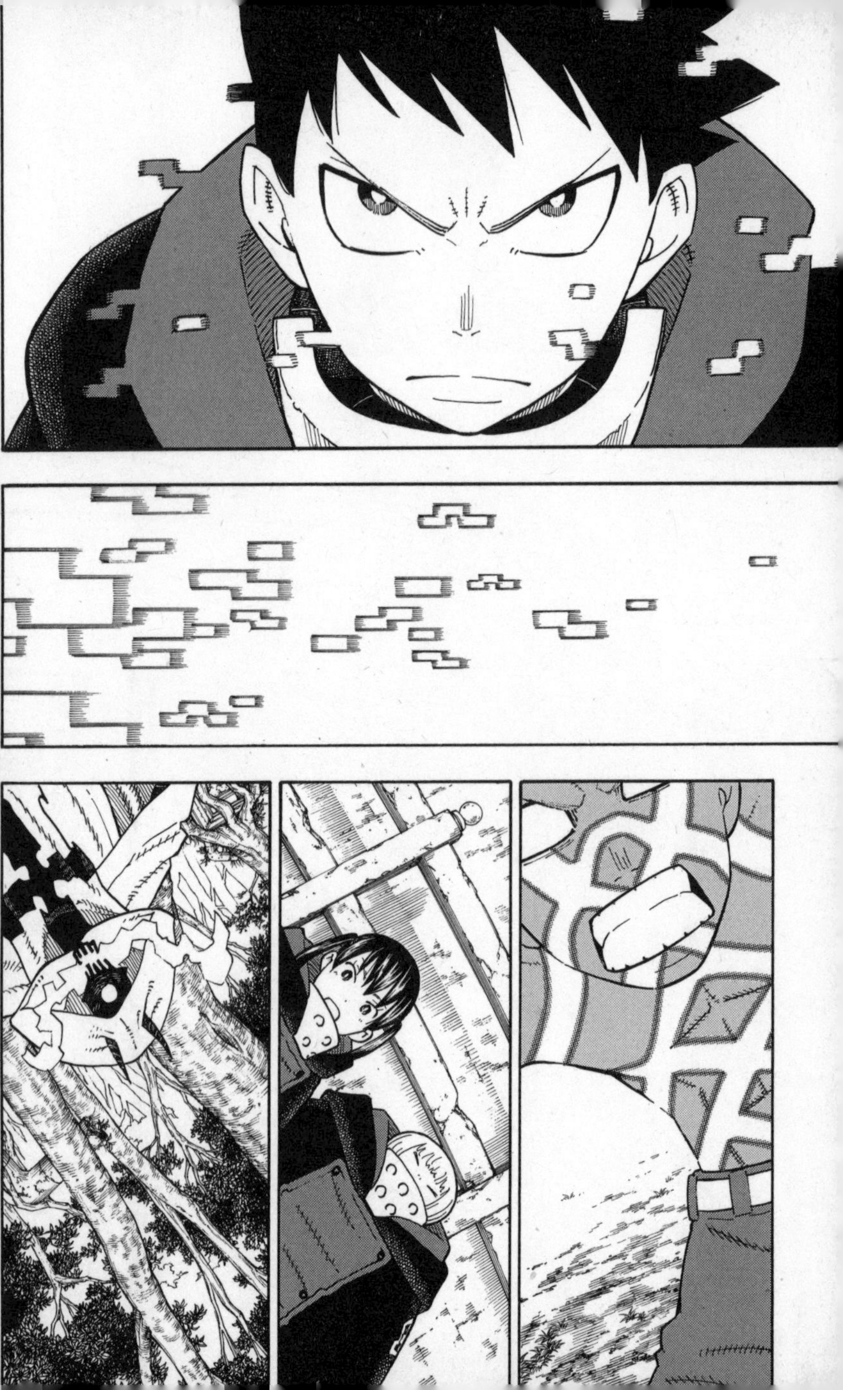

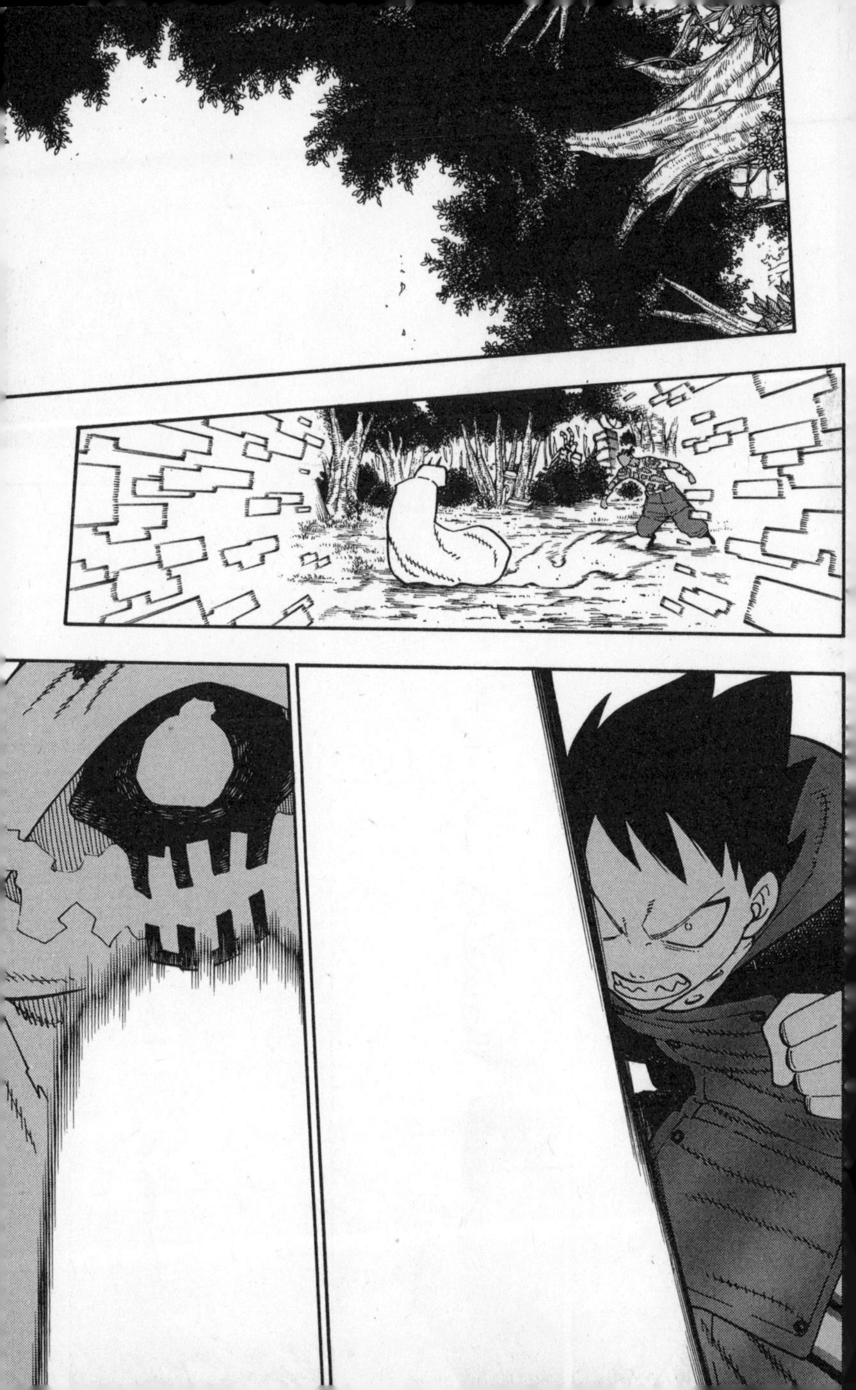

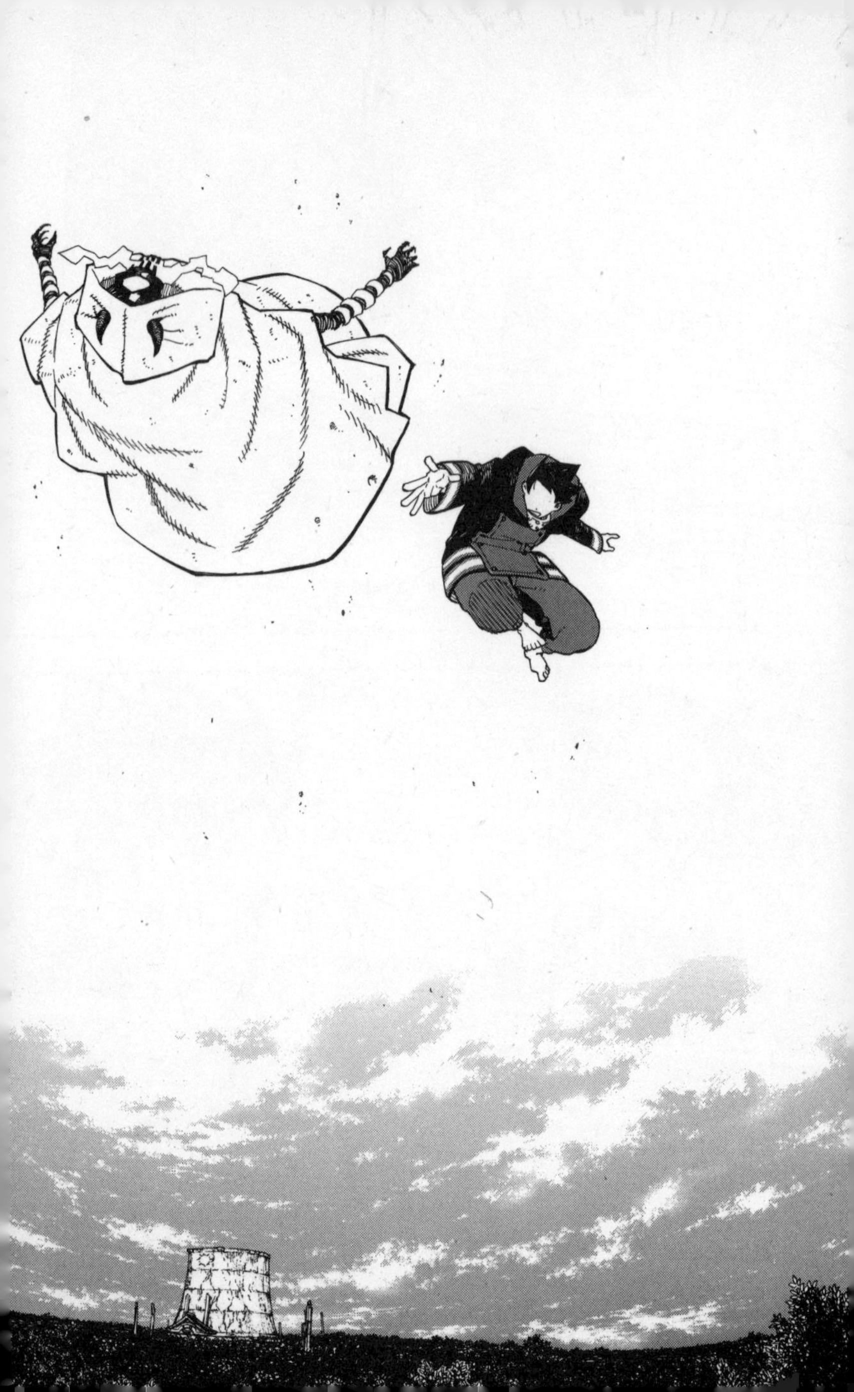

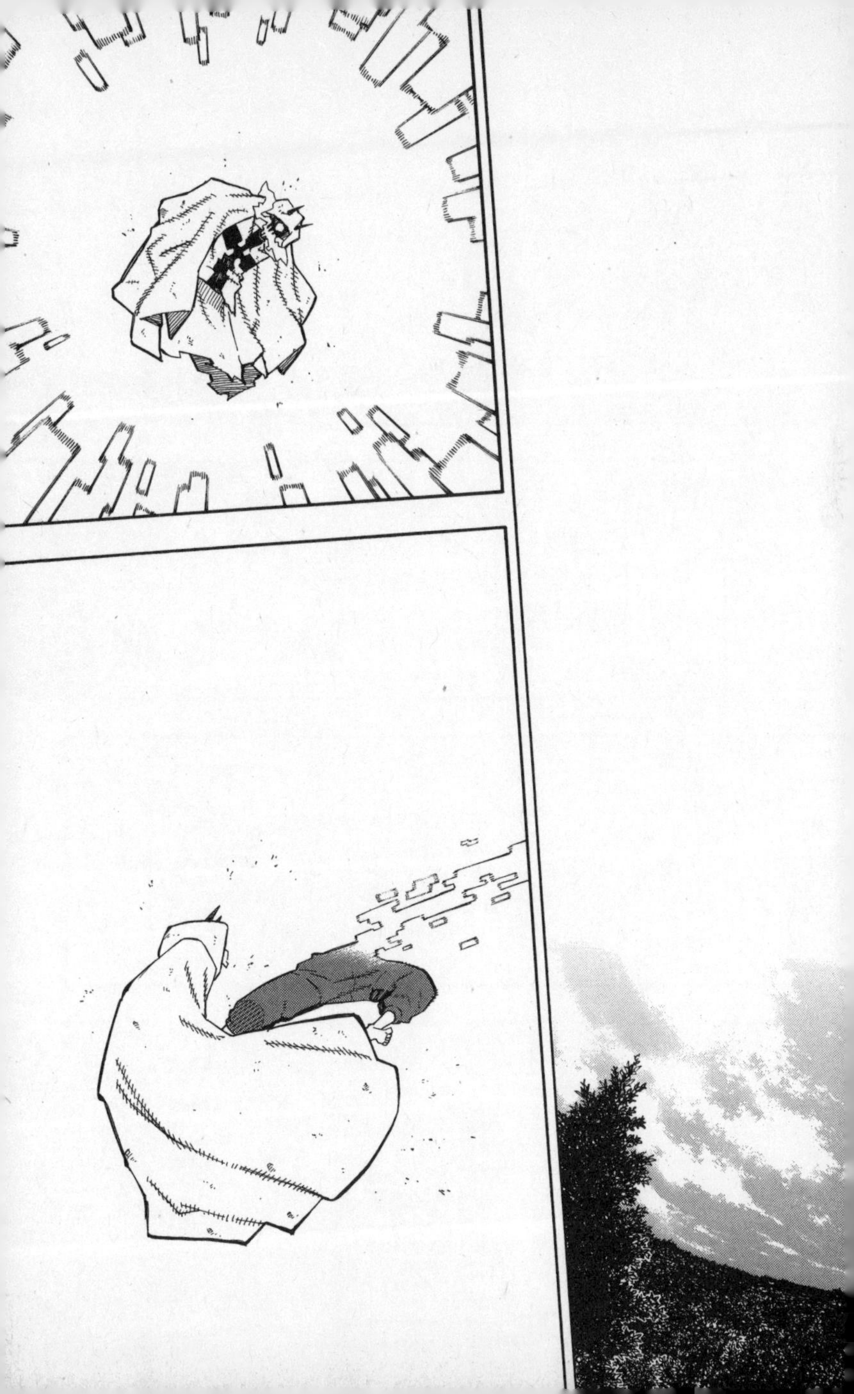

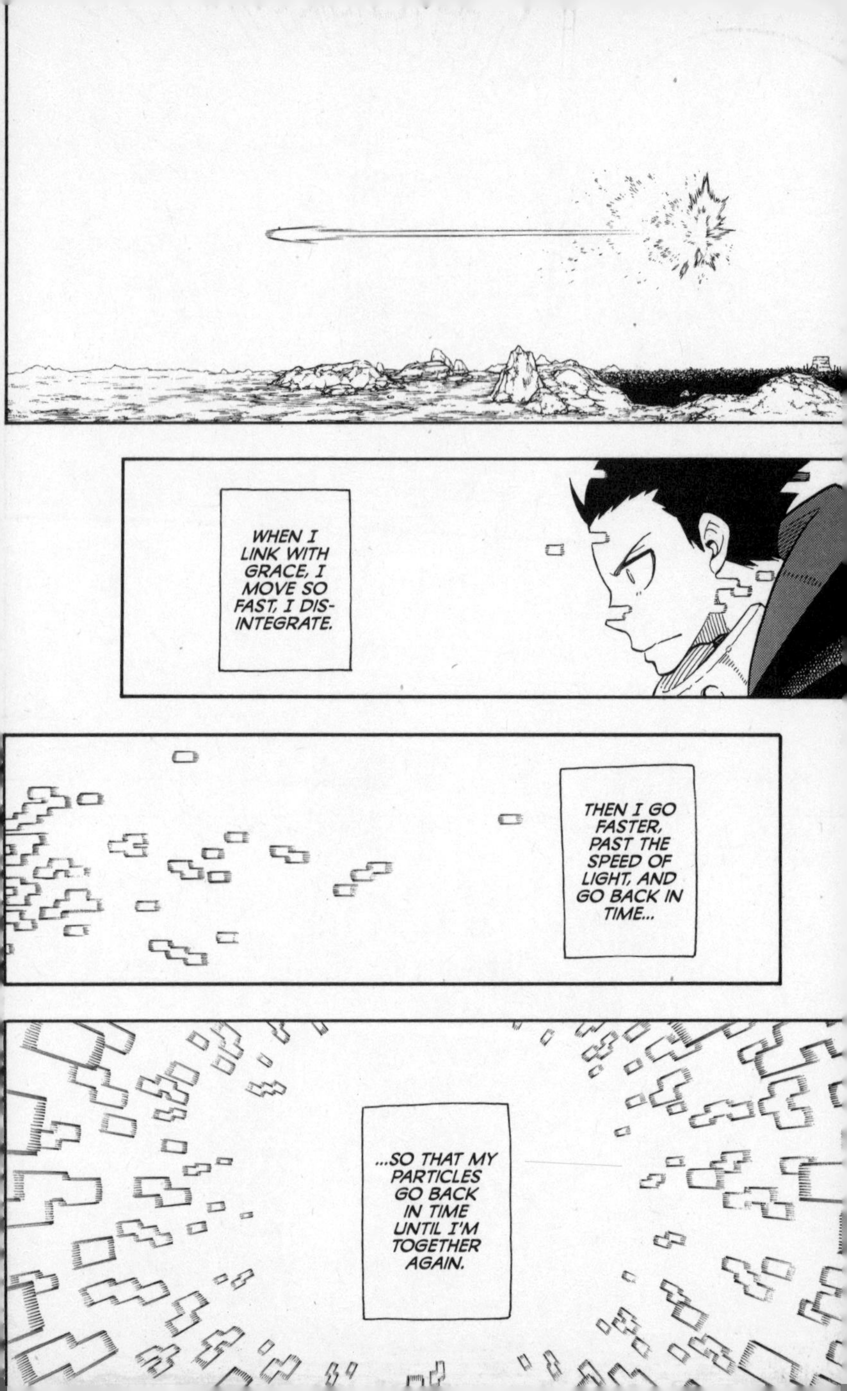
WHEN I LINK WITH GRACE, I MOVE SO FAST, I DIS-INTEGRATE.
THEN I GO FASTER, PAST THE SPEED OF LIGHT, AND GO BACK IN TIME...
...SO THAT MY PARTICLES GO BACK IN TIME UNTIL I'M TOGETHER AGAIN.

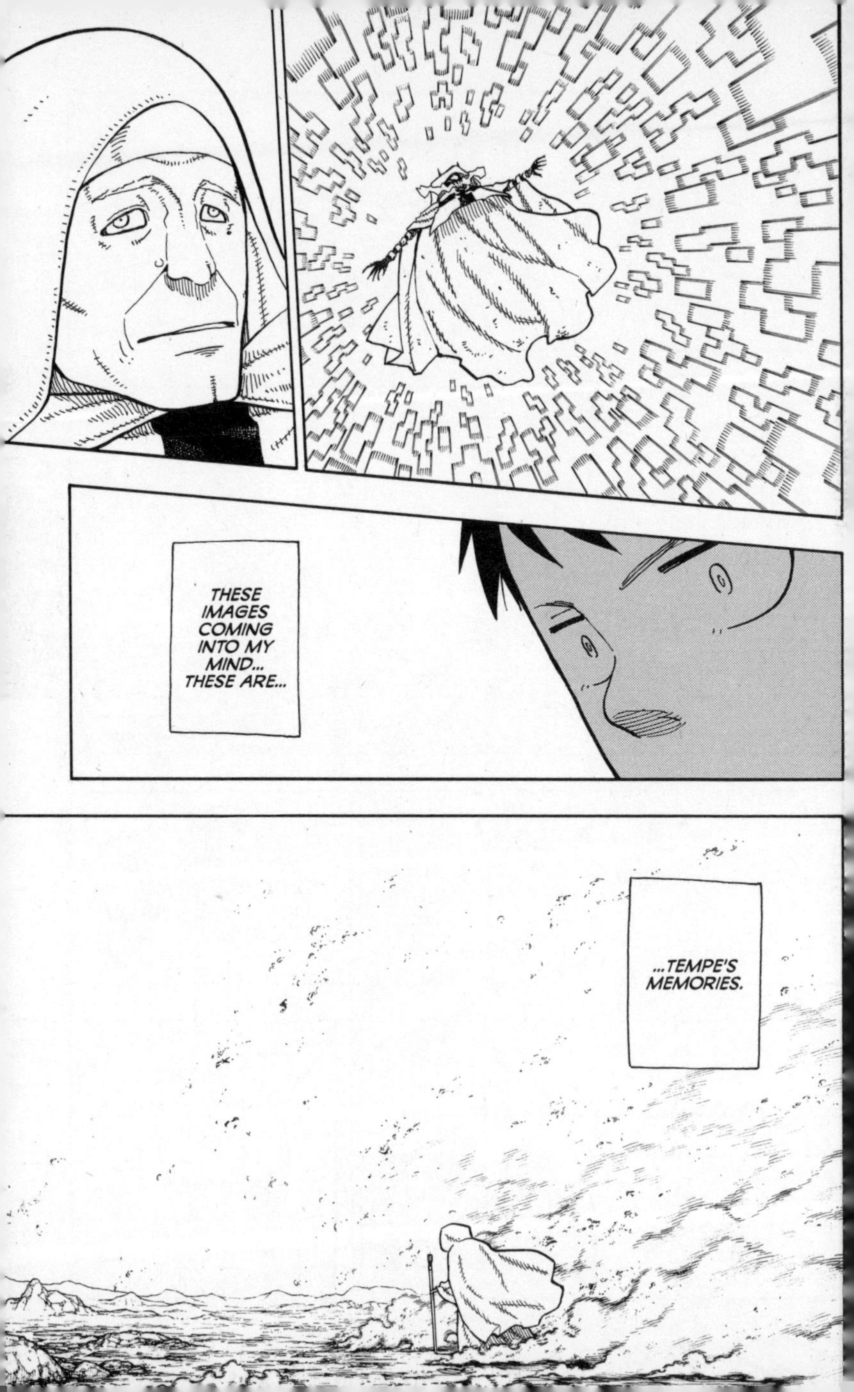
THESE IMAGES COMING INTO MY MIND... THESE ARE...
...TEMPE'S MEMORIES.

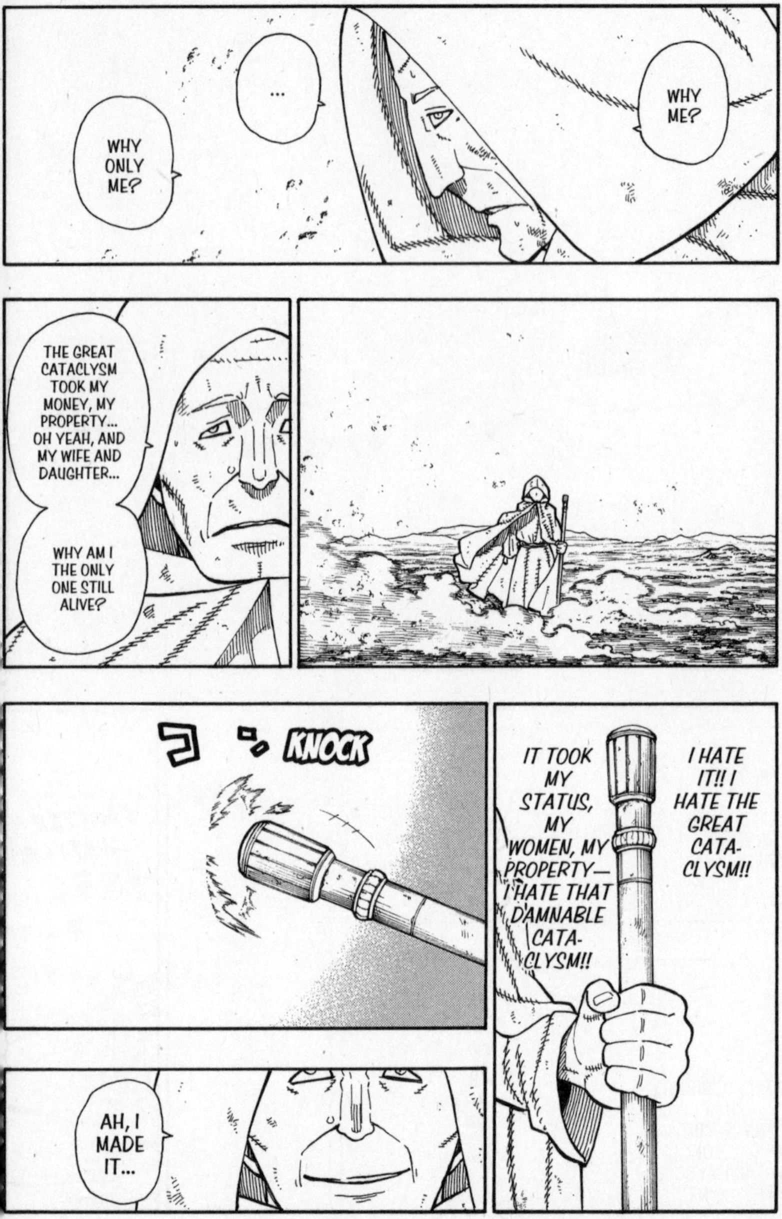
WHY ME?
...
WHY ONLY ME?
THE GREAT CATACLYSM TOOK MY MONEY, MY PROPERTY... OH YEAH, AND MY WIFE AND DAUGHTER...
WHY AM I THE ONLY ONE STILL ALIVE?
I HATE IT!! I HATE THE GREAT CATA-CLYSM!!
IT TOOK MY STATUS, MY WOMEN, MY PROPERTY— I HATE THAT DAMNABLE CATA-CLYSM!!
KNOCK
AH, I MADE IT...

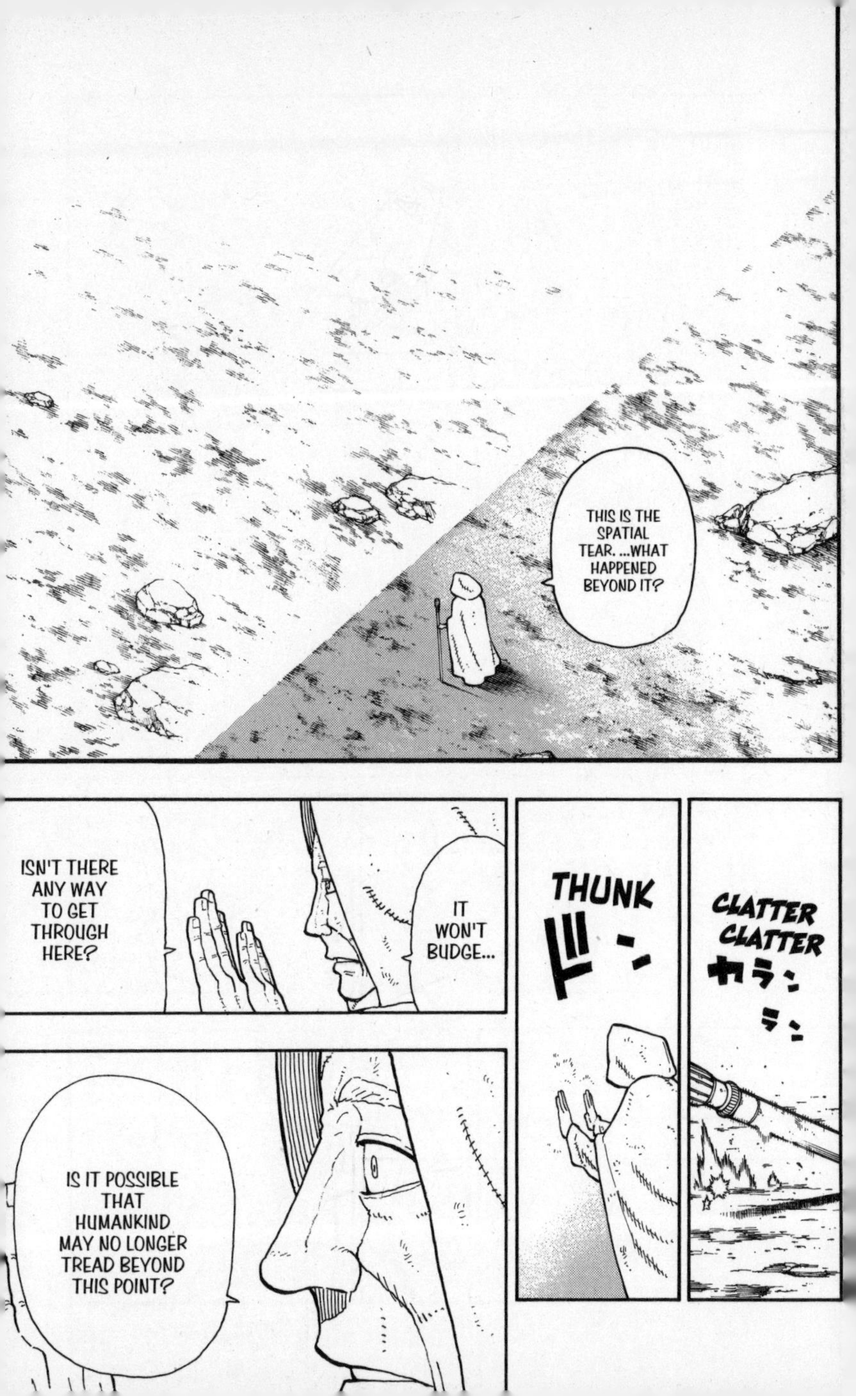
THIS IS THE SPATIAL TEAR. ...WHAT HAPPENED BEYOND IT?
CLATTER CLATTER
カラン ラン
THUNK
ドン
IT WON'T BUDGE...
ISN'T THERE ANY WAY TO GET THROUGH HERE?
IS IT POSSIBLE THAT HUMANKIND MAY NO LONGER TREAD BEYOND THIS POINT?

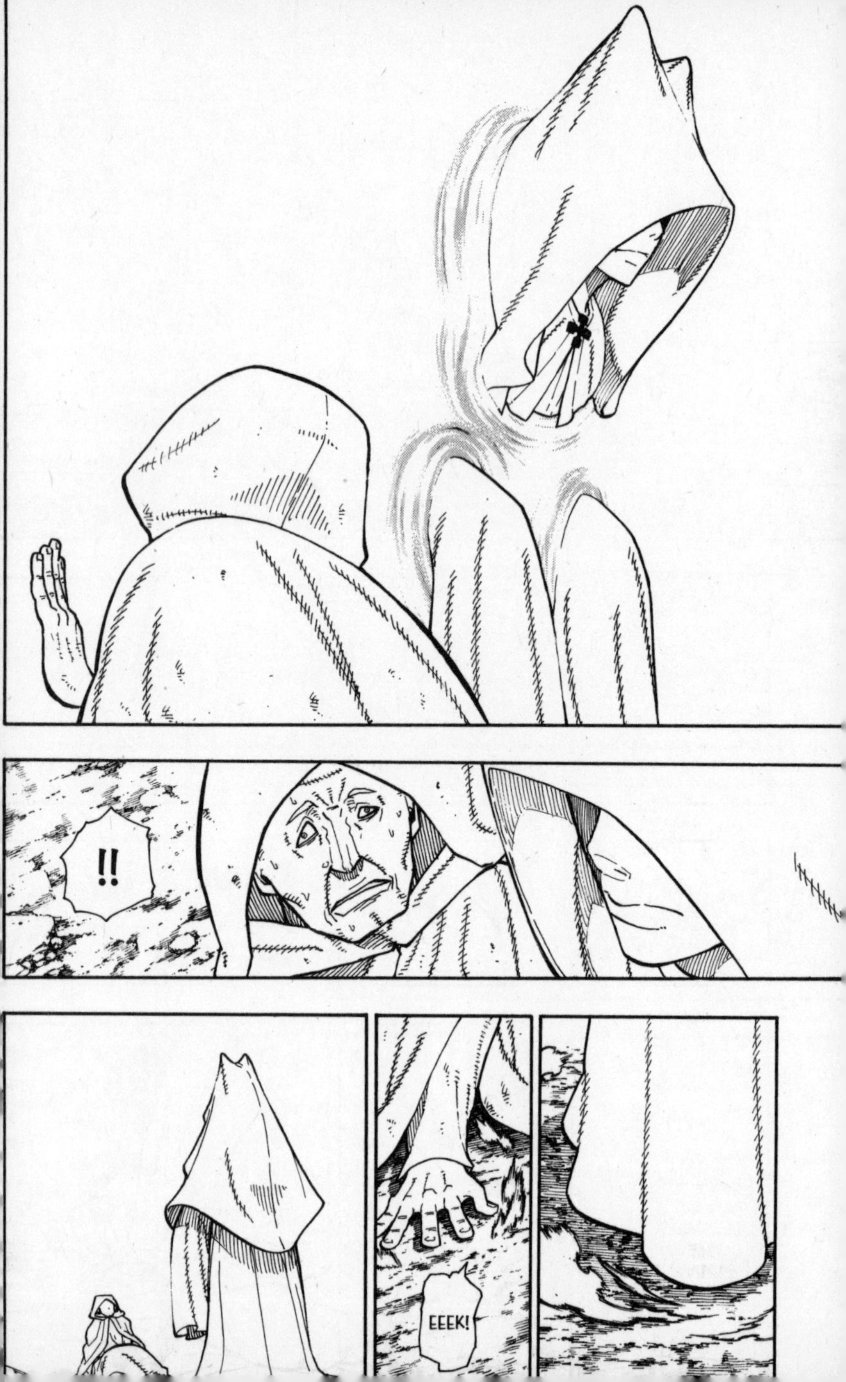
!!
EEEK!

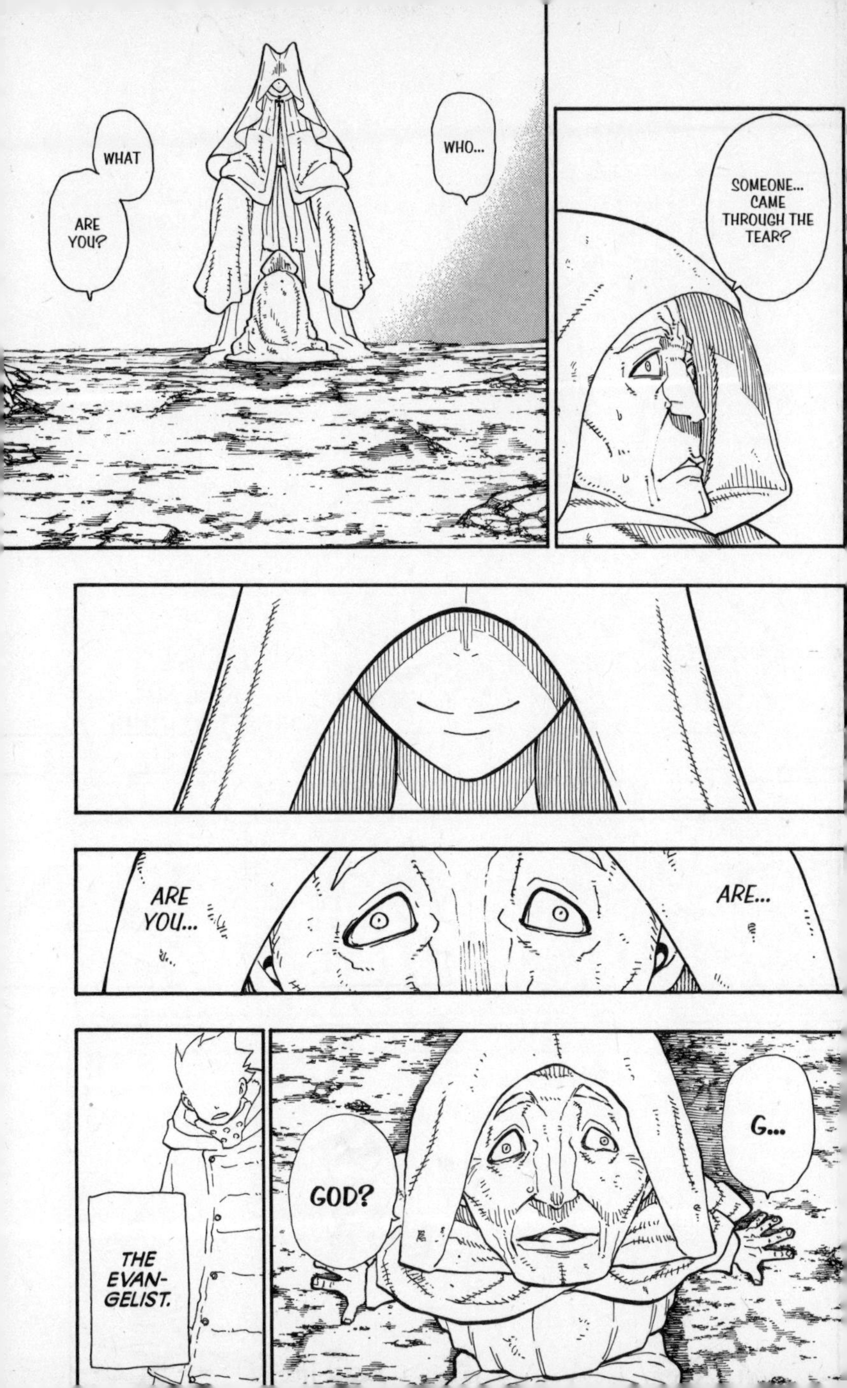
SOMEONE... CAME THROUGH THE TEAR?
WHO...
WHAT ARE YOU?
ARE...
ARE YOU...
G...
GOD?
THE EVANGELIST.

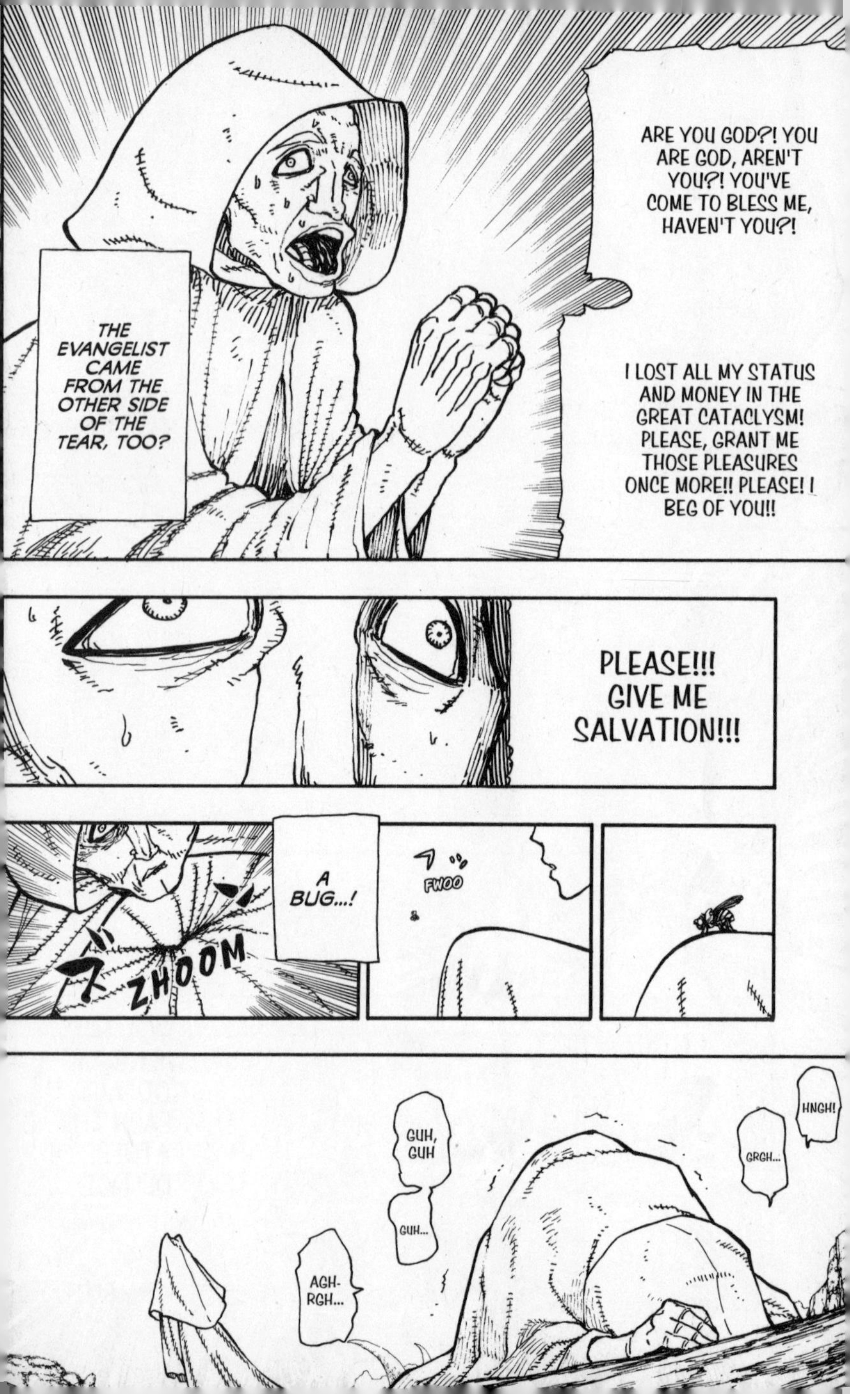
ARE YOU GOD?! YOU ARE GOD, AREN'T YOU?! YOU'VE COME TO BLESS ME, HAVEN'T YOU?!
I LOST ALL MY STATUS AND MONEY IN THE GREAT CATACLYSM! PLEASE, GRANT ME THOSE PLEASURES ONCE MORE!! PLEASE! I BEG OF YOU!!
THE EVANGELIST CAME FROM THE OTHER SIDE OF THE TEAR, TOO?
PLEASE!!! GIVE ME SALVATION!!!
FWOO
A BUG...!
ZHOOM
HNGH!
GRGH...
GUH, GUH
GUH...
AGH-RGH...

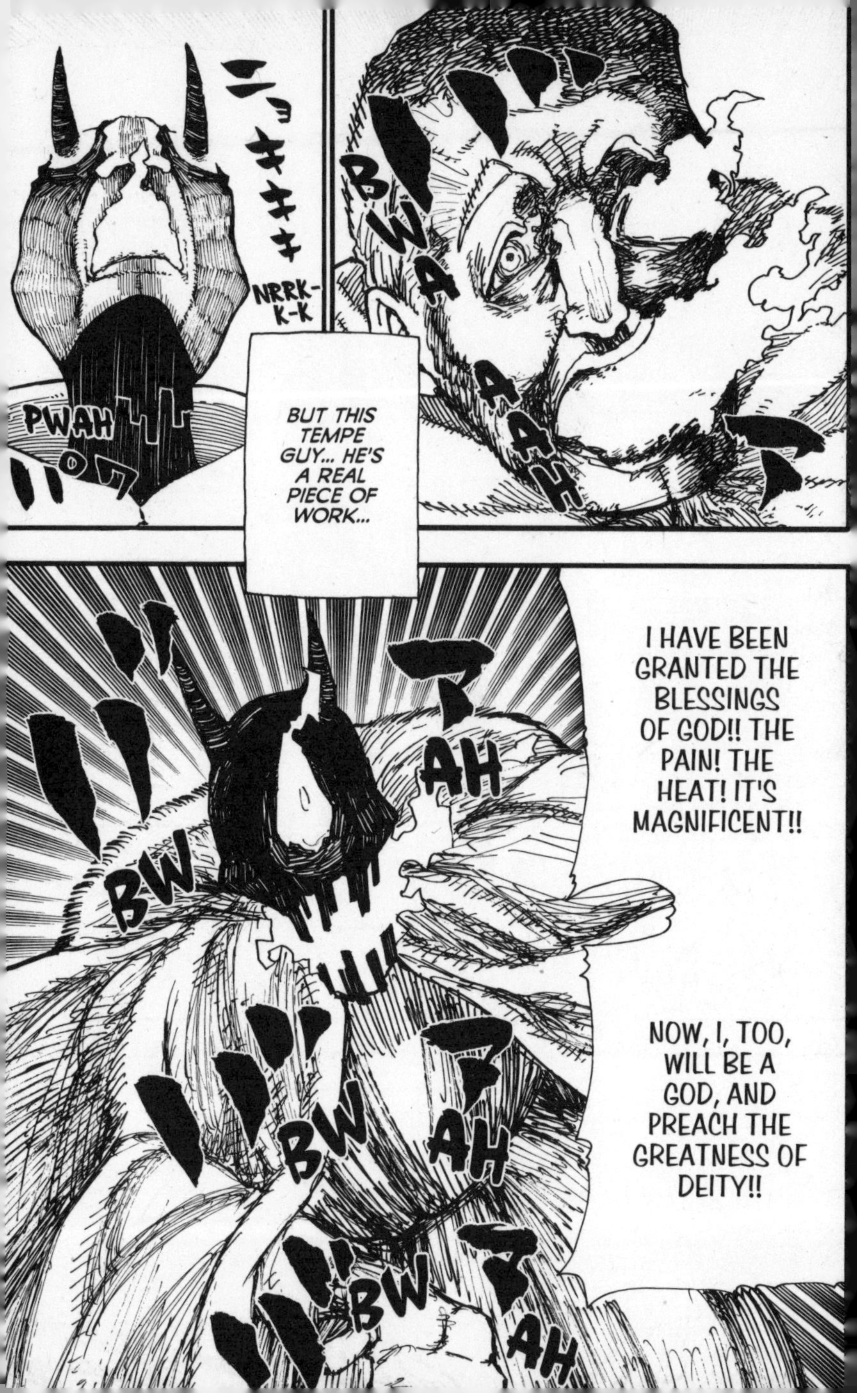
BWAAAAH
ニョキキキ
NRRK-K-K
PWAH
BUT THIS TEMPE GUY... HE'S A REAL PIECE OF WORK...
I HAVE BEEN GRANTED THE BLESSINGS OF GOD!! THE PAIN! THE HEAT! IT'S MAGNIFICENT!!
BW AH
NOW, I, TOO, WILL BE A GOD, AND PREACH THE GREATNESS OF DEITY!!
BW AH
BW AH

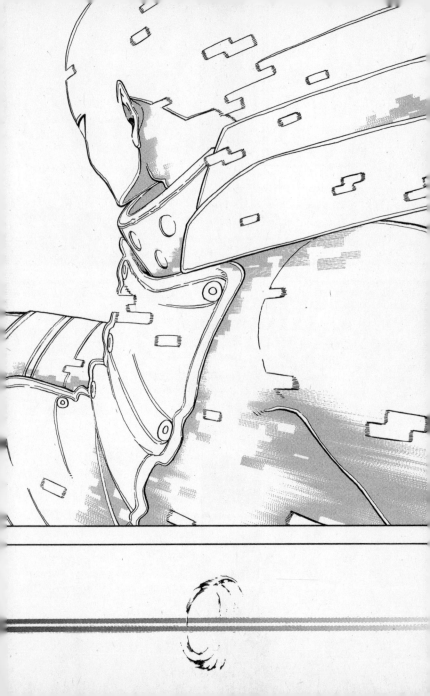

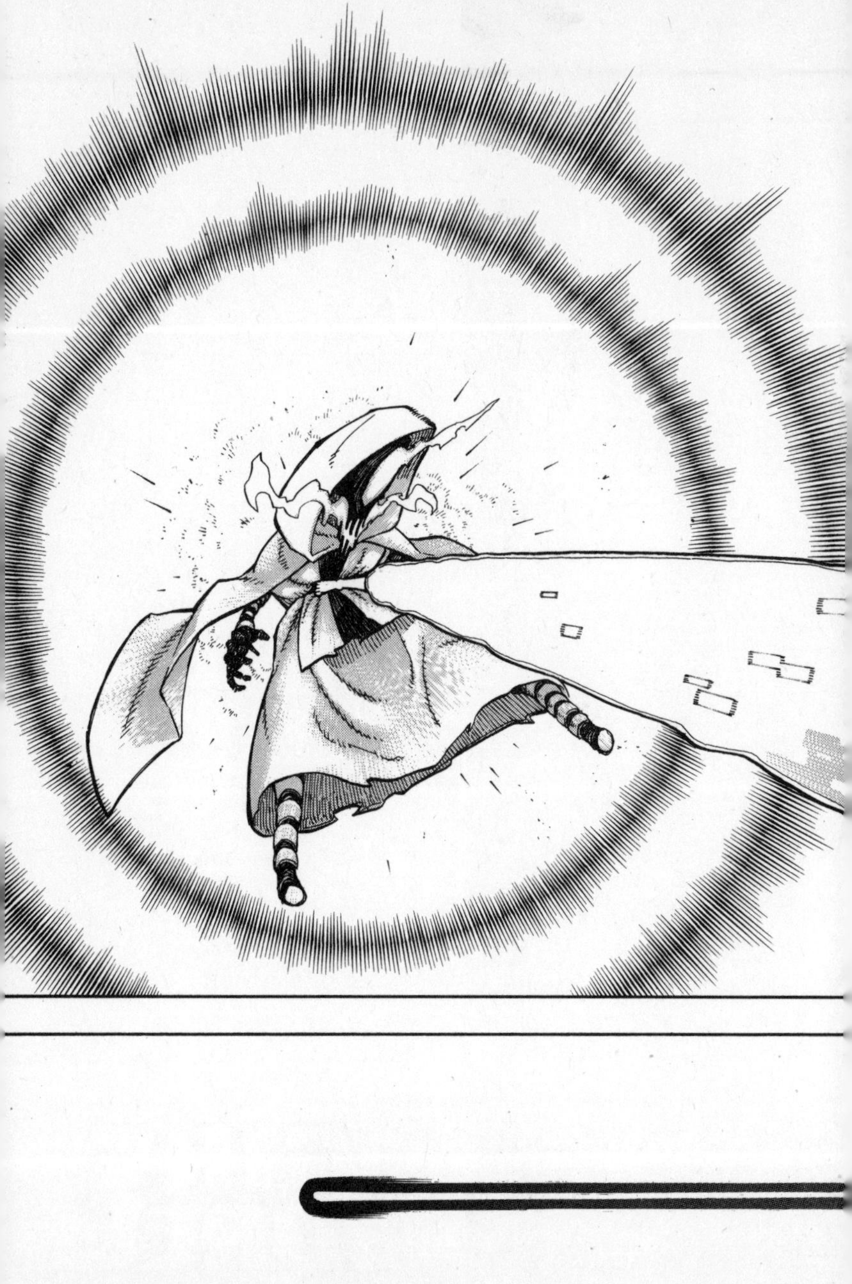

FIRE FORCE

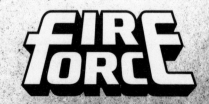

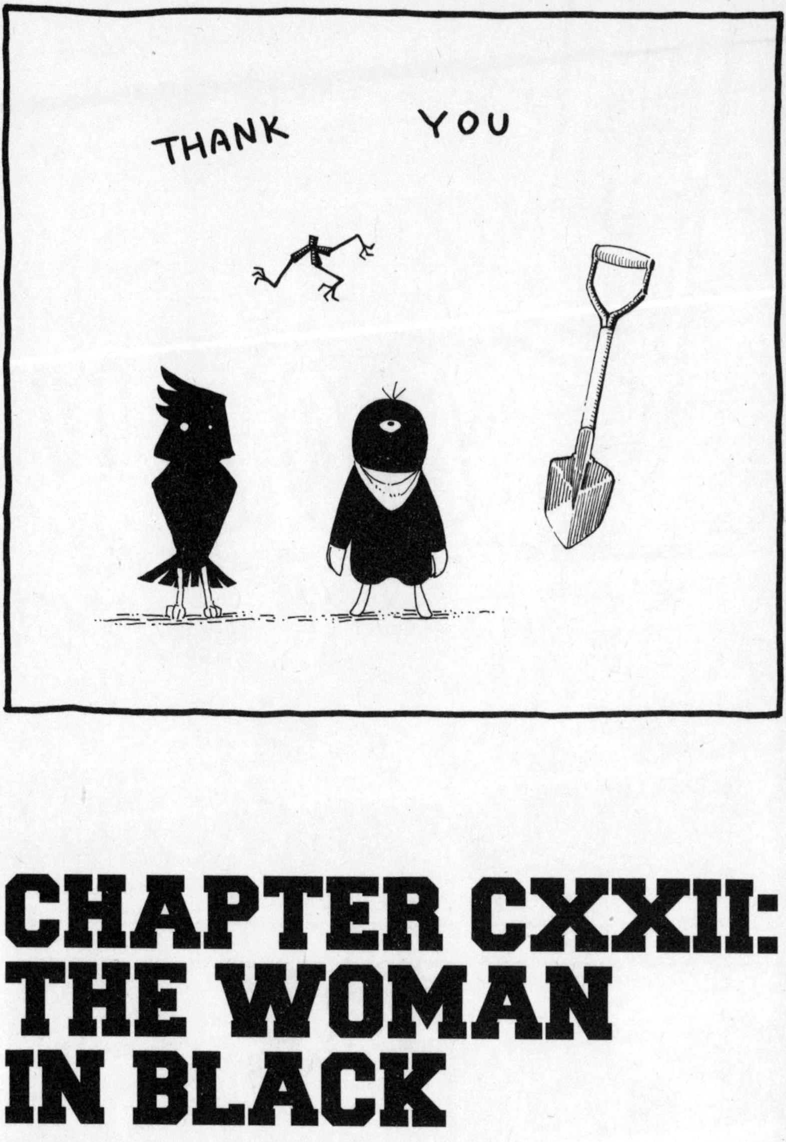
THANK
YOU

CHAPTER CXXII: THE WOMAN IN BLACK

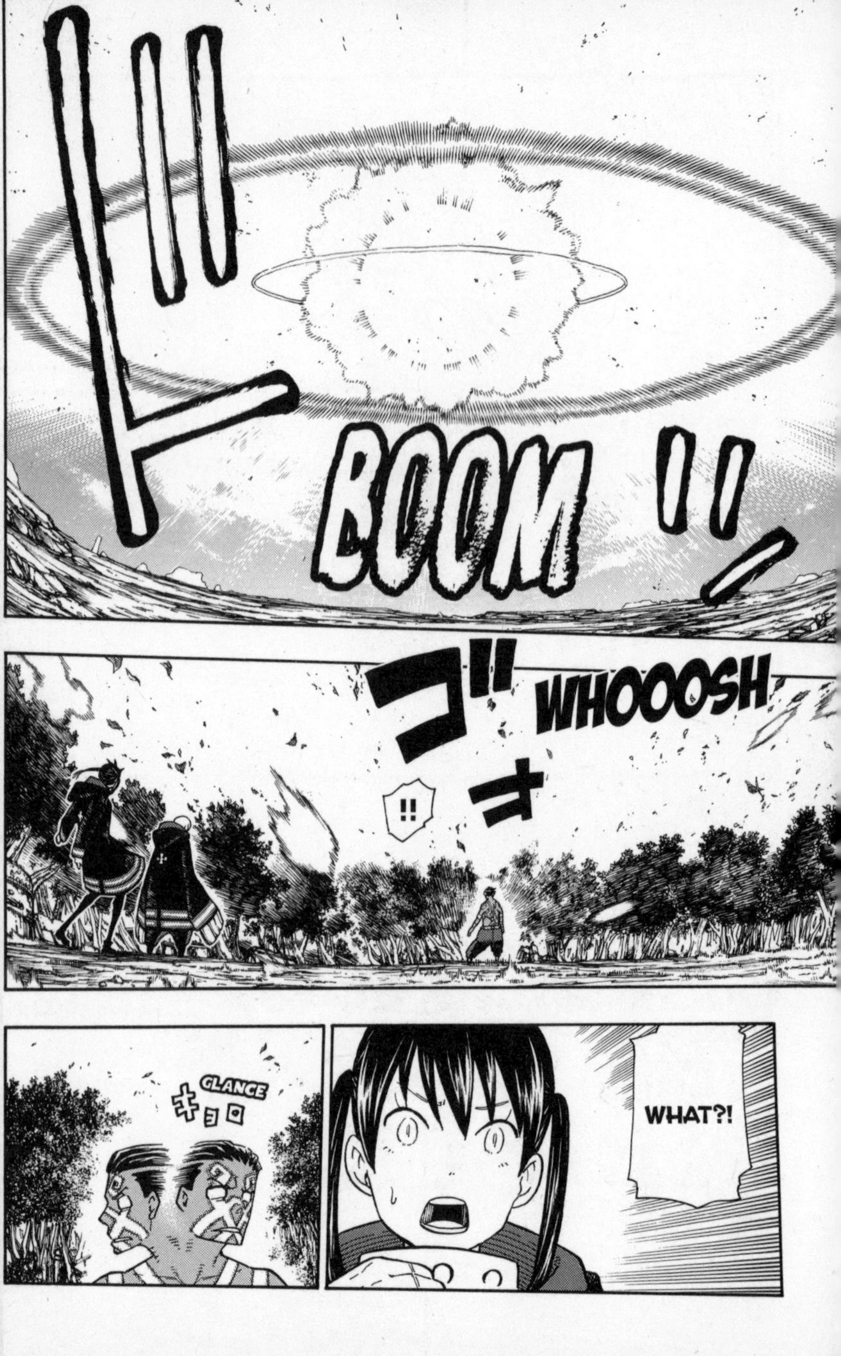

BOOM!!
WHOOOSH
!!
WHAT?!
GLANCE

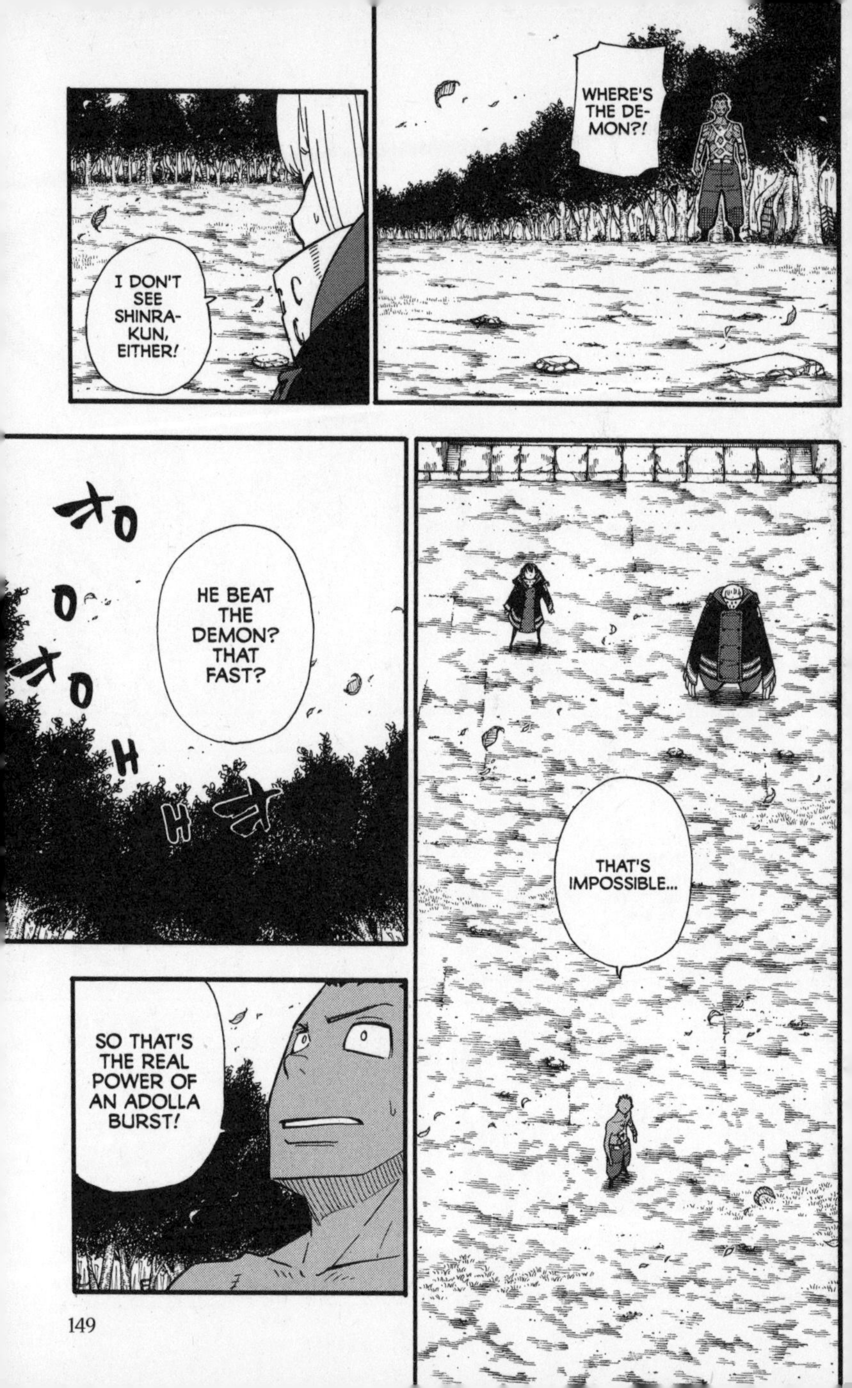
WHERE'S THE DE-MON?!
I DON'T SEE SHINRA-KUN, EITHER!
THAT'S IMPOSSIBLE...
HE BEAT THE DEMON? THAT FAST?
SO THAT'S THE REAL POWER OF AN ADOLLA BURST!

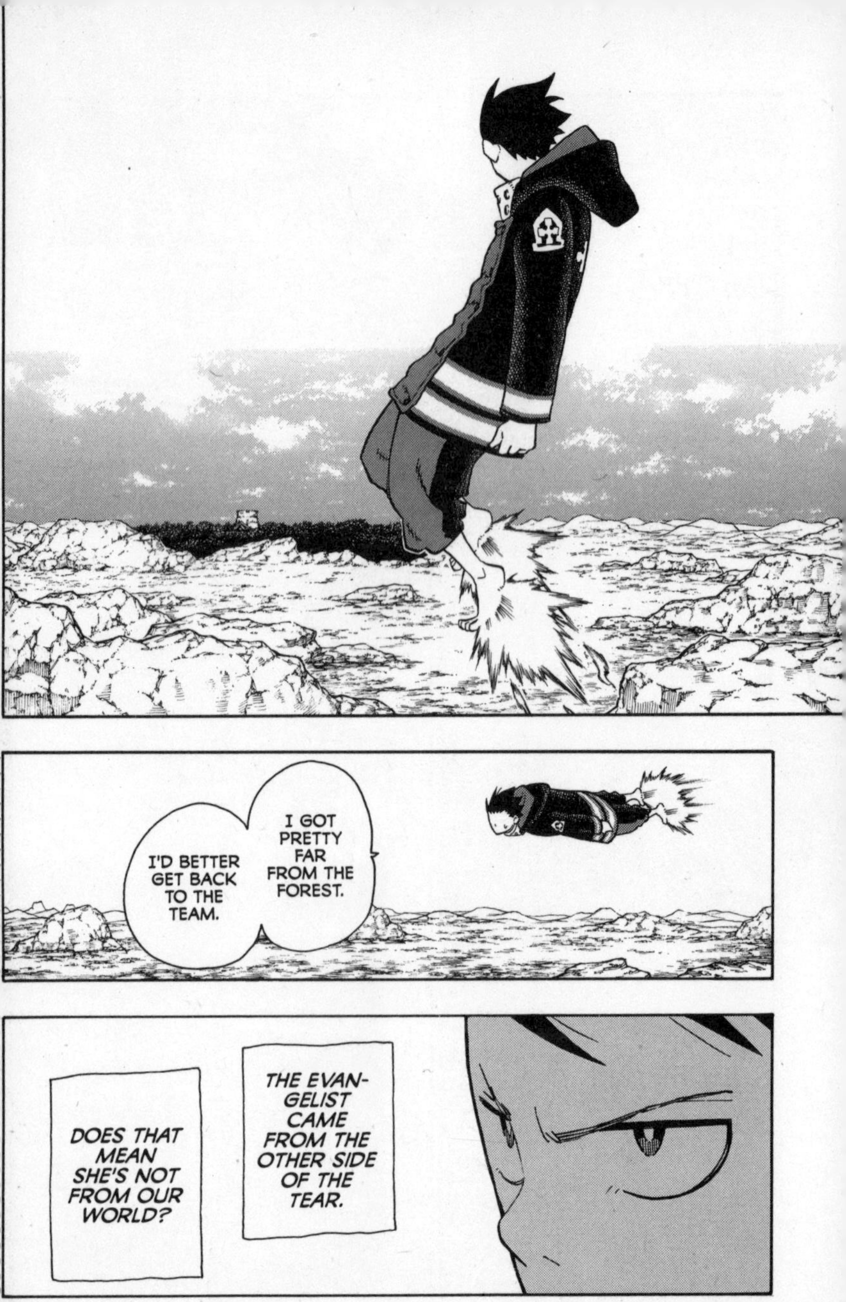
I GOT PRETTY FAR FROM THE FOREST.
I'D BETTER GET BACK TO THE TEAM.
THE EVAN-GELIST CAME FROM THE OTHER SIDE OF THE TEAR.
DOES THAT MEAN SHE'S NOT FROM OUR WORLD?

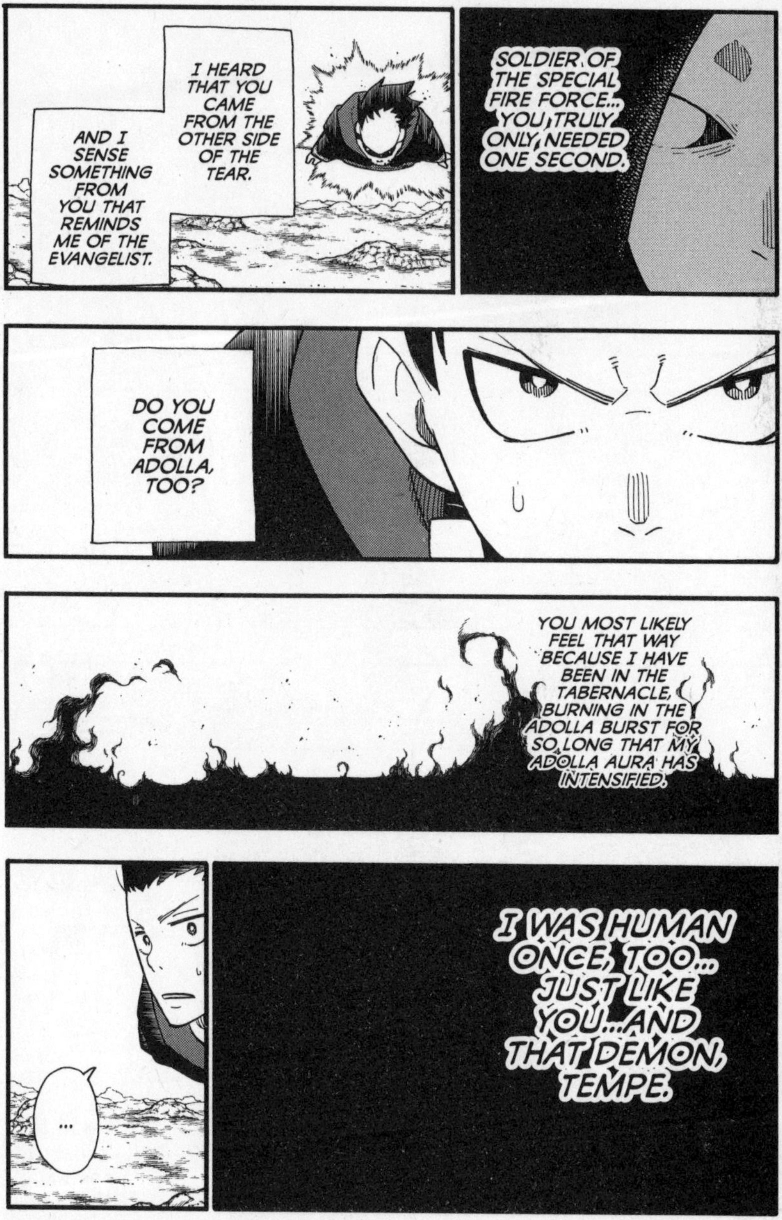
SOLDIER OF THE SPECIAL FIRE FORCE... YOU TRULY ONLY NEEDED ONE SECOND.
I HEARD THAT YOU CAME FROM THE OTHER SIDE OF THE TEAR.
AND I SENSE SOMETHING FROM YOU THAT REMINDS ME OF THE EVANGELIST.
DO YOU COME FROM ADOLLA, TOO?
YOU MOST LIKELY FEEL THAT WAY BECAUSE I HAVE BEEN IN THE TABERNACLE, BURNING IN THE ADOLLA BURST FOR SO LONG THAT MY ADOLLA AURA HAS INTENSIFIED.
I WAS HUMAN ONCE, TOO... JUST LIKE YOU...AND THAT DEMON, TEMPE.
...

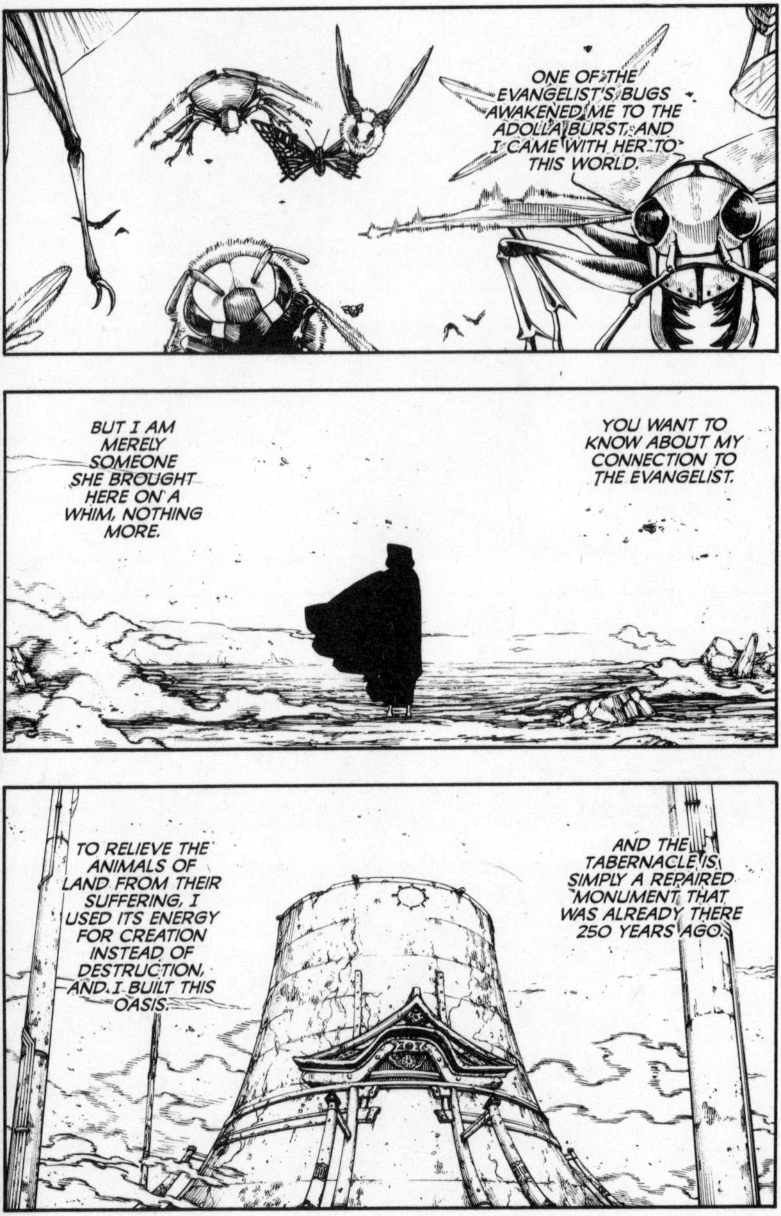

ONE OF THE EVANGELIST'S BUGS AWAKENED ME TO THE ADOLLA BURST, AND I CAME WITH HER TO THIS WORLD.
YOU WANT TO KNOW ABOUT MY CONNECTION TO THE EVANGELIST.
BUT I AM MERELY SOMEONE SHE BROUGHT HERE ON A WHIM, NOTHING MORE.
AND THE TABERNACLE IS SIMPLY A REPAIRED MONUMENT THAT WAS ALREADY THERE 250 YEARS AGO.
TO RELIEVE THE ANIMALS OF LAND FROM THEIR SUFFERING, I USED ITS ENERGY FOR CREATION INSTEAD OF DESTRUCTION, AND I BUILT THIS OASIS.

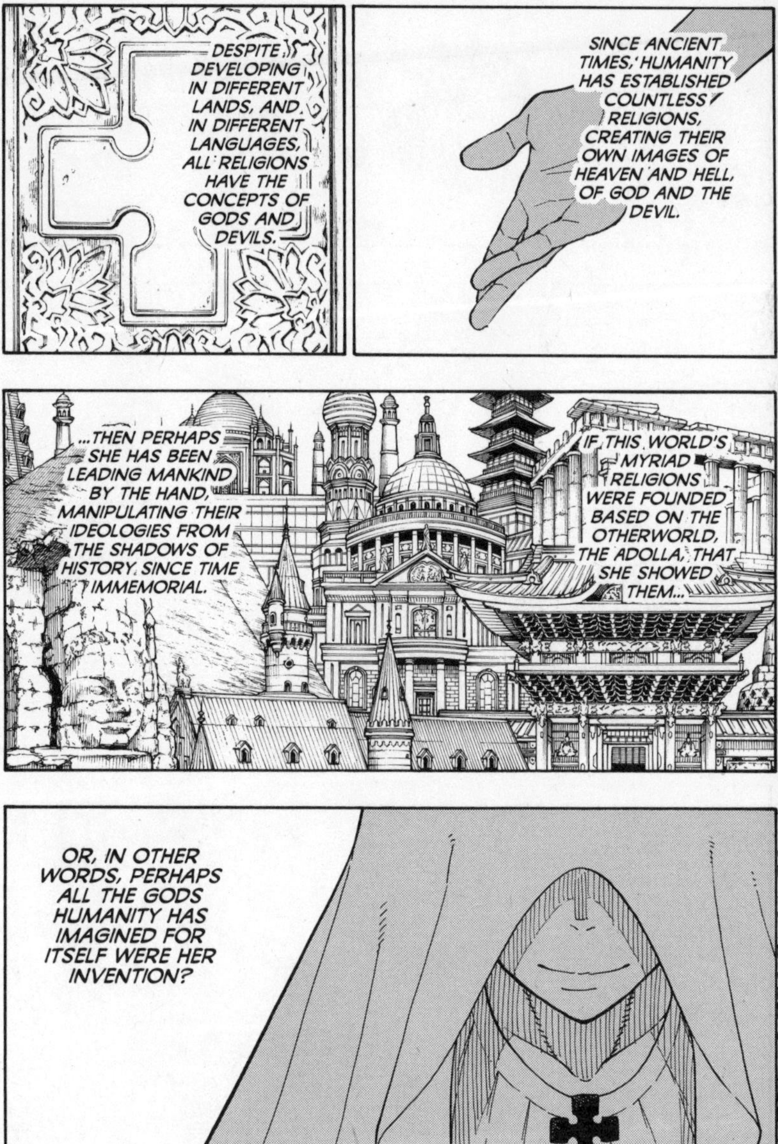
SINCE ANCIENT TIMES, HUMANITY HAS ESTABLISHED COUNTLESS RELIGIONS, CREATING THEIR OWN IMAGES OF HEAVEN AND HELL, OF GOD AND THE DEVIL.
DESPITE DEVELOPING IN DIFFERENT LANDS, AND IN DIFFERENT LANGUAGES, ALL RELIGIONS HAVE THE CONCEPTS OF GODS AND DEVILS.
IF THIS WORLD'S MYRIAD RELIGIONS WERE FOUNDED BASED ON THE OTHERWORLD, THE ADOLLA, THAT SHE SHOWED THEM...
...THEN PERHAPS SHE HAS BEEN LEADING MANKIND BY THE HAND, MANIPULATING THEIR IDEOLOGIES FROM THE SHADOWS OF HISTORY SINCE TIME IMMEMORIAL.
OR, IN OTHER WORDS, PERHAPS ALL THE GODS HUMANITY HAS IMAGINED FOR ITSELF WERE HER INVENTION?

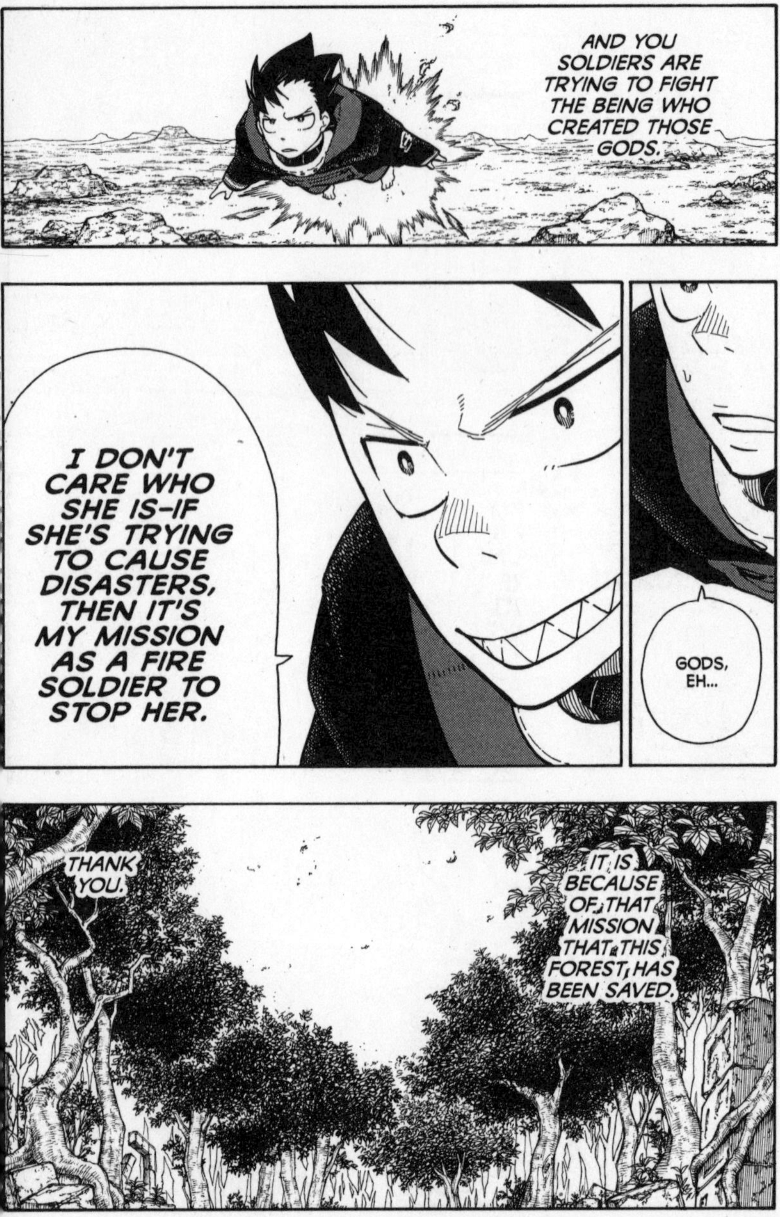
AND YOU SOLDIERS ARE TRYING TO FIGHT THE BEING WHO CREATED THOSE GODS.
GODS, EH...
I DON'T CARE WHO SHE IS–IF SHE'S TRYING TO CAUSE DISASTERS, THEN IT'S MY MISSION AS A FIRE SOLDIER TO STOP HER.
IT IS BECAUSE OF THAT MISSION THAT THIS FOREST HAS BEEN SAVED.
THANK YOU.

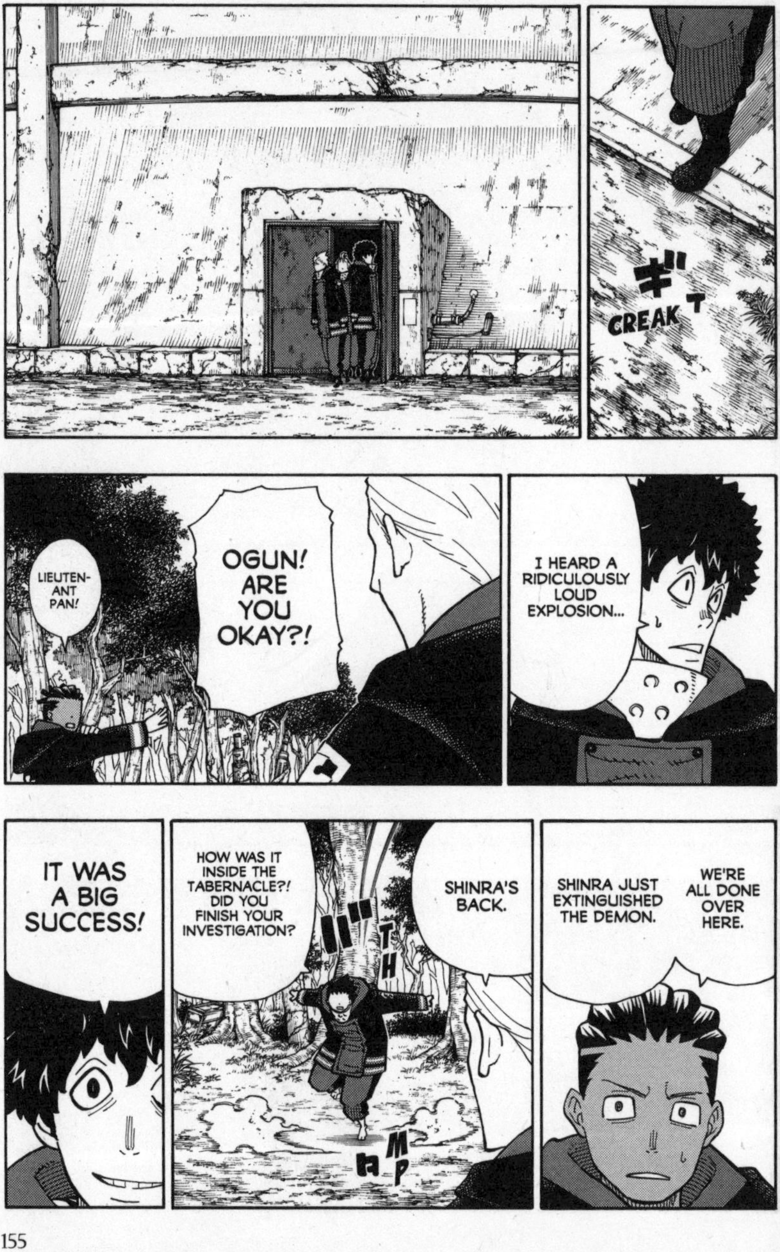
CREAK
I HEARD A RIDICULOUSLY LOUD EXPLOSION...
OGUN! ARE YOU OKAY?!
LIEUTEN-ANT PAN!
WE'RE ALL DONE OVER HERE.
SHINRA JUST EXTINGUISHED THE DEMON.
SHINRA'S BACK.
HOW WAS IT INSIDE THE TABERNACLE?! DID YOU FINISH YOUR INVESTIGATION?
IT WAS A BIG SUCCESS!

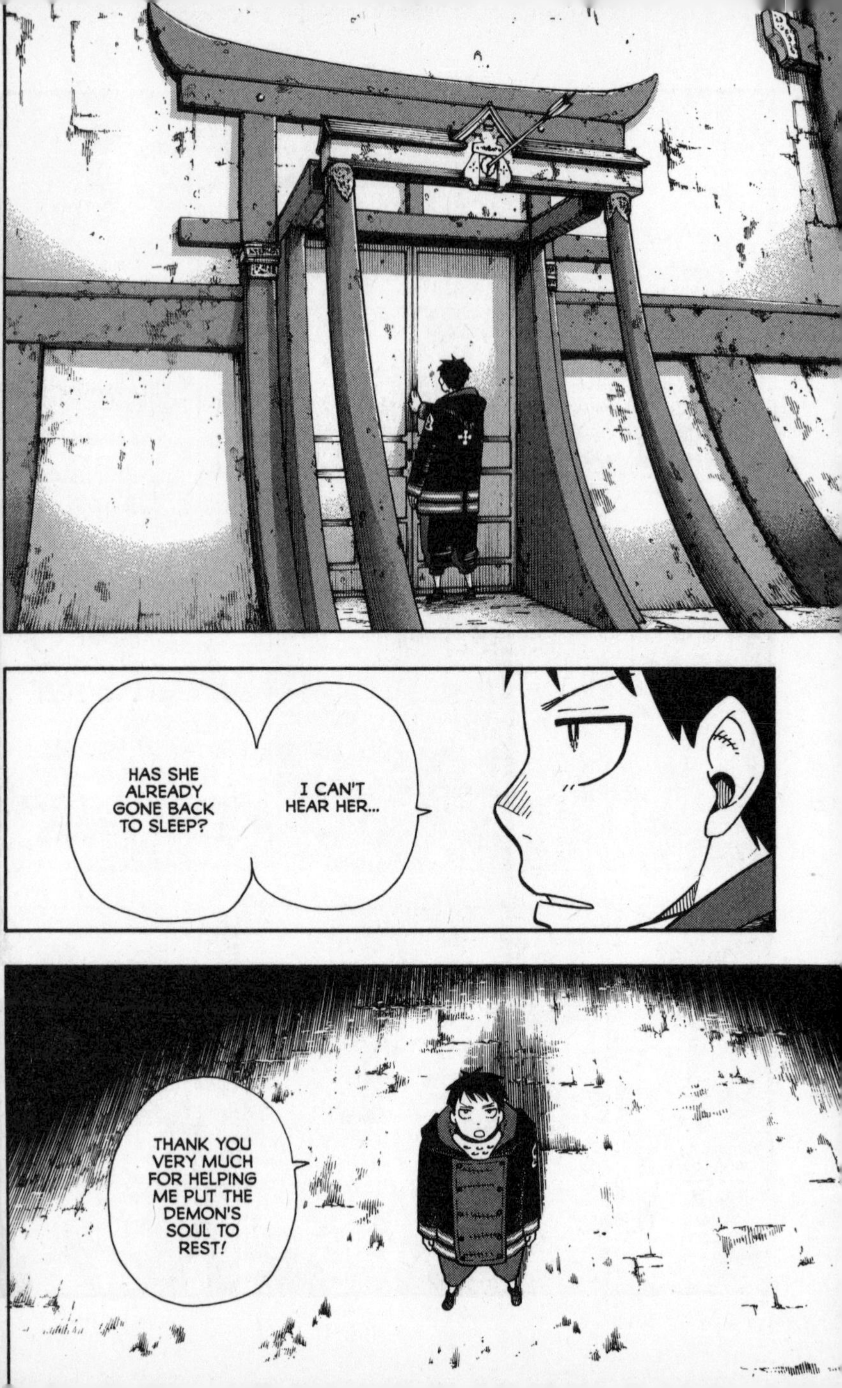
I CAN'T HEAR HER...
HAS SHE ALREADY GONE BACK TO SLEEP?
THANK YOU VERY MUCH FOR HELPING ME PUT THE DEMON'S SOUL TO REST!

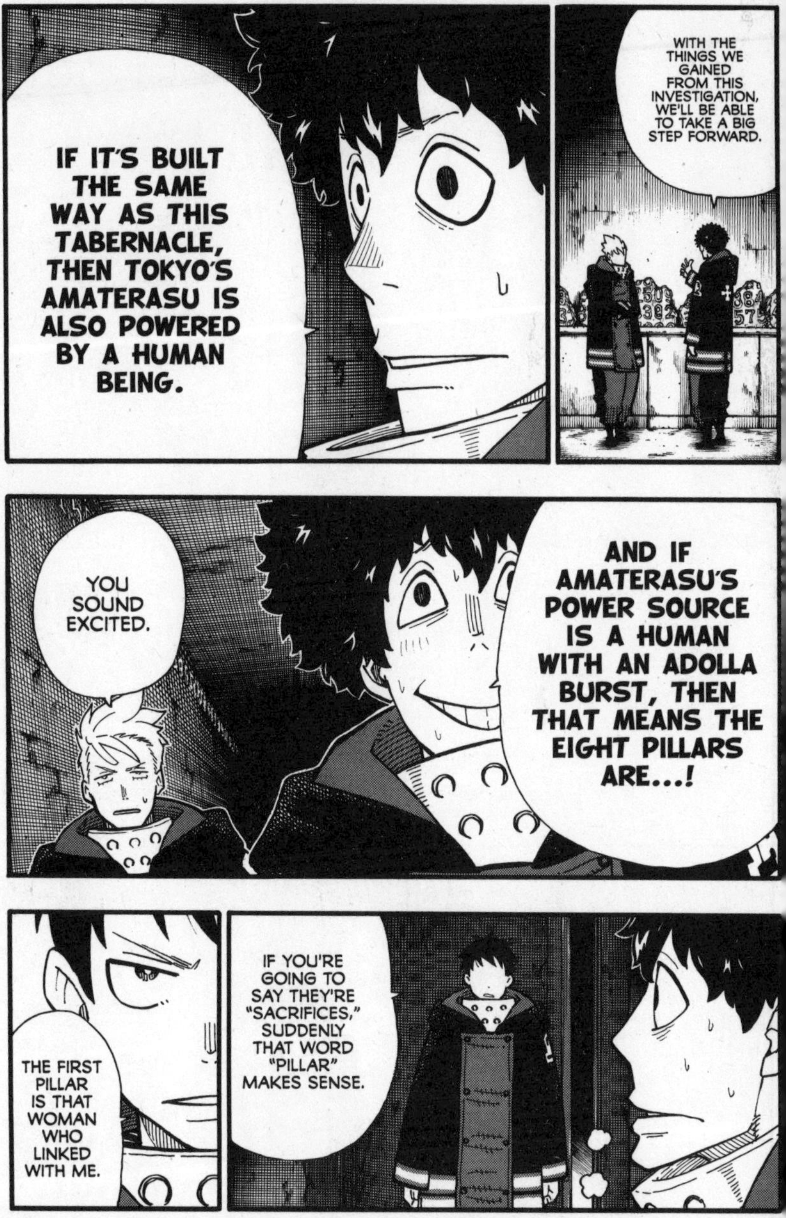
WITH THE THINGS WE GAINED FROM THIS INVESTIGATION, WE'LL BE ABLE TO TAKE A BIG STEP FORWARD.
IF IT'S BUILT THE SAME WAY AS THIS TABERNACLE, THEN TOKYO'S AMATERASU IS ALSO POWERED BY A HUMAN BEING.
AND IF AMATERASU'S POWER SOURCE IS A HUMAN WITH AN ADOLLA BURST, THEN THAT MEANS THE EIGHT PILLARS ARE...!
YOU SOUND EXCITED.
IF YOU'RE GOING TO SAY THEY'RE "SACRIFICES," SUDDENLY THAT WORD "PILLAR" MAKES SENSE.
THE FIRST PILLAR IS THAT WOMAN WHO LINKED WITH ME.

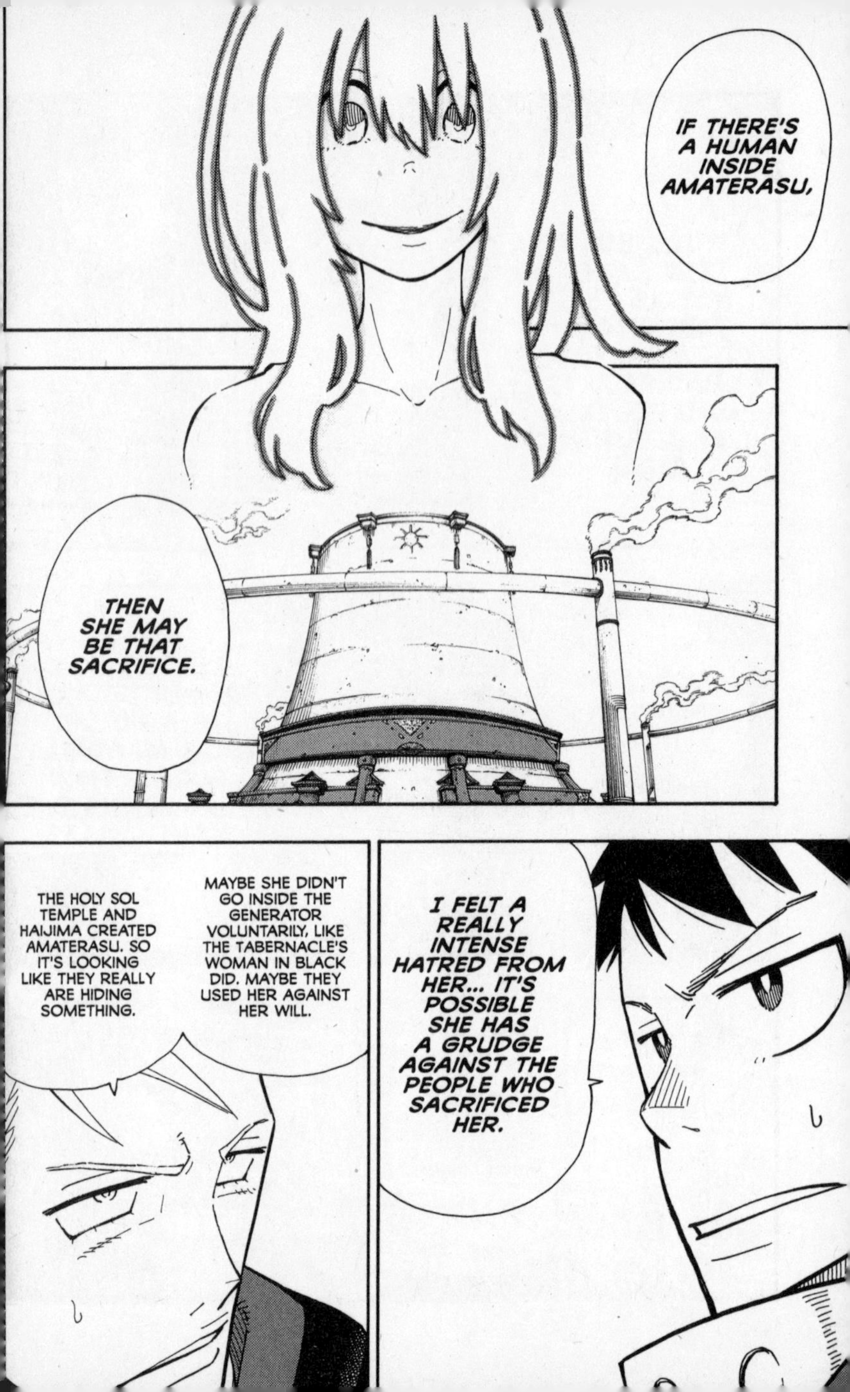
IF THERE'S A HUMAN INSIDE AMATERASU,
THEN SHE MAY BE THAT SACRIFICE.
I FELT A REALLY INTENSE HATRED FROM HER... IT'S POSSIBLE SHE HAS A GRUDGE AGAINST THE PEOPLE WHO SACRIFICED HER.
MAYBE SHE DIDN'T GO INSIDE THE GENERATOR VOLUNTARILY, LIKE THE TABERNACLE'S WOMAN IN BLACK DID. MAYBE THEY USED HER AGAINST HER WILL.
THE HOLY SOL TEMPLE AND HAIJIMA CREATED AMATERASU. SO IT'S LOOKING LIKE THEY REALLY ARE HIDING SOMETHING.

THE EIGHT ARROWS IN THE HEART OF THE TABERNACLE...

I'M GUESSING THEY'RE SOME KIND OF KEY.

THAT FLASH DRIVE DR. GIOVANNI TOOK FROM VULCAN.

MAYBE IT HAS DATA ON IT RELATED TO AMATERASU'S VERSION OF THOSE ARROWS.

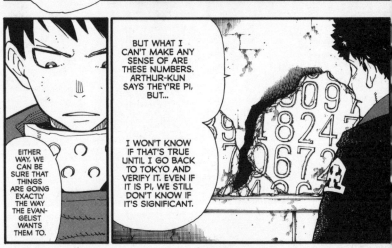

BUT WHAT I CAN'T MAKE ANY SENSE OF ARE THESE NUMBERS. ARTHUR-KUN SAYS THEY'RE PI, BUT...

I WON'T KNOW IF THAT'S TRUE UNTIL I GO BACK TO TOKYO AND VERIFY IT. EVEN IF IT IS PI, WE STILL DON'T KNOW IF IT'S SIGNIFICANT.

EITHER WAY, WE CAN BE SURE THAT THINGS ARE GOING EXACTLY THE WAY THE EVANGELIST WANTS THEM TO.

159

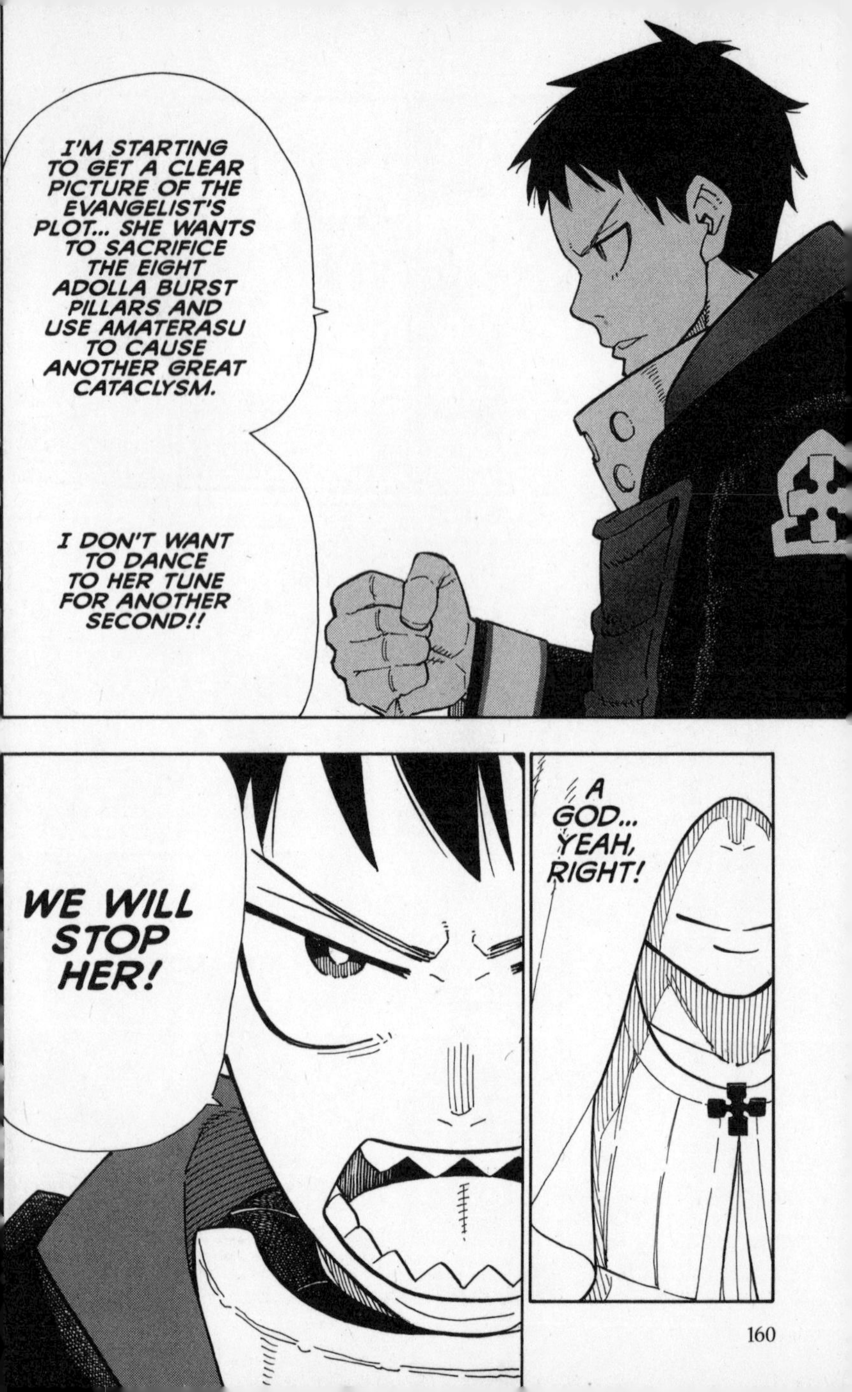
I'M STARTING TO GET A CLEAR PICTURE OF THE EVANGELIST'S PLOT... SHE WANTS TO SACRIFICE THE EIGHT ADOLLA BURST PILLARS AND USE AMATERASU TO CAUSE ANOTHER GREAT CATACLYSM.
I DON'T WANT TO DANCE TO HER TUNE FOR ANOTHER SECOND!!
A GOD... YEAH, RIGHT!
WE WILL STOP HER!

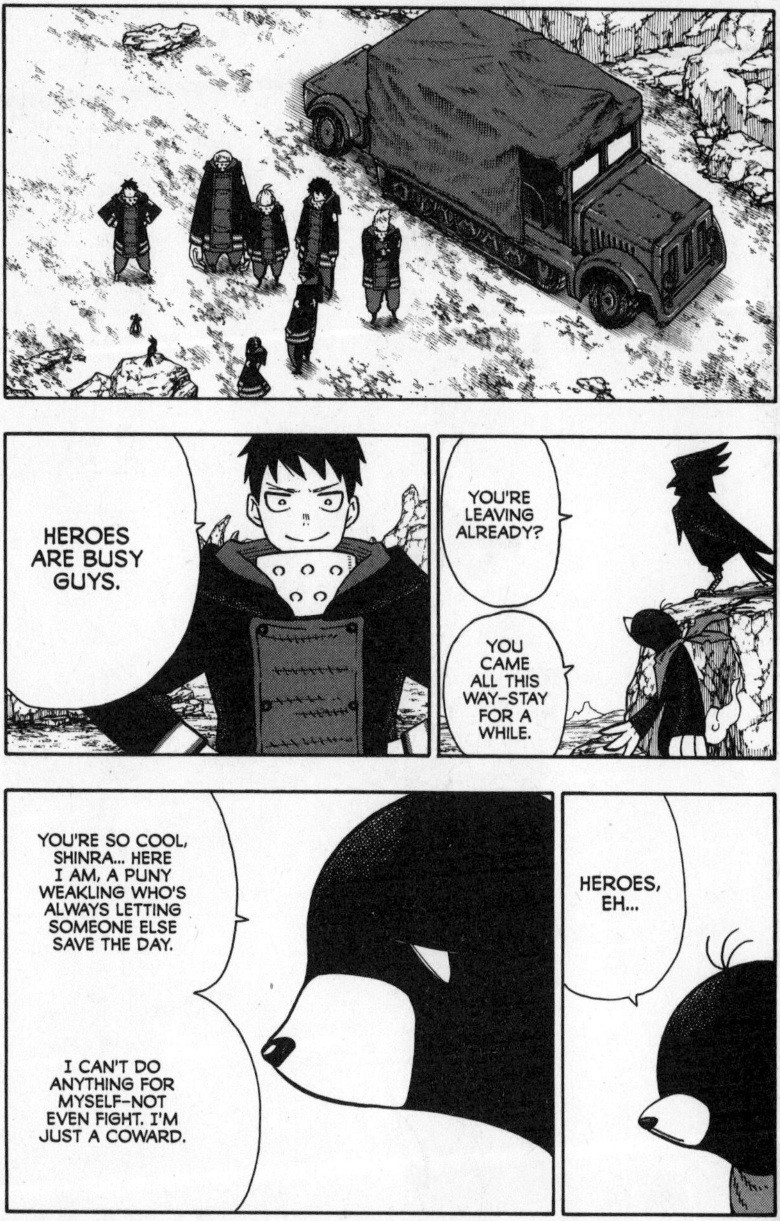
YOU'RE LEAVING ALREADY?
YOU CAME ALL THIS WAY—STAY FOR A WHILE.
HEROES ARE BUSY GUYS.
HEROES, EH...
YOU'RE SO COOL, SHINRA... HERE I AM, A PUNY WEAKLING WHO'S ALWAYS LETTING SOMEONE ELSE SAVE THE DAY.
I CAN'T DO ANYTHING FOR MYSELF—NOT EVEN FIGHT. I'M JUST A COWARD.

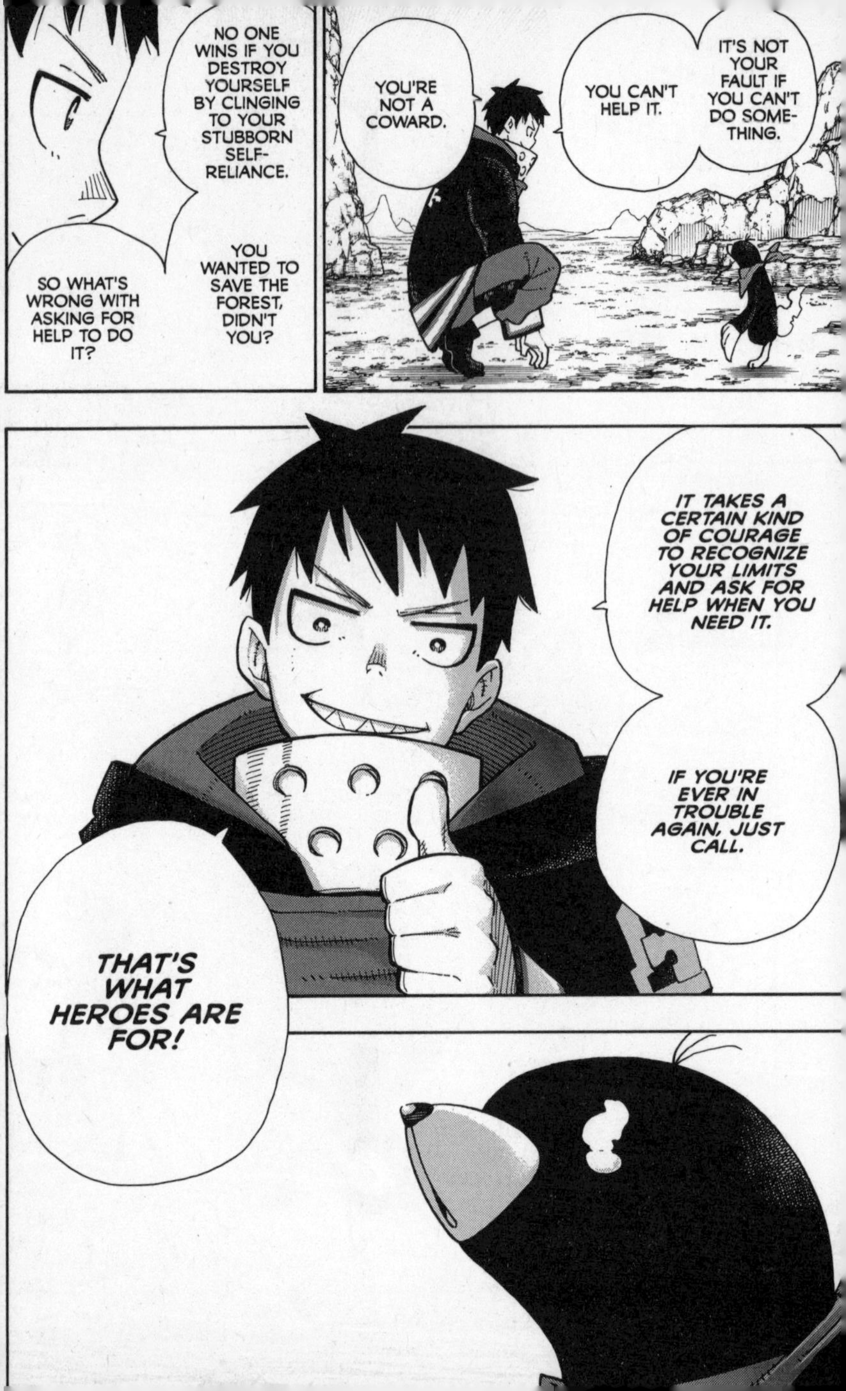
IT'S NOT YOUR FAULT IF YOU CAN'T DO SOME-THING.
YOU CAN'T HELP IT.
YOU'RE NOT A COWARD.
NO ONE WINS IF YOU DESTROY YOURSELF BY CLINGING TO YOUR STUBBORN SELF-RELIANCE.
YOU WANTED TO SAVE THE FOREST, DIDN'T YOU?
SO WHAT'S WRONG WITH ASKING FOR HELP TO DO IT?
IT TAKES A CERTAIN KIND OF COURAGE TO RECOGNIZE YOUR LIMITS AND ASK FOR HELP WHEN YOU NEED IT.
IF YOU'RE EVER IN TROUBLE AGAIN, JUST CALL.
THAT'S WHAT HEROES ARE FOR!

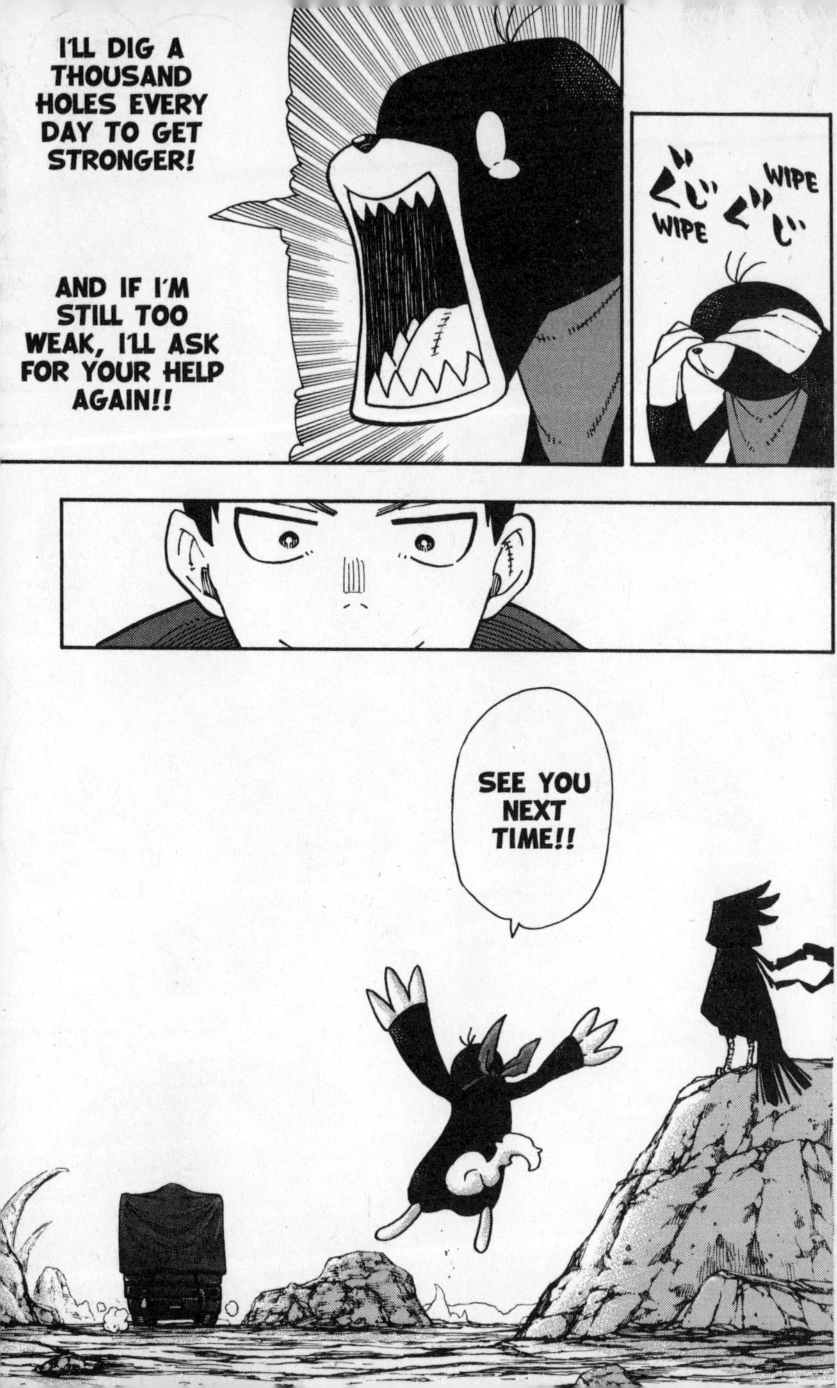
WIPE
WIPE
I'LL DIG A THOUSAND HOLES EVERY DAY TO GET STRONGER!
AND IF I'M STILL TOO WEAK, I'LL ASK FOR YOUR HELP AGAIN!!
SEE YOU NEXT TIME!!

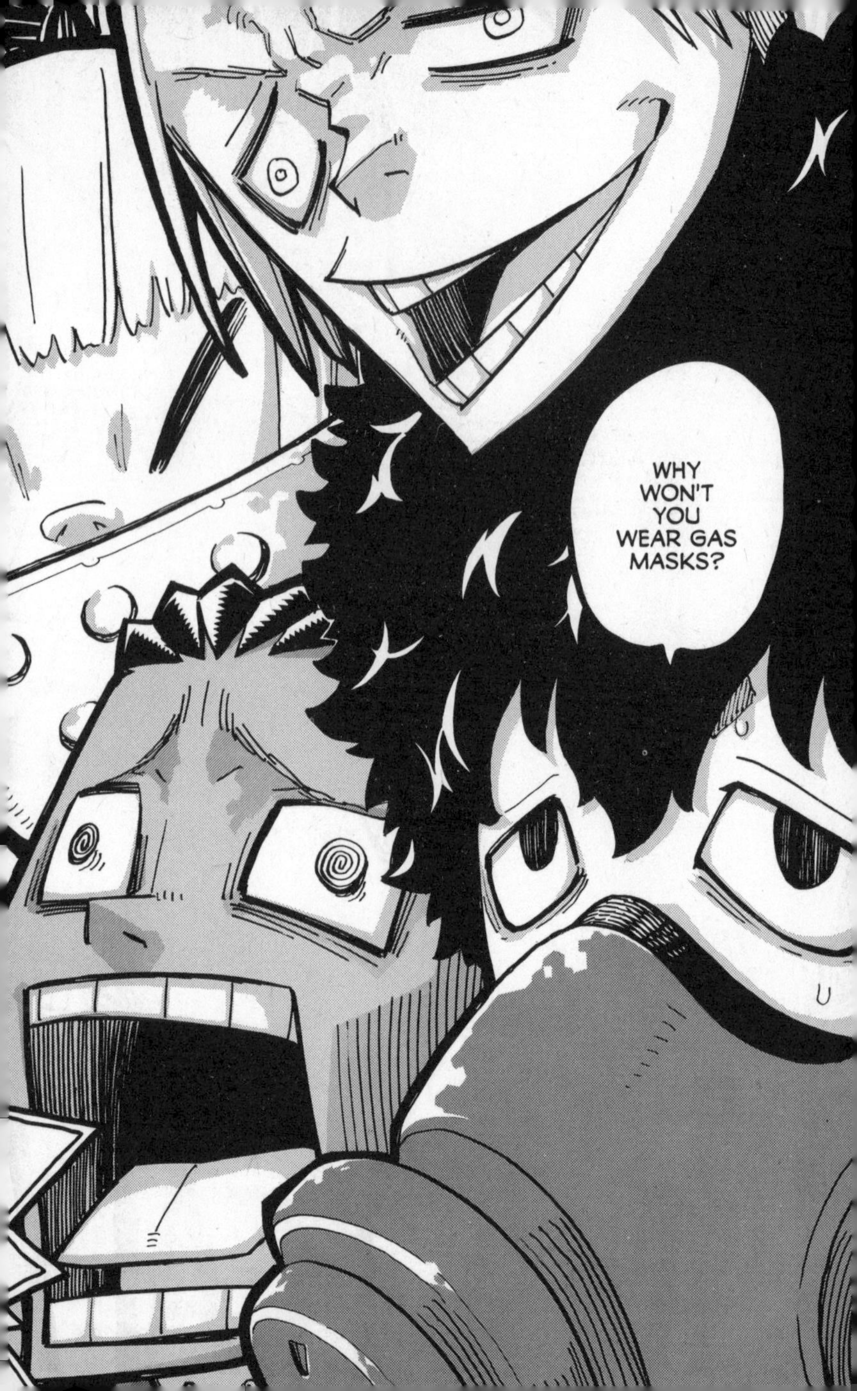
WHY WON'T YOU WEAR GAS MASKS?

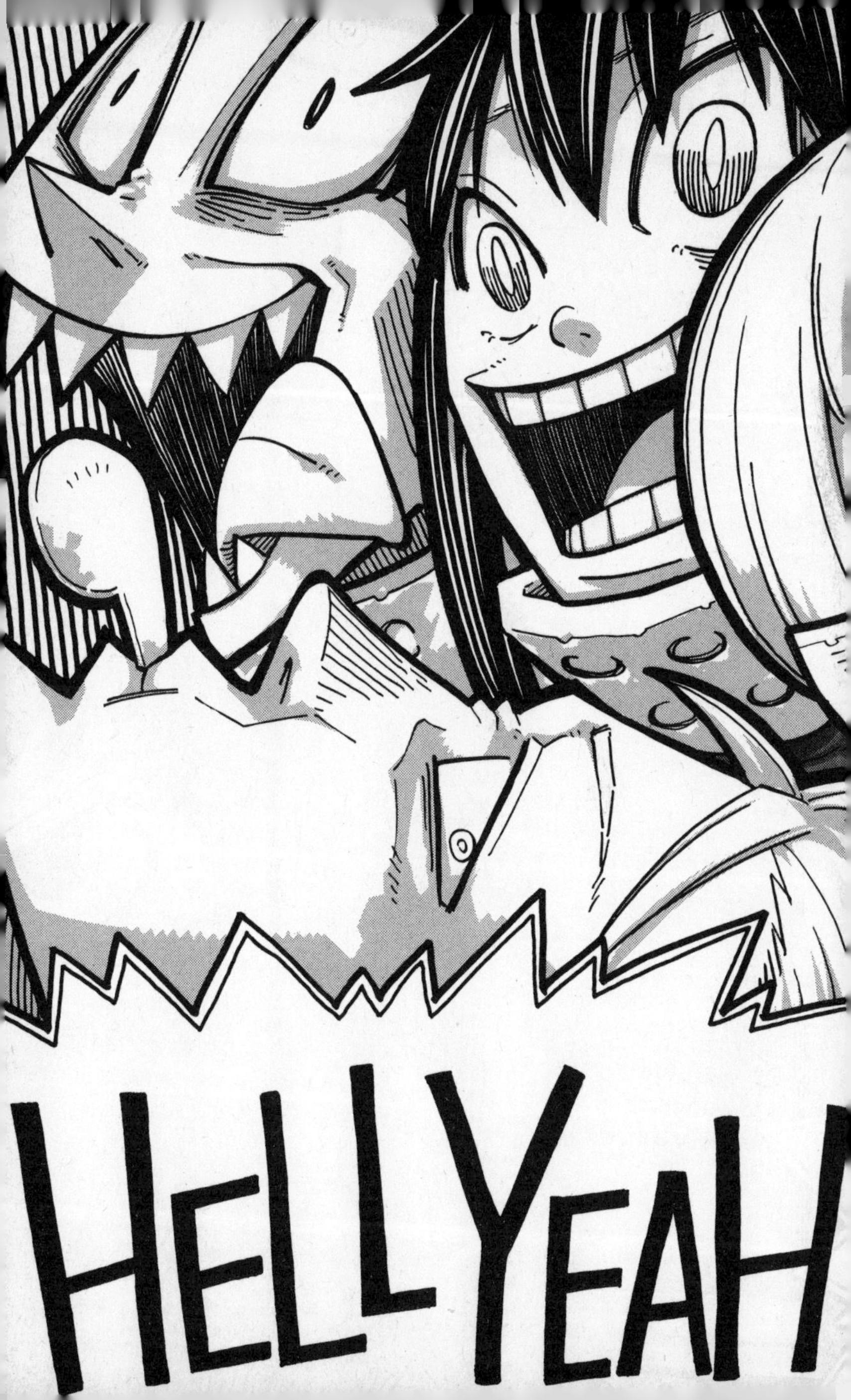
HELL YEAH

FIRE FORCE

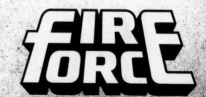

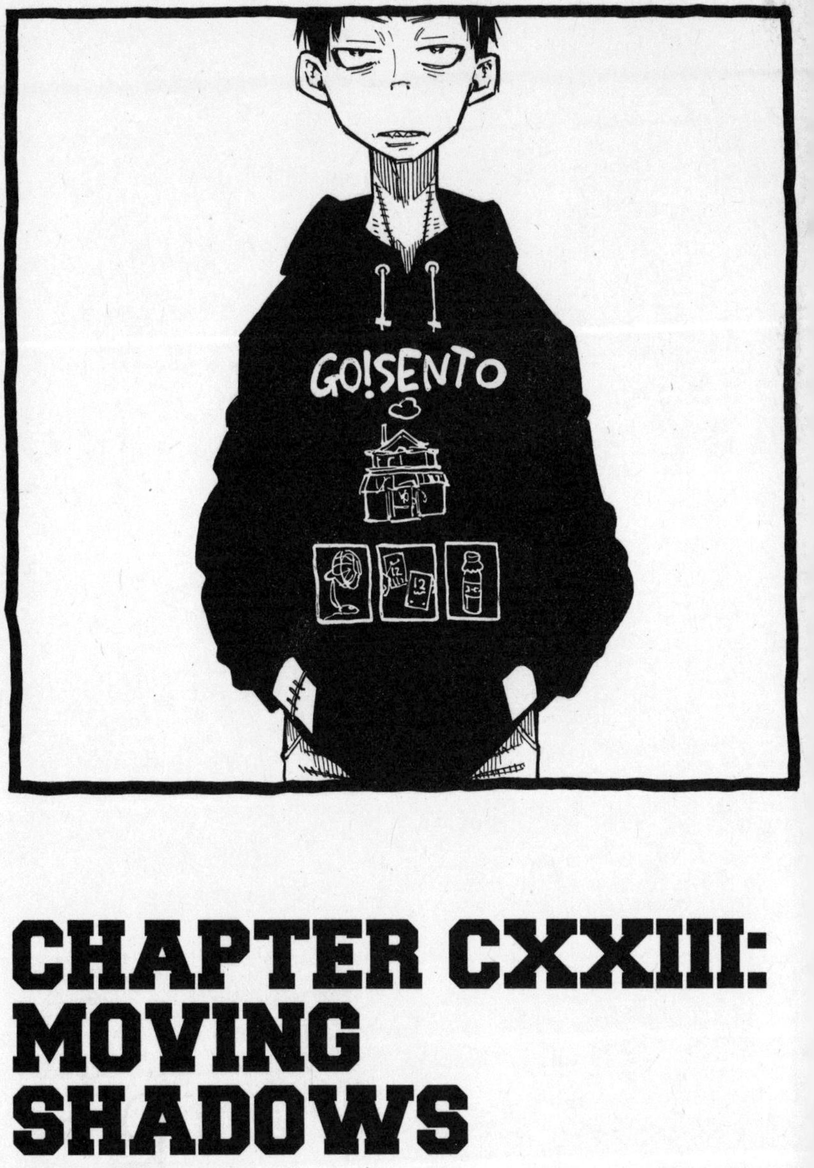
GO!SENTO

CHAPTER CXXIII: MOVING SHADOWS

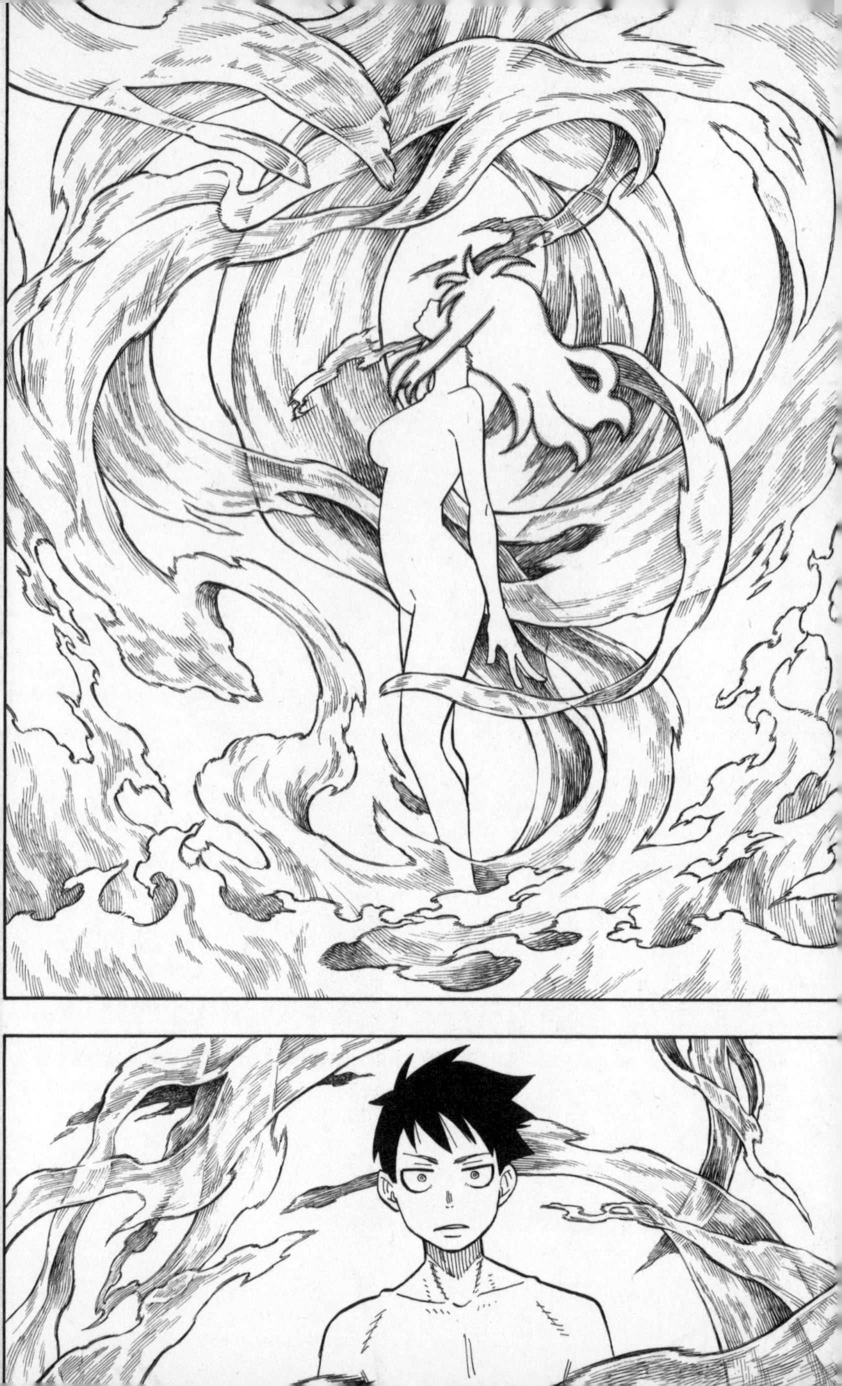

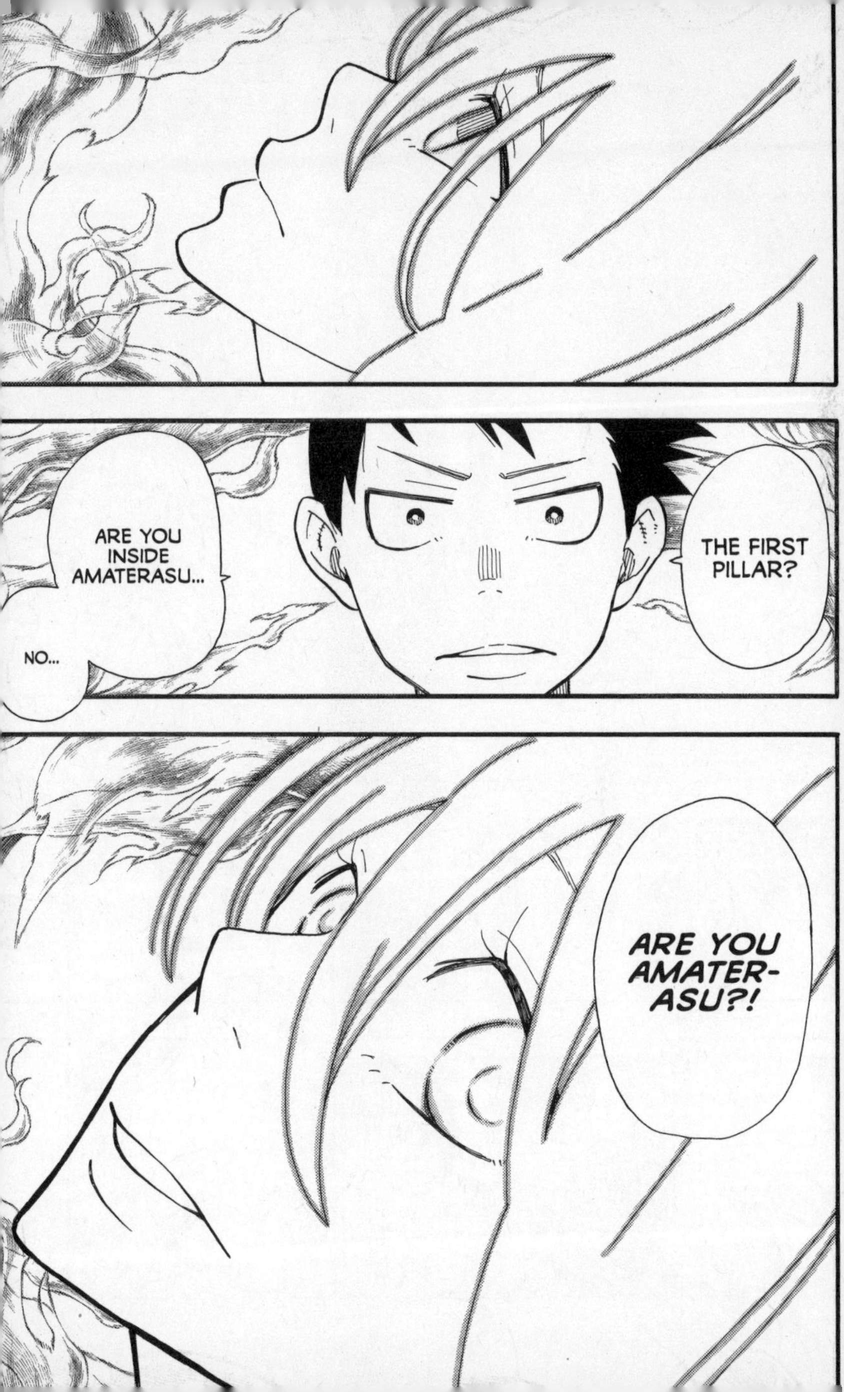
THE FIRST PILLAR?
ARE YOU INSIDE AMATERASU...
NO...
ARE YOU AMATER-ASU?!

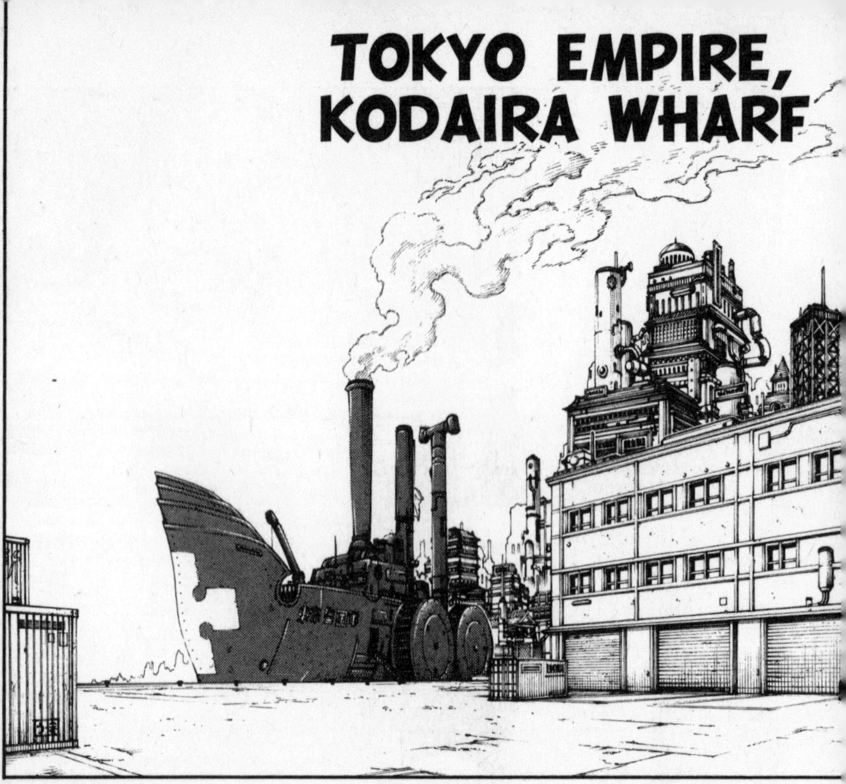
TOKYO EMPIRE, KODAIRA WHARF

Ship: Tokyo imperial Army

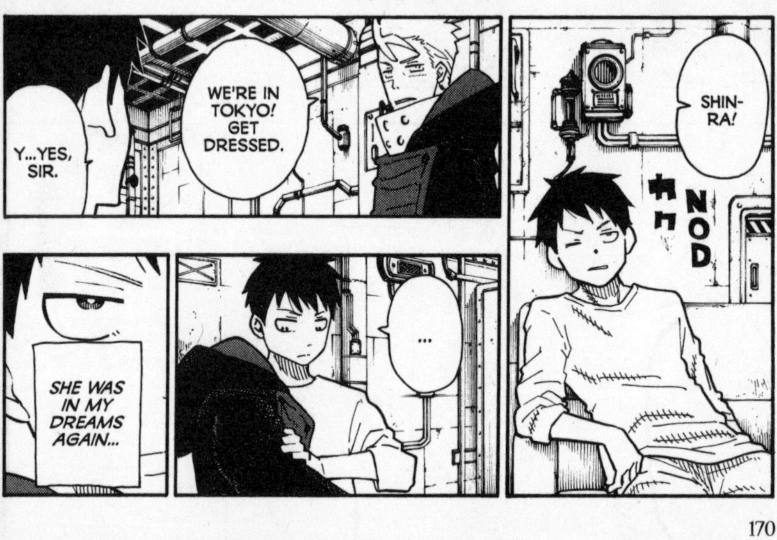
SHIN-RA!
NOD
WE'RE IN TOKYO! GET DRESSED.
Y...YES, SIR.
...
SHE WAS IN MY DREAMS AGAIN...

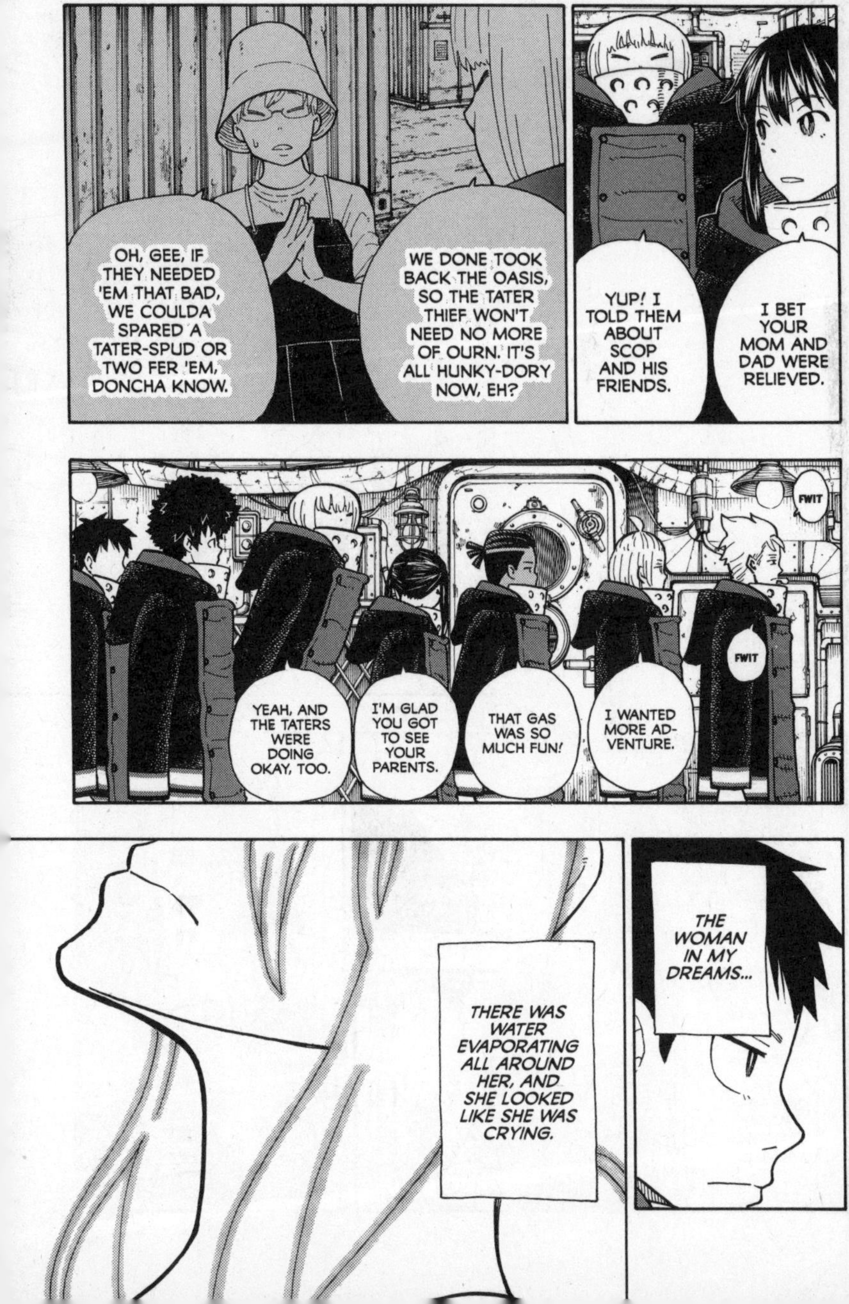
I BET YOUR MOM AND DAD WERE RELIEVED.
YUP! I TOLD THEM ABOUT SCOP AND HIS FRIENDS.
WE DONE TOOK BACK THE OASIS, SO THE TATER THIEF WON'T NEED NO MORE OF OURN. IT'S ALL HUNKY-DORY NOW, EH?
OH, GEE, IF THEY NEEDED 'EM THAT BAD, WE COULDA SPARED A TATER-SPUD OR TWO FER 'EM, DONCHA KNOW.
FWIT
FWIT
I WANTED MORE AD-VENTURE.
THAT GAS WAS SO MUCH FUN!
I'M GLAD YOU GOT TO SEE YOUR PARENTS.
YEAH, AND THE TATERS WERE DOING OKAY, TOO.
THE WOMAN IN MY DREAMS...
THERE WAS WATER EVAPORATING ALL AROUND HER, AND SHE LOOKED LIKE SHE WAS CRYING.

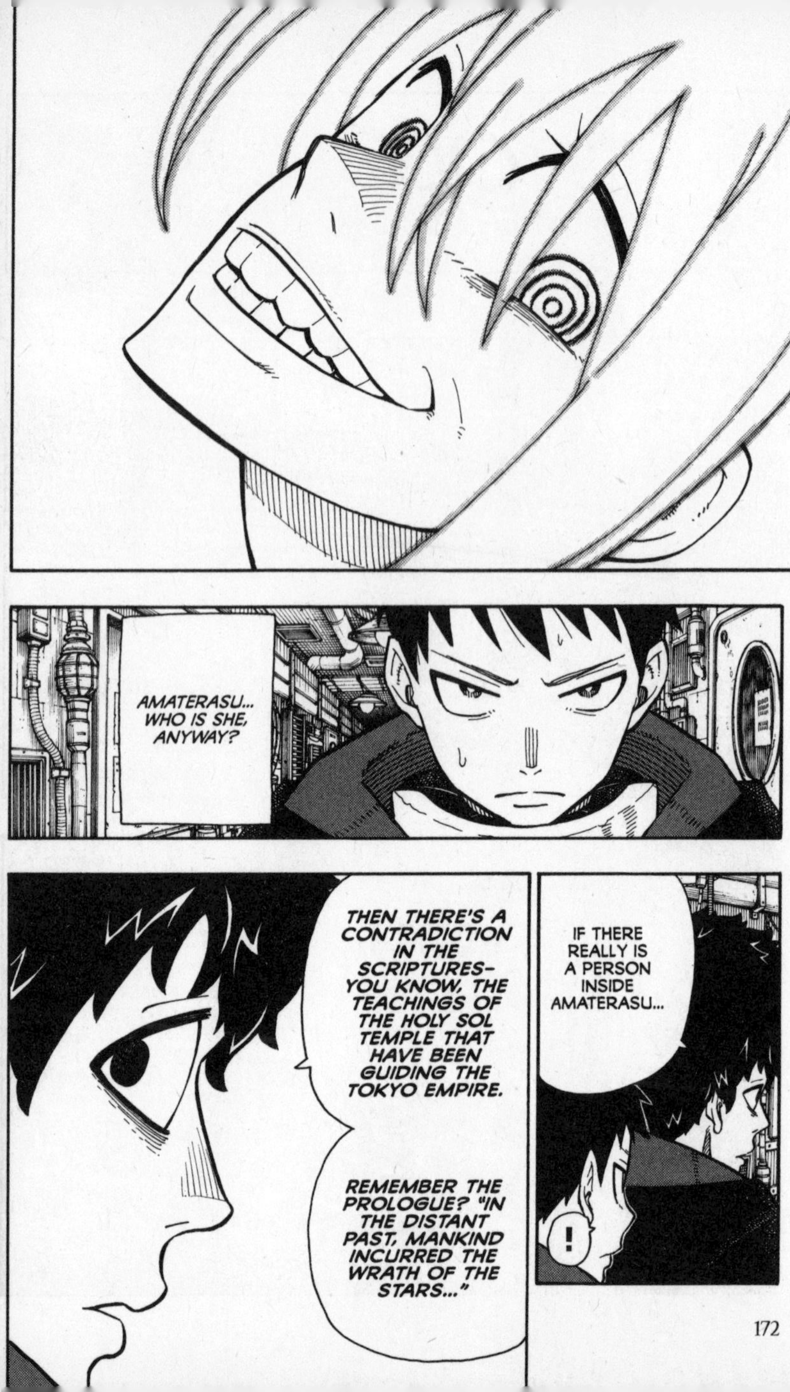
AMATERASU... WHO IS SHE, ANYWAY?
IF THERE REALLY IS A PERSON INSIDE AMATERASU...
!
THEN THERE'S A CONTRADICTION IN THE SCRIPTURES–YOU KNOW, THE TEACHINGS OF THE HOLY SOL TEMPLE THAT HAVE BEEN GUIDING THE TOKYO EMPIRE.
REMEMBER THE PROLOGUE? "IN THE DISTANT PAST, MANKIND INCURRED THE WRATH OF THE STARS..."

PROLOGUE
~ THE GREAT CATACLYSM ~

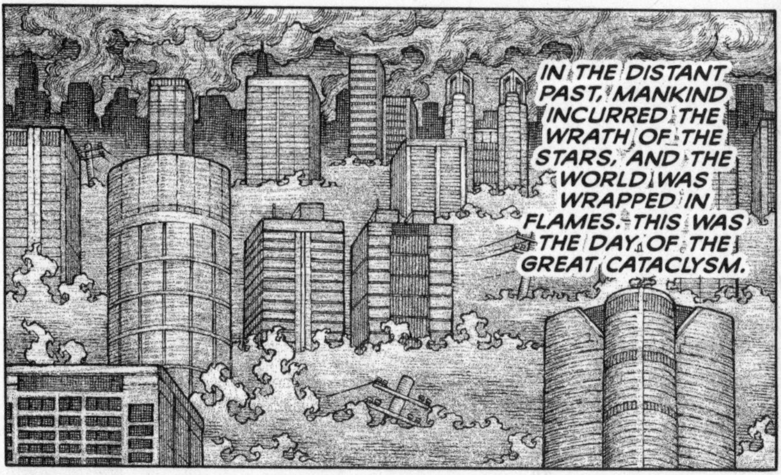
IN THE DISTANT PAST, MANKIND INCURRED THE WRATH OF THE STARS, AND THE WORLD WAS WRAPPED IN FLAMES. THIS WAS THE DAY OF THE GREAT CATACLYSM.

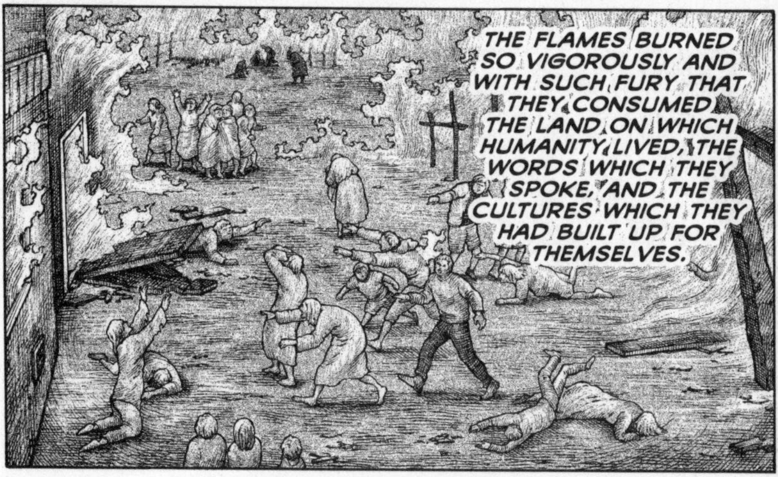
THE FLAMES BURNED SO VIGOROUSLY AND WITH SUCH FURY THAT THEY CONSUMED THE LAND ON WHICH HUMANITY LIVED, THE WORDS WHICH THEY SPOKE, AND THE CULTURES WHICH THEY HAD BUILT UP FOR THEMSELVES.

CHAPTER 1

~ HOLY FIRE ~

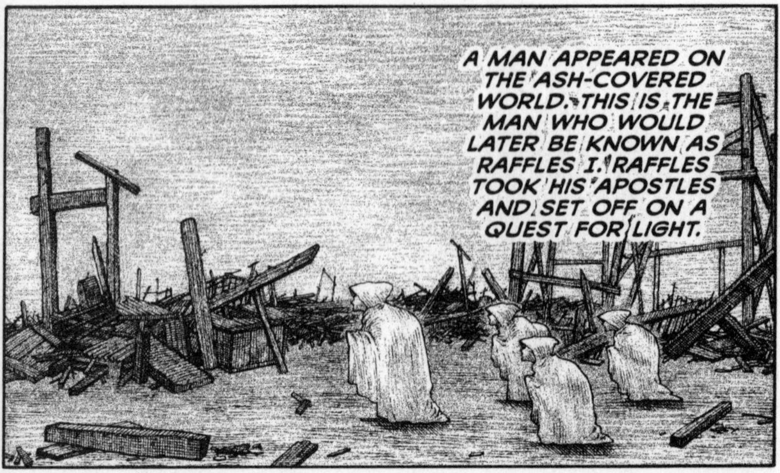
A MAN APPEARED ON THE ASH-COVERED WORLD. THIS IS THE MAN WHO WOULD LATER BE KNOWN AS RAFFLES I. RAFFLES TOOK HIS APOSTLES AND SET OFF ON A QUEST FOR LIGHT.

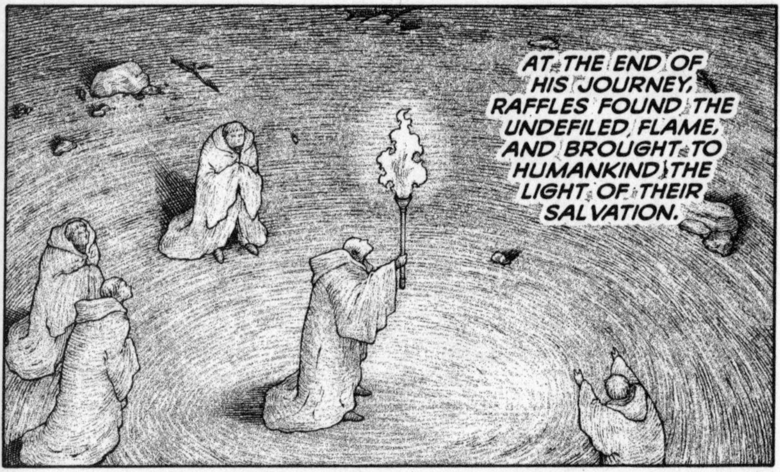
AT THE END OF HIS JOURNEY, RAFFLES FOUND THE UNDEFILED FLAME, AND BROUGHT TO HUMANKIND THE LIGHT OF THEIR SALVATION.

CHAPTER 2
~ AMATERASU ~

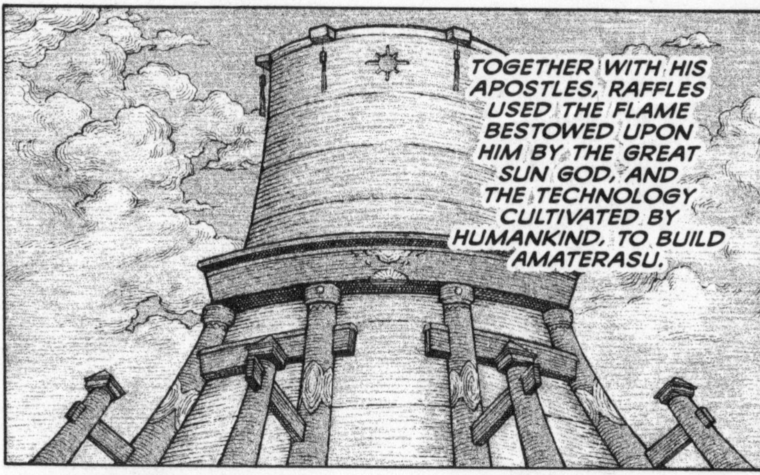
TOGETHER WITH HIS APOSTLES, RAFFLES USED THE FLAME BESTOWED UPON HIM BY THE GREAT SUN GOD, AND THE TECHNOLOGY CULTIVATED BY HUMANKIND, TO BUILD AMATERASU.

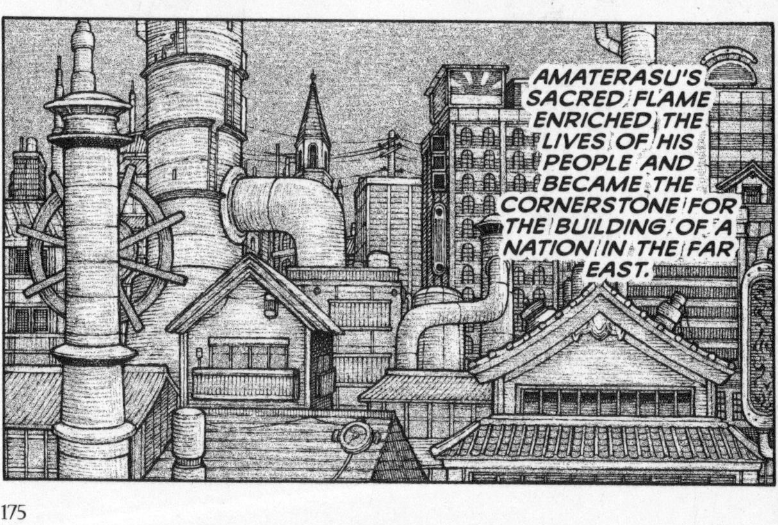
AMATERASU'S SACRED FLAME ENRICHED THE LIVES OF HIS PEOPLE AND BECAME THE CORNERSTONE FOR THE BUILDING OF A NATION IN THE FAR EAST.

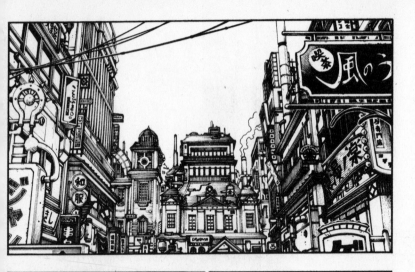

AMATERASU IS RUNNING NORMALLY TODAY.

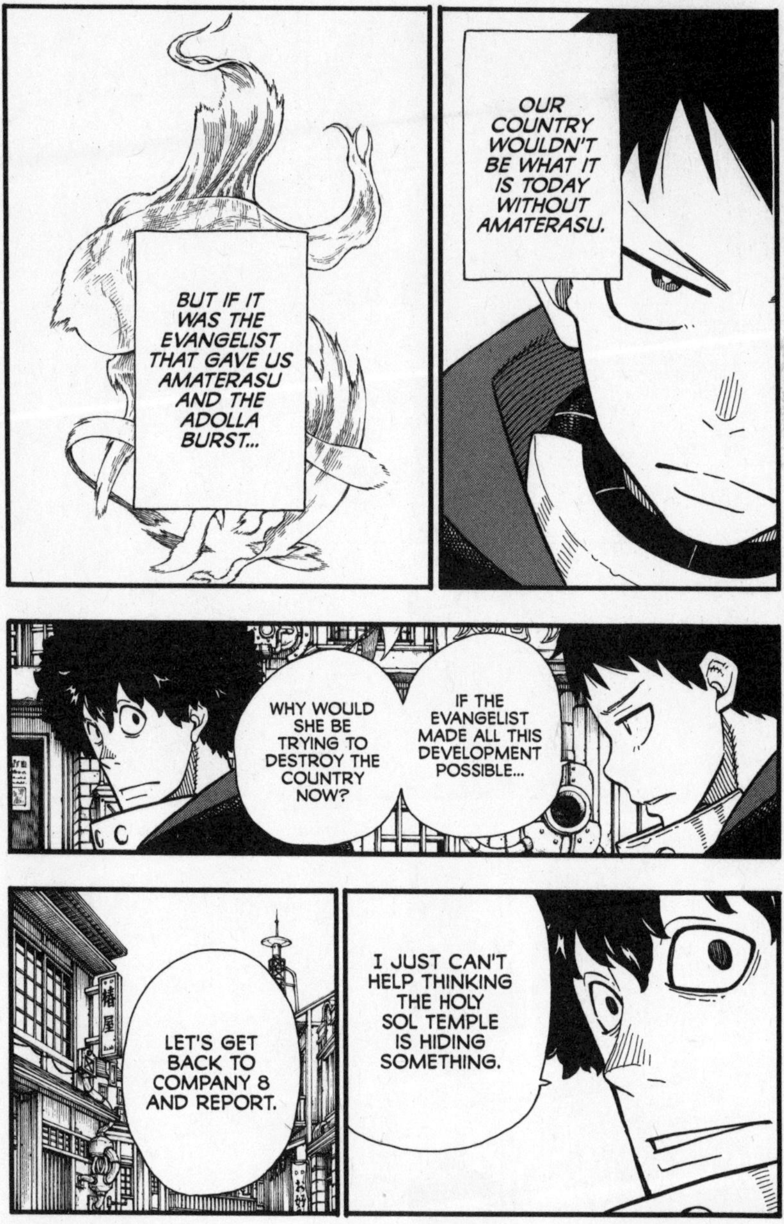
OUR COUNTRY WOULDN'T BE WHAT IT IS TODAY WITHOUT AMATERASU.
BUT IF IT WAS THE EVANGELIST THAT GAVE US AMATERASU AND THE ADOLLA BURST...
IF THE EVANGELIST MADE ALL THIS DEVELOPMENT POSSIBLE...
WHY WOULD SHE BE TRYING TO DESTROY THE COUNTRY NOW?
I JUST CAN'T HELP THINKING THE HOLY SOL TEMPLE IS HIDING SOMETHING.
椿屋
LET'S GET BACK TO COMPANY 8 AND REPORT.

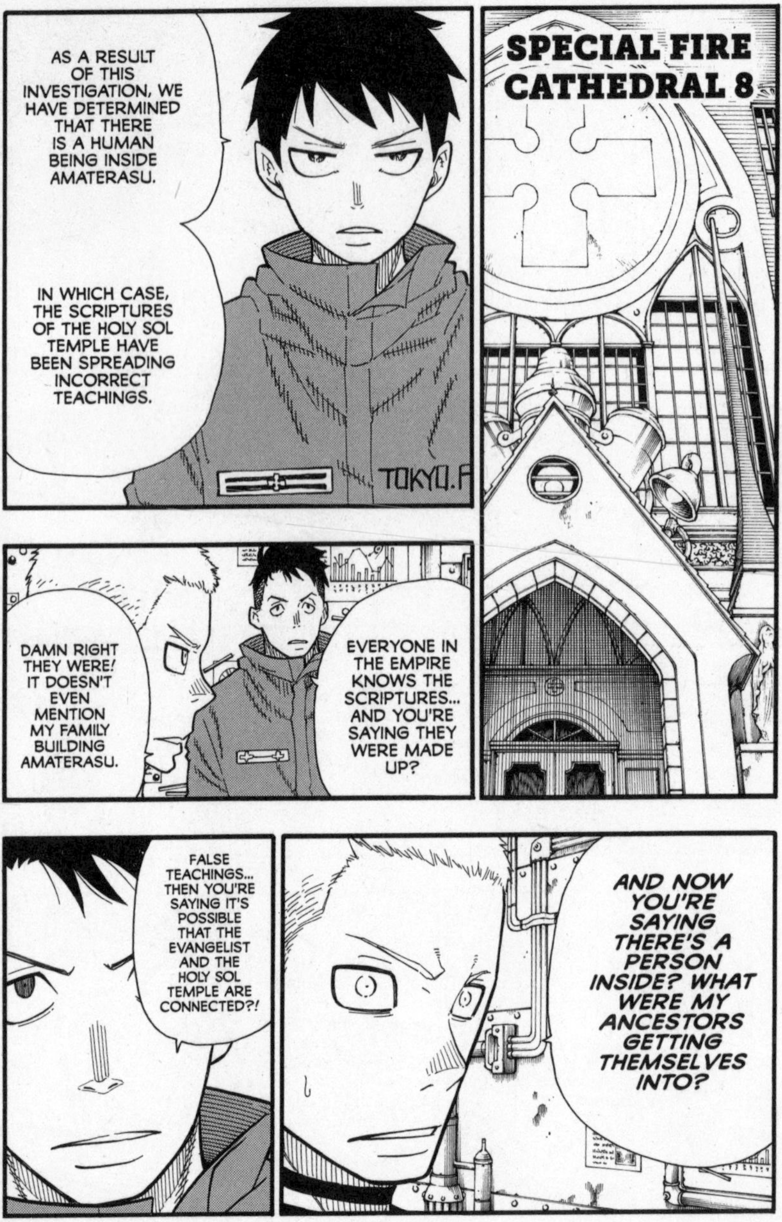
SPECIAL FIRE CATHEDRAL 8
AS A RESULT OF THIS INVESTIGATION, WE HAVE DETERMINED THAT THERE IS A HUMAN BEING INSIDE AMATERASU.
IN WHICH CASE, THE SCRIPTURES OF THE HOLY SOL TEMPLE HAVE BEEN SPREADING INCORRECT TEACHINGS.
TOKYO.F
EVERYONE IN THE EMPIRE KNOWS THE SCRIPTURES... AND YOU'RE SAYING THEY WERE MADE UP?
DAMN RIGHT THEY WERE! IT DOESN'T EVEN MENTION MY FAMILY BUILDING AMATERASU.
AND NOW YOU'RE SAYING THERE'S A PERSON INSIDE? WHAT WERE MY ANCESTORS GETTING THEMSELVES INTO?
FALSE TEACHINGS... THEN YOU'RE SAYING IT'S POSSIBLE THAT THE EVANGELIST AND THE HOLY SOL TEMPLE ARE CONNECTED?!

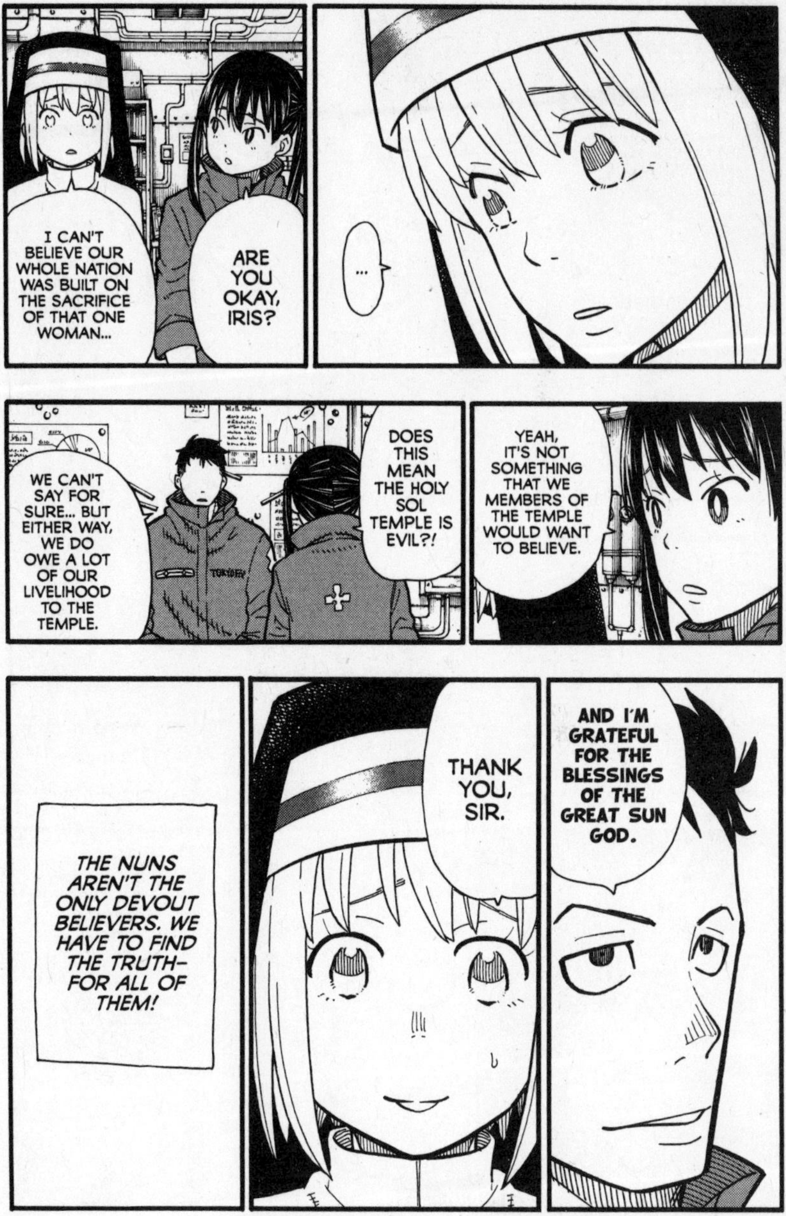
...
ARE YOU OKAY, IRIS?
I CAN'T BELIEVE OUR WHOLE NATION WAS BUILT ON THE SACRIFICE OF THAT ONE WOMAN...
YEAH, IT'S NOT SOMETHING THAT WE MEMBERS OF THE TEMPLE WOULD WANT TO BELIEVE.
DOES THIS MEAN THE HOLY SOL TEMPLE IS EVIL?!
WE CAN'T SAY FOR SURE... BUT EITHER WAY, WE DO OWE A LOT OF OUR LIVELIHOOD TO THE TEMPLE.
AND I'M GRATEFUL FOR THE BLESSINGS OF THE GREAT SUN GOD.
THANK YOU, SIR.
THE NUNS AREN'T THE ONLY DEVOUT BELIEVERS. WE HAVE TO FIND THE TRUTH—FOR ALL OF THEM!

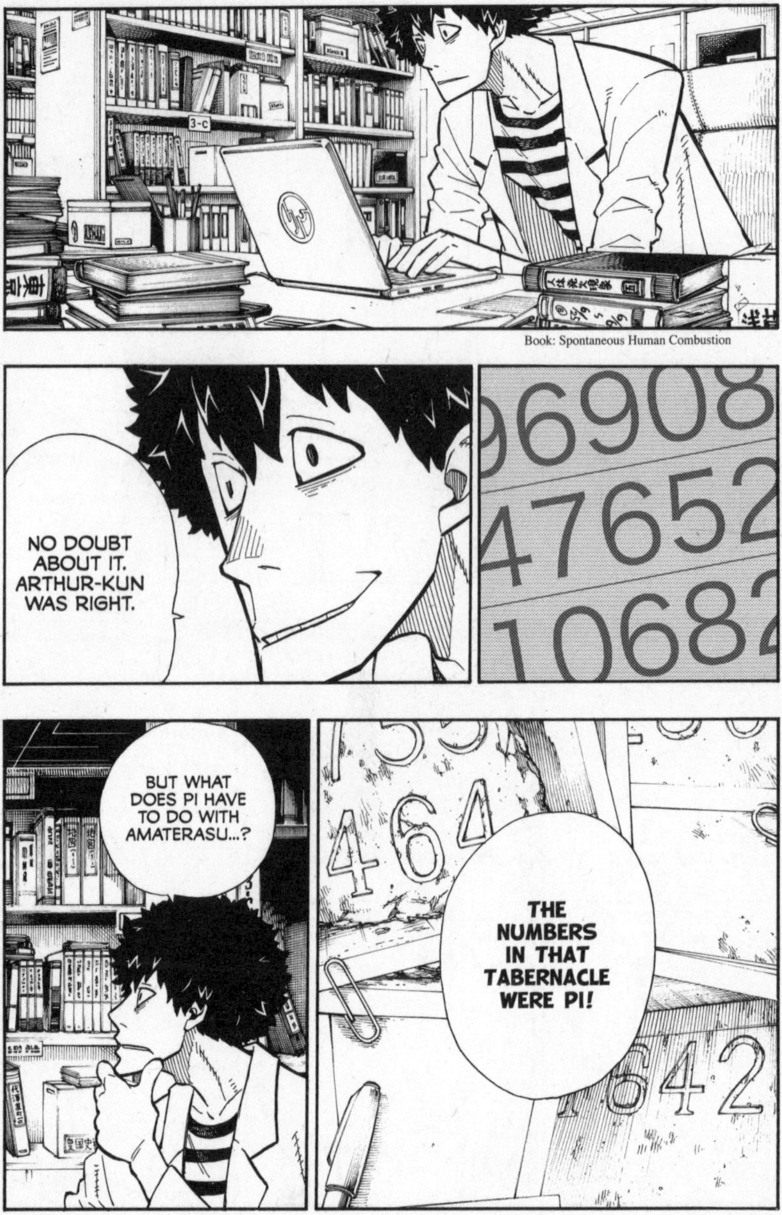
NO DOUBT ABOUT IT. ARTHUR-KUN WAS RIGHT.
THE NUMBERS IN THAT TABERNACLE WERE PI!
BUT WHAT DOES PI HAVE TO DO WITH AMATERASU...?

Book: Spontaneous Human Combustion

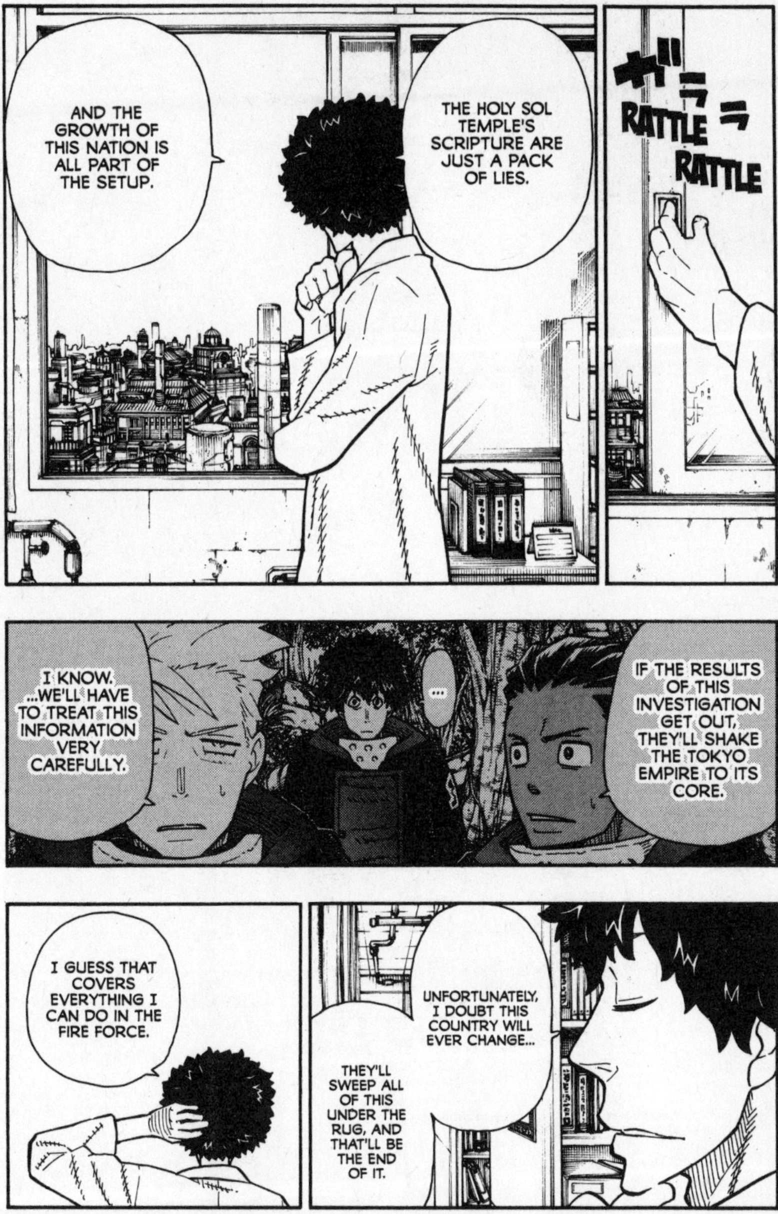
RATTLE
RATTLE
THE HOLY SOL TEMPLE'S SCRIPTURE ARE JUST A PACK OF LIES.
AND THE GROWTH OF THIS NATION IS ALL PART OF THE SETUP.
IF THE RESULTS OF THIS INVESTIGATION GET OUT, THEY'LL SHAKE THE TOKYO EMPIRE TO ITS CORE.
...
I KNOW. ...WE'LL HAVE TO TREAT THIS INFORMATION VERY CAREFULLY.
UNFORTUNATELY, I DOUBT THIS COUNTRY WILL EVER CHANGE...
THEY'LL SWEEP ALL OF THIS UNDER THE RUG, AND THAT'LL BE THE END OF IT.
I GUESS THAT COVERS EVERYTHING I CAN DO IN THE FIRE FORCE.

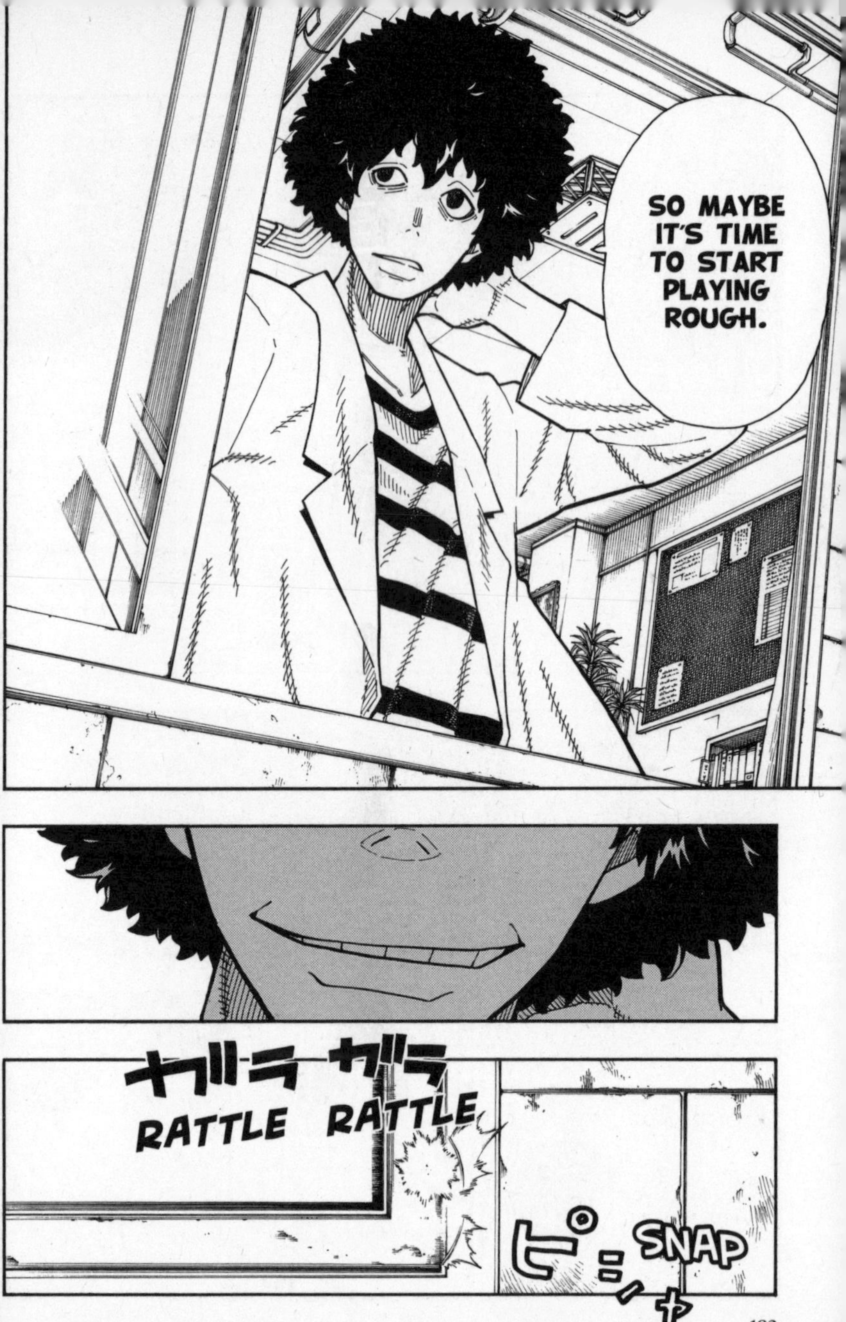
SO MAYBE IT'S TIME TO START PLAYING ROUGH.
ガラ ガラ
RATTLE RATTLE
ピシッ
SNAP

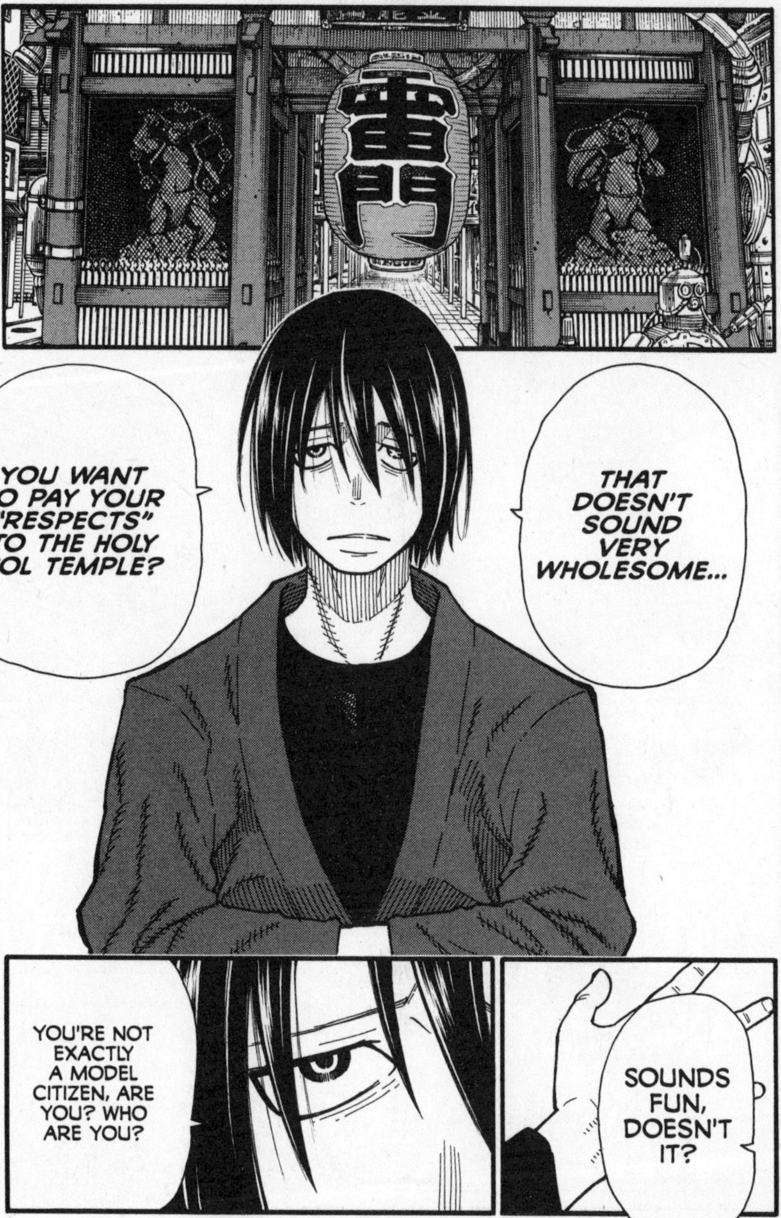
YOU WANT TO PAY YOUR "RESPECTS" TO THE HOLY SOL TEMPLE?
THAT DOESN'T SOUND VERY WHOLESOME...
SOUNDS FUN, DOESN'T IT?
YOU'RE NOT EXACTLY A MODEL CITIZEN, ARE YOU? WHO ARE YOU?

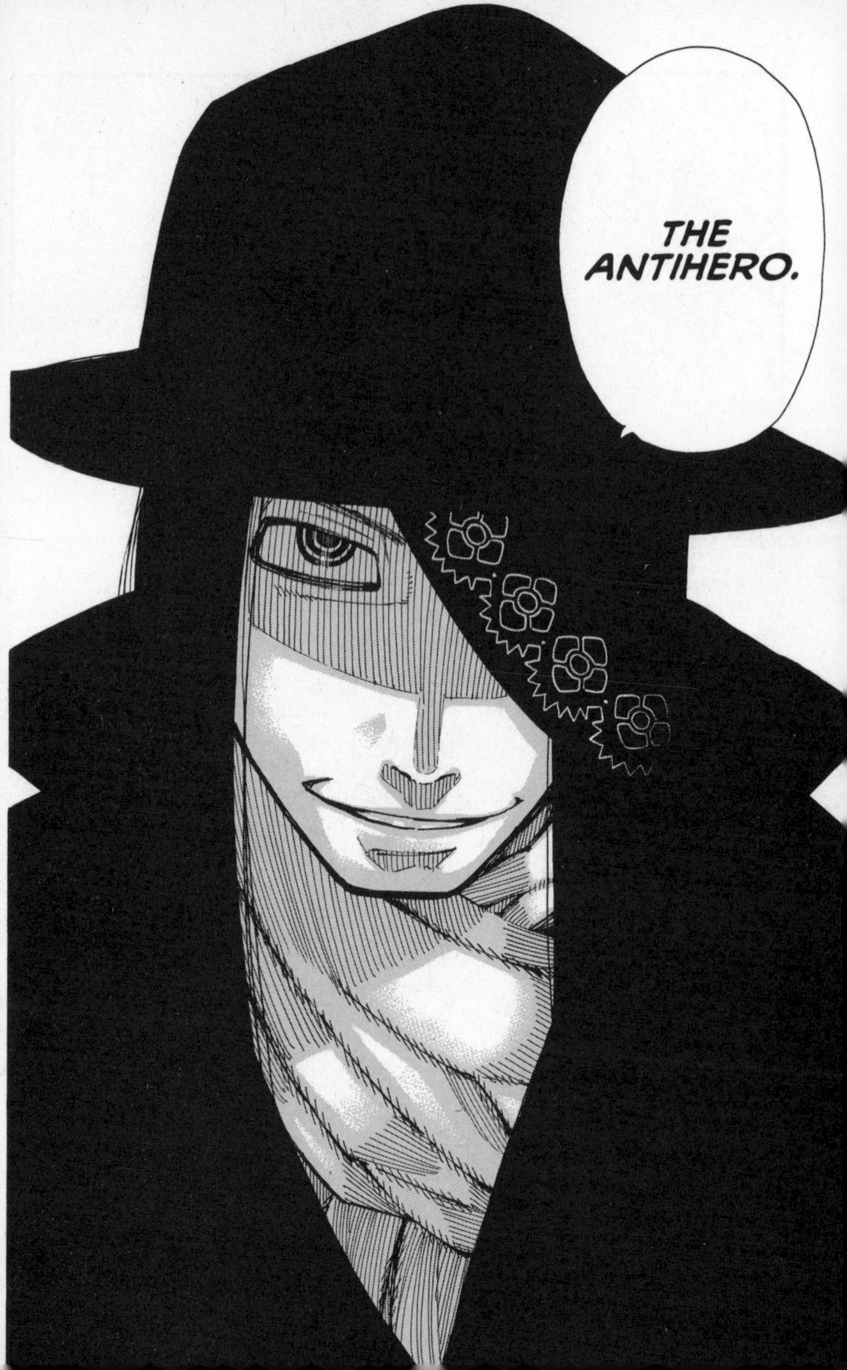
THE ANTIHERO.

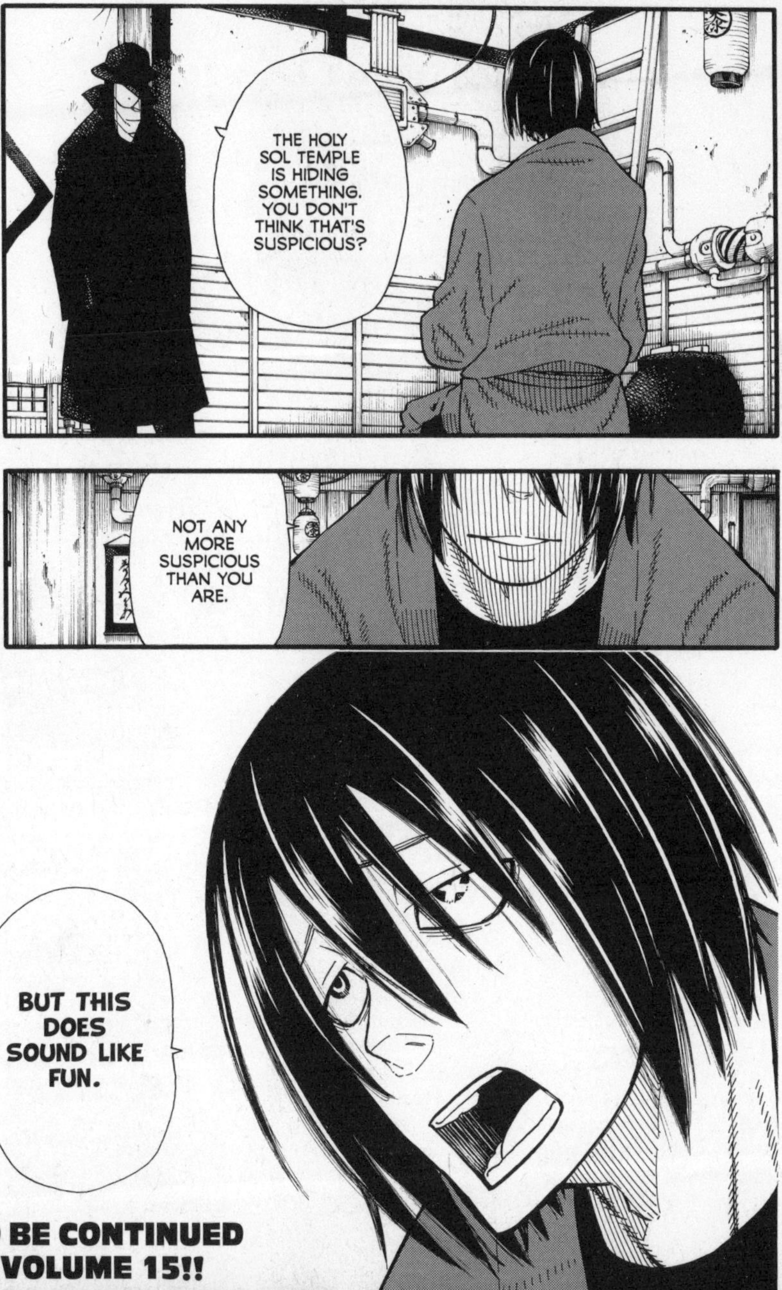
THE HOLY SOL TEMPLE IS HIDING SOMETHING. YOU DON'T THINK THAT'S SUSPICIOUS?
NOT ANY MORE SUSPICIOUS THAN YOU ARE.
BUT THIS DOES SOUND LIKE FUN.

TO BE CONTINUED IN VOLUME 15!!

Translation Notes:

Infernal dog vs Hell Hound, page 20

The Japanese word for Infernal is *homurabito*, a combination of *homura*, meaning "flame," and *hito*, meaning "person." When Shinra sees these new creatures, he describes them as "*homurabito* dogs," keeping the "person" part of the term intact. Arthur thinks this is ridiculous, and advises Shinra to drop the *hito* and refer to the dogs as *homura-inu*, or *homura dogs*.

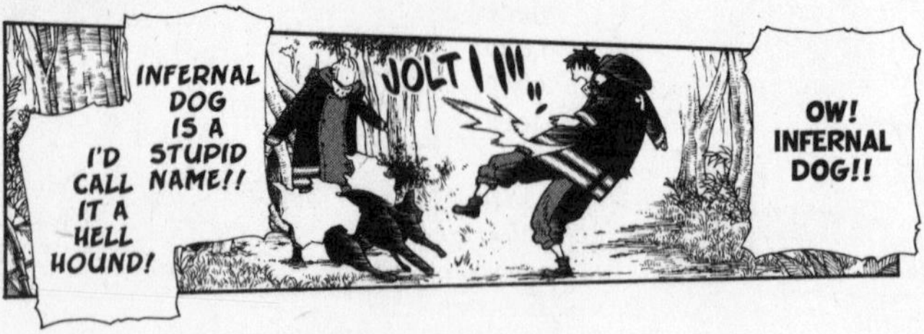
OW! INFERNAL DOG!!
JOLT!!!
INFERNAL DOG IS A STUPID NAME!!
I'D CALL IT A HELL HOUND!

Arthur's poem, page 86

The most common representation of pi is 3.14159, making Arthur's recognition of it seem incorrect, and his poem out of place. However, pi is still being calculated past the millionth digit, and the string 34102515 appears in the number at least three times. In order to memorize the whole(?) thing, Arthur has used Pilish, a mnemonic device in which the lengths of words correspond to the decimal digits of pi. In Pilish, zero is represented by a ten-letter word, and can be combined with the next digit (in this case, "mythologized" represents 0 and 2). Arthur, of course, would choose knightly words to remember the digits!

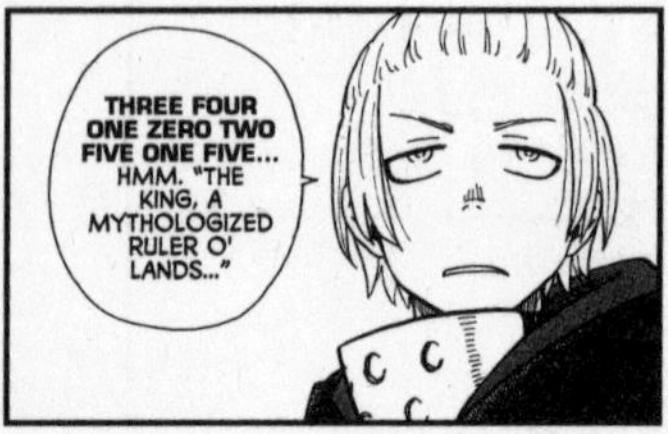
THREE FOUR ONE ZERO TWO FIVE ONE FIVE... HMM. "THE KING, A MYTHOLOGIZED RULER O' LANDS..."

Who is Sir Cumference, page 89

The translators confess to altering Arthur's confusion somewhat. In the original Japanese, Arthur explains that he has studied things related to *en* (roundness), which he associates with the *en-taku*, or Round Table. These words for "round" and "table" are not the ones used most commonly in Japanese dialogue, and so despite his obsession with all things knightly, he has yet to figure out what the *entaku* is. Unfortunately, in order to use English terms that would make Arthur's confusion more understandable, the translators would have to remove the obvious reference to the knights of Camelot, and so they resorted to a different play on words.

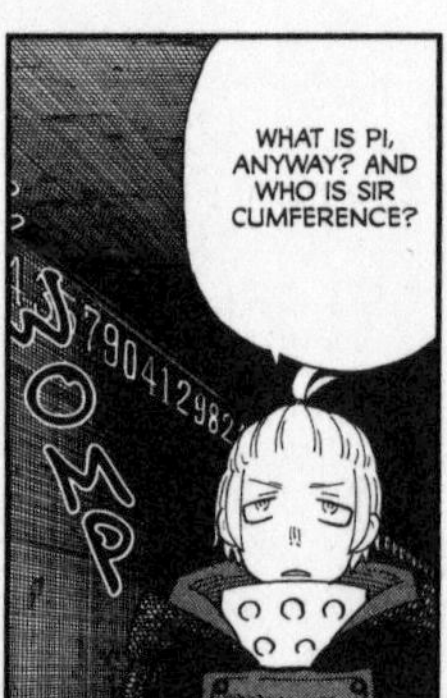
WHAT IS PI, ANYWAY? AND WHO IS SIR CUMFERENCE?
WOMP
790412982

Human pillar, page 112

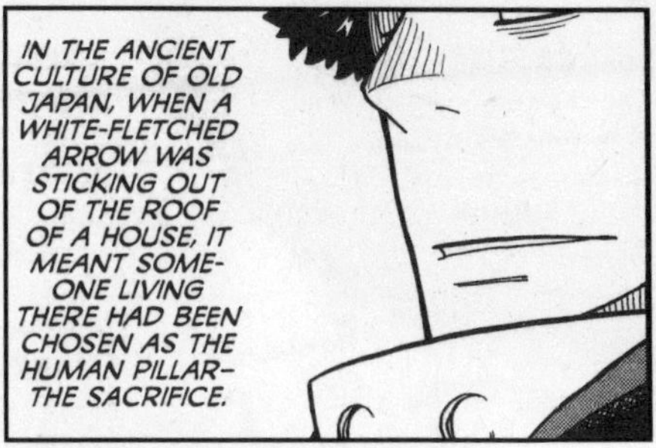
IN THE ANCIENT CULTURE OF OLD JAPAN, WHEN A WHITE-FLETCHED ARROW WAS STICKING OUT OF THE ROOF OF A HOUSE, IT MEANT SOME-ONE LIVING THERE HAD BEEN CHOSEN AS THE HUMAN PILLAR—THE SACRIFICE.

Hitobashira, or "human pillar," is a word for human sacrifice. These sacrifices were generally made at the commencement of important construction projects, either by burying the victim alive or drowning them (most likely in the case of bridge construction). The word pillar, or *hashira*, may refer to the sacrifice being a type of support for the new structure, but it's worth noting that *hashira* is also a counter (a suffix attached to numbers when counting, such as one *hashira*, two *hashira*, etc.) used when stating a number of deities. This may be because the victim, upon being sacrificed, is elevated in status to something more than mere mortal.

Shinra's shirt, page 167

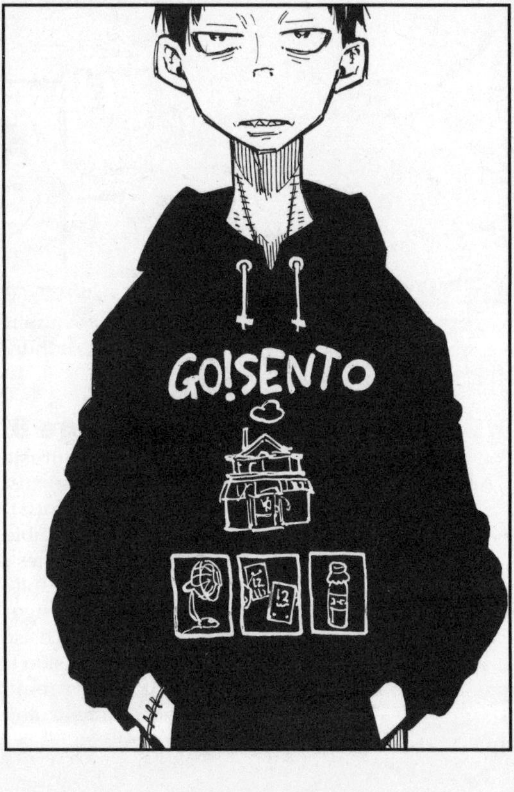
GO!SENTO
12
12

A *sento* is a public bathhouse, as pictured under the text on Shinra's shirt. As the name suggests, this is a place of communal bathing. They may not be necessary in modern times, as most people have baths in their homes, but some people find social benefits to communal bathing, and they're useful at the end of a long day spent out of town. Also pictured on the shirt are items representing things one can find at a *sento*, including a fan, numbered keys for shower lockers, and coffee-flavored milk.

AFTERWORD MANGA: ATSUSHIYA

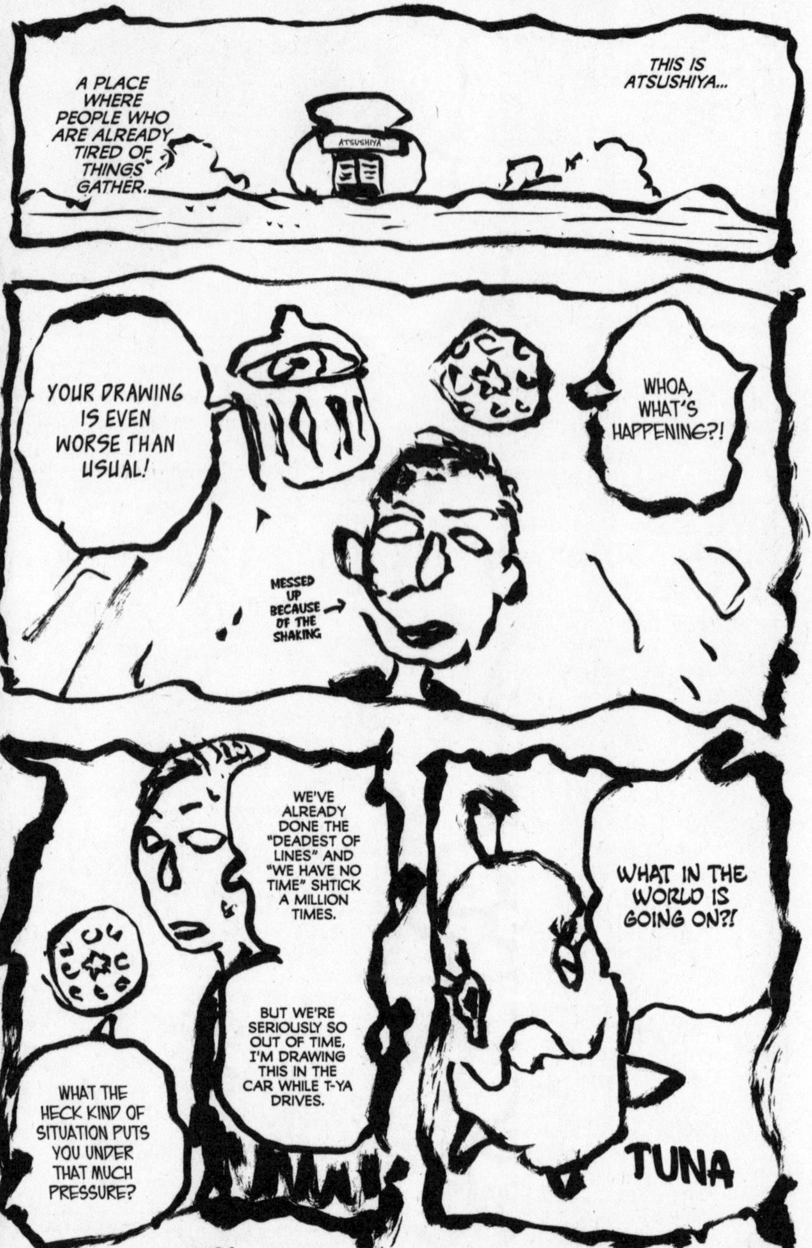
THIS IS ATSUSHIYA...
A PLACE WHERE PEOPLE WHO ARE ALREADY TIRED OF THINGS GATHER.
ATSUSHIYA
WHOA, WHAT'S HAPPENING?!
YOUR DRAWING IS EVEN WORSE THAN USUAL!
MESSED UP BECAUSE OF THE SHAKING
WHAT IN THE WORLD IS GOING ON?!
TUNA
WE'VE ALREADY DONE THE "DEADEST OF LINES" AND "WE HAVE NO TIME" SHTICK A MILLION TIMES.
BUT WE'RE SERIOUSLY SO OUT OF TIME, I'M DRAWING THIS IN THE CAR WHILE T-YA DRIVES.
WHAT THE HECK KIND OF SITUATION PUTS YOU UNDER THAT MUCH PRESSURE?

WE WERE ON PUBLIC ROADS UP UNTIL THIS POINT.

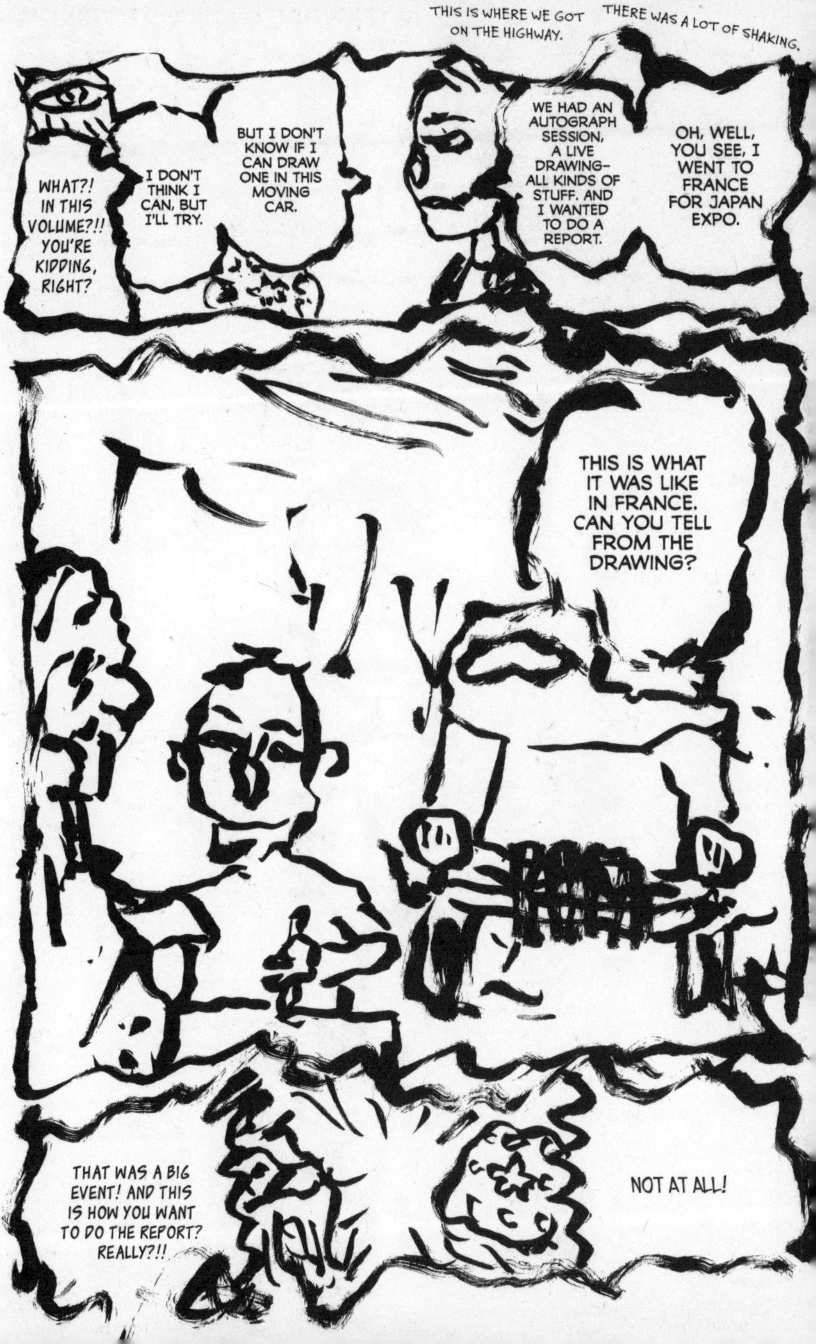
THERE WAS A LOT OF SHAKING.
THIS IS WHERE WE GOT ON THE HIGHWAY.
OH, WELL, YOU SEE, I WENT TO FRANCE FOR JAPAN EXPO.
WE HAD AN AUTOGRAPH SESSION, A LIVE DRAWING– ALL KINDS OF STUFF. AND I WANTED TO DO A REPORT.
BUT I DON'T KNOW IF I CAN DRAW ONE IN THIS MOVING CAR.
I DON'T THINK I CAN, BUT I'LL TRY.
WHAT?! IN THIS VOLUME?!! YOU'RE KIDDING, RIGHT?
THIS IS WHAT IT WAS LIKE IN FRANCE. CAN YOU TELL FROM THE DRAWING?
NOT AT ALL!
THAT WAS A BIG EVENT! AND THIS IS HOW YOU WANT TO DO THE REPORT? REALLY?!!

SPECIAL FIRE FORCE DISTRICT MAP!!

THERE ARE EIGHT SPECIAL FIRE FORCE COMPANIES THAT KEEP THE TOKYO EMPIRE SAFE. WE NOW PRESENT TO YOU THEIR JURISDICTIONS IN MAP FORMAT!!

JURISDICTION MAP

ITABASHI WARD
KITA WARD
ADACHI WARD
NERIMA WARD
COMPANY 6
TABATA
ARAKAWA WARD
COMPANY 8
KATSUSHIKA WARD
COMPANY 4
TOSHIMA WARD
KOMAGOME
BUNKYO WARD
IRIYA
TAITO WARD
ASAKUSA
NAKANO WARD
SUGINAMI WARD
COMPANY 1
UENO
SUMIDA WARD
AKIHABARA
CHIYODA WARD
EDOGAWA WARD
MINATO WARD
COMPANY 5
COMPANY 3
KOTO WARD
SHINJUKU WARD
CHUO WARD
CENTER
SETAGAYA WARD
MEGURO WARD
COMPANY 7
SHIBUYA WARD
COMPANY 2
OTA WARD

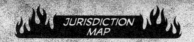

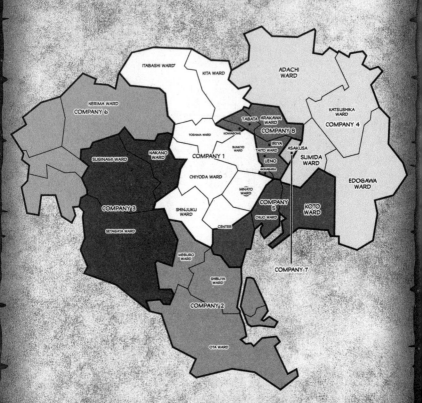

TOP SECRET FILES NOW REVEALED!!

SPECIAL FIRE FORCE

SIMPLIFIED CHART

WE'VE PUT TOGETHER A QUICK LOOK AT THE CHARACTERISTICS OF EACH SPECIAL FIRE FORCE COMPANY!!

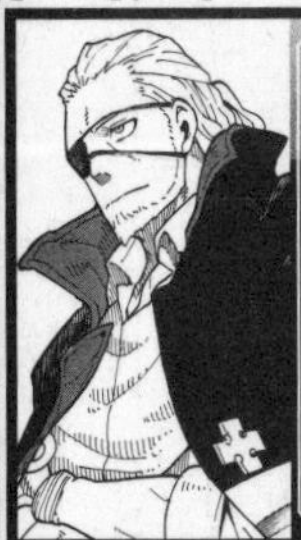

SPECIAL FIRE FORCE COMPANY 1

Captain: Leonard Burns.
This company is centered around the Holy Sol Temple, and is a group of the most elite fire soldiers in the force.

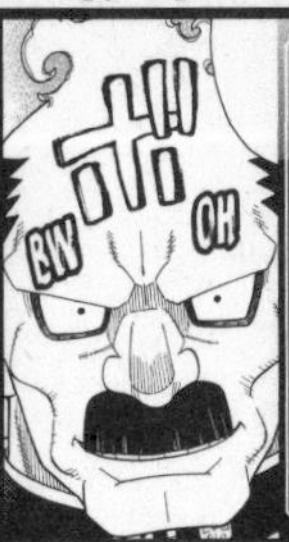

SPECIAL FIRE FORCE COMPANY 2

Captain: Gustav Honda.
This company is centered around the Tokyo Imperial Army. Juggernaut is assigned here as a new recruit.

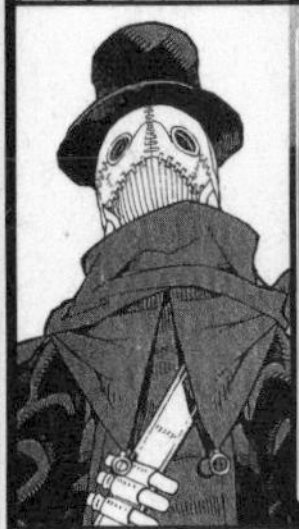

SPECIAL FIRE FORCE COMPANY 3

The company once captained by Dr. Giovanni, a follower of the Evangelist. The company is centered around Haijima Industries, but it currently has no captain?

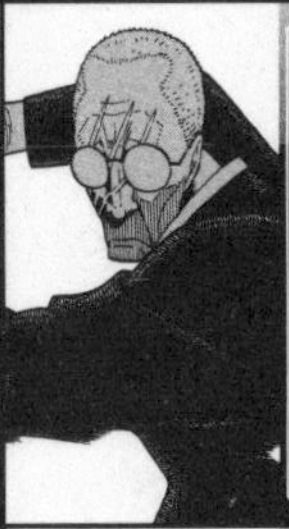

SPECIAL FIRE FORCE COMPANY 4

Captain: Sōichirō Hague.
This company is built mainly of former members of the Fire Defense Agency. This is also the company that runs the Academy where Shinra trained.

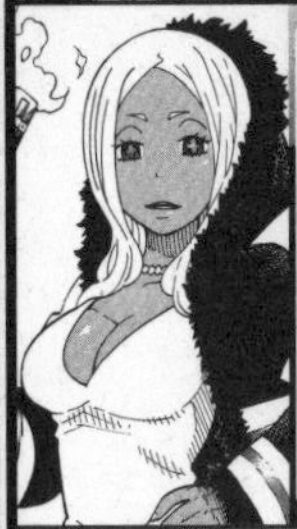

SPECIAL FIRE FORCE COMPANY 5

Captain: Princess Hibana.
This company is centered around Haijima Industries. Its captain, Hibana, is helping Company 8 unofficially.

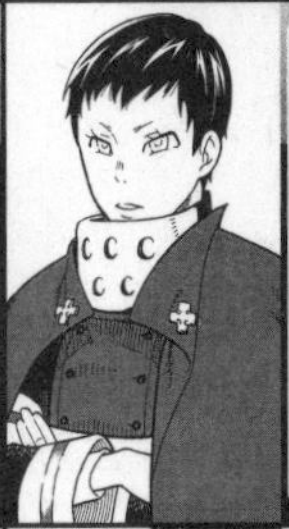

SPECIAL FIRE FORCE COMPANY 6

Captain: Kayoko Huang.
This company is responsible for healthcare in the Special Fire Force. Its captain, Huang, is a skilled physician, second to none in healing other pyrokinetics.

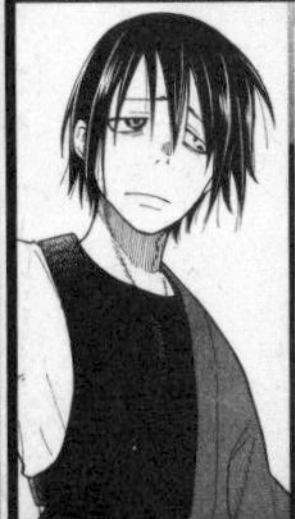

SPECIAL FIRE FORCE COMPANY 7

Captain: Shinmon Benimaru.
A company with a strong vigilante element due to its members coming from the hikeshi of Asakusa. Their captain, Benimaru, is known as the toughest soldier on the force.

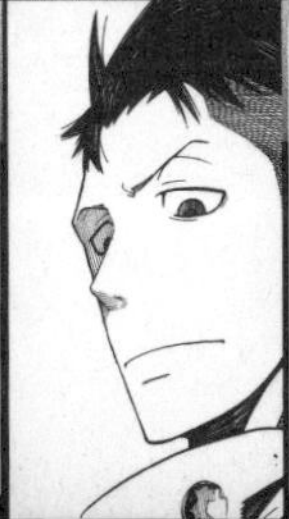

SPECIAL FIRE FORCE COMPANY 8

Captain: Akitaru Ōbi.
This is the company our hero Shinra works for, and is an unorthodox company that was formed to investigate the other companies.

Fire Force volume 14 is a work of fiction. Names, characters, places, and products of the author's imagination or are used fictitiously. Any resemblance to actual events, locales, or persons, living or dead, is entirely coincidental.

A Kodansha Comics Trade Paperback Original.

Published in the United States by Kodansha Comics, an imprint of Kodansha USA Publishing, LLC, New York.

Publication rights for this English edition arranged through Kodansha Ltd., Tokyo.

First published in Japan in 2018 by Kodansha Ltd., Tokyo.

ISBN 978-1-63236-721-1

Printed in the United States of America.

www.kodanshacomics.com

9 8 7 6 5 4 3 2

Translation: Alethea Nibley & Athena Nibley
Lettering: AndWorld Design
Editing: Lauren Scanlan
Kodansha Comics edition cover design: Phil Balsman